CW00503041

Questioning Gender Politics

Questioning Gender Politics: Contextualising Educational Disparities in Uncertain Times showcases contemporary thinking on pressing aspects of gender equalities, such as patriarchal culture, sexual harassment, trans rights, queer pedagogies, and sex education in various educational settings and international contexts.

This book illustrates how education is an important physical, material and ideological site for understanding and challenging stubborn gender inequalities. *Questioning Gender Politics* positions itself within existing theorisations and research outlining how gender issues and sexist power cultures have in many cases changed from plain to more insidious inequalities. The notion of education is also expanded to include a broader understanding of how gender issues impinge on education. The range of work explored in this volume includes contributions on modern conceptualisations of gender, feminism and education, transnormativities, queer theory, intersectional pedagogy, postheteronormativity in education, and more.

Questioning Gender Politics: Contextualising Educational Disparities in Uncertain Times will be of great value to undergraduate and postgraduate students of Gender and Education, as well as seasoned educators.

Jessie A. Bustillos Morales is a senior lecturer in the Education Division at London South Bank University (LSBU). She holds a PhD in Education from University College London (UCL). She has worked in academia for over thirteen years across several institutions in the UK.

Teaching with Gender

The series is a collection which has a long standing tradition of publications of theoretical reflections and case studies that address the pedagogical, conceptual and political dimensions of teaching and learning about gender. First linked to its predecessor, the ATHENA network, the Teaching with Gender book series is now coordinated by ATGENDER - the European Association for Gender Research, Education and Documentation. A wide range of international scholars have contributed to the edited volumes in this series, offering teaching tools and seminar exercises that give students and teachers valuable sources for the teaching and studying of gender and sexuality.

Teaching Gender: Feminist Pedagogy and Responsibility in Times of Political Crisis
Beatriz Revelles Benavente and Ana Maria González Ramos

Decolonization and Feminisms in Global Teaching and Learning
Sara de Jong, Rosalba Icaza and Olivia U. Rutazibwa

Feminist Perspectives on Teaching Masculinities
Learning Beyond Stereotypes
Sveva Magaraggia, Gerlinde Mauerer and Marianne Schmidbaur

Homonationalism, Femonationalism and Ablenationalism
Critical Pedagogies Contextualised
Edited by Angeliki Sifaki, C.L. Quinan and Katarina Lončarević

Questioning Gender Politics
Contextualising Educational Disparities in Uncertain Times
Edited by Jessie A. Bustillos Morales

https://www.routledge.com/Teaching-with-Gender/book-series/TWG

Questioning Gender Politics

Contextualising Educational Disparities in Uncertain Times

Edited by
Jessie A. Bustillos Morales

Routledge
Taylor & Francis Group

LONDON AND NEW YORK

Designed cover image: Devenorr, Getty Images

First published 2025
by Routledge
4 Park Square, Milton Park, Abingdon, Oxon OX14 4RN

and by Routledge
605 Third Avenue, New York, NY 10158

Routledge is an imprint of the Taylor & Francis Group, an informa business

© 2025 selection and editorial matter, Jessie A. Bustillos Morales; individual chapters, the contributors

The right of Jessie A. Bustillos Morales to be identified as the author of the editorial material, and of the authors for their individual chapters, has been asserted in accordance with sections 77 and 78 of the Copyright, Designs and Patents Act 1988.

British Library Cataloguing in Publication Data
A catalogue record for this book is available from the British Library

Library of Congress Cataloging-in-Publication Data
Names: Bustillos Morales, Jessie, 1983- editor.
Title: Questioning gender politics : contextualising educational disparities in uncertain times / edited by Jessie A. Bustillos Morales. Description: Abingdon, Oxon ; New York, NY : Routledge, 2025. |
Series: Teaching with gender | Includes bibliographical references and index.
Identifiers: LCCN 2024013041 (print) | LCCN 2024013042 (ebook) |
ISBN 9781032502328 (hardback) | ISBN 9781032502298 (paperback) |
ISBN 9781003397502 (ebook)
Subjects: LCSH: Gender identity in education. | Sexism in education. |
Sexual minorities--Education. | Gender non-conforming people--Education.
Classification: LCC LC212.9 .Q47 2025 (print) | LCC LC212.9 (ebook) |
DDC 370.81--dc23/eng/20240423
LC record available at https://lccn.loc.gov/2024013041
LC ebook record available at https://lccn.loc.gov/2024013042

ISBN: 978-1-032-50232-8 (hbk)
ISBN: 978-1-032-50229-8 (pbk)
ISBN: 978-1-003-39750-2 (ebk)

DOI: 10.4324/9781003397502

Typeset in Sabon
by Taylor & Francis Books

Contents

Contributors

Amina Ali is an A-level English teacher at London Academy of Excellence, Tottenham. Amina's research is foundational in decolonisation. She is interested in decolonising her classroom, through pedagogy and curriculum. Her current practice is grounded in relearning and expanding perceptions of what constitutes good classroom practice.

Iraia Elorduy Alverde is a student in the RMA Gender Studies programme at Utrecht University researching childhood sexual abuse and the impact it has on the body, the brain and the psyche. Their research and practices are in the field of feminist, political, and post-materialism theory.

Erika Bernacchi is an adjunct professor in Sociology of Education at the University of Florence, Education Department. She is also a researcher at Istituto degli Innocenti of Florence. Her research themes concern gender stereotypes in education, gender-based violence, masculinity, and postcolonial studies.

Sebastian Bernhard is a research associate and PhD candidate at the Research Group Gender and Diversity in Engineering (GDI). His PhD project is funded by the German Research Foundation (DFG) and deals with gendered experiences within the so-called engineering culture from an interdisciplinary perspective of experimental philosophy.

Mart Busche a professor for General Pedagogy and Social Work at Alice-Salomon University of Applied Sciences. Their research focus is on gender and sexual diversity, critical masculinity studies, sexualised violence, and queer studies. They earned their PhD in Sociology with a study on boys and non-violence (University of Kassel, Germany).

Isaura Castelao-Huerta is a researcher at the Centre for Research and Advanced Studies (Cinvestav, Mexico), Deparment of Educational Research (DIE). She has instructed various workshops on the gender perspective for staff of public and private institutions.

Naomi Davis is a PhD student at Solent University specialising in women's experiences of sexual harassment in Higher Education. Her research develops the use of walking methodologies to explore the ways in which women on university campuses experience sexist encounters with others, including intimidation and sexual abuse.

Antonio Raimondo Di Grigoli is a junior researcher in Educational Studies at the University of Florence and a consultant at the Istituto degli Innocenti of Florence. His main research focuses on critical studies on men and masculinities and queer and intersectional pedagogy as theoretical fields to analyse heteronormativity as a cultural construct.

Ayla Fedorchenko is a research assistant and PhD student in the research group "Gender 3.0 – Gender Diversity at School" at European University Flensburg, Germany. She has a Master of Education in the subjects English, Sport/Sport Science and Philosophy/Ethics.

Tamás Jules Fütty is a junior professor in the Department of Education Science at European University Flensburg, Germany. He is an interdisciplinary senior researcher and leader of the research group "Gender 3.0 – Gender Diversity at School".

Rachel Levi Herz is a teaching fellow in the Gender Studies Programme at Bar-Ilan University, Israel. She specialises in sexualities, subjectivity, agency, vulnerability theory, gender-based education, and social activism. Her recent publications focus on young women's sexual subjectivity and agency, analysed through the lens of vulnerability and affect theory.

Daniel Holtermann is a researcher and educator at Dissens Institute for Education and Research, Berlin. He is working to transfer knowledge from gender studies into pedagogical practices in EU-funded projects like "Boy in Care – Strengthening Boys to Pursue Care Occupations" and "ECaRoM – Early Care and the Role of Men".

Majda Hrženjak is a researcher and project leader at the Peace Institute at the Institute for Contemporary Social and Political Studies, Slovenia. Her research explores the concept of care in relation to intersectional inequalities, citizenship, migration and feminist ethic of care, and gender studies, including critical studies of men and masculinities.

Scott Kerpen is a Sociology lecturer at Bath Spa University. His research explores digital empowerment, with a primary focus on the online practices of gender and sexual minorities. His work adopts participatory methods, collaborating with marginalised groups to explore opportunities for community building, identity exploration, and activism.

Sophie Lehner is an aspiring researcher in the field of Educational Sciences and Queer Pedagogies. Having completed their MA in Helsinki, Finland, Sophie is now based in Vienna, Austria. Sophie's work has focused on queer pedagogies, invisibility of queerness in higher education and innovative educational approaches.

Carmen Leicht-Scholten is Director of the RRI Hub at RWTH Aachen University and holds the Chair of Gender and Diversity in Engineering. She is based at the Faculty of Civil Engineering and has a second seat at the Faculty of Arts and Humanities.

Brian McDonough is a course leader of Sociology at Solent University. His research specialises in the sociology of the body, technology, and work. He is co-editor of *Sociology, Work and Organisation: A Global Context* (2024) and author of *Flying Aeroplanes and Other Sociological Tales: An Introduction to Sociology and Research Methods* (2021).

Tabitha Millett is an assistant professor of Arts, Creativities and Education at the University of Cambridge. Her current research interests are in areas of art and design education and arts-based research. Tabitha is also a practising artist who is working with galleries in London, LA, Munich, and Barcelona.

Domitilla Olivieri is an assistant professor in the Graduate Gender programme in Utrecht University's Media and Culture Studies department. Their research focuses on documentary practices, time and spaces of the everyday, forms of social and political relationality and contestation, activist interventions in neoliberal academia, and rhythm in (documentary) media.

Jan Parker is the head of department for Social Sciences and Nursing at Solent University. Her research specialises in social inequalities within Social Work and Higher Education (HE), investigating the ways in which young people on university placements develop resilience to prepare themselves for careers in social work.

And Pasley is a Marsden research fellow and lecturer at the University of Auckland. Based in Aotearoa, New Zealand, And's present research collaborates with trans students to imagine what it might mean for (whole-school) sexuality education to be decolonised and centre trans students' interests.

Catherine Phipps is a senior lecturer in Education and Sociology at Solent University in Southampton. She has published in the areas of gender, sexuality, and gender identity in the sport and physical education contexts and has been involved in work aiming to tackle sexual harm in educational settings.

Diana Fernández Romero is a senior lecturer in Communications and Media Studies at Rey Juan Carlos University in Madrid, Spain. Her research interests include Discourse Analysis, Communication and Gender, Gender-based Violence, Feminist Pedagogies and Digital Feminist Activism.

Miri Rozmarin is a senior lecturer in the Gender Studies Programme at Bar-Ilan University. She is also a senior research fellow and the Head of the Research Lab 'Contemporary Feminist Political Subjectivity' at the Van Leer Jerusalem Institute. Her research interests include vulnerability, political subjectivity, and post-Oedipal kinships.

Elli Scambor is a sociologist and Managing Director of the Institute for Masculinity Studies and Gender Research at the Verein für Männer- und Geschlechterthemen Steiermark (Association for Men's and Gender Issues). She has been coordinator of numerous international studies focusing on the role of men and gender equality, and gender and violence prevention.

Camilla Stanger is an educator and researcher based in London, currently coordinating an academic and creative enrichment programme across different schools in Tottenham, North London. This is alongside her research and teaching at Goldsmiths College (University of London), where she contributes to the BA Education and Secondary Teacher Education programmes.

Philippa Velija is a professor and the deputy dean of The School of Arts, Humanities and Social Sciences at the University of Roehampton. Her research analyses inequality and power in sport and leisure settings. She is also interested in the ways in ways to tackle misogyny and 'lad' cultures in education settings.

Zixi Zuo is a PhD student at the Institute of Education at University College London. Her research explores gendered and sexual subjectivities among contemporary Chinese young people through their practice of intimacy. Her research critically examines the system of heteronormativity in Chinese higher education settings.

Acknowledgements

My warmest and most sincere thanks to all contributors in this book. You engaged with the review process so reflexively and diligently and allowed for this book to grow and explore gender disparities in a reflexive and scholarly manner. Your chapters offer so many challenges and pedagogical points of departure and bring hope to those who want to teach and resist the systemic everydayness of educational inequalities. As I engaged with the editorial process for this book, I have come to question my own reasons for wanting to edit such a book; I wanted to create something I could use with my own students, but I now realise that the pressing issues portrayed here transcend any need for pedagogical, curricular, or even scholarly development. The narratives, qualitative data, and multidisciplinary analyses from various international contexts are a powerful statement as to how damaging gender inequalities are for all. The book would not have been possible without the many years of nurturing and scholarly feminist sisterhood I have had the pleasure to share with Dr Shiva Zarabadi, Dr Hanna Retallack, Dr Camilla Stanger and Naty Rios. Similarly, I draw so much strength from the many years of caring friendship I have shared with excellent educators, Brigitte Dang and Simona Caba. I would like to thank AtGender for giving me the opportunity to contribute to the Teaching with Gender book series and for their guidance throughout the editorial process. A last very special thanks to the three people who bring me light and endless joy every day, Brian, Huxley and Blake.

1 Introduction

Questioning Gender Politics in Education

Jessie A. Bustillos Morales

Education and schooling continue to be a very important site where gender relations and gender politics take place (Mac an Ghaill, 1994; Mac an Ghaill, 1996; Haywood and Mac an Ghaill, 1996; Lesko, 2000; Renold, 2005; Ringrose and Renold, 2012; Mendes et al., 2022). This book explores the role of education amidst persisting gender inequalities within educational sectors. By referring to gender politics in education, the aim of the book is to illustrate chapter by chapter the alternative ways of interpreting and explaining what goes on in education; therefore, the chapters are prisms through which we gaze at a politics in education which is characterised by myriad gendered disparities. Yet, it is also important to point to how education in this book is wide-ranging, not just contained within schools. The approach to politics in this book is revisiting established concepts and relations that we traditionally associate with education to demonstrate how disparities and disadvantages can allow us to see both where gender frictions, tensions, and inequalities are and where educational implications are located in the issues identified by contributors.

Thus, this book will present theoretical explorations, case studies, and emerging research mapping out some of the oppressive heteronormative, sexist, and patriarchal cultures affecting educational lives today in educational settings and across various international contexts. The book also hosts an international forum on contemporary thinking on the role of gender in education and the inequalities that characterise processes of education around the world. The chapters will provide a modern look into education, looking at pressing gender and sexuality issues in educational sectors. In previous works, a critical feminist approach has been suggested for education (Weiler and Arnot, 1993; Ng et al., 1995; Ringrose 2013), yet it is important to continue to explore the shifting issues and concerns of the feminist theoretical debates in order to help shape future feminist agendas that are better suited for our changing international educational landscapes.

Crucially, the book also provides theoretical and empirical responses to critical questions needed to frame education differently. Some of these questions are: How can education be redefined to be more inclusive? Are there any ways in which more opportunities to challenge toxic student and staff cultures can open up in education? What modes of collaboration and resistance enable an

DOI: 10.4324/9781003397502-1

ethical response to gender inequalities in education? What concepts can be utilised beyond traditional concepts to better address gender inequalities in education? Through its international contributions the book helps to rethink education and learning beyond what is officially in the curriculum and instead create an understanding of how gender inequalities in education are embedded in practices, cultures, pedagogies, and institutional arrangements.

Emergent inequalities in gender are associated with the interpretation of gender identities as binary opposites. This book will present scholarly challenges to these binaries, which continue to uncritically construct idealised femininities and masculinities as the only possibilities to enact gender and as necessarily oppositional. In doing this, the book is contributing to the discourse of 'deconstruction of binaries', which is best understood through feminist scholarly research and theory (Sedgwick, 2008; White et al., 2017; Youdell, 2006). Consequently, the book will develop its themes guided by some of the critical questions posed previously but with a focus on contemporary formations of gender identity.

In this way the book aims to illustrate how education is an important physical, material, and ideological site for understanding and challenging stubborn gender inequalities. Contrary to postfeminist discourses that claim gender equity has been achieved and therefore feminism is redundant, the book positions itself within existing research outlining how gender issues and power cultures have in many cases changed from plain to more insidious inequalities (Ringrose and Epstein, 2015). The notion of education is also expanded in this book, with a focus on more alternative forms of education, such as, youth activisms, creative pedagogies, and media research. The book will provide conceptual as well as pedagogical contributions which will help students and educators understand current debates and issues around gender, whilst also reflecting critically on the role of education in turbulent times.

In Chapter 2 Pasley and Lehner set the scene for the discussions around gender by bringing into sharp focus how gender discourses and gender relations are ubiquitous. The chapter offers several possibilities to think about gender and sexuality beyond the social order, and the narrative of this chapter challenges how gender and sexuality are understood as inherently different and separate. Pasley and Lehner conceptually and theoretically explore how gender and sex are 'conflated via a biological essentialism' and as a result, biological sex can be differentiated from psychological gender. However, through this approach the naturalisation of gender continues to serve the heteronormative and established social order. By troubling the acceptance that we can now 'better' understand gender and sex through a biological essentialist logic, taking a modern look at gender identities, this chapter warns of how there is a risk in reproducing hegemonic gender discourses and relations in the form of transnormativities.

The focus then shifts to queer theory in Chapter 3, where Millett explores how queer theory fits into curricular and pedagogical contexts. The educational implications of queer theory are articulated against the backdrop of what

Millett argues is a conservative educational agenda in the UK. Millett evidences the conservative nature of curriculum and pedagogy in the UK by exploring aspects of educational policy and the hierarchies of knowledge that make inclusive practice challenging in education. Chapter 3 also seeks to establish a queer pedagogy genealogy by both exploring the discourse of conservatism within education in the UK, but also by exploring the work of Pinar (2012), Kumashiro (2002), and Halberstam (2011) . The focus on queer theory then pushes the reader to move beyond affirmation of identities to a more critical stance on how identities are constituted or normalised.

The next chapter delves into intersectional pedagogy and practice both theoretically and empirically. Stanger and Ali carefully narrate intersectional research encounters with young Black women in three settings: a girls' dance and discussion project, a poetry and spoken word group, and a series of book clubs. Chapter 4 presents an example of reflexive research theoretically infused with interconnected concepts such as, 'liberation', 'home', 'community' and 'voice'. The chapter presents reflexivity in research by drawing from previous research centred on belonging and community (hooks, 1990, 1994; Brown, 2009; Sears, 2010). Stanger and Ali offer a carefully narrated and research-informed pedagogical example of how critical pedagogy can be used to de-centralise power in education and create inclusive and co-created pedagogies and practice.

Chapter 5 presents findings from a research project analysing educational policies in Germany aimed at making schools more sensitive to the needs of students experiencing inequalities of gender or sexuality. The chapter proposes a post heteronormative approach to challenge what they present in their findings as the individuation of inclusion. The chapter examines the ways in which education in schools continues to perpetuate heteronormative cultures and how efforts to make schools more inclusive have resulted in educational policies around sex education that focus heavily on self-responsibility and self-determination. This overt shift towards agency is presented as problematic as it does not challenge cis-heteronormative cultures and relations in education. Through an analysis of the sex education curriculum in Germany, Fütty, Fedorchenko and Busche argue that the current approach contributes to the invisibility of gender diversity whilst also passing accountabilities and responsibilities to students because of their gender or sexual identity.

The concept of caring masculinities is explored in Chapter 6 to make sense of the early childhood education sector and how gender identity constructions can be understood through a framework that recognises the unchecked sexism still existing in the environments in which young children learn. The chapter departs from findings from two research projects and introduces the concept of hegemonic masculinity to understand how it influences gender relations in ways that subjugate and oppress any form of gender identity outside of hegemonic masculinity. Caring masculinities is explored conceptually and practically in Chapter 6, embedding the notion of care in Fraser's (1996) and Tronto's (1993, 1995) complex definitions of societal caring practices and the disparities in the distribution of caring responsibilities. Defining the praxis of caring masculinities, the chapter offers conceptual and empirical explorations of what a gender sensitive pedagogy could look like in an early childhood education setting. Whilst there are various obstacles to implementing a gender sensitive pedagogy in schools, Chapter 6 highlights the excessive focus on child-centredness as a contributing factor to teacher complacency and acceptance of gender roles in early childhood education. Whilst there is a need to allow child exploration and play, the focus on child-centred pedagogies is argued to become a vehicle for the reproduction of gender inequalities and gender stereotyping in childhood.

Velija and Phipps turn to physical education (PE) and gender in Chapter 7, using the theoretical approach of figurational sociology (Elias, 1978) to explore how the education of future educators can shed light on the pervasive nature of gender inequalities. Gender relations are discussed as carrying power which has roots in social, cultural, and historical processes. Focusing on the teaching of teachers within the context of PE, Velija and Phipps explain how gender knowledge is embedded in sets of gender relations which seem unproblematic but are influenced by naturalistic assumptions about binary opposites, such as the male and female bodies, lad culture in Higher Education and the lack of gender sensitive subject knowledge in PE. The chapter analyses data from a qualitative study carried out in higher education courses where future PE teachers are trained. The findings point to uneasy learning experiences where gender roles and stereotypes are unchallenged both in curricular delivery and pedagogical practice. Velija and Phipps's chapter throws a spotlight on the need to develop subject specific gender knowledge which can both further subject knowledge in PE but can also help address some of the inequalities documented in the chapter.

Whilst inequalities of gender in education tend to focus on students' experiences, it is also very important to examine how institutions account for the experiences of staff. Chapter 8 explores the experiences and responsibilities of care in the Higher Education sector and how the 'accelerated academy' can reproduce unequal structures that affect those who find themselves at the caregiving end of relationships in academia (Gravett et al., 2021, p. 5). With an incisive illustration of how neoliberalism governs academic structure, Castelao-Huerta brings into sharp focus the resulting rationalities that create a hostile environment for those who care for others, both at work and at home, and the way in which caring is recast through a neoliberal logic. To challenge some of the resulting neoliberalised ways of perceiving care, Castelao-Huerta's chapter draws on Motta and Bennett's (2018) definition of care in academia as more than just a relation but involving an affective praxis which continues to be disregarded within the sector. The chapter argues that care practices in academia are marked by precarity because those who provide too much care tend to pay the costs, mainly through the lack of recognition of their caring responsibilities and also through a lack of career development. These inequalities are also compounded by the fact that care is still a relation which is perceived as having little economic value within a capitalist model that is enabled and survives because of ongoing gender inequalities.

In Chapter 9 experiences of sexual harassment are examined through Merleau-Ponty's (2014) philosophy and its ontological distinctions between the body as object and the body as the lived, existential body. The chapter's theorisation of the body incites an analysis of experiences of sexual harassment in Higher Education as more than discursive, but also highly affective and material. The chapter illustrates how the context of Higher Education continues to struggle to question unequal gender relations. The qualitative data presented is affectively charged, narrating carefully how young females navigate and subvert sexual harassment experiences through a lived Merleau-Pontian grip on such situations. The chapter also exemplifies how the Foucauldian (Foucault, 2003) concept of the 'gaze' can be used to explain how the material and discursive university experiences are still governed by patriarchal cultures.

The contributions that feminist scholarship brings into education are explored in Chapter 10. Olivieri and Elorduy Alverde present their feminist caring pedagogy in Higher Education with a focus on students' experiences and how they are affected by inequalities of access, opportunity, and circumstance in the Netherlands. Although many of the inequalities narrated are overlooked by the neoliberal university, Olivieri and Elorduy Alverde make visible the discourses that disadvantage students in Higher Education by exploring how students are constructed as consumer citizens. The neoliberal logic of self-accountability and responsibility make the educational environment unresponsive to the basic needs identified in students' lives. The chapter provides an analysis of qualitative data pointing to how, instead, the precarity of being a student in times of social and economic hardship requires that the academy shift from relationships of productivity and profit to a feminist pedagogy of care. The experiences of students and staff are conflated through the hostility that accelerated academia creates for both groups. And the chapter seeks to recast the teacher–student relationship through a feminist pedagogy of care. Chapter 10 argues that if a pedagogy of care is to disrupt the idealised student situations on which universities create their systems, then there is a need to resist the speeds at which staff and students are expected to work. Equally, a feminist pedagogy of care troubles the speeds at which students are expected to learn. The chapter argues that slowing down is resistance. However, the chapter also explores how slowing down is also a privilege in modern institutions.

Fernández Romero presents, in Chapter 11, an empirical evaluation of how interventions can help address inequalities in education, based on feminist scholarship. Discussing results from an initiative to depatriarchialise and decolonise power relations with Higher Education faculty staff, Fernández Romero highlights the complexities of introducing a gendered perspective in educational practice. Chapter 11 argues that feminist pedagogy and scholarship are leading praxis-based bodies of knowledge that help challenge the false neutrality of the academy and institutional arrangements. The chapter narrates feminist praxis in context and movement, tracing resistances, transgressions, opportunities and positionalities in teaching and learning which move from the theoretical to the embodied to the praxis of educators in Higher Education. Some of the key findings point to the need to embed intersectional praxis if universities are committed to decolonising institutions and challenging patriarchal culture.

In Chapter 12, Zuo examines the cultural, social, educational, and political landscape of sex education in Chinese universities. Whilst there is a marked shift in recognising the need for sex and sexuality education, Zuo's chapter outlines the difficulties and shortcomings of the current approach to engage young people in sex education. Zuo's chapter examines multiple educational media and materials to discuss the problematic sexism and misogyny which continues to responsibilise young women for the consequences of a male desire problematically perceived as inevitable. The chapter also presents these findings against the backdrop of a complex socio-political context which portrays a progressive attitude but is still heavily permeated by a misogynistic moralising ideology. Youth sexuality is then recognised, but only within the strict parameters of a cis-heteronormative and a patriarchal set of gender and sexual relations which subjugates female sexuality to male sexuality.

Levi Herz and Rozmarin build on the theme of sex education to include sexual practices based on vulnerability. Levi Herz and Rozmarin argue that gender-based vulnerabilities are among the most persistent forms of social vulnerability that shape the lives of women and minorities but also use vulnerabilities as point of departure from which to understand empowering practices. By focusing on vulnerability as an affective response of bodies to their surroundings, Chapter 13 demonstrates how vulnerability operates as a resource for young women to manage risk while developing their abilities to express themselves sexually. The chapter explores selected youth affective relations, which are perceived as risky, but which also offer insights into how sexual expression must be conceptualised beyond the lens of vulnerabilities, particularly when thinking about appropriate sex education for young people.

Kerpen presents two case studies with LGBTQIA+ youth from the United Kingdom in Chapter 14, to make sense of how cis-heteronormativity can drive young people to exploitative online encounters. The chapter contextualises how LGBTQIA+ youths are at a higher risk of engaging in risky online behaviours, not just because of the ubiquitous use of online media and the anonymity that characterises it, but more importantly, because of the missed opportunities to protect cis-heteronormative societal expectations. The chapter also examines how current relationships and sex education (RSE) continues to serve the interests of a normative heterosexual matrix. The exclusion of LGBTQIA+ sexual agency and experiences in RSE is a failed opportunity to educate young people on how to recognise and manage risky online encounters.

Bernhard and Leicht-Scholten discuss the ongoing and historical gender disparities that continue to disadvantage women in STEM subjects. The lack of diversity in engineering is explored in Chapter 15 to approximate how the subject is marked by a culture which contributes to gender disparities. The chapter explores the ways in which disparities in STEM are explained through the notion of choice and historical stereotypes around self-concept of ability in STEM which are sexist and discriminatory. Bernhard and Leicht-Scholten argue that the subject of engineering and its culture are governed by a hegemonic masculinity paradigm but also by other forms of gender oppression that continue to responsibilise women for choosing to self-exclude or drop out of STEM courses.

References

Brown, R.N. (2009) *Black Girlhood Celebration: Toward a Hip Hop Feminist Pedagogy*. New York: Peter Lang.

Elias, N. (1978). *What Is Sociology?* New York: Columbia University Press.

Foucault, M. (2003) *The Birth of the Clinic: An Archaeology of Medical Perception*. London: Routledge.

Fraser, N. (1996) Gender equity and the welfare state: A post-industrial thought experiment, in: S. Benhabib (Ed.), *Democracy and Difference. Contesting the Boundaries of the Political*. Princeton: Princeton University Press, pp. 218–242.

Gravett, K., Taylor, C.A., and Fairchild, N. (2021) 'Pedagogies of mattering: reconceptualising relational pedagogies in higher education'. *Teaching in Higher Education*, 29(2), pp. 388–403.

Halberstam, J. (2005) *In a Queer Time and Place: Transgender Bodies, Subcultural Lives*. New York; London: NYU Press.

Halberstam, J. (2011) *The Queer Art of Failure*. Durham, NC: Duke University Press.

Haywood, C. and Mac an Ghaill, M. (1996) Schooling masculinities, in: M. Mac an Ghaill (Ed.) *Understanding Masculinities*. Buckingham: Open University Press, pp. 50–60.

hooks, b. (1990) *Yearning: Race, Gender and Cultural Politics*. Boston: South End Press.

hooks, b. (1994) *Teaching to Transgress: Education as the Practice of Freedom*. London: Routledge.

Kumashiro, K.K. (2002) *Troubling Education Queer Activism and Antioppressive Education*. New York: Routledge Falmer.

Lesko, N. (Ed.) (2000) *Masculinities at School*. London; Thousand Oaks: Sage.

Mac an Ghaill, M. (1994) *The Making of Men: Masculinities, Sexualities, and Schooling*. Buckingham: Open University Press.

Mac an Ghaill, M (1996) 'What about the boys? Schooling, class and crisis masculinity', *Sociological Review*, 44(2), pp. 381–397.

Mendes, K., Horeck, T. and Ringrose, J. (2022) 'Sexual violence in contemporary educational contexts', *Gender and Education*, 34(2), pp. 129–133. doi:10.1080/09540253.2022.2032537.

Merleau-Ponty, M (2014) *Phenomenology of Perception*. London: Routledge.

Motta, S.C. and Bennett, A. (2018) 'Pedagogies of care, care-full epistemological practice and "other" caring subjectivities in enabling education'. *Teaching in Higher Education*, 23(5), pp. 631–646.

Ng, R., Staton, P. and Scane, J. (1995) *Anti-Racism, Feminism and Critical Approaches to Education*. London: Praeger Publications.

Pinar, W.F. (2012) Understanding curriculum as gender text: Notes on reproduction, resistance and male–male relations, in: W. Pinar (Ed.) *Queer Theory in Education*. Hoboken: Taylor and Francis, pp, 183–202.

Renold, E. (2005) *Girls, Boys and Junior Sexualities: Exploring Childrens' Gender and Sexual Relations in the Primary School*. London: Routledge Falmer.

Ringrose, J. (2013) *Postfeminist Education? Girls and the Sexual Politics of Schooling.* Foundations and Futures of Education. London: Routledge.

Ringrose, J. and Epstein, D. (2015). Postfeminist educational media panics and the problem/promise of 'successful girls', in: *Introducing Gender and Women's Studies.* London: Macmillan, pp. 188–204. doi:10.1007/978-1-137-31069-9_11.

Ringrose, J. and Renold, E. (2012) 'Slut-shaming, girl power and 'sexualisation': Thinking through the politics of the international SlutWalks with teen girls'. *Gender and Education*, 24(3), pp. 333–343. doi:10.1080/09540253.2011.645023.

Sears, S. (2010) *Imagining Black Womanhood: The Negotiation of Power and Identity in the Girls Empowerment Project.* Albany: State University of New York Press.

Sedgwick, E.K. (2008) *Epistemology of the Closet.* Berkeley: University of California Press.

Tronto, J. (1993) *Moral Boundaries: A Political Argument for an Ethic of Care.* New York: Routledge.

Tronto, J. (1995) Women and caring: What can feminists learn about morality from caring?, in: V. Held (Ed.). *Justice and Care: Essential Readings in Feminist Ethics.* Boulder: Westview Press, pp. 101–116.

Weiler, K. and Arnot, M. (1993) *Feminism and Social Justice in Education.* London: Routledge.

White, R.D., Wyn, J. and Robards. B. (2017) *Youth and Society.* 4th ed. Melbourne: Oxford University Press.

Youdell, D. (2006) 'Subjectivation and performative politics – Butler thinking Althusser and Foucault: Intelligibility, agency and the raced–nationed–religioned subjects of education'. *British Journal of Sociology of Education* 27(4), pp. 511–528.

2 Exploring the Pedagogical Possibilities of Various Gender Ontologies

And Pasley and Sophie Lehner

Introduction

This chapter unpacks the various historical and ongoing conceptualisations of gender and explores the pedagogical possibilities that these gender ontologies offer learners. First, the chapter delineates a history of the terminology that has been used to refer to gender/sex/sexual difference to highlight the situatedness of these terms. Thereafter, a brief discussion of some non-Western and/or pre-colonial ontologies of 'gender' is provided to highlight the situatedness of the very possibility of gendered epistemologies and denaturalising any notion of their inherence. Leading from this, Lugones' (2007) colonialities of gender are unpacked, examining the colonial co-production of race and gender via biological essentialism as part of the modern/colonial project's justification of global domination. The chapter then explores how these orders have constituted endocisheterosexism – that is, the privileging of bodies that conform to binary male/female sex categories (Fausto-Sterling, 2000), gender assigned at birth (Butler, 1990), and attraction to the 'opposite' sex (Sedgwick, 1990) – and the associated gender hegemonies (Lugones, 2007). This enables us to unpack the boundaries that mark feminist resistances to these orders, including the four 'waves' of feminism, queer theory, trans studies, and relational/posthuman/new materialist approaches to gender, and to what extent they resist readings of gender that are based in the (modern colonial) humanist Genres of Man (Wynter, 2003). For each section, the pedagogical possibilities and consequences of each of these approaches is considered, affording educators a sense of the gender possibilities they offer their students.

This chapter is designed as a cursory overview of the different gender possibilities offered by various movements and theories. It is by no means all-encompassing, yet the chapter recognises a vast breadth of theory that has emerged in response to gender systems and inequalities. It is designed to offer a range of implications that emerge from a selection of perspectives to empower educators to take a more critically informed stance in relation to how they conceptualise gender and institute practices that render certain ways of doing gender im/possible. In doing so, we hope that educators can engage more effectively with their students and empower their engagements with the complex inheritance of gender.

DOI: 10.4324/9781003397502-2

Terminology, Coloniality, and More-Than-Western Worlds

The ubiquity of gender discourses in present day discussions, from hegemonic masculinities and femininities in popular magazines (Favaro and Gill, 2018) to the 'Transgender Tipping Point' (Steinmetz, 2014), disguises the reality that 'gender' is a recent concept, developed less than 70 years ago (Money, 1955). Gender's omnipresence is a product of the naturalisation of a social order oriented around sexual difference (Stryker, 1994), but it is by no means inherent. While current definitions tend to differentiate between biological sex and psychological gender (and sexuality), it would be a mistake to understand such distinctions as progressions along a linear, predetermined trajectory, wherein gender and sex were conflated via biological essentialism (Fausto-Sterling, 2000) but are now 'better' understood as separate. Instead, this chapter asks readers to trouble the givenness of how one knows and does gender.

As a case in point, it is important to recognise that most societies around the world have historically not relied and/or presently do not rely on the Western social orders of gender or any gender/sex differentiation for that matter. For example, Oyěwùmí (1997, p. 31) describes how 'gender was not an organising principle in Yoruba society prior to colonisation by the West'. Tagalog notions of *bakla* do not make the same ontological distinctions between gender and sexuality, understanding them as co-constitutive (yet quite unlike heteronormative conflations of gender and sexuality; binaohan, 2014). Similarly, Supawantanakul (2018) discusses how Thai understandings of *kathoey* exceed the simplistic translation as 'transgender', accounting for more-than-binary possibilities. Laing (2021) describes how *two-spirit* has become the umbrella term to refer to complex genders and sexualities among North American/Turtle Island Indigenous people, though these meanings vary considerably. Picq and Tikuna (2019) describe how, '[i]n Juchitán, Mexico, *muxes* are neither man nor woman, but a Zapotec gender hybridity [and, in] Hawai'i, the *māhū* embrace both the feminine and masculine'. In Australia, sistergirl and brotherboy present First Nations peoples' renegotiation of the colonialities of gender that afford a more expansive, kinship-based sense of gender diversity (O'Sullivan, 2021). In Aotearoa New Zealand, takatāpui recognises the fluid, relational constitution of gender, sex, and sexual expression that resists the essentialisation of self (Kerekere, 2017; Pasley and Tupaea, In Press). This is by no means an exhaustive list, but it clearly demonstrates the non-universality of Western notions of gender. Notably, Supawantanakul (2018) cautions against reading non-Western gender systems through Western lenses, recognising the situated nuance that defines these ways of knowing and being, often operating outside Modernist imaginaries. Indeed, even referring to them as gender systems is often a misnomer. Likewise, Ratel-Khan (2020) contends that the 'third gender/sex' framing of Indigenous gender reinforces colonialities of gender. Furthermore, Puar (2013) identifies how homonationalism construes present-day 'civilised society' as necessarily accepting of queerness, despite the largely colonial imposition of queerphobia, thereby reinstituting colonial hegemonies and naturalising the colonial paradigm on which queerphobia is built.

The gendering of Western society, based on biological essentialism, was an invention with an agenda. Lugones (2007) unpacks the ways in which the heterosexual matrix (Butler, 1990) – the fiction of a biological binary that maps seamlessly onto gender roles and sexual attraction, enforcing cisheteronormativity – equated (Western) gender etiquette with 'performing humanity', which served to justify the colonisation of those who did not perform Western gender roles (and were therefore read as 'less-than-human'). Simultaneously, this incentivised white women's justification of patriarchal inequalities to maintain the privileges of white supremacy. Patriarchal and white supremacist orders are designed to maintain one another. The ongoing inheritance of these (racialised) gendered social orders that have become inscribed across the world through global capitalism is known as the colonialities of gender (Lugones, 2007), entangled with broader colonialities of power (Quijano, 2000) and being (Wynter, 2003). These colonialities are important for thinking about what gender justice might look like. Furthermore, because all norms are entangled, it means that other hegemonies, including class, disability, and education (Puar, 2015), affect whether gender is read as 'adequate'. In/adequacy translates into the level of in/accessibility to participate in society (De La Cadena, 2010; Jaramillo-Aristizabal, 2022). Whether or not resistance movements have been able to recognise these dynamics has affected how they have manifested and the limits of the gender imaginaries that they have offered.

The Four 'Waves' of Feminism: Dismantling the Master's House with the Master's Tools to Moving Beyond Binaries

First wave feminism describes the movement in the 19th and 20th century that fought for legal rights for women, such as the right to vote. The movement was predominantly led by and for white, middle-class cis women and dominant feminist discourse in this era did not tend to concern itself with issues of class, race, sexuality, disability, etc. In the wake of the French revolution, Mary Wollstonecraft's (1792/1992) *A Vindication of the Rights of Women* lay the foundations for much of the suffragette movement, which is evident in the works of suffragettes like Kate Sheppard and Kate Edger (NZ), Elizabeth Cady Stanton and Susan B. Anthony (US), Emmeline, Christabel, Sylvia and Adela Pankhurst (UK); the work of her daughter, Mary Wollstonecraft Shelley, and other feminist writers, such as Virginia Woolf, the Brontë sisters, and Sylvia Plath (who was a major inspiration for the second wave). This era of feminism saw the establishment of women's colleges in universities (previously male-only spaces), the ability for women to own property (and no longer be considered property themselves), and the start of their inclusion within political spaces, among many other advances (Woolf, 1929).

Women gained the right to vote in Mauretania (1961), Algeria (1962), Morocco (1963), Libya (1964), Sudan (1964), Yemen (1970), Jordan (1974), Iraq (1980), and Djibouti (1986), demonstrating that this 'wave' did not impact all places at the same time. Moreover, some examples are not as clear cut as they might seem, such as women's right to vote in Aotearoa New Zealand being instituted by the New Zealand (settler) government in 1893, which neglects the reality that wāhine (Māori women) had political agency prior to colonisation. One can imagine the incredulity at being informed that your people are being liberated from the system of oppression that was imposed by your 'liberators'. While these might seem far-off concerns in present-day Western classrooms, it is important to account for the historical precedence that underlies these movements. Also, in globalised classrooms with many international students, some students may hark from contexts where many of these concerns remain present (World Bank, 2019). Moreover, these issues rematerialise in the form of financial abuse, domestic violence, wage gaps, and the ongoing unequal distribution of domestic labour (UN Women, 2023). Notably, critiques around the wave metaphor for feminist movements identify that this comparison treats feminist advancements as linear progressions along predetermined lines towards 'liberation' (Reger, 2017; Rome, O'Donohoe, and Dunnett, 2019), rather than acknowledging non-linear and alternative strategies or differences in what liberation can mean (Sundberg, 2014).

Second wave feminism arose in the early 1960s and marked a shift in feminist discourse from 'women can do what men can', invested in accessing established patriarchal structures, towards resisting the patriarchal order that subjugates 'woman' relative to 'man'. This is evident in the broadening of the concerns of the feminist movement, concerning itself with issues such as reproductive rights, family, domestic violence, rape, and workplace harassment and inequalities. However, it remained a white, middle-class cis women's movement. Catalysed by Betty Friedan's (1963/1982) *The Feminine Mystique* and in response to post-Second-World-War efforts to re-entrench patriarchal order after the independence that wartime tended to grant women, the second wave extended the fight for legal rights to self-determination over one's own body and rights to protect women in both family and workplace settings. A significant component of shifting gender role expectations was through fighting for the right to work, and a major milestone of feminist movement was the approval of the contraceptive pill that allowed women to have greater control of their reproductive agency. Emerging from the United States, this movement included the outlaw of marital rape, the establishment of legal precedents for abortion access via the Roe v. Wade (1973) decision and equal pay via the Equal Pay Act (1963), which were replicated elsewhere. In Germany, second wave feminism was responsible for engraining the equality of men and women in the constitution, the first female federal minister, the opening of women's centres, the establishment of the first chair for women's and gender studies at a German university, and the creation of ADEFRA, one of the first associations for Black German women, in the post-war period.

The issue common to first and second wave feminism is that they operate on the terms established by the colonialities of gender. That is, they perpetuate the mythology of biological essentialism, maintaining a binary construction of sexual difference/gender, based on assumed biological binaries. In this way, gender becomes 'a property of individuals' (Linstead and Pullen, 2006, p. 1288).

There is substantial work that demonstrates not only the fallacy of biological binaries but that the attributions accorded to gender/sex are largely arbitrary and founded in the misogynistic ideologies that were inherited through the coloniality of gender (Fausto-Sterling, 2000, 2012; Pasley, 2020, 2021). That being said, it is important to acknowledge that these movements were responding to deeply entrenched colonialities of gender, which they did not necessarily have the tools to dismantle. Moreover, while the relatively privileged subjects at the forefront of these movements appear problematic in hindsight, it is interesting to consider that they were often seeking to dismantle the fundamentally classist, patriarchal white supremacist systems that afforded them their relative privilege. However, these essentialist approaches to gender risk more serious consequences because of how they treat gendered power as a zero-sum game, whereby inequalities become a tug of war between supposed 'privileges' afforded to men/women and boys/girls. In education, this remains evident in ongoing debates around the 'feminisation' of education fostering boys' 'underperformance' (Ringrose, 2007) or the United Nation's (binary) gender equality goals' focus on uplifting girls' access to education (cf. UNHCR Gender Equality Toolkit, 2020). These conceptions of bodies and power neglect the complex patterns of relations that differentiate experiences of bodies and gender, producing (cis)normative assumptions around what sorts of bodies do what sorts of activities and neglecting the violent, racialised origins of this order of things (aka colonisation).

When biological essentialism is used to measure womanhood, for example, trans women are excluded from feminist agendas, despite their disproportionately greater exposure to gendered violence (Veale et al., 2019). The conflation of sex and gender affords a misattribution of patriarchal violence to bodily form and confuses sexual similarity with allyship. This is a 'fundamental attribution error' (Jones and Harris, 1967), wherein the disproportionate association of violence with male bodies leads these bodies to be equated with violence, which fosters sanctioned ignorance around violence perpetrated by female bodies or of the fact that male bodies are not inherently violent or privileged. This stance often referred to as trans exclusionary radical feminism (TERF; PearceErikainen, and Vincent, 2020), though Williams (2016) notes that radical feminism also has a rich history of trans inclusion, and most trans exclusion is not perpetrated in the name of 'feminism'. Notably, this reduction of people to their genitals is precisely how misogyny treats cis women. To sympathise, the scale and severity of patriarchal violence means that this misattribution is often coming from a place of trauma and/or protectionism; however, disproportionately higher rates of violence experienced by trans people globally (Balzer and Berredo, 2016) illustrate that this perspective not only buys into the colonialities of gender, but also enforces the boundaries of biological essentialism. To be clear, sympathising with trans exclusionary positions should not provide a platform to 'debate' trans lives – trans exclusionary perspectives are unfounded and those who hold these perspectives, even from a place of fear, need to be accountable for the violence that they enact when they take these positions. It is important for educators to ensure that they are helping students unpack these prejudices and resist the proliferation of biologically essentialist perspectives.

The effects of biological essentialist thinking are not limited to trans people. For example, Rahimi and Liston (2011) found that teachers' stereotypes around sexualised black bodies led them to ignore the sexual violence experienced by black girls or blame them for their victimisation. Black bodies are not permitted to inhabit gender in the same way white bodies are. Gender was designed to privilege certain (white, cisgender, heterosexual, middle-class, able, etc.) bodies, producing hegemonies of gender performativity, which it evidently continues to do. Despite the colonial origins of these social organising principles (Kerekere, 2017), settler nations and other postcolonial contexts have often become willing participants in the perpetuation of these social orders. Educational systems, which largely remain part of the colonial machinery (Ashcroft, 2001; Coloma, 2013), often operate to maintain these social orders via rewarding 'appropriate' gender performativity and punishing 'deviance' (Pascoe, 2005; Allen, 2004). Despite these disciplinary forces, the colonialities of gender have been adopted and adapted by Others; however, essentialist understandings of gender do not have the capacity account for this variation (Linstead and Pullen, 2006). Subsequently, educators need to be careful how they participate in these colonialities.

Emerging in the 1990s, third wave feminism presented a critique of second wave feminism's essentialising tendencies, attending to the numerous ways in which gender operates, incorporating perspectives that acknowledge gender's intersection with other experiences, such as race (Crenshaw, 1989), class (Spencer-Wood, 2011), trans rights (Serrano, 2007; Stone, 1991), and sexual liberation (cf. SlutWalks; Ringrose and Renold, 2012). This is not to say that these perspectives did not predate the 90s, but that this is when they came to the fore. For many, the third wave is synonymous with riot grrrl, zines, Bitch magazine, reclaiming 'women's crafts' like knitting, and space to experiment with masculinity and femininity (Karaian and Mitchell, 2010; Garrison, 2000). It presented the emergence of feminist critique of popular culture and media and more clearly articulated consent discourses and rape culture (Nguyen, 2013). Emerging alongside neoliberalism, feminism was marketed as desirable, with slogans like 'girl power'. Gill (2007) contends that the collusion with neoliberalism gave rise to postfeminist sentiment, whereby inequalities are written off with 'choice' discourses. For example, Wolf (1993) claims that the second wave victimises women and exaggerates inequalities, which ignores systemic patterns of gendered violence. Other critiques have focused on failure to recognise that these 'choices' were only possible because of the struggles of the former waves (Evans, 2013). Similarly, Angulo (2019) identifies how the marketisation of feminism reified classist, racialised, and heteronormative divides as the 'liberated' woman was coded as normatively successful. Some critiques have tended to focus on the diffuseness of third wave foci, which diluted feminist unity and perhaps diminished the unity of the cause, though this was partly intentional insofar as it recognised the diversity and non-uniformity of needs across feminisms (Evans, 2014). The emergence of intersectionality enabled a paradigm shift in the ontological possibilities of gender that third wave feminism offered.

Kimberlé Crenshaw (1989) coined the term 'intersectionality' in response to anti-sexism and anti-racism legal structures that were incapable of addressing dynamics where sexism and racism intersected, such as those experienced by black women in the United States. These dynamics were emblematic of the failures of society and women's rights movements, like second wave feminism, to conceive of gender beyond a (white, middle-class, heterosexual, cisgender, able-bodied, etc.) normative frame, failing to account for marginalised women and account for the relative privilege that white women potentially held over other marginalised groups (Phipps, 2021). Simultaneously, Black rights movements had not specifically addressed the need for black women's rights either, mostly led by and for black men. In this way, Crenshaw (1989) recognised that black women's multiple marginalities meant that they were not accounted for in either feminist or Black rights movements. Intersectionality aims to highlight this intersection, double/multiple oppression, and foster what Lugones (2007) has called deep coalition, recognising a shared struggle for justice across injustices. In Aotearoa, the Identify Survey (Fenaughty et al., 2022) has explored the status of trans students who have experienced state care, demonstrating how this double marginality means that they are less likely to have positive educational experiences (Fenaughty et al., In Press). Importantly, this research demonstrates that neither their gender nor care-experienced status alone that causes these elevated levels of disadvantage; their status as trans students who have experienced state care exposes them to unique experiences. For example, being in care and trans was associated with their carers being more likely to know about their gender, possibly because of the reduced privacy of young people in care, but less likely to be supportive of them. Educators need to be aware of how there is no one-size-fits-all approach to students based on any single identity.

Evans-Winters (2021, p. 2) contends,

> the intent of theoretically framing and analyzing educational problems and issues from an intersectional perspective is to better comprehend how race and gender overlap to shape (a) educational policy and discourse, (b) relationships in schools, and (c) students' identities and experiences in educational contexts.

However, while the introduction of the concept of intersectionality was revolutionary for many social justice movements, there remains room for critique. Because intersectionality remains structural in nature, employing essentialising categories (such as blackness and womanhood), it is unable to account for the immanent nature of power, which poststructuralism had so poignantly demonstrated (Foucault, 1979). The multiplicity of potential intersections presents an unfeasible set of contingencies, even if structuralism is assumed. Subsequently, third wave approaches often devolve into what could be referred to as 'Spice

Girls Feminism', wherein the Spice Girls formed a collection of tokenised versions of femininity, united by 'girl power'. On the surface, the possibilities of 'woman' appear to expand but in fact operate to reinforce not only the gender binary but also the normative configuration of femininity by creating examples, if not caricatures, of feminine deviance (Linstead and Pullen 2006; compare Mayo, 2009). Grotesquely, this includes the normative whiteness of femininity as black femininity is labelled 'scary spice', reinforcing the colonialities of gender. Despite these pitfalls, it remains an important theoretical development insofar as it challenges the monolithic conceptualisation of identity in social structures, highlighting the need to account for the differentiation of identity. In the classroom, educators should be mindful of the ways in which gender is differentiated by experiences of racialisation (Rahimi and Liston, 2011), disability (Puar, 2015), class (Spencer-Wood, 2011), sexuality (Kondelin, 2014), religion (Poveda Guillén, 2017), and more. In this way, even if students possess similar experiences in one regard, not all of them have the same needs and resources, and classrooms become sites of ongoing (re)negotiations of power.

While bearing many similarities with third wave approaches, Parry, Johnson, and Wagler (2018) contend that the fourth wave differentiates the feminist movement through its technological character, emerging from the increased accessibility of online mass media and tools, such as Facebook, the platform formerly known as Twitter, and Tiktok. Globalisation has facilitated an immense diversification of narratives, providing countless examples that resist the totalising effects of the colonialities of gender. Indeed, the capacity for non-institutionalised storytelling has become a powerful mode of information preservation and dissemination, enabling commentary and contributions from communities that had less access in previous movements. For example, young Indigenous people have used Tiktok to educate others on Indigenous gender practices, reaching audiences in numbers and ways that were not previously possible (Marino, 2023; Carlson and Mongibello, 2021). In the mainstream, the #MeToo movement gained traction, designed to support survivors of sexual violence and hold perpetrators accountable, with notable targets including US President Donald Trump and film mogul Harvey Weinstein (Pellegrini, 2018). Simultaneously, these technologies have been taken up by influential figures with misogynistic talking points, such as Jordan Peterson and Andrew Tate, which has fostered a resurgence of patriarchal values in younger generations of (largely) men and fed the entitlement of 'Incel' (involuntarily celibate) communities who feel spurned by feminist denial of men's entitlement to women's bodies (Trifan, 2023). For example, the 2014 Gamergate controversy emerged from the 'men's rights movement', designed to silence critiques of misogyny and other injustices in videogame culture (O'Donnell, 2020). While distasteful, such sentiments are not exactly new and are in fact driven by the imagination of a 'return' to traditional patriarchal orders.

Parry, Johnson, and Wagler (2018) note that there is less theoretical nuance in the fourth wave, blurring the boundaries between movements, illustrating a limitation of the wave metaphor, failing to capture the dis/continuity of feminism. Indeed, some commentators discuss intersectionality as a defining tool of the fourth wave (Zimmerman, 2017), which perhaps suggests that the fourth wave is defined more by changes in circumstance than an ideological paradigm shift. Given that this movement is still in its infancy, it is perhaps too early to know how it might otherwise modify the possibilities of knowing and doing gender; however, the change in circumstances and the tools available already present a range of intriguing ways in which feminists are taking up and enacting new possibilities for gender justice. Educators who are engaging with these dynamics need to develop an awareness of the tools their students are engaging with and raise questions around the potential precarity of content driven by algorithms that may not have their best interests at heart and/or create echo chambers that can impede their critical engagement (Bouvier, 2022).

Queer Theory: A Means of Reconstituting Gender, Not Just Rearranging the Furniture

Queer theory emerged in the early 1990s as a form of resistance to mainstream trends in lesbian and gay studies, borrowing heavily from poststructural theory (Foucault, 1976/1990; Butler, 1990; Sedgwick, 1990; Duggan, 2002; Halberstam, 2005; Rich, 1980; Muñoz, 2009; Namaste, 2009). While this theoretical oeuvre is inspired by and borrows from queer communities' experiences of marginality, queer theory refers to an epistemological approach, rather than necessitating queer content, though gender has often been the focus of this work. At the core of queer theory on gender is a recognition of the imbrication of sex, gender, and sexual norms via biological essentialism that plagued the feminist movements that preceded it (Butler, 1990; Sedgwick, 1990), which Butler dubbed the heterosexual matrix. Compulsory heterosexuality (Rich, 1980) or heteronormativity (Warner, 1993) recognised how heterosexuality (and, by extension, endosex and cisgender bodies) was privileged, allowing endo/cis/heteronormative bodies greater access to a world that was contoured in accordance with their interests. queer theory recognises how these normativities become knowable when we violate or queer them but that to queer norms is to disrupt what is thinkable and open up nuanced possibilities (Butler, 1990). A critical distinction is that gender is by no means inherent to bodies but is instead a matter of what Butler (1990) called *gender performativity*, which is not about performance, per se, but about the ways we are compelled by discourse to enact ourselves. In this way, gender is achieved through repetition and ritual, rendering someone recognisable. Queerness and queering operate to renegotiate the boundaries of intelligibility and therein the possibilities of gender. Jones (2023, p. 10) denotes that 'queer theory offers a lens through which we can call into question hegemonic practices that otherwise remain invisible due to repetition and tradition'. Muñoz (2009) contends that queer utopia is not something that can be achieved – always on the horizon – as we continue to renegotiate the boundaries of normativity and unsettle established orthodoxies in the ongoing pursuit of more just power relations.

Reflecting the queer theory that it is derived from, queer pedagogy rethinks pedagogy and knowledge to challenge, question, and restructure current (endocisheteronormative) education systems (Britzman, 1995), interrogating, dismantling, and unsettling educational structures and the normativities that constitute them. It extends beyond simply integrating queer topics into current educational systems, towards critically questioning and disrupting normativities (Quinlivan, 2018). Quinlivan et al. (2014) contend that inclusion grounded in the cunning of liberal recognition risks the corruption of what it means to be queer by coding queerness in normative terms. Duggan (2002) attends to how homonormativity mimics heteronormative structures, such as gay couples being expected to have one partner who is 'the man'/dominant and the other who operates as 'the woman'/submissive. Pasley, Hamilton, and Veale (2022) similarly draw attention to how the ways transnormative pressures influence trans people to imitate binary cis orders of gender. Liberal progressive sexuality education seeks to recuperate queerness into normative structures to make it palatable to cisheteronormative students, teachers, and society. Queer pedagogy offers educators a new lens through which to inspect not only their surroundings but also their own actions and urges educational institutions not to 'attach themselves to one set model since these ideals end up alienating and excluding certain individuals' (Nemi Neto, 2018, p. 591). Quinlivan's (2018) queer pedagogy draws on Halberstam's (2011) notion of the queer art of failure, finding ways of conceptualising success beyond the boundaries of normative qualification. In this way, queer pedagogy can help educators and their students to identify (by crossing) and playing with (or queering) the gender possibilities their classrooms offer.

Prescribing how one might implement queer pedagogy is somewhat contra to the very notion of this praxis. Indeed, Britzman (1995, p.152) queries whether there is such a thing, suggesting that there is perhaps a 'possibility of articulating pedagogies that call into question the conceptual geography of normalization'. They note the paradoxical nature of how queering norms serves 'both to recuperate and to exceed the stereotypes that contain and dismiss' (p. 153); a double gesture that operates to (re)signify impropriety. In reality, calling it queer theory disguises the wily tactic of exposing the mechanisms that naturalise heterosexuality or any other hegemonic identity, for that matter, and how the norm requires the Other to exist. From this, Britzman (1995, p. 165) suggests that queer pedagogy becomes that which enacts a refusal of

> normal practices and practices of normalcy, [beginning with] an ethical concern for one's *own* reading practices... exploring what one cannot bear to know... the imagining of a sociality unhinged form the dominant conceptual order ... so that all bodies matter.

The conclusion of Kumashiro's (2002) *Troubling Education: Queer Activism and Anti-Oppressive Pedagogy* is perhaps the most fitting end to a book on queer pedagogy insofar as it walks the talk, refusing closure and resisting convention or even authoritativeness; 'an ending that would make it difficult for readers to read and to finish reading my book in traditional ways' (p. 200). Kumashiro (2002) invites readers to read his text through other lenses, undermining any essential meaning or value of the work, and to embrace the refusal of finality in any 'lessons'. The conclusion confronts the teacher's dilemma of desiring to control what cannot be controlled: what is learnt, how it is learnt, and what change emerges. Instead, it remains open to meeting learners/readers where they are and allowing the lessons to take them where they need to go if they can transport them there. Rather than prescribing who learners become, Kumashiro hopes that their queer pedagogy opens new paths for who they might become. Indeed, returning to the question of whether there is a queer pedagogy (Britzman, 1995), Kumashiro (2002, p. 202) contends 'teachers and students must simultaneously enact different antioppressive forms of education while troubling those very forms; simultaneously be antioppressive in some ways while troubling those very ways of being'.

The double gesture of queer pedagogy is not without risk. Linstead and Pullen (2006) caution against queer theory's appearance of breaking the binary but actually leaving the boundaries that are crossed undisturbed. For example, the recognition of trans people, but privileging those who replicate cisnormativities, erases any sense of disruption and maintains the gender binary (Pasley, Hamilton, and Veale, 2022; Gill-Peterson, 2018; Vipond, 2015). Mayo (2009) describes how the extraordinary focus on queer and trans students in sexuality education can reinforce the sense of their Otherness, while silences around cisgender, heterosexual experiences simultaneously indicate their givenness. This is evident in the way 'gender diversity' is assumed to not include cisgender students, suggesting that 'diversity' is simply code for Other. Similarly, non-binary genders are often treated categorically, lumping all differences into one group, rather than addressing the multiplicitous variation that exists beyond the binary. Therein, Linstead and Pullen (2006) demonstrate that having a 'third' option does not inherently do the work of disrupting the gender binary. Educators should take care to ensure that their praxis does not reinscribe the undesirability of becoming otherwise. Moreover, queer theory's reliance on the intelligibility of discourse (Mitchell, 2008) presents the predicament of the violence of recognition when unintelligible expressions of gender are read through established lenses, leading to the erasure of the terms on which people understand themselves. Educators need to find strategies to understand students' gender on their own terms (Pasley, 2022, 2021; Hoskins, 2010), rather than contorting them into forms that makes sense to educators' pre-established understandings.

Trans Studies and the Risk of Transnormativities

Trans studies shares much with queer theory (and to make a stark distinction would be fallacious) but the distinction reflects an ideological rupture in the post-Stonewall Riots era, wherein predominantly wealthy, white gay men used their relative privilege to campaign for gay inclusion based on shared hegemonic statuses (Duggan, 2002; Pasley, Hamilton and Veale, 2022). In short, this entailed positioning gay people who sought to achieve heteronormative standards (e.g., marriage, children, property, active/passive relationship dynamics) as 'good queers', whereas those who resisted heteronormativity (and other entangled hegemonies, including trans people) were cast as 'bad queers'. This led to the subsequent distinction between queerness as sexual, while transness concerned gender. Transfeminism responds to the ensuing disproportionate gender violence experienced by trans people (Balzer and Berredo, 2016; Fenaughty et al., 2022) and the medical systems that have been gatekeeping gender affirming procedures since the middle of the 20th century (Stone, 1991; Vipond, 2015; Pasley, Hamilton, and Veale, 2022). 'Transgender' was reclaimed to signal trans people's agency to determine their own gender, in opposition to the medically sanctioned term, 'transsexual'; however, it is also important to recognise that many within the trans community continue(d) to use medical terms and/or remain invested in access to medical infrastructures. The work of key trans theorists recognised the historical presence of trans people, resisted biological narratives, and embraced the possibility of trans as contra to the heterosexual matrix (rather than simply conforming to it; Stone, 1991; Bornstein, 1995; Stryker, 1994). While cis/trans distinctions are a product of the colonialities of gender, when trans is a proxy for the possibilities of doing gender otherwise, it can do the work of denaturalising cisnormativities (Pasley, 2022). Despite the valiant efforts of these theorists, Vipond (2015) highlights the way trans access remains striated along intersections of race, disability, and other normative expectations. Gill-Peterson (2018) highlights how pressures to enact gender in particular ways extend to trans children, particularly because of the potential to erase any trace of gender non-conformity with early transition (while continuing to restrict children's agency in these processes). Pasley (In Press) demarcates how the value of embracing gender diversity and non-conformity extends to both cis and trans children, reducing pressure to conform and bullying in response to non-conformity, so teachers should have strategies to help young people embrace difference.

As (hegemonic expressions of) trans citizenship has gained traction (Steinmetz, 2014), normative institutions have incorporated trans foci, often concerned with issues of infrastructure, policy, access, measuring trans well-being (often relative to cisgender standards), and undermining systemic inequalities and discrimination (e.g., Boe et al., 2020; Veale et al., 2019; Balzer and Berredo, 2016). Often, the narrowness of these foci is a product of the state of survival that many trans people have been put in by the colonialities of gender. Pasley, Hamilton and Veale (2022) account for how trans people have often been inculcated into participating in colonialities of gender by systems that require them to perform transnormative embodiments of gender or by a society that marginalises gender non-conformity. Educators should consider how their practices reproduce narrow models of gender. Trans children are often held to more strict standards of gender role conformity to be treated well by their peers and staff (Pasley, 2022), so educators should consider ways in which they might resist cis- and transnormativities in the classroom, such as refusing to incorporate binary gender practices, such as boys' and girls' lines, sports, and uniforms (Pasley, In Press, 2022; New Zealand Ministry of Education, 2020).

Ashley (2019a) emphasises the importance of supporting trans and gender creative students' exploration of gender possibilities, recognising that delaying transition comforts the anxieties of adults at the expense of children's well-being. 'Desistance', which requires young people to prove their gender by sustaining their identity in case their gender is 'just a phase', ignores the hypocrisy that we are prepared to believe cisgender children's sense of gender (Ashley, 2022). Moreover, the gatekeeping of access to blockers and hormone replacement dehumanises trans people (Ashley, 2019b). However, Ashley (2019c) recognises that medical access alone will not avert homelessness for trans young people – a statistic in which they are over-represented (Fraser et al., 2021) – and broader factors that support trans well-being need to be addressed. Fenaughty et al. (2022) demonstrate that trans students in Aotearoa face significantly greater educational barriers across the board, even compared to their cisgender queer counterparts. Notably, Pasley (2022) has cautioned that, while research that accounts for inequality is important and such discrepancies should not be ignored, deficit model research risks reducing trans lives to suffering and reinforcing trans people's status as Other. Educators should seek ways to engage with diversity in their classrooms through strengths-based approaches that do not single out trans children as different (Mayo, 2009; Quinlivan, 2018).

Understanding Gender Relationally

Linstead and Pullen (2006) argue for a conception of gender as relationally constituted, whereby all gender is understood as heterogeneous and the possibilities multiplicitous. What gender can become proliferates through the ongoing reconfiguration of relations. In this way, gender cannot be fitted into existing conceptualisations but can only be understood through the continual mapping of relations. A relational approach moves gender beyond subject–object dualisms and allows gendered subjectification to be understood as co-constitutive. To conceptualise this, Linstead and Pullen (2006) draw on Deleuze and Guattari's (1987) notion of the Body without Organs, which resists the positivist understanding that gender exists 'out there', waiting to be found, or that the matter or definition of gender can be settled, in contrast to essentialist notions that have dominated Western paradigms. Gender is never complete, always in the middle of becoming itself. This allows for a much more capacious understanding of gender and what it can become, unrestrained by any obligation to a pre-established binary.

While Linstead and Pullen (2006) employ Deleuze and Guattari (1987) to explore gender in this relational sense, other feminist materialist approaches have taken up similar theories, such as agential realism (Barad, 2007). Of note is their capacity to account for the more-than-human relations that co-constitute gender, which is integral to accounting for the ways in which gender emerges from relations that exceed human intentionality or intelligibility (Pasley, 2022). These theories, applied to notions of gender/sex/sexuality/sexual difference, have been variously unpacked by Lane (2009), Jagger (2015), Højgaard et al. (2015), and Pasley (2022). For Pasley (2022), agential realism calls us to attend to the ways in which present gender possibilities emerge from the confluence of pasts that (never) were and futures that might (not) be. Gender is always already haunted (cf. Derrida, 1994). Subsequently, understanding what it means to ethically engage with gender is a matter of tracing the entangled temporalities that produce present possibilities (Pasley, 2022). In classrooms, educators might engage students in questions around what produced the gender dynamics that they are wrestling with. Unlike queer theory, the goal is not necessarily to queer the norms that are entangled in these dynamics, recognising that these norms may be implicated in more capacious responses (Pasley, 2022), but to attend to relations in ways that offer a better sense of how relations might be responded to.

Mohandas and Osgood (2023) produced a bibliography of feminist materialist research in education, from which we provide a few key examples that demonstrate the possibilities such approaches offer. To begin with, Osgood and Giugni/Scarlet (2015, p. 352) offer a wonderful account of the more-than-human constitution of the 'dress–sword–(girl)child–hair–bare-feet–grassy-lawn assemblage' through Haraway's (2004) knotted relations. None of these phenomena can be understood separably (Barad, 2007), as they coalesce in this playful event. The agency is no longer assumed to be solely human, shared with the more-than-human elements that co-produce the boundaries of possibility. Rather than assuming the interference of some pre-figured discourse that contours the meanings of these dynamics, the focus is on tracing what sorts of relations enable this capacious embodiment of gender in a four-year-old (while simultaneously disallowing others). Educators are encouraged to explore what sorts of (gendered) possibilities are produced by the configurations of classrooms, conversations, and how students are entangled in the wider world.

Renold (2019) documents the (ongoing) process of developing AGENDA, a gendered and sexual violence prevention 'anti-guide' that 'departs from the dominant and over-coded policy discourse of "healthy" or "respectful" relationships education' (p. 223; which tends to prescribe 'acceptable' ways of knowing and being oneself). Instead, the resource is designed for users to 'explore their own matters of concern and connect with the concerns of others in ways that might orient them to new ideas and possibilities' (p. 220) , providing 'ideas on *how* to "do something" that mattered to them' (p. 215). The relations that define these dynamics are tapped into through arts-based methods, 'mobilising affirmative pARTicipatory "practices of engagement" to register the complex and relational matters of concern in human and more-than-human worlds' (p. 229). Renold (2019) describes how the project shifts from 'what is' to 'what if', affording a broad range of speculative possibilities, grounded in pragmatic examples of change making. For example, encountering The Rotifer Project, artful approaches facilitated speculative reconfigurations of the rigid binaries so often embedded in schooling praxis, such as uniforms and segregated bathrooms (Renold, 2016; Pasley, 2022). Renold (2019) highlights how these approaches take seriously the ways in which young people's engagements with gender and sexuality are always already threaded through with questions of ethics (cf. Quinlivan, 2018; Barad, 2017). Recognising the relational constitution of violence decentres 'individual responsibility' narratives, refocusing on collective approaches to change. While the differences these reconfigurations afford may appear minor, 'the smallest gesture can make the biggest change' (Renold, 2016, p. 7). Rather than reducing change-making to predefined notions of 'success or failure', the non-linear, 'run-a-way' artistic processes potentiated an array of unanticipated possibilities that could not have been predicted in advance, rendering a more capacious reality for partici-pants. Educators continue to contribute new strategies that potentiate the un/set-tling of gender dynamics (www.agendaonline.co.uk).

Pasley (2022) maps the educational worlds of four trans secondary students to explore possibilities for responding to gender in/justice. Riley, a 16-year-old trans masc non-binary student, rides the bus into school with bags of snacks and drinks for the weekly rainbow group lunch. Despite the opposition from the vice principal, Riley was determined to start the group, carving out an hour of solace in the week for rainbow students, born from their desire for others to not have to endure the isolation that they had. In this configuration of relations, they have the capacity to respond in ways that reconfigure the temporalities that their school has to offer students. Students navigated the frequent inacces-sibility of their aspirations through strategies of *concessional perfectionism*, doing what they could, given the circumstances. An agential realist ethics of response-ability (Barad, 2007) entails the tracing of entangled temporalities to establish what responses are im/possible, affording an openness to becoming otherwise. Subsequently, Pasley (2022) contends that trans genderings are fun-damentally response-able insofar as their enactment necessitates the tracings of temporal entanglements to be rendered im/possible. Educators might use similar strategies to get students to question what sorts of gendered im/possibilities are available to them, the sorts of histories that produced these dynamics, and to speculate around what responses might reconfigure their worlds. Importantly, in each of these examples of relational approaches to gender, there is no response that will resolve (gender) injustice once and for all, as each reconfi-guration begets new im/possibilities (Barad, 2017). Instead, students and edu-cators alike might like to take inspiration from Pasley's (2022) participants, enacting concessional perfectionism in the ongoing pursuit of gender justice.

Conclusion

This chapter affords educators the opportunity to unpack how they relate to the various ways of knowing and doing gender that ongoing feminist approaches have offered in response to the patriarchal orders that were propagated by modern/colonial systems and subsequent colonialities of gender (Lugones, 2007). While each approach has its limitations, if we take as our starting point a commitment to gender justice, this is a good place to query how we might do this better by each other. Importantly, the acknowledgement that justice is only ever partial and that injustice can never be resolved once and for all (Barad, 2017) provides some perspective on why these movements continue to adapt and evolve and perhaps holds some grace for the limitations of those approaches that were doing their best under the circumstances. Barad (in Juelskjær and Schwennessen, 2012) suggests that theoretical developments do not negate what preceded them but give rise to new questions that might be asked. Indeed, tracing the histories that have made developments possible is integral to understanding how we might best respond to current circumstances (Barad, 2007; Pasley, 2022). Our hope is that you never stop, that this text helps you continue your journey and perhaps find allies along the way.

References

Allen, L. (2004) 'Beyond the birds and the bees: Constituting a discourse of erotics in sexuality education'. *Gender and Education*, 16(2), pp. 151–167.

Angulo, S. (2019) *The Feminist Third Wave: Social Reproduction, Feminism as Class Struggle, and Contemporary Women's Movements*. Los Angeles: California State University.

Ashcroft, B. (2001) *On Post-Colonial Futures: Transformations of a Colonial Culture*. London: A & C Black.

Ashley, F. (2019a) 'Thinking an ethics of gender exploration: Against delaying transition for transgender and gender creative youth'. *Clinical Child Psychology and Psychiatry*, 24(2), pp. 223–236.

Ashley, F. (2019b) 'Gatekeeping hormone replacement therapy for transgender patients is dehumanising'. *Journal of Medical Ethics*, 45, pp. 480–482.

Ashley, F. (2019c) 'Puberty blockers are necessary, but they don't prevent homelessness: Caring for transgender youth by supporting unsupportive parents'. *The American Journal of Bioethics*, 19(2), pp.87–89.

Ashley, F. (2022) 'The clinical irrelevance of "desistance" research for transgender and gender creative youth'. *Psychology of Sexual Orientation and Gender Diversity*, 9(4), pp. 387–397.

Balzer, C. and Berredo, L. (2016) *TMM Annual Report 2016*. Berlin: Transrespect versus Transphobia Worldwide.

Barad, K. (2007) *Meeting the Universe Halfway: Quantum Physics and the Entanglement of Matter and Meaning*. Durham, NC: Duke University Press.

Barad, K. (2017) 'Troubling time/s and ecologies of nothingness: Re-turning, re-membering, and facing the incalculable'. *New Formations*, 92, pp. 56–86.

binaohan, b. (2014) *Decolonizing trans/gender 101*, Biyuti Publishing.

Boe, J.L., Ellis, E.M., Sharstrom, K.A., and Gale, J.E. (2020) 'Disrupting cisnormativity, transnormativity, and transmisogyny in healthcare: Advancing trans inclusive practices for medical family therapists'. *Journal of Feminist Family Therapy*, 32(3–4), pp. 157–175.

Bornstein, K. (1995) *Gender Outlaw: On Men, Women, and the Rest of Us*. New York: Vintage.

Bouvier, G. (2022) 'From "echo chambers" to "chaos chambers": Discursive coherence and contradiction in the #MeToo Twitter feed'. *Critical Discourse Studies*, 19(2), pp. 179–195.

Britzman, D.P. (1995) 'Is there a queer pedagogy? Or, stop reading straight'. *Educational Theory*, 45(2), pp. 151–165.

Butler, J. (1990) *Gender Trouble: Feminism and the Subversion of Identity*, New York: Routledge.

Carlson, B. and Mongibello, A. (2021) 'Indigenous resistance in the digital age'. *Anglistica AION. An Interdisciplinary Journal*, 25(1), pp. 1 8.

Coloma, R.S. (2013) 'Empire: An analytical category for educational research'. *Educational Theory*, 63(6), pp. 639–658.

Crenshaw, K. (1989) 'Demarginalizing the intersection of race and sex: A black feminist critique of antidiscrimination doctrine, feminist theory and antiracist politics'. *University of Chicago Legal Forum*, 1989(1), pp. 139–167.

De La Cadena, M. (2010) 'Indigenous cosmopolitics in the Andes: Conceptual reflections beyond "politics"'. *Cultural Anthropology*, 25(2), pp. 334–370.

Deleuze, G. and Guattari, F. (1987) *A Thousand Plateaus*. Trans. B. Massumi. Minneapolis: The University of Minnesota Press.

Derrida, J. (1994) *Specters of Marx*. Trans. P. Kamuf. New York: Routledge.

Duggan, L. (2002) The new homonormativity: The sexual politics of neoliberalism, in: R. Castronovo and D.D. Nelson (Eds) *Materializing Democracy: Toward a Revitalized Cultural Politics*, Durham, NC: Duke University Press. doi:10.1215/9780822383901-007.

Evans, E. (2014) *The Politics of Third Wave Feminisms*. London: Palgrave Macmillan.

Evans, S.M. (2013) 'Feminism's history and historical amnesia'. *Modern Intellectual History*, 10(2), pp. 503–513.

Evans-Winters, V.E. (2021) Race and gender intersectionality and education, in: *Oxford Research Encyclopedia of Education*. doi:10.1093/acrefore/9780190264093.013.1345.

Fenaughty, J., Ker, A., Alansari, M., Besley, T., Kerekere, E., Pasley, A., Saxton, P., Subramanain, P., Thomsen, P., and Veale, J. (2022) *Identify Survey: Community and Advocacy Report*. Identify Survey Team.

Fenaughty, J., Pasley, A., and Kerr, A. (In Press). *Identify Survey Findings for Young People with Oranga Tamariki involvement: Secondary Education Report*. Identify Survey Team.

Fausto-Sterling, A. (2000) *Sexing the Body: Gender Politics and the Construction of Sexuality*. New York: Basic Books.

Fausto-Sterling, A. (2012) *Sex/Gender: Biology in a Social World*. London and New York: Routledge.

Favaro, L. and Gill, R. (2018) 'Feminism rebranded: Women's magazines online and "the return of the F-word"'. *Dígitos: Revista de Comunicación Digital*, 2018(4), pp. 37–65.

Foucault, M. (1976/1990) *The History of Sexuality, Volume 1: An Introduction*. Trans. R. Hurley. New York: Vintage Books.

Foucault, M. (1979) 'Power and Norms', in: M. Morris and P. Patton (Eds) *Power, Truth and Strategy*. New York: Prometheus Books.

Fraser, B., Chisholm, E., and Pierse, N. (2021) '"You're so powerless": Takatāpui/ LGBTIQ+ people's experiences before becoming homeless in Aotearoa New Zealand'. *Plos One*, 16(12), Article e0259799.

Friedan, B. (1963/1982) *The Feminine Mystique*. Harmondsworth: Penguin.

Garrison, E.K. (2000) 'US feminism-grrrl style! Youth (sub) cultures and the technologics of the third wave'. *Feminist Studies*, 26(1), pp. 141–170.

Gill, R. (2007) 'Postfeminist media culture: Elements of a sensibility'. *European Journal of Cultural Studies*, 10(2), pp. 147–166.

Gill-Peterson, J. (2018) *Histories of the Transgender Child*. Minneapolis: University of Minnesota Press.

Halberstam, J.J. (2005) *In a Queer Time and Place: Transgender Bodies, Subcultural Lives*. New York: NYU Press.

Halberstam, J.J. (2011) *The Queer Art of Failure*. Durham, NC: Duke University Press.

Haraway, D.J. (2004) *The Haraway Reader*. London: Psychology Press.

Højgaard, L., Juelskjær, M., and Søndergaard, D.M. (2015) 'The "WHAT OF" and the "WHAT IF" of agential realism–In search of the gendered subject'. *Kvinder, Køn and Forskning*, 2012(1–2). doi:10.7146/kkf.v0i1-2.28069.

Hoskins, T.K. (2010) *Māori and Levinas: Kanohi ki te kanohi for an Ethical Politics* (Doctoral dissertation, ResearchSpace@ Auckland).

Jagger, G. (2015) 'The new materialism and sexual difference'. *Signs: Journal of Women in Culture and Society*, 40, pp. 321–342.

Jaramillo-Aristizabal, A. (2022) 'Critical theory and academia: Ontological im/possibilities for upholding plural worlds'. *Knowledge Cultures*, 10(3), pp. 126–149.

Jones, E.E. and Harris, V.A. (1967) 'The attribution of attitudes'. *Journal of Experimental Social Psychology*, 3, pp. 1–24.

Jones, M.C. (2023) *Queer and Trans Inclusion in Finnish Teacher Education and Educational Research*. Open Access Dissertations. Paper 1516. Available at: https://digitalcommons.uri.edu/oa_diss/1516.

Juelskjær, M. and Schwennesen, N. (2012) 'Intra-active entanglements–An interview with Karen Barad'. *Kvinder, Køn and Forskning*, 2012(1–2), pp. 10–23.

Karaian, L. and Mitchell, A. (2010) Third wave feminisms, in: N. Mandell and J. Johnson (Eds) *Feminist Issues: Race, Class and Sexuality*. London: Pearson, pp. 40–62.

Kerekere, E., (2017) *Part of the whānau: The Emergence of takatāpui Identity-he whāriki takatāpui*. Unpublished Doctoral thesis. Available at: https://static1.squarespace.com/static/5893cf9215d5db8ef4a8dc98/t/590fe54c1e5b6c8e16f8cd01/1494213974577/kerekere+part+of+the+whanau+the+emergence+of+takatapui+identity-1.pdf.

Kondelin, S. (2014) 'Dis/orientations of gender and sexuality in transgender embodiment'. *SQS Journal*, 8, pp. 32–43.

Kumashiro, K.K. (2002) *Troubling Education: Queer Activism and Antioppressive Pedagogy*. London and New York: Routledge.

Laing, M. (2021) *Urban Indigenous Youth Reframing Two-Spirit*. London and New York: Routledge.

Lane, R. (2009) 'Trans as bodily becoming: Rethinking the biological as diversity, not dichotomy'. *Hypatia*, 24, pp. 136–157.

Linstead, S. and Pullen, A. (2006) 'Gender as multiplicity: Desire, displacement, difference and dispersion'. *Human Relations*, 59(9), pp. 1287–1310.

Lugones, M. (2007) 'Heterosexualism and the colonial/modern gender system'. *Hypatia*, 22(1), pp. 186–219.

Marino, F. (2023) '#Twospirit: Identity construction through stance-taking on TikTok'. *Discourse, Context and Media*, 54, Article 100711.

Mayo, C. (2009) Access and obstacles: Gay–straight alliances attempt to alter school communities, in: W. Ayers, T. Quinn, and D. Stovall (Eds) *Handbook of Social Justice in Education*. London and New York: Routledge, pp. 484–497.

Mitchell, K. (2008) 'Unintelligible subjects: Making sense of gender, sexuality and subjectivity after Butler'. *Subjectivity*, 25, pp. 413–431.

Mohandas, S. and Osgood, J. (2023) 'Feminist new materialist approaches to childhood studies'. Oxford Bibliographies. Available at: https://oxfordbibliographies.com/displa y/document/obo-9780199791231/obo-9780199791231-0286xml.

Money, J. (1955) 'Hermaphroditism, gender and precocity in hyperadrenocorticism: psychologic findings'. *Bulletin of the Johns Hopkins Hospital*, 96(6), pp. 253–264.

Muñoz, J. (2009) *Cruising Utopia: The Then and There of Queer Futurity*. New York: New York University Press.

Namaste, V. (2009) 'Undoing theory: The "transgender question" and the epistemic violence of Anglo-American feminist theory'. *Hypatia*, 24, pp. 11–32.

Nemi Neto, J. (2018) 'Queer pedagogy: Approaches to inclusive teaching'. *Policy Futures in Education*, 16(5), pp. 589–604.

New Zealand Ministry of Education (2020) *Relationships and Sexuality Education: A Guide for Teachers*. Wellington, New Zealand: Leaders, and Boards of Trustees.

Nguyen, T. (2013) 'From SlutWalks to SuicideGirls: Feminist resistance in the third wave and postfeminist era'. *Women's Studies Quarterly*, 41(3/4), pp. 157–172.

O'Donnell, J. (2020) 'Militant meninism: the militaristic discourse of Gamergate and Men's Rights Activism'. *Media, Culture and Society*, 42(5), pp. 654–674.

Osgood, J. and Giugni, M./Scarlet, R. R. (2015) 'Putting posthumanist theory to work to reconfigure gender in early childhood: When theory becomes method becomes art'. *Global Studies of Childhood*, 5, pp. 346–360.

O'Sullivan, S. (2021) 'The colonial project of gender (and everything else)'. *Genealogy*, 5(3), p. 67.

Oyěwùmí, O. (1997) *The Invention of Women: Making an African Sense of Western Gender Discourses*. Minneapolis: University of Minnesota Press.

Parry, D.C., Johnson, C.W. and Wagler, F.A. (2018) Fourth wave feminism: Theoretical underpinnings and future directions for leisure research, in: D. Parry (Ed.) *Feminisms in Leisure Studies*. London and New York: Routledge, pp. 1–12.

Pascoe, C.J., (2005) '"Dude, you're a fag": Adolescent masculinity and the fag discourse'. *Sexualities*, 8(3), pp. 329–346.

Pasley, A. (2020) 'The effects of agential realism on sex research, intersexuality and education'. *Sex Education*, 21(5), 504–518.

Pasley, A. (2021) The effects of agential realism on gender research and education, in: L. Jackson (Ed.) *The Oxford Encyclopaedia for Philosophy of Education*. Oxford: Oxford University Press.

Pasley, A. (2022) *Spacetimegenderings: How Trans Secondary School Students Matter in Aotearoa NewZealand*. Aotearoa New Zealand: Doctoral Thesis. ResearchSpa- ce@Auckland. University of Auckland.

Pasley, A. (In Press) (Trans)genderings, in: M. Tesar (Ed.) *The SAGE Encyclopedia of Social Justice in Early Childhoods and Childhood Studies*. Thousand Oaks: SAGE.

Pasley, A., Hamilton, T., and Veale, J.F. (2022) Transnormativities: Reterritorialising Perceptions and Practice, in: L. Johnston and P. Doan (Eds) *Rethinking Transgender Identities*. London and New York: Routledge, pp. 160–171.

Pasley, A. and Tupaea, M. (In Press) Takatāpui and Rainbow Māori, in: *Rainbow Family and Sexual Violence Prevention in Aotearoa New Zealand: An Overview*. Rainbow Violence Prevention Network.

Pearce, R., Erikainen, S., and Vincent, B. (2020) 'TERF wars: An introduction'. *The Sociological Review*, 68(4), pp. 677–698.

Pellegrini, A. (2018) '#MeToo: Before and after'. *Studies in Gender and Sexuality*, 19(4), pp. 262–264.

Phipps, A. (2021) 'White tears, white rage: Victimhood and (as) violence in mainstream feminism'. *European Journal of Cultural Studies*, 24(1), pp. 81–93.

Picq, M.L. and Tikuna, J. (2019) 'Indigenous sexualities: Resisting conquest and translation'. *Sexuality and Translation in World Politics*, 57.

Poveda Guillén, O. (2017) *According to Whose Will: The Entanglements of Gender and Religion in the lives of Transgender Jews with an Orthodox Background*. Uppsala: Acta Universitatis Upsaliensis.

Puar, J. (2013) 'Rethinking homonationalism'. *International Journal of Middle East Studies*, 45(2), pp. 336–339.

Puar, J.K. (2015) 'Bodies with new organs: Becoming trans, becoming disabled'. *Social Text*, 33(3), pp. 45–73.

Quijano, A. (2000) 'Coloniality of power and Eurocentrism in Latin America'. *International Sociology*, 15(2), pp. 215–232.

Quinlivan, K. (2018) *Exploring Contemporary Issues in Sexuality Education with Young People: Theories in Practice*. Cham: Springer.

Quinlivan, K., Rasmussen, M.L., Aspin, C., Allen, L., and Sanjakdar, F. (2014) 'Crafting the normative subject: Queerying the politics of race in the New Zealand Health education classroom'. *Discourse: Studies in the Cultural Politics of Education*, 35, pp. 393–404.

Rahimi, R. and Liston, D. (2011) 'Race, class, and emerging sexuality: Teacher perceptions and sexual harassment in schools'. *Gender and Education*, 23(7), pp. 799–810.

Ratel-Khan, J. (2020) *Decolonizing Transgender: Deconstructing Western Framings of Indigenous Gender-Diverse Identities*. (Doctoral dissertation, Syracuse University).

Reger, J. (2017) 'Finding a place in history: The discursive legacy of the wave metaphor and contemporary feminism'. *Feminist Studies*, 43(1), pp. 193–221.

Renold, E. (2016) *AGENDA: A Young People's Guide to Making Positive Relationships Matter*. Cardiff University, Children's Commissioner for Wales, NSPCC Cymru, Welsh Women's Aid and Welsh Government.

Renold, E. (2019) 'Becoming AGENDA: The making and mattering of a youth activist resource on gender and sexual violence'. *Reconceptualizing Educational Research Methodology*, 10(2–3), pp. 208–241.

Rich, A. (1980) 'Compulsory heterosexuality and lesbian existence', *Signs*, 5(4), pp. 631–660.

Ringrose, J. (2007) 'Successful girls? Complicating post-feminist, neoliberal discourses of educational achievement and gender equality'. *Gender and Education*, 19(4), pp. 471–489.

Ringrose, J. and Renold, E. (2012) 'Slut-shaming, girl power and "sexualisation": Thinking through the politics of the international SlutWalks with teen girls'. *Gender and Education*, 24(3), pp. 333–343.

Rome, A.S., O'Donohoe, S., and Dunnett, S. (2019) Rethinking feminist waves, in: S. Dobscha (Ed.). *Handbook of Research on Gender and Marketing*, Cheltenham: Edward Elgar Publishing, pp. 252–260.

Sedgwick, E.K. (1990) *Epistemology of the Closet*. Oakland: University of California Press.

Serrano, J. (2007) *Whipping Girl. A Transsexual Woman on Sexism and the Scapegoating of Feminity*. London: Hachette.

Spencer-Wood, S.M. (2011) 'Commentary: How feminist theory increases our understanding of the archaeology of poverty'. *Historical Archaeology*, 45(3), pp. 183–193.

Steinmetz, K. (2014) 'The transgender tipping point'. *TIME*, (29 May). Available at: https://time.com/135480/transgender-tipping-point.

Stone, S. (1991) The Empire Strikes Back: a posttranssexual manifesto. in: J. Epstein and K. Straub (Eds) *Body Guards: The Cultural Politics of Gender Ambiguity.* New York: Routledge, pp. 280–304.

Stryker, S. (1994) 'My words to Victor Frankenstein above the village of Chamounix: Performing transgender rage'. *GLQ: A Journal of Lesbian and Gay Studies*, 1(3), pp. 237–254.

Sundberg, J. (2014) 'Decolonizing posthumanist geographies'. *Cultural Geographies*, 21 (1), pp. 33–47.

Supawantanakul, N. (2018) *Queer Glocalisation and Intersectionality: In the Cases of Thailand and Japan.* (Doctoral dissertation, ResearchSpace@ Auckland).

Trifan, E. (2023) 'Searching for authenticity: Critical analysis of gender roles and radical movements in personal development practices in contemporary society'. *Studia Universitatis Babes-Bolyai-Sociologia*, 68(1), pp. 75–101.

UNHCR (2020) *UNHCR Gender Equality Toolkit.* United Nations High Commissioner for Refugees.

Veale, J., Byrne, J., Tan, K.K., Guy, S., Yee, A., Nopera, T.M.L., and Bentham, R. (2019) *Counting Ourselves: The Health and Wellbeing Of Trans and Non-Binary People in Aotearoa New Zealand.* Transgender Health Research Lab.

Vipond, E. (2015) 'Resisting transnormativity: Challenging the medicalization and regulation of trans bodies'. *Theory in Action*, 8(2), p. 21–44.

Warner, M. (1993) *Fear of a Queer Planet: Queer Politics and Social Theory.* Minneapolis: University of Minnesota Press.

Williams, C. (2016) 'Radical inclusion: Recounting the trans inclusive history of radical feminism'. *Transgender Studies Quarterly*, 3(1–2), pp. 254–258.

Wolf, N. (1993) *Fire with Fire: The New Female Power and How It Will Change the 21st Century.* New York: Random House.

Wollstonecraft, M. (1792/1992) A vindication of the rights of woman, in: *The Works of Mary Wollstonecraft.* London: Penguin.

Woolf, V. (1929) *A Room of One's Own.* London: Hogarth Press.

UN Women (2023) *Women, Peace, and Security 2020–2021 Annual Report.* United Nations Entity for Gender Equality and the Empowerment of Women.

World Bank (2019) *The Little Data Book on Gender.* Washington, DC: World Bank.

Wynter, S. (2003) 'Unsettling the coloniality of being/power/truth/freedom: Towards the human, after man, its overrepresentation—An argument'. *CR: The New Centennial Review*, 3(3), pp. 257–337.

Zimmerman, T. (2017) '#Intersectionality: The fourth wave feminist Twitter community'. *Atlantis: Critical Studies in Gender, Culture and Social Justice*, 38(1), pp. 54–70.

3 Making Sense of the Need to Queer Curriculum, Pedagogy, and Practice

Tabitha Millett

Introduction: What is Queer Theory?

There is not a single definition of queer theory, as such a definition would go against queer theory's political stance of pushing against standardisation of any sort. And whilst it is not in the remit of this chapter to fully unpack the genealogies of queer theory, I have stated elsewhere (Millett 2021), that queer theory can be viewed as a 'being' *and* a 'doing'. Today, the term 'queer' is usually used as an identity category or an umbrella term for LGBTQIA+[1] people, by LGBTQIA+ people, to reappropriate a once derogatory term. Equally, the term queer has roots within the 1970s/80s' gay rights movement, which saw some LGBTQIA+ people break away from the assimilatory politics at the time to critically question the notion of a unified gay and lesbian identity. In other words, queer aimed to trouble ideas of essentialism and biological determinism *and still does*. Therein, to account for this past, one could describe themselves as 'being' queer, to acknowledge themselves outside of the categories of gay and lesbian. Within Western academia, the term queer has roots within poststructuralism, and is often used as a verb to interrogate structures, be that heteronormative or otherwise. This definition by David Halperin (1995), provides a more open definition for queer, one which I will align with for the chapter:

> Queer is by definition *whatever* is at odds with the normal, the legitimate, the dominant. *There is nothing in particular to which it necessarily refers.* It is an identity without an essence.
>
> (Halperin, 1995, p. 62).

Here, queer can be viewed as a 'doing', rather than a 'being', a process that has no arrival. If you have arrived at queer, it is not queer anymore (Millett, 2021). In other words, queer is a constant state of becoming to create difference, as through the disorder, newness *could* be created (Millett, 2021). Some of this difference/newness might be perceived as good or bad, yet what is important is that it is explored, as doing so, might make more meanings and connections for more people.

DOI: 10.4324/9781003397502-3

With the repeal of the Section 28 of the Local Government Act 1988, which forbade the teaching of homosexuality as an acceptable family relationship, 20 years ago in the UK, and the new changes to Sex and Relationship Education in 2020, making the teaching of LGBTQIA+ people compulsory in primary and secondary state schools – now marks Britain's most promising time for schools to respond proactively to LGBTQIA+ provision. Yet, from the most recent Stonewall school report in 2017, key findings still suggest that 45% of LGBTQIA+ students experience bullying. This figure might come as no surprise considering how schools approach gender and sexuality. Over the past ten years, schools have welcomed support from LGBTQIA+ charities to provide anti-bullying education during assembly days and tutor time, yet arguably such measures have fallen short of troubling the heteronormativity embedded within school structures, leaving deeper explorations of gender and sexuality uninvestigated within the formal curriculum (Millett, 2021). Therefore, over the course of this chapter, I will be discussing a pedagogy that aims to adopt aspects of queer theory (discussed further below), as a way of moving beyond and *queering* current anti-bullying provisions in schools to disrupt heteronormativity. The aim is to propose a pedagogy which queers holistically, which means not only focusing on content discussed but also on *how* that content is explored with students. This queering of pedagogy may be more important than ever, as schools face extreme government accountability and educational standards that are overwhelmingly market driven, which has arguably restricted how knowledge is explored and created with students. In what follows, I will discuss the downfalls of LGBTQIA+ provisions in schools when adopting a queer lens, then I will provide a brief overview of what has been previously written on queer pedagogy together with propositions of my own. The latter section will provide examples from empirical research of queering in practice.

LGBTQIA+ Initiatives in Schools: Essentialism vs Representationalism

Since the overturn of Section 28 in the UK in 2003, researchers have become increasingly interested in reporting homophobia and LGBTQIA+ student experiences in UK schools (Guasp, 2014; METRO, 2014; Bradlow et al., 2017; GLSEN, 2018; Harris Wilson-Daily, and Fuller, 2021). Nonetheless research findings have been rather varied, some findings have suggested positive experiences for LGBTQIA+ students in schools (McCormack and Anderson, 2010; Morris, McCormack, and Anderson, 2014; White, Magrath, and Thomas, 2018) whilst other studies have suggested LGBTQIA+ students experience harassment or even danger (Vega, Crawford, and Van Pelt, 2012; Bradlow et al., 2017). Yet there has been criticism regarding some of the research methodologies (Monk, 2011, Warwick and Aggleton, 2014; Millett, 2021), as some studies are overwhelmingly researcher-led, leading the researcher to define what homophobia is.

For example, decisions were made even down to language use, which arguably is highly subjective, especially within adolescent intentions, i.e., 'That's so gay!' (Warwick and Aggleton, 2014). More pressing, however, is the inability to recognise the intersections of identity like race and class, which may contribute to other factors like school attendance or academic performance (Formby, 2015). Nevertheless, this body of research has meant educational institutions have needed to respond proactively with regards to LGBTQIA+ students (Millett, 2021). Many schools invite outside LGBTQIA+ charities to support with assembly talks on anti-bullying or the creation of PHSE resources/posters along celebratory lines (Millett, 2021). For example, pictures of happy gay celebrities like Ellen Degeneres and her wife or famous gay athletes usually decorate school corridors. More recently, within Physical, Social and Health Education (PSHE) across the school, the teaching of pronouns and the different identity labels within the LGBTQIA+ acronym are now seen as fundamental for learning about gender and sexuality (Millett, 2021; TES, 2023).

Nevertheless, there has been noticeable criticism of the anti-bullying approaches, as all LGBTQIA+ students tend to be grouped together as all experiencing the same issues, often labelling LGBTQIA+ students as tragic victims, isolating them further (Monk, 2011; McCormack, 2012; Formby, 2015; Harris, Wilson-Daily, and Fuller, 2021; Millett, 2021). Moreover, such anti-bullying and decorative celebratory discourses work to aid and support heteronormativity. For example, whilst it is important to have representation of LGBTQIA+ in the curriculum, successful and somewhat homonormative celebrities (like Ellen and her wife) create a discourse where to be seen as a successful a gay person means conforming to heterosexual ideals – monogamy/gender conforming, leading to an exclusion of those who do not want to conform to such norms (Marston, 2015; Millett, 2021). Not only this, such anti-bullying discourses, create an 'us' vs. 'them' dichotomy, positioning LGBTQIA+ as 'other' compared to their normal heterosexual peers (Marston, 2015; Millett, 2021). Therefore, how sexuality and gender is explored in schools is problematic from a queer perspective, as it does little to trouble heteronormativity *or normativity* of any kind. Instead, such LGBTQIA+ celebratory discourses are welcomed by schools under the umbrella of 'inclusion', as the examples above do little to trouble the existing heteronormative structures. For instance, the importance given to the learning of identity labels and pronouns still supports heteronormativity and 'born this way' narratives, as doing so bypasses any deeper understandings of gender and sexuality construction, positioning identity as fixed and stable. More worryingly, such content can often underscore individualism, which arguably has been mounting in certain areas of the LGBTQIA+ identity politics, largely supported by the increasing neoliberalism within contemporary society. Thus, having more complex explorations of gender and sexuality in the formal curriculum that offer alternatives to anti-bullying discussions, assembly days and the obsession with identity politics might be a good place to begin. Not only does addressing LGBTQIA+ subjects in the formal curriculum give them greater importance, as opposed to only addressing them in more peripheral subjects like PSHE/assembly day, but it could also provide new knowledges for exploring gender and sexuality – as each curriculum subject will offer different avenues to investigate these. Hence, it could be argued that the curriculum needs 'queering', which would mean troubling the legitimate, the dominant, and the known, thus reaching beyond identity labels and anti-bullying discourses towards more nuanced and dynamic ways of understanding gender and sexuality construction. Yet, in order to queer, schooling, school pedagogical cultures, and teachers' practice must think holistically. It is one thing to discuss gender and sexuality constructions with students, but, very importantly, it is another to think about *how* teachers and schools teach this with students. I now turn to the next section on queering pedagogy.

Making Sense of the Need to Queer Curriculum, Pedagogy, and Practice

Over the past four decades, consecutive governments in the UK have removed themselves from educational responsibilities, giving rise to private educational organisations, like Ofsted, Policy Exchange, and the Education Policy Institute. This neoliberal move from public to private has meant that schools are overwhelmingly market driven, answering to targets, standards, and league tables, which has resulted in increased pressure and competition and the monitoring of staff and students (Ball, 2017; Biesta 2010; 2017, Perryman et al., 2018). However, within this rhetoric of educational performance and standards, which measures the 'quality' of teaching and learning as reflected in 'good' exam results, a discourse is established of what effective learning and teaching is (Biesta 2010; Atkinson, 2011; Millett, 2021). Such a discourse has seen the rise in the last ten years of conservative educational policies influenced heavily by E.D Hirsch (2016). For instance, this was apparent in 2014 when the Secretary of State for Education at the time, Michael Gove, made changes to the national curriculum championing the use of a 'structured stock knowledge' (Coughlan, 2013), followed by the Minister of State for Schools, Nick Gibb, who produced essays on Hirsch through right-wing 'think tank', *Policy Exchange*. Hirsch's (2016) ideas are largely predicated on having a knowledge-rich curriculum, which necessitates the learning of a core knowledge. This core knowledge is often lauded as paramount for effective teaching and learning, providing students with 'cultural capital' and thereafter social mobility. Drawing on Foucault (1977), it is knowledge that holds power, in that power is constituted through what is accepted as certain forms of knowledge. Therefore, one could argue, within this rhetoric of what effective teaching and learning is, where the learning of recognised forms of knowledge is equated to becoming a successful citizen, students are made citizens of the state – conformist, conservative, and, moreover, people who can be easily monitored/examined. On the Department for Education's website, published in 2021, Nick Gibb positions his educational reforms with Hirsch, by providing an example of an economics lecturer at Cardiff university giving a short history test to undergrad students stating that:

> 60% did not know Brunel's profession; 65% did not know who the reigning monarch was at the time of the Armada; 83% did not know that Wellington led the British army at Waterloo and 88% couldn't name a single nineteenth century prime minister.
>
> Department for Education, 2021

When reflecting on this example, one can only assume the types of histories or knowledges that are held in greater esteem over others. Of course, such histories have been criticised in detail for excluding more marginalised groups such as LGBTQIA+ people and people of colour. Thankfully, some positive steps have been made by universities recently, in response to the Black Lives Matter movement, to decolonise their curriculums, yet arguably, more acknowledgement is needed in UK schools. For example, in a speech given at the Social Market Foundation thinktank in 2021, Nick Gibb stated:

> A curriculum based on relevance to pupils is to deny them an introduction to the best that has been thought and said. And, of course, there is no reason why the work of a dead white man is not appropriate for children from ethnic minorities to learn about.
>
> Department for Education, 2021

Again, this rhetoric of 'best' and what counts as 'best' is troubling and equally a misunderstanding of how decolonising actually works. Therefore, as practitioners, it is important to question why these gatekeepers of knowledge have an invested interest in keeping the status quo. However, perhaps a more pressing point (and a point that is pertinent to this chapter) is that the way knowledge is viewed is deeply problematic. Knowledge and pedagogy are understood as static, fixed, and singular. Within the Hirschian model, knowledge is an established and objective fact, separated in its specific domains, something to be delivered from teacher to student, to then be regurgitated for examinations. As long ago as the 1960s, thinkers like Paulo Freire (1996) have suggested that this type of practice within education is highly problematic, as pedagogy is reduced to prescriptive and recognised bodies of knowledge, giving little agency to teachers and students. To escape this framework of recognition, where the government, schools, and governing bodies like Ofsted hold such value, it is important to develop a pedagogy that ruptures these systems, to allow for difference, teacher and student agency and new knowledges – it is here that queer theory can contribute. Building on queer's disruptive nature could transform pedagogy from state of recognition to states of unknowingness. States of unknowingness are important for pedagogy because a more open pedagogy allows for a more democratic approach to teaching and learning as there is a mutual negotiation of knowledge between teacher and student. Moreover, it is within this negotiation that new subjectivities, new ways of thinking, and new knowledges can thrive.

Yet this is not the first time, a queer pedagogy has been suggested – nor is it likely to be the last. Two texts pivotal to queer's pedagogy genealogy are William Pinar's (2012) *Queer Theory in Education* and Kevin Kumashiro's (2002) *Troubling Education Queer Activism and Antioppressive Education*. Both texts advocate for the strange and unfamiliar, a pedagogy that de-centres and displaces (Pinar, 2012) and a pedagogy that acknowledges uncomfortable knowledges placing crisis at the centre of learning (Kumashiro, 2002). Both texts also look beyond the affirmation of identities, instead advocating for ways to confront how identities are constituted as normal or natural. Kumashiro (2002) even pushes for self-reflexivity for students, where students use new knowledge explored and relate it to their own lives. Therefore, both texts encourage teachers and students to leave safe and recognised bodies of knowledge and enter different perspectives that are unfamiliar from traditional ways of knowing. Here, we can see similarities with Jack Halberstam's (2011) *The Queer Art of Failure*, which asks its readers to escape from the usual dominant discourses to focus on life's failures – and it is here that experiences of failure in life can open new and productive ways of thinking. Whilst only drawing on three texts here, all are essential for thinking through applying queer theory in education. All propose an epistemology and pedagogy outside of orthodox ways knowing, where knowledge is seen as an encounter with the unknown, a making between student and teacher, which ultimately challenges learning in schools today.

Of course, advocating for such unprescribed ways of working may not fit with the strict assessment practices and educational targets that govern schools currently, as such unintelligible knowledge is unrecognised by those very practices. Even Michael Young (2020), another advocate for powerful knowledge, is quick to make his rebuttal known:

> The first are the left-wing, anti-racist and feminist thinkers who see 'powerful knowledge' as another way of imposing an alien culture on those who are assumed to have either no culture of their own or the wrong culture. My response to these criticisms is not that they should be dismissed – they highlight the major inequalities of our society. It is that their criticism becomes criticism for its own sake. They point to the limitations of any attempt to shift the unequal distribution of knowledge through the curriculum but offer no alternative except radical changes that are always on the next horizon.
>
> Young, 2020, p. 27

Assuming this chapter fits within Young's (2020) grouping of 'left-wing, anti-racist and feminist thinkers', I propose that there are alternative pedagogies that can be included in the formal curriculum alongside other more systematic knowledges. Moreover, this chapter champions 'criticism, for criticism's sake', as to work with queer theory is to constantly interrogate what you are surrounded by – one should never rest, one should always be in a state of becoming, a state of no arrival. Or as Judith Butler (1999) states: 'a term in process, a becoming, a constructing that cannot rightfully be said to originate or to end. As an ongoing discursive practice, it is open to intervention and resignification' (p. 45). Therefore, this openness to intervention and resignification is where practices of criticality can constitute new pedagogies resulting in new subjectivities and new becomings.

Queering Pedagogy *in Practice*

This section provides two small vignettes from empirical research from a project in a North London school (Millett, 2021), which was based on queering understandings of gender and sexuality through art as part of a GCSE Art and Design unit. The unit was examined formally and was a body of work that was very much within the present day and certainly not on Young's (2020) the 'next horizon'. These examples from empirical research, which have all been pseudonymized, contribute to the current lack of examples of queering the curriculum and educational practice.

Much like the Hirsch model, there have been inherent conservativisms in Art and Design as a subject in school since the early 20th Century, where mechanical drawings, technical skills, and representation are valued as paramount to art learning. This legacy has meant that skill-based approaches and replication discourses are still omnipresent today in art and design departments up and down the country – supported by dominant didactic, Hirschian-like pedagogies (Burgess, 2003; Grant, 2019; Millett, 2021). For example, it is common to see pastiches of famous dead white male painters and known movements like pop art decorating the art rooms. It is the belief of many art teachers, that students must learn the traditional knowledges first to be provided with the necessary tools for expression later, much like the importance of learning how to use a dark room for photography or learning grammar to write a sentence (Atkinson, 2011; Millett, 2021). Whilst this argument has some merit, there are problems with viewing learning as linear, not to mention the overemphasis on developing skills to engender self-expression. The concept of self-expression, usually applied in terms of originality underpins a modernist discourse, as Atkinson (2011) states: 'The crucial point here is that the discourse of self-expression allied to discourses of technical skill and their associated practices of representation constitute the discursive framing of art practice, art object and artist in much school art education' (p. 50).

Therefore, art practice is arguably chained to recognised bodies of knowledge, which leads to misrecognition of other knowledges that fall outside of this matrix of intelligibility. Conversations with colleagues in other subjects reveal that this pedagogy is not unique to art, and nor would it be with the Hirschian model being lauded in schools. Therefore, the project in North London aimed to queer pedagogy holistically by: exploring outside traditional practices in art and design, through making work with students in less predictable ways; the teacher and students working collaboratively during the learning process; the project queering content, specifically queering ideas of gender and sexuality, to move beyond celebratory discourses.

Queering Content

Whilst the North London project wanted to move beyond celebratory and anti-bullying discourses and pull away from the fixation with learning identity labels and pronouns, the project still worked with the topic of identity (due to it being a common art and design theme) and specifically gender and sexuality. Yet, the aim was to have a queerer approach, one where the practices of identity construction were explored, but there was also an exploration of learning outside representation, as representation often leads to essentialism and thus misrecognises the complexities of sexuality, desire, and gender (Getsy, 2015). In other words, the body is culturally marked, and based on those significations, we hold certain assumptions based on the form known as gender. Thereafter, bodies are made legible, then binarised and regulated based on that form. Thus, the aim of the project was to resist the categorisation that often regulates non-heteronormative subjects, by working with ideas of the abstraction.

One of the tasks the students were given to do was to relate gender and sexuality to everyday objects, objects that had more heteronormative readings, like toy cars, and then objects and artworks that had more ambiguous readings, like a bucket or Eva Hesse's sculptures. The aim here was to have students question the hidden assumptions we make about gender and sexuality in the everyday and then look to move past those assumptions through applying more fluid and plural readings to ambiguous forms. It is important to highlight that this activity was open-ended, with the teacher asking the students *if* they could read gender and sexuality into different forms and objects. There was no correct answer nor any clear objectives. Students found it relatively easy matching stereotypical objects to gender and sexuality stereotypes. For example, many students connected washing-up liquid bottles with women due to social connotations of housework being women's work. Additionally, students, through conversations with their teacher, were able to associate the shapes, materials, and functions of the objects to gender and sexuality. For instance, students began to associate metal/steel rods with masculinity due to the hardness of the materials and the angular shapes, whilst others associated porcelain vases with femininity due to the fragility and shape of the object. Therefore, students were able draw heteronormative readings from everyday objects in a manner which did not trouble them. Yet, when moving onto the more obscure artworks and objects, like (Eva Hesse sculpture and tights with old foam stuck into them mixed with wood shavings) interestingly their responses were largely of defiance and confusion:

STUDENT PARTICIPANT 1: I think this art is trash, I don't like it. How can you associate that random thing to gender?

STUDENT PARTICIPANT 2: If you can link these artworks with gender and sexuality, you can link these with anything. I could link this with a bucket.

STUDENT PARTICIPANT 2: It's literally they take a piece of wood and make this.

STUDENT PARTICIPANT 3: Exactly, art requires skill, they just ... clearly didn't put effort into it.

STUDENT PARTICIPANT 3: ... the thing is they planned TRASH! They planned absolute trash.

In the eyes of an Ofsted examiner, or even Hirsch, one could read the above example as unsuccessful, the students were clearly dismissive of the exercise, and there is no clear learning objective or even a clear example of learning occurring. Yet, when reading with a queer lens, a lens which cradles failures, one could argue that the students were constituted differently, as the task punctured their prior knowledges regarding gender and sexuality and art. For instance, for the students, art requires skill, as they are indoctrinated into the epistemology of school art, and gender and sexuality require something that is recognisable and representative. In other words, due to the reconfiguration of prior knowledges, new subjectivities came to the fore, as both the objects/artworks and the students, were constituted as something different. This constitution occurred through the students' reaction to being asked to read the objects in terms of gender and sexuality, as their own epistemological understandings of art and gender and sexuality were changed. Therein, the learning occurring here was outside of prescribed bodies of knowledge, a learning that pierced prior understandings, a queering of learning.

After the task, students were given the next 5–6 weeks to make artwork that related to the subject of gender and sexuality. The students were given the choice to work collaboratively, (often not encouraged in art and design in school) and students were allowed to make what they wished based on the class conversations that had taken place. Most of the work made was of an abstract nature with complex reasons for why they had chosen specific materials and ways of presenting their work. The work created was a triumph, as not only were there elements of a queer resistance to representation when exploring gender and sexuality, but the artwork itself had a sense of complexity and maturity, unlike the prescribed examples of school art usually seen. Whilst it is not in the remit of this chapter to discuss their work more in depth, more from this project can be seen in Millett (2021).

Queering How to Teach

The tasks above gave students a space to make their own knowledges regarding gender and sexuality, as there were no prescribed outcomes or units of established knowledge to be learned. For example, students were not asked to learn specific knowledge about LGBTQIA+ people or how to apply specific and established art skills. Instead, there was an openness to their learning; therefore *how* the content is explored is just as important as the content itself. It is important to mention the teacher here too, as she was just as instrumental to the content and how it was explored. The statement below is what she said about the project when asked how she found exploring gender and sexuality in art and design:

TEACHER PARTICIPANT: Well yeah, it's not, it's not anything that's been in the forefront of discussions that I've had in my life … I've never been, you know, had any kind of issues with anybody else's sexuality or gender. It's never been something I've really discussed, but it's something that I've had to talk about, as a teacher it's almost like you're expected to have some knowledge on things, as soon as you open your mouth, there's a feeling that you're the expert in the room. And I suppose I wasn't the expert in the room, and probably some of these kids, well, absolutely a lot of these kids are way more advanced in knowing some of the stuff that they know. It's, it's, it's put me on more of an equal standing, I think. A path of discovery along with the kids, as opposed to me imparting my 'wise' knowledge on them.As the above implies, the teacher was very much on a path of discovery with the students, as she had no prior interest in the topics of gender and sexuality herself. She continues:

TEACHER PARTICIPANT: I think there's a lot of, there's a lot of, we're in a big time of change at the moment, there's a lot of you know, if, unless it's something that is directly affecting you in your life, it's not something you would necessarily know much about or discuss much about, and so there's a lot of kind of, it's difficult for people to discuss those kinds of things or approach them whilst talking to kids, when you're teaching PSHE, it can be an awkward conversation, and I think actually, we're not directly dealing with, this is a PSHE subject, we're dealing with art, and this is what we can talk about in art, and in fact, there's a lot of subjects that we can talk about it, giving the kids as much freedom, without directly, err you know pressuring them into discussing things. I don't know if that makes sense? I've certainly been brought out of my comfort zone discussing things with the kids, not in a bad way, you know, I've never, it's something that people don't normally discuss too much particularly when it comes to you know working with children.

Interestingly, the teacher found exploring the subjects through art, a non-linguistic medium, more freeing, than approaching it in PSHE, where she believes the delivery can be too forced. Equally, she mentioned again being brought out of her comfort zone when discussing gender and sexuality. Echoing perhaps the legacy of section 28, where the presumed safety of children can only be within heterosexual culture, The teacher participant highlights the uneasiness that many teachers face when discussing these topics with students (which is perhaps why these subjects tend to be avoided in the formal curriculum). Yet, at the same time, the teacher participant explored gender and sexuality in her own subject, which allowed her some confidence and a space to learn alongside the students.

Drawing on aspects of Butler's (2005) ethics, she purports that we ask ourselves and others to maintain a coherent identity through holding passionate attachments to norms, such as how teachers are expected to be 'all knowing' (echoing the teacher participant's words above). By holding on to these attachments, we are constituted as an intelligible subject and therefore coherent to one another and ourselves. For instance, the teacher may hold attachments to knowing key foundational skills in art (norms), in order to be recognised by herself and others as an art teacher. Yet, Butler (2005) discusses the importance of momentarily withholding from this coherence to enter into states of unknow-ingness in order to relate to ourselves and others more ethically. For Butler, doing this offers us a chance of 'becoming human' (p.136). When relating Butler (2005) to the teacher participant's declaration above, it is apparent that partaking in a pedagogy that was less prescriptive and discussing topics she felt less knowl-edgeable about made her feel as if she was not the 'expert in the room'. Here, I argue that the teacher participant became momentarily less of a coherent teaching subject to herself and her students (from the excerpt above we see students questioning the lesson). Thus, as she is pushed outside her comfort zone, we begin to see an ethical meeting as she was 'on a path of discovery along with the children' or an 'equal standing'. In other words, I argue that both the teacher and her students entered into an unknowing state of learning which opened up a space for creating knowledge together – a queering of pedagogy.

Queering Futures

Over the course of the chapter, I have rejected the assumption of core or final knowledges in the pursuit of unknowingness and uncertainty. Whilst it is important to resist giving an overview of what a queer pedagogy *is*, as this would not be very queer at all, I have suggested how we might approach queering school. I have outlined the issues with current approaches to LGBTQIA+ in schools, as such essentialist approaches stunt deeper explorations of gender and sexuality and do little to challenge heteronormativity. I have also proposed that as educators, we do not search for final truths *for* our students but search for how things come to be seen as true *with* our students. Education is arguably becoming more neoliberal, where rote learning and core knowledge are held as the epitome of a successful education. Therefore, now is the time to embrace different spaces for learning to ensure a broad and deeper learning experience for both teachers and students. In the two small vignettes discussed above, I demonstrated how pedagogy could be done differently whilst still meeting formal curriculum criteria. I believe the examples suggest how we might create a class-room that not only resists regulatory powers that make others, 'others', but a classroom that seeks different knowledges which may be more exciting for all.

Note

1 LGBTQIA+ lesbian, gay, bisexual, trans, queer/questioning, intersex, asexual/ other sexuality non-conforming.

References

Atkinson, D. (2011) *Art, Equality and Learning: Pedagogy against the State*. Rotterdam: Sense.
Ball, S. (2017) *The Education Debate*. 3rd ed. Bristol: Policy Press.

Biesta, G.J.J. (2010). *Good Education in an Age of Measurement: Ethics, Politics, Democracy*. London: Paradigm Publishers.

Biesta, G.J.J. (2017) *The Rediscovery of Teaching*. London and New York: Routledge.

Bradlow, J., Bartram, F., April, G., and Jadva, V. (2017). *Stonewall School Report*. London: Stonewall. Available at: https://www.stonewall.org.uk/school-report- 2017 (Accessed 15 October 2020).

Burgess, L. (2003) Monsters in the playground: contemporary art in schools, in: N. Addison, and L. Burgess (Eds) *Issues in Art and Design Teaching*. London and New York: Routledge, pp. 108–121.

Butler, J. (1999) *Gender Trouble Feminism and the Subversion of Identity*. (10th anniversary edition). London and New York: Routledge.

Butler, J. (2005). *Giving an Account of Oneself*. New York: Fordham University Press.

Coughlan, S. (2013) 'Gove sets out "core knowledge" curriculum plans'. *BBC News*. Available at: https://www.bbc.co.uk/news/education-21346812 (Accessed 13 July 2023).

Department for Education (2021) 'Speech: The importance of a knowledge-rich curriculum'. Available at: https://www.gov.uk/government/speeches/the-importance-of-a -knowledge-rich-curriculum (Accessed 15 October 2020).

Formby, E. (2015) 'Limitations of focussing on homophobic, biphobic and transphobic 'bullying' to understand and address LGBT young people's experiences within and beyond school'. *Sex Education*, 15(6), pp. 1–15.

Foucault, M. (1977) *Discipline and Punish: The Birth of the Prison*. New York: Vintage Books.

Freire, P. (1996). *Pedagogy of the oppressed*. London; New York: Penguin Books. (Originally published in Spanish in 1968).

Getsy, D.J. (2015) *Abstract Bodies: Sixties Sculpture in the Expanded Field of Gender*. New Haven: Yale University Press.

GLSEN (2018) *The 2017 National School Climate Survey: The Experiences of Lesbian, Gay, Bisexual, Transgender, and Queer Youth in Our Nation's Schools*. Available at: https://files.eric.ed.gov/fulltext/ED590243.pdf.

Grant, W. (2019) 'Liberal ideals, postmodern practice: A working paradox for the future of secondary school art education in England?'. *The International Journal of Art and Design Education*, 39(1), pp. 56–68.

Guasp, A. (2014) *The Teachers' Report 2014*. London: Stonewall. Available at: https://www. stonewall.org.uk/system/files/teachers_report_2014.pdf (Accessed 15 October 2020).

Halberstam, J. (2011) *The Queer Art of Failure*. Durham, NC: Duke University Press.

Halperin, D. (1995) *Saint Foucault: Toward a Gay Hagiography*. Oxford: Oxford University Press.

Harris, R., Wilson-Daily, A.E., and Fuller, G. (2021) 'Exploring the secondary school experience of LGBT+ youth: an examination of school culture and school climate as understood by teachers and experienced by LGBT+ students'. *Intercultural Education*, 32(4), pp. 368–385.

Hirsch, E.D. (2016) *Why Knowledge Matters: Rescuing Our Children From Failed Educational Theories*. Cambridge, MA: Harvard Education Press.

Kumashiro, K. (2002) *Troubling Education Queer Activism and Anti-Oppressive Education*. New York and London: Routledge.

Marston, K. (2015) 'Beyond bullying: The limitations of homophobic and transphobic bullying Interventions for affirming lesbian, gay, bisexual and trans (LGBT) equality in education'. *Pastoral Care in Education*, 33(3), pp. 161–168.

McCormack, M. (2012) *The Declining Significance of Homophobia*. Oxford: Oxford University Press.

McCormack, M. and Anderson, E. (2010) '"It's not acceptable any more": The erosion of homophobia and the softening of masculinity at an English Sixth Form'. *Sociology*, 44(5), pp. 843–859.

METRO (2014) *Youth Chances Summary of First Findings: The Experiences of LGBTQ Young People in England*. London: METRO. Available at: http://www.mermaidsuk.org.uk/assets/media/youth%20chances%20experiencies%20og%20lgbt%20youth_2014.pdf (Accessed 15 October 2022).

Morris, M., McCormack, M., and Anderson, E. (2014) 'The changing experiences of bisexual male adolescents'. *Gender and Education*, 26(4), pp. 397–413.

Millett, T.V.P. (2021) *Queering the Art Classroom*. (PhD Thesis. University College London). Available at: https://discovery.ucl.ac.uk/id/eprint/10130350/1/Millett_10130350_Thesis_redacted.pdf (Accessed: 13 October 2022).

Monk, D. (2011) 'Challenging homophobic bullying in schools: The politics of progress'. *International Journal of Law in Context*, 7, pp. 181–207.

Perryman, J., Maguire, M., Braun, A. and Ball, S. (2018) 'Surveillance, governmentality and moving the goalposts: The influence of Ofsted on the work of schools in a post-panoptic era'. *British Journal of Educational Studies*, 66(2), pp. 145–163.

Pinar, W.F. (2012) Understanding Curriculum as Gender Text: Notes on Reproduction, Resistance and Male-Male Relations, in: W. Pinar (Ed.) *Queer Theory in Education*. Hoboken: Taylor and Francis, pp. 183–202.

TES (2023) 'Pronouns and gender PSHE'. Available at: https://www.tes.com/teaching-resource/pronouns-and-gender-pshe-12791615 (Accessed 15 October 2022).

Vega, S., Crawford, H.G., and Van Pelt, J.L. (2012) 'Safe schools for LGBTQI students: How do teachers view their role in promoting safe schools?'. *Equity & Excellence in Education*, 45(2) pp. 250–260.

Warwick, I., and Aggleton P., (2014) 'Bullying, "cussing" and "mucking about": Complexities in tackling homophobia in three secondary schools in south London, UK'. *Sex Education*, 14(2), pp. 159–173.

White, A.J., Magrath, R., and Thomas, B. (2018) 'The experiences of lesbian, gay and bisexual students and staff at a Further Education college in South East England'. *British Educational Research Journal*, 44(3), pp. 480–495.

Young, M. (2020) From powerful knowledge to the powers of knowledge, in: C. Sealy (Ed.) *The ResearchED Guide to the Curriculum: An Evidence-Informed Guide for Teachers*. (1st ed.). Woodbridge: John Catt Educational Ltd.

4   The Power of Extracurricular Pedagogies with Young Black Women in 21st Century British Schools

'we grow, we relearn, we redefine'

Camilla Stanger and Amina Ali

Introduction

That Black girls and young women face often unacknowledged and unaddressed barriers to success within the British education system is a key premise of this chapter and speaks to research tracing this group's educational marginalisation from the late 20th century to the present decade (Mac an Ghaill, 1988; Mirza, 1992, 2009; Wright, 2005; Youdell, 2006; Archer, Hollingworth, and Mendick, 2010; Phoenix, 2010; Stanger 2019). The findings consider, for example, how young Black women face a higher rate of school exclusions than their peers, how Black girls are positioned as 'hypersexual', 'aggressive', and altogether 'inappropriate' within the classroom and the corridor (by peers and staff), and how forms of Black, feminine working-class culture and knowledge are underrepresented and undervalued within the British school curriculum. A second premise for this chapter, however, is the sheer commitment to and investment in education that many young Black British women make, with Heidi Mirza and Diane Reay (2000) identifying a particular 'desire' and 'consuming passion' (p. 521) for education that underpins Black British feminine identities and communities of practice. Taken alongside this group's educational marginalisation, Mirza is brought to ask the following question: 'why is it that those who are the most committed to education often struggle the most to succeed?' (Mirza, 2006, p. 137). The passion for education is captured in this poem by research participants, titled, Amplify:

> Through words we connect and through laughter we shine, we relate, through stories, through words, we are seen. The sense of freedom, this sense of power fills the classroom we are fearlessly and constantly evolving. It's like magic, the way that we see beneath our skin's surface, amidst our differences. And mirror each other in appearance and substance, by unapologetically being ourselves in the face of adversity. And falsifying expectations, we grow, we relearn, we redefine, and project our voices so all the world has to hear, so all the world has to listen.
>
> (Poem by participants in College B's 'Freethinkers' extracurricular project)

DOI: 10.4324/9781003397502-4

While Mirza's question is a relevant starting point for this chapter, and we are indebted to her work and that of others in being able to ask it, we ultimately ask another: what might be done? Specifically, what might be done to alleviate the 'struggle' Black girls have been found to face within UK schools, and facilitate a space in which their educational desires, passions, investments, and capacities might better flourish? In order to offer one potential answer to this question, we explore the experiences and seek the views of two small groups of Black British girls studying in two sixth-form colleges – namely the last step of UK compulsory education prior to university or employment – located in the same area of inner London.

The young women we researched with all identified as 'Black' in relation to their diasporic cultural and familial heritages, inclusive of West African (Ghanaian and Nigerian), East African (Somali and Kenyan), and African Caribbean (Jamaican). All displayed, to a strong degree, Mirza's notion of a clear educational 'desire', and yet all experienced a similar 'struggle to succeed' within their college: either being positioned as, or experiencing themselves in some way, however subtle, as educationally 'inferior', a label that has followed the Black British community for decades (Mirza and Reay, 2000). Research focusing on 21st century schooling tends to understand this enduring inequality as both nuanced for and veiled within what has been defined as a 'neoliberal' British education system (Mirza, 2006; Archer, Hollingworth, and Mendick, 2010). This would be a system that is increasingly target-driven, individualised, grounded in ideas of meritocracy, and in being so, masks its function as a system of White governance. Upon this basis, we turn our attention to exploring a pedagogical approach that strived to alleviate this increasingly complicated struggle, in making room for our research participants and the institutions themselves to '*grow [...] relearn [...] redefine*'.

The pedagogical approach we articulate in this chapter is one that foregrounds young Black women's voices and forms of identity, their practices of sisterhood and community, and is built upon the assumption that Black girls have much to contribute both creatively and academically. We critically explore three examples of such an approach, which all took place outside timetabled curriculum lessons: a girls' dance and discussion project, a poetry and spoken word group, and a series of book clubs, all of which we conceive through deeply interconnected ideas of 'liberation', 'home', 'community', and 'voice' (hooks, 1990, 1994; Brown, 2009; Sears, 2010).

In developing research around the experiences of young Black women however, we do not mean to rarify or essentialise the being, or becoming, of a Black girl. Instead, we understand this, and any, identity as a socially constructed yet lived reality, as something multifaceted that is partially directed by and can thus be mobilised and reimagined by the subject themselves in powerful and hopeful ways (Ahmed, 2002). We also acknowledge that terms such as 'Black' and 'girl' are identifiers that have been constructed to serve a function within a system of, as bell hooks (2003) puts it, 'imperialist white-supremacist capitalist patriarchy' (p. v). We therefore pay attention not only to how our research participants take ownership of these identifiers for themselves, how they move within and beyond them, but also to how our own social and institutional positionality has shaped this research.

Articulating a Research Practice of Reflexivity and Care: The Research Sites and Methods

What connects us as co-researchers is first and foremost that we are teachers who care, and who wish to research our own practice in service of that care. As proposed by Christina Sharpe (2016) to care would mean to acknowledge the structurally violent histories that shape young people's lives and commit to finding ways to support young people with this understanding. A helpful starting point in this respect is articulated by Ruth Nicole Brown (2009) who, in the context of her teaching and research with African-American girls, suggests 'the problem is that Black girls are not typically included in the conversations that shape our lives and destiny' (p. 2). We thus aim to place the voices and perspectives of our research participants at the centre of our discussions and interpretations. Then, to complement Sharpe's (2016) understanding of care, we also adopt an approach to 'reflexivity' as a second guiding principle for our research. This reflects what Mayor (2022) defines as 'anti-racist research praxis', namely 'an iterative process of self-reflexivity and relational accountability to reflect, theorize, and act differently during feminist [...] research' (p. 625). Similarly, we posit that critically reflecting upon our respective social positions can serve a practice of caring and careful research, as well as being mobilised towards more nuanced and critical knowledge production. We thus briefly introduce the complications and possibilities of our respective positions now as a foundation for the research narratives we share later in the article.

For the first author, Camilla, there is a particular need for care and reflexivity within this study. This chapter portrays my efforts as an educator to work with and write about Black girls' experiences in a manner that is loving and celebratory of their 'power and genius' (Brown, 2009, p. 3), whilst also recognising that I do so through the structurally violent lens of someone who is White and otherwise privileged within the education system. Three strategies I thus employ to mitigate the harms and embrace the possibilities of this positionality are as follows. Firstly, prioritising the perspectives, languages, and theorisations of Black women and girls, with a particular commitment to learning/unlearning when those perspectives challenge my own. Secondly, finding opportunities to name, expose, and critically unpick Whiteness and how it operates as something I have lived insight into and as a key focus of my work. Thirdly, through entering a space of mutually supportive and critical dialogue and co-thinking with my co-author Amina.

For the second author, Amina, as a Black Muslim woman and first-generation immigrant who is now a teacher in the British state education system, I have experienced the reality of being a Black girl through the education system that I am now turning a critical eye to as a researcher. This means that alongside drawing on my lived experiences as a guide, I also retain a level of respect and respectful boundaries for my students, as I understand our differences as well our sameness, allowing myself to be taught by them. It also means that, as someone who is both politically and emotionally engaged, I am bold in allowing my emotional connectedness to the subject matter to drive my research and ways of expressing it. I understand emotion can be sidelined within academia (Ahmed, 2004, 2012), but as hooks (2003) puts it, 'by making the personal political, many individuals have experienced major transformations in thought' (p. vi). This would all be in service of relearning and reimagining what education in the UK can be, especially for Black girls.

The two research sites are located in an area of inner London that houses some of the poorest wards in the country, offering pre-university courses and qualifications for young people aged 16–19. Camilla's research site, College A, in which she taught English and dance, has a highly inclusive admissions policy, often enrolling students whose school-leaver grades do not give them access to other providers in the borough, and with a strong focus on preparing students for the workplace. Camilla researched with six young women who studied in College A between 2014 and 2015, all of whom were aged 17–19 at the time of research and studied vocational courses, mostly in Health and Social Care. Camilla worked as a classroom assistant in the young women's lessons and took this as an opportunity to present her research questions, extending an open invitation to anyone who wished to join as participants and 'consultants': (1) what barriers to educational success do young Black women face in a college and society like this? (2) can we work together to create a dance project that might make a difference? Initially four students offered to take part, with a further three (friends of the original four), joining later on. The outcome was a dance project, which she and the girls met weekly to develop, and which culminated in a performance for International Women's Day.

Amina's research began during her time as a Teacher of English at College B, an academically selective 6th form in the same area of London, which enrols a comparatively smaller cohort of young people who attain well above the national average in their national school-leaver examinations, with a particular focus on academic 'excellence' and preparing for entry to high-tariff selective universities. Alongside her teaching, Amina facilitated different reading clubs as part of the college's compulsory extracurricular offer. It is important to note that Amina did not create these clubs with the intention of researching them; however, once she noticed their power for particular students, she personally invited students to be interviewed about their experiences. Seven young women took part, all of whom had started their studies at College B in 2022 and will finish in 2024: all were aged 16–17 at the time of research and are studying three to four A-levels one of which is English Literature.

A key part of the research process was a series of interviews that took place variously as one-to-ones, pairs or small groups, depending on the young women's preferences. After some initial pre-planned questions, the interviews in both Camilla's and Amina's respective research came to be shaped around matters that the participants (mainly 'interviewees' but also 'interviewers') felt were pressing and filling their thoughts that day, thus becoming far more dialogical than a series of questions and answers. This was supported by the fact that the 'interviewers' were part of the community being researched rather than professionalised outsiders (Milligan, 2016). These interviews soon became spaces for sharing, exchange, and sense-making that responded to the immediate context, aligning with what Gunaratnam (2003) discusses as a need for listening and co-learning rather than asking and extracting within an anti-racist approach to empirical research. Camilla also interviewed senior staff members in her research site, as part of an additional aim of exploring how Whiteness operated through this institution. All names as they appear in this chapter are pseudonyms, either of the young women's or authors' choosing.

The research also took place within and 'about' different extracurricular projects, which meant that another research key method was observing; a practice that is embodied, invested, and never-neutral (Fitzpatrick, 2013). The observations offered insights into the young women's and our own embodied and transformative experiences of being, talking, and/or moving with our students outside the codified spaces of the curriculum lesson. This period of observations helped the authors understand the complicated and shifting institutional perspectives marked by their 'insider-outsider' navigations throughout the research stages (Milligan, 2016, p. 235).

Mapping the experience of Black British girls in the research sites

Returning to the research cited at the start of this chapter, namely that which traces the educational marginalisation of Black girls: the findings suggest that British schools still do operate via White, middle-class, patriarchal norms, with regards to, variously, curriculum content, modes of assessment and codes of conduct, dress, and even hairstyling within the school building. However, within a 'neoliberal' system, these norms of Whiteness govern more covertly, firstly by imagining social structures of oppression as barriers that can be climbed or neutralised through the right kind of hard work and self-fashioning within a mythical context of choice. This framework therefore holds up certain codified norms (such as the fluent use of Standard English in an academic exam or particular ways of expressing oneself within a classroom debate) as freefloating forms of cultural capital, up for grabs by anyone who sufficiently applies themselves. One outcome is a deficit or pathologised view of those who do not 'succeed' – or do not succeed quickly and quietly enough – in such 'DIY projects of the self' (Kelly, 2000, p. 468), and thus the system works to keep at the bottom those whose forms of knowledge, learning, and conduct do not align with the dominant cultural norms. This deficit view has affected Black girls in British schools in particular ways, both in how they are understood by their school and how they understand themselves. This was certainly true for our research participants.

College A's Health and Social Care cohort (hereafter referred to as HSC) comprised almost exclusively young women from global majority communities, many of whom had strong aspirations to work in the HSC sector, commonly as early years educators, youth workers, nurses, or midwives. Two of the college's Assistant Principals, explain these aspirations in a particular way. Mark says, 'this is impressionistic – but you can see some of the things that have driven them to the caring side of things are issues they've had with their own being cared for', whilst Paul suggests, 'maybe the HSC students are doing the course to give back – because of some of the support they have had from that sector'. Although tentative, Mark's and Paul's words suggest an impression that HSC students have had a history of 'need' and state intervention which forms the basis of their aspirations within the sector. In alignment with this narrow if not deficit-based view of the young women's ambitions, it was also the case that certain members of this cohort had acquired a particular reputation in the college. Phrases I had heard staff use to describe this student group, and had also myself used at times, ranged from 'vulnerable' and 'needy' to 'hard work', 'loud', and 'crazy', with another Assistant Principal sharing, in an informal conversation about a corridor altercation, 'Camilla, I hate to say it, but it's usually the Black girls in the cohort'. This all speaks to research suggesting that young Black women are often positioned as 'problem girls' or 'at risk' in UK schools (Wright, 2005; Ball, Maguire, and Macrae, 2000), with less attention paid to the contexts shaping their interactions or to their strengths and successes. Another stark example of this is that, at the time of research, young Black women who studied HSC did not feature in any of the college's marketing materials, with the college's marketing officer sharing she had been directed to 'keep her camera away' from 'some' students. This is despite this particular cohort making up a significant minority of the college's student population, alongside achieving some notable academic success.

Indeed, in terms of college achievement rates, the HSC cohorts performed comparatively highly each year and their teachers rarely discussed the challenges of teaching this cohort in relation to the quality of their work. It was also clear that a 'consuming passion' for education (Mirza and Reay, 2000, p. 521) characterised how my research participants engaged with their studies. All took a meticulous, proud and driven approach to their college work, which Kayla, a student on the HSC course emphasises in interview:

INTERVIEWER: Do you take pride over your work?
KAYLA: [smiles broadly] very [laughs] extremely. Like even just like [picks up the pace, with another smile] if it's on the computer like – I like it to all be aligned correctly. Like I hate messy work.

An excitable drive for not just good but perfect work was also evident in the amount of detailed content and high-level analysis Cairo and Winter would put into their assignments, despite being told by their teachers that this often far exceeded what they needed to do for the pass criteria. Felicia indeed indicates the pleasure she felt in doing a piece of work not just well, but at its very best:

INTERVIEWER: So what does your work mean to you?
FELICIA: Everything. I just love doing the work and getting it right. I love it. I even get competitive with it.

And when asked to describe themselves as learners, all four girls position education as central to their identities: 'I am just someone that wants to learn' (Kayla); 'education really matters to me' (Cairo); 'I'm a hardworking student' (Felicia); 'I'm self-educated!' (Winter). Despite this however, a clear deficit discourse still operated in relation to a view of the girls' educational commitments, 'intelligence' and indeed the very value of their course. This was something that the students themselves engaged with, enacting a complicated relationship with their choice of course:

WINTER: First I wanted to be a lawyer, so I was gonna do A Levels, but then I got [pause] a U in maths [small laugh] so I couldn't. So then I had to go and do like BTEC ... but now I know what I want to do.
INTERVIEWER: And what is that?
WINTER: Midwife.
INTERVIEWER: I can imagine you being an excellent midwife because ...
WINTER: But I think a lot of people stereotype.
INTERVIEWER: [pause, feeling suitably checked by Winter] Go on ...
WINTER: Like, when I say I want to be a midwife everyone says, 'ahh every Black girl wants to be a midwife' it's annoying. Or like, 'every Black girl does HSC'.
KAYLA: Yeah.
INTERVIEWER: How do you think your course is viewed in the college then?
KAYLA: Yeah [pause] everyone looks at you like 'oh you're dumb' [pause] like bottom of the pile, [whereas] the A Level students – like people who are like [pause] the smart, smart people [trails off].

This all reflects Mirza's (1992, 2009) research with Black working class young women who discuss their own 'choices' to study HSC, a sector they respect yet understand as being undervalued, and explain these choices as part of their 'dynamic rationalisation' (2009, p. 26) of the education system they find themselves in, with its limited options for girls 'like them'. Meanwhile, Amina's research participants at College B can be understood as 'the A Level students [...] the smart people' Kayla refers to, the ones who might escape pathologisation as 'at risk' or 'bottom of the pile'. However, this did not mean that they were immune to a 'myth of Black intellectual inferiority' (Fordham, 1996, cited in Mirza and Reay, 2000, p. 524), as Amina's research suggests.

College B is an academically selective sixth form in which many students aspire and are encouraged to attend high-tariff universities, including Oxbridge, and pursue careers in Medicine, Law and Finance. The college seeks to implement a strong ethos of 'academic rigour', and students generally have high expectations for themselves and seek to achieve the highest possible grades. However, it is openly spoken about among staff and students that a sense of 'imposter syndrome' is endemic within College B, with many counselling referrals being related to anxieties around academic performance and aptitude. This was experienced and articulated by Amina's research participants in particular ways. Firstly, through a discourse of gratitude amongst the students, specifically feeling 'grateful' for having been selected for and being able to attend a 'college like this'. Secondly, this continued into a sense of needing to live-up to the college's expectations, which manifested in a particular fear for a number of the girls: the fear of being understood, or labelled, as 'lazy', 'not bright enough', or 'not resilient enough' by their teachers.

As Fatimah puts it:

> I don't know how to speak with big words ... lots of teachers will say you're going to feel imposter syndrome and I always still feel it [...] if I'm worried about my work and how my grades are looking, then I'm not going to feel comfortable in that environment. I find myself not talking and not contributing in the class and being one of the quiet kids because my mind is so worried about my grades and how I'll come across.

This all speaks to decades of research suggesting that Black children are constructed through ideas of 'intellectual inferiority' and 'laziness' within UK and US schools (Mirza, 2006; Fordham 1996), with these becoming labels that young people can variously internalise and work to actively avoid.

So it seems that young Black women across both colleges engaged in a dynamic rationalisation of their choices and options which stemmed from a 'fear' of being exposed as not deserving the educational opportunities available to them. The young women, whether studying at more inclusive or selective colleges, displayed drive and even 'gratitude', but also an apprehension of being exposed as an 'imposter' or 'dumb' if they failed in their attempts to succeed educationally. Therefore, what our research participants have in common as young Black women who study in 21st-century neoliberal schools is feeling in some way not worthy of, or inferior in relation to, dominant cultures of educational success within their school. This was while also being extremely committed to and passionate about their studies. So what might be done?

Co-creating hooksian Homeplaces for Black Girls: Dance, Literature and Voice

The critical and hopeful pedagogy of bell hooks (1990, 1994) is central to the spaces and practices we explore in this chapter. hooks herself locates the beginning of her pedagogy in her reading of Paulo Freire, explaining that 'one sentence of Freire's became a revolutionary mantra for me: "we cannot enter the struggle as objects in order later to become subjects"' (1994, p. 46). This goal resonates with combinations of subjection and striving our research participants felt in their educational contexts. The resulting vision of education that Freire offers hooks can be articulated as 'a shared consciousness of oppression and a shared commitment to … finding [a] path to liberation' (Jackson 1997, p. 464). hooks' own intersectional approach reimagines the term 'liberation' as freedom from and within intersecting racist, sexist, and classist processes of oppression, thus entailing the decentring of 'race', gender, and class-based privilege within education systems (Carolissen et al., 2011). We adopt this hooksian vision of 'liberation' as a goal for education whereby, as Mirza puts it in discussing Black British supplementary schools, 'education is not about the process of learning or teaching; it is about refutation' (2006, p. 153).

A key practical approach hooks takes forward from Freire's work in service of 'liberation' is privileging the personal, lived experiences of students within the learning process. In doing this, a traditional 'banking concept' (Freire, 1996, p. 53) of education, in which the teacher imparts their privileged/dominant form of knowledge to the students, is disrupted in prioritising what the students already know through their lived experiences. Central to this process is also the practice of 'dialogue', namely, 'the encounter between [students], mediated by the world, in order to name the world' (Freire, 1996, p. 69), in which teacher-as-knowledge-holder is disrupted, and in which 'students-of-the-teacher' become 'students-teachers' (Freire, 1996, p. 61). hooks (2003) develops these ideas through her concept of learning communities working together against 'continuing institutionalized systems of dominance' (p. 1). Importantly, hooks (2003) places community as both the heart and goal of a liberatory education: 'progressive education, education as the practice of freedom […] enables us to restore our sense of connection [and] teaches us how to create community' (p. vii-viii). This offers a final hooksian approach: that of an 'engaged pedagogy' (1994, p. 7). Central to an engaged pedagogy, one that facilitates 'connection' and 'liberation', is 'the notion of pleasure in the classroom' (hooks, 1994, p. 7) and its liberatory effects in 'stimulating serious intellectual … engagement' (p. 7). In this, hooks advocates for a sensual, physical and emotional 'energy' that can charge a learning process and 'excite the critical imagination' (p. 195), meaning there is an important capacity for acutely embodied experiences of pleasure, joy and anger to mobilise change, community and 'liberation'.

With respect to where such pedagogical approaches might take place, and how they might feel for Black women and girls in particular, hooks (1990) employs the metaphor of 'home', specifically the 'homeplace' to articulate separate, safe, and sanctuary-like spaces Black women and girls have historically co-created. However, as Leigh Kelly (2020) puts it, 'while for hooks homeplace is a site of healing and resistance outside of the physical spaces that reinforce racial oppression, homeplaces can also be created within such spaces' (p. 451). We now propose two pedagogical practices towards creating such 'homeplaces' for Black girls very much within 21st-century schools, drawing on the radical and creative pedagogical practice of Ruth Nicole Brown (2009) and Stephanie Sears (2010).

Brown (2009) and Sears (2010) worked collaboratively with fellow Black women and girls to create after-school projects in the US: Brown's project 'Saving Our Lives, Hearing Our Truths' (SOLHOT), and Sears' 'Girls Empowerment Project' (GEP). The authors' discussions of their projects provide useful reference points for the goals of our research. Namely, Black-girl-centred learning communities that challenge dominant discourses, embrace relationships and emotion, and offer new ways of thinking and being. With ideas of community and belonging running through their work, it is no surprise that Brown and Sears also employ the metaphor of 'home' and 'homeplace' to conceptualise the sanctuary-like feeling of the spaces that opened up for and with their project members. They explore how, within these 'homeplaces', young Black women came to feel connected, free to engage in their own cultural practices and question dominant forms of knowledge.

The particular practices that shaped these spaces are similar to those that we employ in our own projects. Firstly, dance is foregrounded as a deeply embodied yet 'metaphysical' (Sears, 2010, p. 3) practice through which Black girls and women can 'access their power' (Sears, 2010, p. 66) and through which 'the power and genius of Black girls' (Brown, 2009, p. 3) can be celebrated and felt in visceral ways. An understanding of dance as a liberating practice in the face of White, patriarchal discourses that enact violence upon Black feminine bodies (Gottschild, 2003; Stanley Niaah, 2010) also shows itself within a small body of research around critical education for, with, and by young Black women (Youdell, 2006; Atencio, 2008; Hickey-Moody, 2013; Stanger, 2016). These 'homeplaces' also make space for a direct critical education that names power relations in 'intellectual, textual' ways (Luke, 2004, p. 26), for example, discussion and creative writing activities around media representations of Black women. Indeed, various acts of verbal expression, through group discussion and writing, take a central role in Brown's and Sears' projects. Both writers employ the term 'voice' in discussing these practices, a significant term within Black feminist theory (Hill Collins, 2000; hooks, 1994) through which exercising one's voice means expressing and asserting one's social position, with this also therefore being a way to speak back to silencing racist and sexist discourses. The notion of a visceral and emotionally engaged sense of community is also key here, with Sears (2010) in particular discussing the importance of argument and laughter within the GEP, citing the 'critical thinking' (p. 105–106) and 'self-love' (p. 103–104) that opens up through these acutely political acts for Black women in the face of racist and sexist oppression. Amina and Camilla worked with different groups of young women to co-create similar forms of 'homeplace' within their respective research sites in ways that offer particular challenges and possibilities to consider for future practice.

College A: An International Women's Day Dance Project

A key dance practice that emerged within Camilla's research with the HSC girls, one of 'coming together' and 'acting on our own behalf' (Brown, 2009), was in preparing for an International Women's Day (IWD) dance performance.

During the six weeks of preparation for this event, Camilla witnessed a particular experience of learning and community, one rooted in a Black girl-directed, playful, and culturally marked creative space.

Notably, a group of young women with different West-African heritages formed their own subgroup to create an 'Afrobeats medley' piece for the show. Camilla was witness to the girls engaging in lively, not uncompetitive, and choreographically productive conversations around their respective countries, during which they shared music, language, and dance steps, a dialogic 'encounter between [students], mediated by the world, in order to name the world' (Freire, 1996, p. 69). The young women spent an increasing amount of time in the dance studio, rehearsing their creation with meticulous attention to detail. This was not dissimilar to the efforts they would put into their college coursework, but with an additional sense of 'wholeness' (hooks, 1994, p. 14) that dancing in tribute to one's culture might bring, especially when the creative work emerged through much laughter, debate, and play with one's friends. As one participant from this group of young creators put it: 'we rehearsed ... we was serious ... yeah – they're my girls'. The seriousness of the girls' playful work did not go unappreciated within the event itself, with the audience erupting into applause and cheering as soon as the girls entered the stage and with one of the college's Assistant Principals turning to me mid-performance exclaiming, 'We have some really good dancers, don't we?'.

These are arguable examples of how a hooksian 'energy' might charge a space in order to 'excite the critical imagination' (hooks, 1994, p. 195) in this instance through reframing how these students were understood within the college: as 'good', 'serious', and worthy of applause, rather than 'vulnerable', 'crazy', or in need of intervention. This sense of seeing, or being seen, differently was also felt by the girls themselves. In the interviews Camilla conducted in the days after the performance, all research participants had the same thing to say about the experience: that it 'brought us together', with the words 'proud' and 'pride' repeatedly being used. This was a rare occasion in which the young women's forms of educational and creative striving were publicly acknowledged within the college and in a way that made the girls feel 'proud' to be who they were, rather than embarrassed or 'stereotyped'.

Interestingly though, this sense of pride, pleasure, and energy did not characterise the entirety of the dance project. In the early stages of the dance studio work, Camilla had taken more of a central role: leading warm-ups, teaching choreographic techniques, as per Freire's 'banking concept' (1996, 53), and co-teaching dance steps/styles alongside different members of the group. The atmosphere of these sessions sometimes felt a little 'awkward', as Felicia generously put it, with moments where students opted out of dancing entirely, saying they felt 'uncomfortable' doing so in front of others – perhaps in yet another space where White forms of knowledge were inscribing what counted as 'good' work. It was only as Camilla came to take a more peripheral role – during the IWD devising period – that more energy, enthusiasm, flow, and creative work was generated. Returning to the words of Felicia, 'Miss, really and truly, that's when it started being fun – when we were putting ourselves into it'. Indeed, the more Camilla's position was decentred, the more the terrain of the project could be reinscribed by the young women's culturally rooted work with each other, as something closer to a 'Black girl centered experience' (Brown, 2009, p. 6). In this sense, it was not just the girls who had the opportunity to 'grow, relearn, redefine'. Once Camilla moved to the periphery of the space, at times trying out elements of the girls' routines under their guidance, she too found herself in a position where she could feel and see things differently: specifically in experiencing the young women as leaders. This sense of the young women as guides to Camilla's own learning again disrupted the deficit narrative surrounding their educational identities within the college. It is also reminiscent of Youdell's (2012) discussions of how 'the White teacher [can become] a "humble learner" in a cross-race dialogue – thus creating "dissonance" in Whiteness and offering White educators "other ways of being White"' (p. 145).

However, one of the teachers, herself a Black woman, shared a particular concern with Camilla following the IWD project: that the students' new visibility in this way might perpetuate a stereotype that 'dance is all Black women can do', a pertinent concern within a neoliberal system that doubts their 'serious' intellectual and economic potential. In this respect, a new question arises: how best to support the students, in the midst of an important period of 'growth, relearning, and redefining', to still navigate the demands and codes of the neoliberal school and classroom? Indeed, the girls' form tutor, who had been a staunch supporter of the dance project, reported to Camilla in the weeks following the IWD project that the girls were now 'too empowered' in their regular lessons, stating that 'answering back' and 'shouting out' were now taking place more than usual. Interestingly, these were practices that Camilla had begun to experience more so as 'speaking up' and 'joining in' without the 'homeplace' that had evolved over the weeks of the project. A key example of this was the final session of the project: in this farewell session, the group used the secluded space of the dance studio for what became a lively and impassioned debate on education and its role in women's lives, clearly displaying how 'education is a consuming passion' (Mirza and Reay, 2000, p. 521) for young Black women. This aligns with how Brown (2009) understood her young participants' bold and often overlapping forms of dialogue as 'embodying types of knowledge about the ways the world works for Black girls' (p. 27). And so perhaps the question can be more pertinently phrased as follows: how best to support the neoliberal school and classroom in adjusting to and making space for a group of young Black women who have 'grown, relearned, redefined'? It is clear there is still thinking and experimenting to do regarding the interactions and reactions of the White neoliberal institution to such 'homeplaces'. The experiences of students in College B help shed further light on this.

College B: Reading and Writing Clubs

The three clubs the research participants from College B attended included 'Reading Revolution', 'Lit Lit', and 'Freethinkers', the latter facilitated by

Amina's colleague. Amina's reading clubs were essentially spaces for students to reignite their love for reading and expose them to a range of literature outside the curriculum. The staff member who facilitated 'Freethinkers' describes it as 'a creative enrichment club in which those who have taken an active interest in poetry and spoken word are able to write and share their creative ideas without fear or worry [...] in a world trying to censor our self-expression at times, we strive to have our voices heard [...] creating a release in the art form that is poetry and spoken word'. The power of this space was continuously discussed in Amina's interviews hence the inclusion of it in our research; it also generated the poem that opens our chapter and gave it its title. While these spaces were not exclusively for Black girls, young Black women did emerge as the dominant student group who chose these spaces as their compulsory extracurricular club; something that the hooksian pedagogies detailed above shed light on.

Amina's vision was to create a joyful and authentic reading space for students, in a way that echoes hooksian discussions of 'engaged' 'homeplaces' (hooks, 1990, 1994). Certainly, Amina's own lived experiences of attending neoliberal (arguably neocolonial) schools as a Black girl informed what these spaces would look like and how they would feel. Specifically, Sharpe's (2016) work shaped her pedagogy in considering the thin line between performative actions and real care; this was in an attempt to offer what Amina felt was missing from her own educational experience. For Amina, it was necessary to reimagine spaces where compassion and care were foundational. As such, the clubs centred on identifying and fostering sources of joy among Black students, in response to the lack of joy prevalent in a society 'permeated by mundane and extreme racism and punctuated by incessant microaggressions' (Smith, Yosso, and Solórzano 2011, p. 212). Indeed, prior to creating the clubs, students had often mentioned to Amina that they had 'lost their love for reading', or were in a 'reading slump', with a hooksian experience of pleasure notably absent from their educational experiences. This is what incentivised Amina to create reading spaces, alongside being intrigued to find out why so many young people at an academically rigorous sixth form had fallen out of love with reading. Undoubtedly, there were various reasons, but Amina's initial understanding, one rooted in her own educational experiences, was that while these students valued reading, the pressures of a target-driven system, filled with a Eurocentric literary curriculum (Elliott, 2014) had alienated them. As one student explained, not only did she have 'no time for reading', but she felt unable to access prescribed texts with a sense of 'enjoyment', which we can read in relation to hooksian ideas of 'pleasure' and 'wholeness' that can be lost under conditions of White supremacy (hooks, 1994, p. 195).

Amina tried different methods in order to reignite a love for literature, the most popular being providing extracts from a range of novels including *My Sister the Serial Killer* (2018) by Oyinkan Braithwaite, *The Bastard of Istanbul* (2006) by Elif Shafak and *The Thing Around Your Neck* (2009) by Chimamanda Ngozi Adichie. This approach is reminiscent of Mirza's (2006) discussions of Black British supplementary schools which centre 'on Black history and knowledge' (p. 142). Ultimately, such educational spaces and curricula are places 'where Whiteness is displaced and Blackness becomes the norm, creating a sanctuary for the Black child in which [...] she is celebrated and recentred' (Mirza, 2006, p. 142). Indeed, Amina's research participants expressed shock, and delight, at the variety of literature that existed: 'It felt shocking seeing these texts. I never knew that could be a thing, and I discovered different ways literature can be created'. For the girls, finding these extracts 'revealed that I am part of something way bigger than myself'. It is helpful here to lean on the words of Bishop (1990, p. ix), which supported Amina's selection of novels:

> books are sometimes windows, offering views of worlds that may be real or imagined, familiar or strange. These windows are also sliding glass doors, and readers have only to walk through in imagination to become part of whatever world has been created or recreated by the author.

The club would always have 40 minutes dedicated to reading and 20 minutes to discussion, which invariably became honest conversations centred around the young women's own experiences. This approach to reading also therefore became opportunities for Black girls who were unintentionally looking for community, through being in a space they could see themselves mirrored, speak freely, present as their authentic selves and create their own narratives:

MARIAM: I loved reading club, reading club was probably the best club I've been to [...]. We would be talking about so many different things and we would have to cut it short. I feel like it was also to do with the people I was with – they knew how to articulate themselves and how to speak, so when we're discussing, the conversation flowed naturally ... the conversations are what I loved.

Amina also witnessed how these conversations were springboards, quite often sparking important dialogue for the girls around navigating the college: ranging from how they articulated themselves, how they were perceived, and the 'invisible rules' of the institutional space. Within these recurring conversations Amina observed how they would advise each other around how to talk without being worried about how their speech was received, and how much they 'were all in this together'. Key to this was that the girls were 'excited to be in an environment where there are people like me'. Indeed, a strong and initially unexpected outcome from these interviews was the girls' repetition of the need for 'community' and finding a sense of belonging through 'each other'.

These experiences are again reminiscent of Mirza's (2006) and Mirza and Reay's (2000) research around the liberatory potential of Black British supplementary schools, namely in communities of Black women coming together to continue legacies of Black female empowerment through education. The girls in College B's experiences are also reminiscent of Mirza's findings regarding the complicated matter of how Black girls might successfully navigate the demands of the neoliberal school system. Mirza's answer is that young Black women adopt seemingly neoliberal ideals of meritocracy in their striving for educational success, something identifiable in how Mariam describes her peers: 'they knew how to articulate themselves and how to speak'. However, they do so not as part of an individualist system of competition, but as a way of 'strategically employ[ing] every means at their disposal in the educational system and the classroom to achieve a modicum of mobility in a world of limited opportunities' (Mirza, 2009, p. 11). Mirza discusses this 'strategic rationalisation' as enacted by the individual Black girl as nothing less than a political act, operating within the very same framework of a community-oriented model of education as Black female empowerment. In this, there is a 'paradoxical pattern of personal educational desire and collective community commitment' (Mirza, 2009, p. 106). The girls in College B arguably took this a little further and in fact mobilised the power of community and communal spaces in order to engage in school with a firmer sense of self and motivation. Indeed, despite the academic pressure 'providing stress' or 'anxiety' because they were falling behind and were scared to be labelled 'lazy', the girls understood that in order to go on to the destinations of choice, they must commit and thrive in this educational setting, while feeling it was through their connections with each other they had the capacity to do so.

It is in this, however, that a particular limitation surfaces. The young women who participated in this research must still navigate themselves through the entire college and wider society. Although their literary 'homeplaces' and their sense of community helped the students tackle 'the myth of Black intellectual inferiority', these young women must still go on and continue to complete their studies and pursue their aspirations even when the extracurricular spaces no longer exist. As Mariam puts it, 'the only thing I didn't like about the reading club was that it was only one hour'. So, how best can teachers and institutions continue to support their students when 'the hour' is over?

Conclusion

In their critical discussion of the role academia might play in decolonising the world for Black women and girls, Edwards, McArthur, and Russell-Owens (2016) call for a 'humanizing' approach to research that considers the 'multiple oppressions Black girls face' (cited in Leigh Kelly, 2020, p. 451), while also trying to create spaces in which joy is at the centre. This kind of work would start from the premise that systemic barriers exist within the UK education system, while placing young Black women's histories, desires, creativity, and voices at the centre of the conversation. This is something we have aimed to achieve in our research. Firstly, through critically explaining the stresses, fears and injustices young Black women face in their education providers, finding that neoliberal forms of schooling allow 'the myth of Black intellectual inferiority' to continue unchecked and in covert ways that invite Black girls to engage in their own 'dynamic rationalisation' of both internalised and externalised prejudice. Secondly, key to our research is an exploration and creation of liberatory pedagogical practices that hold and make space for young Black women's 'power and genius' (Brown, 2009, p. 3), specifically through co-created spaces that invite embodied, creative, and joyous critical thinking and expression that both emerge from and reaffirm Black feminine communities. We ultimately posit that minority students, especially in this case Black girls, can and should be able to bring their authentic selves to schools without fear of being labelled. Our research has shown that while this looks different for different communities, one solution is the 'homeplaces' we articulate as powerful spaces that can complement and re-energise young Black women's authentic and 'whole' (hooks, 1994) engagement with school and schooling.

However, as the limitations raised in both our research narratives suggest, the mere existence of 'homeplaces' in neoliberal schools is not enough. If those in the neoliberal institution itself, including teachers, are not supported to '*grow [...] relearn [...] redefine*' through and with such 'homeplaces', the young women's growth is at best resigned to the margins and, at worst, subsumed back into discourses of 'problem girls'. We hope our research has shown that through holistic and 'engaged' forms of teacher education, research and participation, where all members of the institution are invited to be caring (Sharpe, 2016), whole (hooks, 1994), and humble learners (Youdell, 2012), the beginnings of such change might be possible.

References

Ahmed, S. (2002) Racialised bodies, in: M. Evans and E. Lee (Eds) *Real Bodies: A Sociological Introduction*. Hampshire: Palgrave, pp. 46–63.

Ahmed, S. (2004) *The Cultural Politics of Emotion*. Edinburgh: Edinburgh University Press.

Ahmed, S. (2012) *On Being Included: Racism and Diversity in Institutional Life*, Durham, NC and London: Duke University Press.

Archer, L., Hollingworth, S., and Mendick, H. (2010) *Urban Youth and Schooling*. Maidenhead: Open University Press.

Atencio, M. (2008) '"Freaky is just how I get down": Investigating the fluidity of minority ethnic feminine subjectivities in dance'. *Leisure Studies*, 27(3), pp. 311–327.

Ball, S.J., Maguire, M. and Macrae, S. (2000) *Choice, Pathways and Transitions Post-16: New Youth, New Economies in the City*. London: Routledge Falmer.

Bishop, R.S. (1990) 'Mirrors, windows, and sliding glass doors'. *Perspectives*, 6(3), pp. ix–xi.

Brown, R.N. (2009) *Black Girlhood Celebration: Toward a Hip Hop Feminist Pedagogy*. New York: Peter Lang,

Carolissen, R., Bozalek, V., Nicholls, L., Leibowitz, B., Roleder, P., and Swartz, L. (2011) 'bell hooks and the enactment of emotion in teaching and learning across boundaries: A pedagogy of hope?'. *SAJHE*, 25(1), pp. 157–167.

Edwards, E., McArthur, S.A., and Russell-Owens, L. (2016) 'Relationships, being-ness, and voice: Exploring multiple dimensions of humanizing work with Black girls'. *Equity & Excellence in Education*, 49(4), pp. 428–439.

Elliott, V. (2014) 'The treasure house of a nation? Literary heritage, curriculum and devolution in Scotland and England in the twenty first century'. *The Curriculum Journal*, 25(2), pp. 282–300.

Fitzpatrick, K. (2013) 'Ethics, Power, Representation, and Socially Just Research'. *Critical Pedagogy, Physical Education and Urban Schooling*, 432, pp. 53–72.

Fordham, S. (1996) *Blacked Out: Dilemmas of Race, Identity, and Success at Capital High*, Chicago: University of Chicago Press.

Freire, P. (1996) *Pedagogy of the Oppressed*. London: Penguin Books.

Gottschild, B. (2003) *The Black Dancing Body: A Geography from Coon to Cool*. New York: Palgrave Macmillan.

Gunaratnam, Y. (2003) *Researching 'Race' and Ethnicity: Methods, Knowledge and Power*. London: SAGE.

Hickey-Moody, A. (2013) 'Tradition, innovation, Fusion: Local Articulations of Global Scapes of Girl Dance' in: A. Hickey-Moody, *Youth, Arts and Education: Reassembling Subjectivity Through Affect*. Abingdon: Routledge, pp. 67–91.

Hill Collins, P. (2000) *Black Feminist Thought*. (2nd Edition). Oxon: Routledge.

hooks, b. (1990) *Yearning: Race, Gender and Cultural Politics*. Boston: South End Press.

hooks, b. (1994) *Teaching to Transgress*. London: Routledge.

hooks, b. (2003) *Teaching Community: A Pedagogy of Hope*. New York and London: Routledge.

Jackson, S. (1997) 'Crossing Borders and Changing Pedagogies: From Giroux and Freire to feminist theories of education'. *Gender and Education*, 9(4), pp. 457–468.

Kelly, P. (2000) 'The dangerousness of youth at risk: The possibilities of surveillance and intervention in uncertain times'. *Journal of Adolescence*, 23, pp. 463–476.

Leigh Kelly, L. (2020) '"I Love Us for Real": Exploring Homeplace as a Site of Healing and Resistance for Black Girls in Schools'. *Equity & Excellence in Education*, 53(4), pp. 449–464.

Luke, A. (2004) Two takes on the critical, in: B. Norton and K. Toohey (Eds) *Critical Pedagogies and Language Learning*. New York: Cambridge University Press, pp. 21–29.

Mac an Ghaill, M. (1988) *Young, Gifted and Black*. Milton Keynes: Open University Press.

Mayor, C. (2022) 'Anti-Racist Research Praxis: Feminist Relational Accountability and Arts-Based Reflexive Memoing for Qualitative Data Collection in Social Work Research'. *Feminist Inquiry in Social Work*, 37(4), pp. 624–644.

Milligan, L. (2016) 'Insider-outsider-inbetweener? Researcher positioning, participative methods and cross-cultural educational research'. *Compare: A Journal of Comparative and International Education*, 46(2), pp. 235–250.

Mirza, H.S. (1992) *Young, Female and Black*. Oxon: Routledge.

Mirza, H.S. (2006) '"Race", gender and educational desire'. *Race, Ethnicity and Education*, 9(2), pp. 137–158.

Mirza, H.S. (2009) *Race, Gender and Educational Desire: Why Black Women Succeed and Fail*. London and New York: Routledge.

Mirza, H.S. and Reay, D. (2000) 'Spaces and places of black educational desire: Rethinking Black supplementary schools as a new social movement'. *Sociology*, 34(3) pp. 521–544.

Phoenix, A. (2010) De-colonising practices: negotiating narrative from racialised and gendered experiences of education, in: H.S. Mirza and C. Joseph (Eds) *Black and Postcolonial Feminisms*. Oxon: Routledge, pp. 101–114.

Sears, S. (2010) *Imagining Black Womanhood: The Negotiation of Power and Identity in the Girls Empowerment Project*. Albany: State University of New York Press.

Sharpe, C. (2016) *In the Wake: On Blackness and Being*. Durham, NC: Duke University Press.

Smith, W.A., Yosso, T.J., and Solórzano, D.G. (2011) Challenging racial battle fatigue on historically white campuses: A critical race examination of race-related stress, in: R.D. Coates (Ed.) *Covert Racism*. Hoboken: Jossey Bass, Brill, pp. 211–237.

Stanger, C. (2016) 'Let me change it into my own style': Cultural domination and material acts of resistance within an inner city dance class, in: A. Hickey-Moody and T. Page (Eds.) *Arts, Pedagogy and Cultural Resistance*, London: Rowman and Little-field, pp. 113–131.

Stanger, C. (2019) *'We rehearsed… we was serious… they're my girls': Developing an Embodied Pedagogy of Hope with Young Black Women 'at Risk' of Exclusion in an Inner London College*. Doctoral thesis, Goldsmiths, University of London.

Stanley Niaah, S. (2010) *Dancehall: From Slave Ship to Ghetto*. Ottawa: University of Ottawa Press.

Wright, C. (2005) Black femininities go to school: How young Black females navigate race and gender in: G. Lloyd (Ed.) *Problem Girls: Understanding and Supporting Troubled and Troublesome Girls and Young Women*. Abingdon: Routledge Falmer, pp. 103–113.

Youdell, D. (2006) *Impossible Bodies, Impossible Selves: Exclusions and Student Subjectivities*. Dordecht, The Netherlands: Springer.

Youdell, D. (2012) 'Fabricating "Pacific Islander": pedagogies of expropriation, return and resistance and other lessons from a "Multicultural Day"'. *Race Ethnicity and Education*, 15(2), pp. 141–155.

5 Heteronormativity Critical Agency
Creating Inclusive Schools

Tamás Fütty, Ayla Fedorchenko and Mart Busche

Introduction

In 2019, a third positive gender marker – 'diverse' – was established in Germany, and another law that allows change of name and legal gender status on the premise of self-declaration is under discussion but still highly contested. The international socio-political context is also characterised by a simultaneity of higher visibility and acceptance of gender diversity and its contestation and restriction – well illustrated by the large number of anti-trans legislative proposals in the USA in the aftermath of the Trump administration. Some countries allow for more equality regarding gender diversity and variations in sex characteristics by changing their legal framework: prohibition of surgeries on intersex children (e.g. Colombia, Germany, Malta), implementation of a third legal status (e.g. Germany, Australia) or even more options (e.g. Austria) apart from 'female' and 'male', or facilitation of the procedure for trans people to change their legal status (e.g. Argentina, Spain). While diversity has become more visible (particularly due to social media and diversity commodification, e.g. on Netflix) and, in Germany, more recognised on scientific and legal levels (Busche and Fütty 2023), this does not yet translate into de facto equality and inclusion of trans, non-binary, intersex and agender people – and this also applies to schools. The quantitative studies regularly undertaken by the European Agency of Fundamental Rights offer empirical data that point to structural discriminations and exclusions regarding gender diversity all over Europe, including in German schools. For instance, half of the intersex (N=341) and trans (N=1968) survey participants (from Germany) were affected by bullying at school, and 26% of intersex and 15% of trans participants changed school due to discrimination or dropped out entirely (FRA, 2020).

Thus, the legal recognition of diversity regarding gender and body characteristics is not yet systematically included and implemented within the German school system. In terms of teaching content, school structure and architecture (changing rooms, toilets), and use of chosen names and pronouns, binary gender and sex norms remain and members of staff are often poorly educated or ignorant (Bittner, 2015; Klocke, Salden, and Watzlawik, 2020; Schmidt and Schondelmayer, 2015). These norms sanction, exclude or discriminate against all those living beyond or between the binary on individual,

DOI: 10.4324/9781003397502-5

interpersonal, and structural levels. In order to implement a broader understanding of diversity regarding gender and body characteristics in schools, the functioning of these norms needs to be understood, analysed, and changed on different levels. As education is a contested field where relationships of power tilt between subjugation and liberation, in this chapter, we will analyse factors that enable and limit the participation of transgender and intersex students at school and explore how the heteronormativity-critical agency of students and teachers can be strengthened. We will start by briefly introducing Judith Butler's deconstructivist theory of becoming subject via subjectivation, with reference to vulnerability and agency. Additionally, a heteronormativity-critical perspective will be proposed in the second section. Based on an empirical example from our research project, in section three, we will interrogate current norms, structures, and conditions in German schools that make students beyond the gender and sex binary systemically invisible, vulnerable, and understood through heteronormativity. Within the binary gendered school structure, we will pay close attention to the agency of students and teachers. To envision a heteronormativity-critical framing of schools that caters to a heterogenous student body, in section four, we will analyse two different sex education curriculum documents from Germany's federal education system which address topics related to gender, sex and sexuality. To go beyond the binary school structure, in section five, a post-heteronormative approach to enabling diversity is proposed.

Exploring a Heteronormativity Critical Agency: Possibilities and Limitations

Binary gender and sex norms are still crucial to grant or withdraw intelligibility and thus social existence (Butler, 1991, 2004). According to Judith Butler, to become a recognisable and intelligible subject, individuals need to undergo subjectivation, which means that they are subjugated under dominant norms that are not chosen; rather they subject, normalise, discipline, and restrict *all* people. These norms and conditions of becoming a recognised and intelligible subject are still significantly binary gendered and sexed (Butler, 1991, 1997, 2004). Gender and sex intelligibility mostly work within a framework of heteronormativity, which – on the basis of a binary gender and sex order – sets heterosexuality as well as cisgender and endosex as the normal and natural form of life. A critique of heteronormativity focusses on norms and practices which make people or bodies that do not conform to dominant medical norms and societal expectations 'the others'. This means that heterosexual, cisgender, and endosex people do not need to come out or position themselves concerning gender, sex, and sexuality because they are constructed as the natural norm.

In this regard, subjectivation and thus norms of recognition go hand in hand with the normative violence of *not* being legally or medically awarded recognition as a 'normal' subject and being relegated to the space of the 'other' (Butler, 1997, p. 26; 2004, p. 100). The denial of recognition within systems and institutions becomes a form of normative violence and creates a structural vulnerability. Within dominant intersectional power relations some people and groups in society, e.g. trans, intersex, nonbinary, people of colour, or people with disabilities, are made normatively and intersectionally more vulnerable to various forms of violence and victimisation than others (Butler, 2004; Fütty, 2019).

At the same time, subjectivation according to Butler (2004) means to become a subject with agency precisely through undergoing subjugating acts of citational becoming under dominant norms of recognition. These ideas are expressed in more detail through Butler's (2009) notion of performativity, which, as a possibility for the production of agency, engages subjects in enacting dominant norms, for example, in their gender performance, to become intelligible in society. Yet, in these repetitions and enactments 'failures' are possible and these can irritate or even shift dominant norms, which will be explored further in the following section based on an empirical example of our research project, Gender 3.0 (Fütty et al., forthcoming).

Ambivalences and Limitations of Heteronormativity-Critical Agency on Interpersonal and Structural Levels

> We only had male and female changing rooms, so together with the trans* student in my class, we wanted to find a solution, where he could get dressed comfortably and, as he preferred, alone. His favoured solution was to get dressed in the teachers' changing room, but this idea was rejected by one of my colleagues who argued that he needed the space himself. We then decided to ask the boys in another class whether they would share a changing room with the boys in my class, so that the spare room could be used by my student. Their changing room would be packed then, but everyone agreed. It was the best solution we could come up with given the rigid binary situation.

The situation above was described by a sports teacher, when asked about her experiences with gender diversity in a German school for our empirical research project 'Gender 3.0: Gender and Sex Diversity in Schools'. The situation has been reported by trainee teachers and support staff several times in similar ways and captures the current state of gender diversity at school. Despite increased visibility and legal recognition in Germany, the *structure* of schools and their architecture (e.g. changing rooms and toilets), as well as dominant practices and forms of interactions and organisation (e.g. dividing groups, separate physical education classes), procedures (e.g. enrolment), and learning content (e.g. materials, examples) remain gendered. Within this heteronormative structure, gender diversity and intersex variation at school is *structurally* made *invisible* and de-thematised because binary options prevail as quasi-natural conditions. The result is that gender diverse and intersex students are often discriminated against or excluded, and their right to participate equally in education is structurally, individually, and interpersonally denied.

The presence of a trans student is often perceived as a problematic *singular case*. Particular needs for diversity and inclusion are often framed as a disturbance of 'smooth' lessons and classroom settings (Krell and Oldemeier 2017, p. 172; Ferfolja and Ullman 2020, p. 8). Nevertheless, what can be framed as structurally generated vulnerability here does not equate to passivity. This particular student came out as a trans man, and this would have required a significant level of individual agency. Whilst this act could be interpreted as progressive, since the student felt that he could disclose his identity, coming out and transitioning (predominantly framed as from one side – female – to the other – male) means that the student becomes partially intelligible and integrated as needing to declare his identity as against the norm. The heteronormative requirement to *come out* marks the trans student as *other* and – in disturbing the binary organisation of education – as *problem*. Thus, subjectivation and agency are shaped by logics of cis-endo-heteronormative norms.

As the excerpt from our research project shows, the existence of trans students challenges the binary order in schools, and this needs individual and collective agency. For the student, his trans life might be more liveable in school now. Also, gender norms are pushed a bit further to integrate another category 'trans' into the school practice on a limited scale. Still, it enacts and reproduces heteronormativity at school: the development of gender positions cannot be carried out in a self-determined way, and the educational opportunities of gender diverse students are structurally restricted. Moreover, as explained in the excerpt, the responsibility for his wellbeing is on the trans student and, after disclosure, on his teacher, instead of the educational and school leadership and entire school organisation. In this regard, Schmidt and Schondelmayer's argument that the absence of addressing gender, sex, and sexual diversity in German schools leaves it as 'nobody's responsibility land' (2015, p. 230) still applies.

While the example does not refer to the background of the student, research states that, in general, gaining self-understanding and agency requires considerable psychological and emotional resources and resilience from young people and needs external support, for instance, support from friends, peers, parents, youth services, and digital communities (Sauer and Meyer, 2016), which many students may not have. Within this individualised and problem-bias framing of gender and sex diversity the *responsibility* to address the structural discrimination/exclusion continues to fall on the student and on teachers. Importantly, when students do not receive support, it can also lead to further exclusions such as dropping out of education, affecting educational attainment and transitions into adulthood. In this regard, a survey by the German youth research institute (DJI) shows that many LGBTQ students decide to *stay invisible* at school to avoid being subject to discrimination and violence or being rejected, shamed, ridiculed, not taken seriously or the evaluation of their educational performance being effected (Krell and Oldemeier, 2015, p. 13).

Moreover, on an interpersonal level, the student needs to *trust* a teacher to approach the topic of transitioning, feeling excluded, or discussing issues at school. As several empirical examples from our projects as well as other research (Kleiner, 2015; Oldemeier, 2021) indicate, the quality of relationship is crucial for students to entrust teachers with their problems and needs. At the same time trust often does not exist, as the national surveys of the German Youth Institute (DJI) show: More than half of the trans and gender diverse participants had witnessed, teachers themselves actively involved in discriminatory behaviour, such as laughing at anti-queer jokes or making fun of students who did not display stereotypically gendered behaviour (Krell and Oldemeier, 2017, p. 172). Additionally, 53.5% of respondents stated that their teachers never showed that they did not tolerate anti-LGBTIQ swearwords and 49.7% of the teachers did not intervene or challenge behaviour when students were teased for being assumed to be LGBTIQ (Krell and Oldemeier 2017, p. 172). It also needs to be considered that many students who do not or cannot conform to dominant notions of Eurocentric masculinity and femininity are sometimes labelled queer, gay, or trans and affected by related discriminations without necessarily identifying with those labels or coming out themselves (Fütty, 2019).

In the excerpt from our research at the beginning of this section, the teacher is asked to *act, take responsibility*, and find an individual solution for the student. As empirical research states teachers often avoid taking responsibility when it comes to addressing gender and sex diversity, including LGBTIQA+ students in the classroom, and preventing peer violence, discrimination, and exclusion. Teachers seem to shy away from this work due to a lack of knowledge, fear of 'concerned parents', or concerns about not having the support of school principals (Klocke *et al.*, 2020, p. 31; Ferfolja and Ullmann 2021, p. 22). Klenk (2023, pp. 49–75) also points out that, if instances of harm or bullying occur, teachers and schools often delegate this responsibility and duty to act directly to affected students, their parents or social workers. Thus, while many teachers are willing to support students (Klenk, 2023; Klocke, Salden, and Watzlawik, 2020), most feel ill-equipped to include gender diversity related content in the curriculum (Hilton and Turnbull, 2010) to provide for those students' needs and also act against anti-LGBTIQA+ school harassment.

To summarise, within the prevailing heteronormative school system, gender-diverse students (as well as students with intersex variations) are made invisible, responsible, and vulnerable to exclusion, discrimination, mobbing, and further violence on a structural as well as an interpersonal and individual level. In this regard, the excerpt points out students' precarious and likewise resistant agency and how crucial the commitment of individual teachers to listen to students, take them seriously, and address their needs for inclusion in education is. While multi-layered explicit and implicit heteronormative policing, restricting, and sanctioning practices and processes shape the conditions for subjectivation in school for all children, at the same time, multi-sited forms of agency and resistance exist. Involving different levels of subjectivation, interaction, and agency. It also points out the necessity of collective efforts, so that one single teacher cannot block a student's right to safety, self-determination, and well-being. Thus, this section highlights the requirement for structural change in schools, including teachers' education on gender diversity and diversity regarding body characteristics. The tensions between subjugation and normalisation in education, as well as enablement/agency related to diversity, are extended further in the next section by investigating school curricula on a macro level.

Structural Conditions for Enabling Diversity Regarding Gender and Sex Characteristics in the German Context: The Example of School Curricula

Based on theoretical and empirical insights on how current school structures and practices shape the schooling experiences of students beyond the limits of heteronormativity, now we will briefly analyse the school curricula, guidelines, and frameworks for sex education of the two federal states, Berlin/Brandenburg and Bavaria, as one key area to support heteronormativity-critical agency. Our goal is to point out how they de/construct heteronormative logics and thereby support or limit the inclusion of gender and sex diversity in sex education and to illustrate the curricular differences between the two federal German states. In doing so, we identify challenges to creating diversity inclusive curricula, particularly concerning the wording and context in which diversity is framed and included.

In Germany's federally organised educational system, gender and sex are only included in few of the general curricula and are predominantly referenced in connection with sex education, which is taught across disciplines in all federal states. In 1993, the federal constitutional court in Germany supported a holistic understanding of sex education in schools based on the WHO guidelines for sexual health, which, besides knowledge on biological processes and contraception, should include teaching on relationships, lifestyles, life situations, and social values (Hilgers, 2004, p.12).

The *Bavarian Guidelines for Family and Sexuality Education* (BSBK, 2016) base their learning objectives almost exclusively on binary oppositional conceptions of gender and sex characteristics and, furthermore, construct the student population as identifying as male *or* female, cis, and heterosexual. For instance, the students shall be able to 'name sex characteristics of boys and girls' as early as the final phase of primary schooling (p. 8). Students are addressed in 'their own gender as boys and girls' (p. 10) and are expected to 'identify with their own body' (p. 10). Mixed education of boys and girls is understood as a pedagogical strategy that, amongst other objectives, enables students to develop 'an equal and responsible partnership' (p. 4). The wording implies a (hetero)sexual/romantic relationship. This reading conforms to the general framing of the guidelines, which are based on the Bavarian school law (BayEUG, 2000, Art. 48 Abs. 1) that defines the promotion of marriage and family as the primary learning objective (p. 2) at a time when same-sex marriage was not yet legally recognised in Germany. Besides mixed education, sex-segregated classroom activities are also suggested as a pedagogical strategy, and how this might negatively affect students, e.g. those who do not identify as either male or female, is not considered. Thus, the text constructs a binary oppositional understanding of sex/gender which derives from a concept of coherence of the gender marker assigned at birth, gender identity and embodiment, and fixed subject positions in which transformations, ambivalences, and fluidities are not included.

There are few instances where the guidelines create space for a more diverse, fluid, and potentially mouldable understanding of gender and sex. However, a close analysis of those *sites of undoing* shows that they are worded in ways that again reinscribe normative ideas of sex and gender and contribute to othering processes. Under the subheading *tasks and objectives*, the guidelines declare that schools shall support students on their way towards 'self-responsibility' and 'self-determination' (BSBK, 2016, p. 3). Pupils shall 'understand, that people can experience their "Geschlechtlichkeit" [a German umbrella term for the mixture of sex, gender, and sexuality] diversely and shape their lives responsibly within the framework of their ethical and moral beliefs' (BSBK, 2016). This opens up space for diverse subjectivities and ways of living and strengthens claims for autonomy irrespective of a person's gender, sex and sexuality. At the same time, the personal belief system is depicted as a supposedly fixed framework, that might allow for or limit students' own ways of living and experiences, rather than as something that students should critically discuss against the background of societal norms and power structures to make self-determination possible. While the legal framework of the Bavarian school law demands tolerance for different values (BayEUG, 2000, Art. 48 Abs. 2), the law also stipulates 'reverence for God' as one of the paramount educational goals, and in accordance with the law, the guidelines provide that students must be educated.

Another example for the inscription of normative ideas of sex and gender is the inclusion of the terms 'transsexuality' and 'intersexuality' as a learning objective for 14- to 15-year-olds: Pupils shall 'respect their own sexual orientation and the sexual orientation of others (hetero-, homo-, and bisexuality) and respect and know of transsexuality and intersexuality' (p. 10). The disruptive potential in this learning goal is hardly achieved as the guidelines use pathologising medical terminology without paying respect to (community-based) self-determinations. Furthermore, gender identity and sex characteristics are conflated with sexuality in the wording (trans/inter*sexuality*) and intersex, despite mostly referring to variants of sex characteristics, is mentioned under the learning area *gender role and gender identity*, not under biological aspects. Moreover, trans and intersex are framed as topics that students should *know of*, rather than as *something that concerns and affects students themselves*. By only mentioning trans and intersex as noteworthy identifications that deviate from the cis-endo-hetero-norm that the guidelines reproduce in the rest of the text, the curricula contribute to othering discourses, which maintain cis and endo as the unmarked norm. Its concept of gender and sex diversity is restricted since endo and cis are obviously not part of this diversity. Thus, while the guidelines mention gender diversity as a topic to learn about, they do so within a limited and pathologising framework, and the implicit binary oppositional understanding of sex/gender as natural norm prevails.

Compared to the Bavarian guidelines the *Framework for Guidance and Action for Comprehensive Sexuality Education/Education for Sexual Self Determination Berlin/Brandenburg* (LISUM, 2021) largely avoids aforementioned othering practices and includes gender and sex diversity from the beginning: 'think diversity by starting from diversity' (Hartmann and Busche 2018a). Gender and sex diversity ways of living are, *as a matter of course*, visible, identifiable, and comprehensible as part of diversity. The framework explicitly mentions different categories of gender, sex, and body diversity that should be taught: e.g. cis, trans, male, female, intersex, endo, non-binary, genderqueer. It adopts a social-constructivist perspective and supports an understanding of gender and sex that works beyond the binary and includes the often unmarked and unnamed norms cisgender and endosex. Thus, othering practices of unmarked heteronormativity or implicit hierarchisation is interrupted. Thereby, the framework contributes to the normalisation and recognition of plural genders, bodies, and sexualities.

However, linguistically it only addresses and mentions female and male students ('Schülerinnen und Schüler') and does not use gender and sex diversity inclusive language that aims to include all students (e.g. 'Schüler*innen'). The framework adds a gender disclaimer to say that the binary form applies to all students 'male, female, and diverse' (p. 4). This might point to political restrictions that curriculum development is affected by, such as prohibitions on the use of inclusive language by the federal senates. Why the gender disclaimer uses terms related to civil status (male, female, diverse) instead of affirmative terms used for self-designations remains questionable. Otherwise, binary distinctions are only discussed as a pedagogical strategy in the guidelines to offer a safe space for students. For example, if they feel insecure talking about sexual topics with students of other genders or forming groups with students who have similar experiences concerning gender and sex diverse socialisation. The authors however warn that those safe spaces might not feel safe for all students and might be particularly challenging for students for whom questions around gender and sex are conflict-laden as well as for students who are affected by peer violence. With regard to the question of how classes can be divided without forcing students into binary gender and sex structures, the authors suggest various options, such as creating a third group or letting the students form the groups based on what they feel comfortable with, and encourage teachers to find individual solutions in the guidelines.

Ultimately, both the Bavarian guidelines and the Berlin/Brandenburg framework provide an argumentative base for teachers to include gender, sex, and sexuality diversity in their sex education classroom. Compared to the Bavarian guidelines the Berlin/Brandenburg documents discuss gender and sex diversity more broadly, deconstruct the binary, and emphasise much more strongly that gender and sex diversity is an issue that concerns everyone and should be regarded as an integral part of school life. It normalises plural identities and works against the curricular silencing of queer perspectives prevalent in school. From the above analysis, it can be seen that school curricula and guidelines should include gender, sex, and sexual diversity as topics across all subjects in a way that treats cisgender, trans, non-binary, or agender as part of gender and sex diversity as along with intersex and endosex as part of body diversity. Affirmative terms should be used to recognise the important work of community groups and activists against pathologising traditions. Furthermore, the wording in curricula and guidelines should help educators understand that gender and sex diversity is more than a topic that students should learn about; it is integral to many of the students' and teachers' lives.

Towards Diversity Inclusion and Post-heteronormative Settings

While guidelines such as those discussed above give structural orientation and function as the formal backbone for gender, sex, and sexual inclusivity education, there are more arenas of action we would like to mention. German and international research identified the general inclusion of LGBTQIA-related content in school as one central dimension of the well-being and sense of security of trans, intersex, nonbinary and other students in school, which can positively affect the school climate (Klocke, Salden and Watzlawik, 2020; Burdge et al., 2013). Students are less likely to hear anti-homo and anti-trans remarks, to feel unsafe, or to miss school if there is an LGBTQ-inclusive curriculum (GLSEN, 2020, p. 9). Studies also point out positive effects of student support groups, such as Gay-Straight-Alliances or Gender and Sexuality Alliances (GSAs) on the well-being of queer students by providing safe(r) spaces on school premises, working against cis-endo-heteronormative school structures, and enabling free gender-diverse development (Lessard, Watson, and Puhl, 2020; Abreu et al., 2022, p. 146). The overall school climate can be enhanced by inclusive non-discrimination policies, comprehensive anti-bullying policies, and policies tailored specifically to the needs of trans, intersex, nonbinary, and agender students. Such measures should also facilitate changing a student's first name on school records, regardless of any legal name change, or using diversity inclusive toilets (GLSEN, 2020; Jones, 2016).

Going beyond logics of heteronormative othering, the development of a pedagogical post-heteronormative approach (Hartmann and Busche 2018a, p. 184; Busche 2021) would entail conditions in which femininity and masculinity and heterosexuality are no longer authoritative frames of orientation and order, so that other genders, bodies and sexualities are no longer presented as deviant or special. Thus, it is important not only to focus on learning processes of students and teachers to address and question gender and sex norms but also to transmit empowerment for marginalised groups (Hartmann and Busche 2018b, p. 25). Crucial within this framing is that it is an outing-free zone. It is about moving beyond prevailing gender, sex, and sexuality norms and their coherence, in ways that explanations of one's own positioning can be omitted, and also about having space for multifaceted gender, sex, and sexuality-related experimentation and enactment. Starting from the de facto existing diversity – even though it is not always obvious – helps to avoid a logic of majority and minority and 'us/them' mindsets.

By making queer lives visible and approachable in everyday life, e.g. by presenting queer biographical experiences with a certain ease as a possibility to choose and shape a (self-)determined way of life, a strategy to establish new self-understandings and to give space to the respective uniqueness of individual life stories can be enabled. In this way, conditions for subjectivation processes can be altered and broadened. This is connected to a basic attitude of being open to new, as yet unknown gender, sex, and sexuality constellations that irritate or undermine the previously valid understandings of gender and sex non-belongings and asexual desires. Every individual is valuable and – in intersectional terms – equipped with different privileges and marginalisations, with different experiences and positionings. In a post-heteronormative space, all diversities are welcome – with special consideration to those that are not known yet. On the one hand, this makes it a learning space to get to know new subject formations, restraints and possibilities, and practices. On the other hand, it lays claim to providing broad and sensitive conditions for subjectivation processes. For post-heteronormative schools it means

> to thematise diverse ways of life in such a way that on the level of the recipients – however they understand themselves and however they live – an opening-emancipative invitation is attached, and on a social or societal level, transformative impulses are triggered insofar as new things can arise in social and societal interactions.
>
> Hartmann 2017, p. 182, transl. M.B.

Conclusion

In this chapter, we highlighted current paradoxes and tension fields concerning the in/visibility of gender and sex diversity at school and the lack of responsibility being taken in addressing it despite Germany's legal recognition and the schools' educational duty to provide equal educational opportunities to all students. As education is a contested field of power between subjugation and liberation, we focused on enabling and limiting factors for gender and sex diversity at school and explored how heteronormativity-critical agency can be understood. Based on Judith Butler's deconstructivist perspective, we argued that gender and sex information communicated to students is still determined within a framework of heteronormativity. By putting the spotlight on an empirical example of our research project, Gender 3.0, in section three, we pointed out that due the prevailing binary school structure, gender and sex diverse students are made at once invisible and other and also structurally vulnerable to discrimination on different levels. Furthermore, we interrogated how heteronormativity-critical agency (of students and teachers) can be understood within this binary school setting as well as within the educational paradox of subjugation and enablement. While reliable teacher–student relationships are crucial for students to disclose problems and needs, requirements for this agency are not necessarily given. By analysing two curricula of Germany's federal school system in section four, it became apparent how differently the thematisation of gender and sex diversity is framed within schooling, considering wording, terminology, and learning goals.

Lastly, moving away from a perspective on visibility and anti-discrimination alone, we proposed a post-heteronormative approach in section five, one that envisions diversity without hierarchisations, a state where no genders, bodies, or sexualities are presented as deviant or special. The aim in doing so was to foster perspectives for inclusion of gender and sex diversity that go beyond a heteronormative framework of othering and delegating responsibility for their well-being to the students themselves. To conclude, to deconstruct heteronormativity at school and thus foster the liveability of LGBTIQA students as along with their access to equal education and job opportunities and thus improved life chances and more self-determination. It is crucial to address, deconstruct, and include gender, sex, and sexual diversity from intersectional perspectives across all disciplines as well as all school practices, regulations, and procedures. It is a cross-sectional task for many agents, policy makers, headteachers, teachers, parents, students, administrative staff, social workers, university staff, etc. to create an education for the future that welcomes the diversity of students and enables more equitable learning opportunities for all.

References

Abreu, R.L., Audette, L., Mitchell, Y., Simpson, I., Ward, J., Ackerman, L., Gonzalez, K., Washington, K. (2022) 'LGBTQ student experiences in schools from 2009–2019: A systematic review of study characteristics and recommendations for prevention and intervention in school psychology journals', *Psychology in the Schools*, 59(1), pp. 115–151. doi:10.1002/pits.22508.

BayEUG – Bayerisches Gesetz über das Erziehungs- und Unterrichtswesen in der Fassung der Bekanntmachung (2000) (GVBl. S. 414, 632, BayRS 2230–2231-1-K), das zuletzt durch § 1 des Gesetzes vom 5. Juli (2022) (GVBl. S. 308) geändert worden ist.

Bittner, M. (2015) *Die Ordnung der Geschlechter in Schulbüchern*, in: A.-C. Schondelmayer, U.B. Schröder and F. Schmidt (Eds) *Selbstbestimmung und Anerkennung sexueller und geschlechtlicher Vielfalt: Lebenswirklichkeiten, Forschungsergebnisse und Bildungsbausteine.* (Springer eBook Collection). Wiesbaden: Springer VS, pp.247–260. Available at: https://doi.org/10.1007/978-3-658-02252-5_20BSBKWK.

BSBK – Bayerischen Staatsministeriums für Bildung und Kultus (2016) *Bekanntmachung des Bayerischen Staatsministeriums für Bildung und Kultus, Wissenschaft und Kunst über die Richtlinien für die Familien- und Sexualerziehung in den bayerischen Schulen vom 15. Dezember 2016.* Available at: https://www.km.bayern.de/download/24053_Richtlinien-f%C3%BCr-die-Familien-und-Sexualerziehung-in-den-bayerischen-Schulen_ver%C3%B6ffentlicht.pdf (Accessed 15 March 2023).

Burdge, H., Snapp, S.D., Laub, C., Russell, S.T., and Moody, R. (2013) *Implementing Lessons That Matter: The Impact of LGBTQ-Inclusive Curriculum on Student Safety, Well-Being, and Achievement.* San Francisco: Gay-Straight Alliance Network and Tucson: Frances McClelland Institute.

Busche, M. (2021) 'Next Stop: Postheteronormativität', *Sozial Extra*, 45(2), pp. 85–89. doi:10.1007/s12054-021-00366-y.

Busche, M. and Fütty, T. (2023) Prekäre Subjektivierungs- und Handlungsbedingungen im Kontext Geschlechterpluralität – Trans*, Inter*, Nichtbinarität und Agender in der Schule, in: M. Kampshoff, B. Kleiner, and A. Langer (Eds) *Trans- und Intergeschlechtlichkeit in Erziehung und Bildung.* (Jahrbuch erziehungswissenschaftliche Geschlechterforschung, Folge 19. Opladen: Verlag Barbara Budrich, pp. 75–90.

Butler, J. (1991) *Das Unbehagen der Geschlechter.* Frankfurt am Main: Suhrkamp.

Butler, J. (1997) *Excitable Speech: A Politics of the Performative.* London: Routledge.

Butler, J. (2004) *Undoing Gender.* New York and London: Routledge.

Butler, J. (2009) *Die Macht der Geschlechternormen und die Grenzen des Menschlichen.* Frankfurt am Main: Suhrkamp.

Ferfolja, T. and Ullman, J. (2020) *Gender and Sexuality Diversity in a Culture of Limitation.* New York: Routledge.

Ferolja, T. and Ullman, J. (2021) 'Inclusive pedagogies for transgender and gender diverse children: parents' perspectives on the limits of discourses of bullying and risk in schools'. *Pedagogy, Culture & Society,* 29(5), pp. 793–810.

FRA – European Union Agency for Fundamental Rights (2020) *A Long Way to Go for LGBTI Equality.* Luxembourg: Publications Office of the European Union.

Fütty, T.J.J. (2019) *Gender und Biopolitik: Normative und intersektionale Gewalt gegen Trans*Menschen.* Dissertation. Bielefeld: transcript.

Fütty, T.J.J., Dehler, S.B., Fedorchenko, A., and Götschel, H. (forthcoming) *Gender 3.0 – Gender Diversity at School. Challenges and Requirements in Teacher Education to Include Gender Diversity, with Special Consideration of the 3rd Civil Status 'Divers',* Ongoing Research Project. Available at: https://www.uni-flensburg.de/en/zebuss/forschung/projekte/aktuelle-projekte/nwg-gender-30-in-der-schule.

GLSEN (2020). *The 2019 National School Climate Survey (Executive Summary).* New York: GLSEN.

Hartmann, J. (2017) *Perspektiven queerer Bildungsarbeit,* in: C. Behrens and A. Zittlau (Eds) *Queer-Feministische Perspektiven auf Wissen(schaft).* (Rostocker Interdisziplinäre Gender und Queer Studien, Band 1). Rostock: Universität Rostock; Universitätsbibliothek, pp.158–181. Available at: https://rosdok.uni-rostock.de/file/rosdok_document_0000010626/rosdok_derivate_0000037729/BehrensZittlau_QFPAW_2017.pdf (Accessed: 09.11.22).

Hartmann, J. and Busche, M. (2018a) Realizing the human right on gender and sexual self-determination in education: A contribution of participatory educational research on diverse gendered and sexual ways of living, in: W. Stankowski, N. Akpinar Dellal, M. Gleitze, and K. Wadon-Kasprzak (Eds) *Contemporary Educational Researches. Education and Human Rights.* Saarbrücken: LAP LAMBERT Academic Publishing, pp. 461–469.

Hartmann, J. and Busche, M (2018b) 'Mehr als Sichtbarmachung und Antidiskriminierung. Perspektiven einer Pädagogik vielfältiger geschlechtlicher und sexueller Lebensweisen', *Sozial Extra 5,* pp. 21–25.

Hilgers, A. (2004) *Richtlinien und Lehrpläne zur Sexualerziehung: Eine Analyse der Inhalte, Normen, Werte und Methoden zur Sexualaufklärung in den sechzehn Ländern der Bundesrepublik Deutschland; eine Expertise im Auftrag der BZgA.* 2003rd ed. (Forschung und Praxis der Sexualaufklärung und Familienplanung Expertise, 4). Köln: Deutsche Digitale Bibliothek.

Hilton, T. and Turnbull, M. (2010) 'Infusing some queer into teacher education'. EdCan Network. Available at: https://www.edcan.ca/articles/infusing-some-queer-into-teacher-education/.

Jones, T. (2016) 'Education policies: Potential impacts and implications in Australia and beyond'. *Journal of LGBT Youth*, 13(1–2), pp. 141–160. doi:10.1080/19361653.2015.1087926.

Kleiner, B. (2015) *Subjekt bildung heteronormativität: Rekonstruktion schulischer Differenzerfahrungen lesbischer, schwuler, bisexueller und Trans*Jugendlicher*. Dissertation. (Studien zu Differenz, Bildung und Kultur, 1). Opladen: Verlag Barbara Budrich.

Klenk, F.C. (2023) *Post-Heteronormativität und Schule: Soziale Deutungsmuster von Lehrkräften über vielfältige geschlechtliche und sexuelle Lebensweisen*. (Studien zu Differenz, Bildung und Kultur, 13). Leverkusen: Verlag Barbara Budrich.

Klocke, U., Salden, S. and Watzlawik, M. (2020) *Lsbti* Jugendliche in Berlin: Wie nehmen pädagogische Fachkräfte ihre Situation wahr und was bewegt sie zum Handeln?* Berlin: Senatsverwaltung für Bildung, Jugend und Familie. Available at: https://bit.ly/3cLe0Iu.

Krell, C. and Oldemeier, K. (2015) *Coming Out und dann …?! Ein DJI Forschungsprojekt zur Lebenssituation von lesbischen, schwulen, bisexuellen und trans* Jugendlichen und jungen Erwachsenen*. Deutsches Jugendinstitut e.V. Available at: https://www.dji.de/fileadmin/user_upload/bibs2015/DJI_Broschuere_ComingOut.pdf (Accessed 1 March 2023).

Krell, C. and Oldemeier, K. (eds.) (2017) *Coming-out - und dann …?!: Coming-out-Verläufe und Diskriminierungserfahrungen von lesbischen, schwulen, bisexuellen, trans* und queeren Jugendlichen und jungen Erwachsenen in Deutschland*. Opladen: Verlag Barbara Budrich.

Lessard, L.M., Watson, R.J. and Puhl, R.M. (2020) 'Bias-based bullying and school adjustment among sexual and gender minority adolescents: The role of Gay-Straight Alliances', *Journal of Youth and Adolescence*, 49(5), pp. 1094–1109. doi:10.1007/s10964-020-01205-1.

LISUM – Landesinstitut für Schule und Medien Berlin-Brandenburg (2021) *Orientierungs- und Handlungsrahmen für das übergreifende Thema Sexualerziehung/Bildung für sexuelle Selbstbestimmung*. Available at: https://www.fpz-berlin.de/OHR_Sexualerziehung_2021-pdf-981027.pdf (Accessed 15 March 2023).

Oldemeier, K. (2021) *Geschlechtlicher Neuanfang: Narrative Wirklichkeiten junger divers* und trans*geschlechtlicher Menschen*. Opladen: Verlag Barbara Budrich.

Sauer, A.T. and Meyer, E. (2016) *Wie ein grünes Schaf in einer weißen Herde: Lebenssituationen und Bedarfe von jungen Trans*-Menschen in Deutschland: Forschungsbericht zu „TRANS* – JA UND?!" als gemeinsames Jugendprojekt des Bundesverbands Trans* (BVT*) e.V.i.G. und des Jugendnetzwerks Lambda e.V.* Berlin: Bundesverband Trans* e.V.

Schmidt, F. and Schondelmayer, A.-C. (2015) Sexuelle und geschlechtliche Vielfalt – (k)ein pädagogisches Thema? Pädagogische Perspektiven und Erfahrungen mit LSBTI, in: A.-C. Schondelmayer, U.B. Schröder, and F. Schmidt (Eds) *Selbstbestimmung und Anerkennung sexueller und geschlechtlicher Vielfalt: Lebenswirklichkeiten, Forschungsergebnisse und Bildungsbausteine*. (Springer eBook Collection). Wiesbaden: Springer VS.

6 Teaching Caring Masculinities in ECEC and Primary Schools

Daniel Holtermann, Erika Bernacchi, Elli Scambor, Majda Hrženjak and Antonio Raimondo Di Grigoli

Introduction: Unpacking Masculinities

Care activities, both paid and unpaid, are mainly provided by women*,[1] and they are either not paid or poorly paid. Gender-based violence is still a normality. Climate change is still ongoing. All three topics are deeply connected to masculinity. Acting like a 'real man' implies being successful, competitive, in control, less empathetic, asserting oneself, and interpreting care as an area that is primarily assigned to women*. The negative consequences of masculinity can be seen on an individual and social level. One concept that tries to change this is 'Caring Masculinities' (Elliott, 2016; Scambor, Wojnicka, and Bergman, 2013). This chapter gives insights on the theoretical background and pedagogic implementation of Caring Masculinities in Early Childhood Education and Care (ECEC) and primary schools.

Current European projects like 'Boys in Care' (BiC – https://www.boys-in-ca re.eu/) and 'Early Care and the Role of Men' (ECaRoM – https://ecarom.eu/) elaborate tools for teaching Caring Masculinities, based on transnational needs analysis results in Europe. In the ECaRoM project an innovative pedagogic approach was implemented which is based on the three dimensions of Mai-Anh Boger's (2017) 'trilemma of inclusion': empowerment, normalization, and deconstruction. The approach will be explained further in subsequent sections. The chapter will specify the implementation of Caring Masculinities in ECEC and primary school. If Caring Masculinities are already fostered from the early stages of education, there is significant potential for tackling the urgent challenges of the gender care gap, gender-based violence, and climate change.

The educational system is crucial to challenge the basis of the mentioned issues: gender stereotypes. It can reproduce gender stereotypes or reduce and support overcoming them (Bernacchi et al., 2022). The earlier gender sensitive education, namely Caring Masculinities, is part of the curriculum, the less likely it is that gender stereotypes will be reproduced. A study in Germany shows that at primary-school age, boys* are already being expected to act as men*, mainly by their parents (Holtermann, 2022). Expectations of masculinity and gendered power inequalities are already being learned in the early years. To challenge these, the educational system plays an important role (Elliott, 2018). Another

DOI: 10.4324/9781003397502-6

study shows that the more boys* are in touch with caring activities and professions, the more likely care will be part of their life (Holtermann 2019).

This chapter problematises the influence of the expectations of masculinity that all those who are perceived as or feel themselves to be boys* have to deal with (Stuve and Debus, 2012). Masculinity is traditionally associated with concepts such as authority, strength, defensiveness, potentiality, and heterosexuality (see, among others, Connell, 1999). This means that those who want to be or should be considered boys* are judged by heteronormative expectations that highlight athleticism, popularity and interest in girls*, both sexual and romantic, respect from boys*/men*, non-femininity, success without excessive effort, lack of mental or physical impairment, sexual potency, whiteness, and so on. The fulfilment of these expectations is accompanied by realistic expectations of enjoying high levels of power, recognition, and security (Rieske, Scambor, and Wittenzellner, 2018, p. 14).

The social relations among men* play an important role in forming pictures about masculinities* and also help to explain boys*' (and later: men*'s) higher overall inclination to violent behaviour: 'Guys hear the voices of the men in their lives – fathers, coaches, brothers, grandfathers, uncles, priests ...' (Kimmel, 2008, p. 47). These ideas are transferred from generation to generation, with a certain self-concept as a result – the *Guy Code*, which is described as a 'collection of attitudes, values and traits' that compose an orientation pattern of 'what it means to be a man' (Kimmel, 2008, p. 45). Kimmel (2008, p. 45) goes on to say:

> ... never showing emotions or admitting to weakness. The face you must show to the world insists that everything is going just fine, that everything is under control, that there's nothing to be concerned about ... Winning is crucial, especially when the victory is over other men who have less amazing or smaller toys. Kindness is not an option, nor is compassion. Those sentiments are taboo.

The so-called *Guy Code* is related to the concept of Hegemonic Masculinity (Connell, 2005, p. 71), an orientation pattern for men* which has influenced gender studies for many years and which explains how often toxic and violent forms of masculinity become the embodiment of privilege and power in different contexts. Hegemony relates to the subordination of women* and other genders and to the subordination of other men*. Among boys*, the creation of a gendered hierarchical order is an important characteristic of differentiation and orientation patterns in the creation and inhabiting of masculinities. Importantly, in this chapter we conceptualise the ways in which education and specifically schooling in the early years is a very important site to understand how Hegemonic Masculinities emerge and how they can be disrupted by Caring Masculinities. It is well known and variously verified that processes in which masculinities are negotiated and represented are closely related to success or failure in the educational system (Budde, 2006; Rieske, 2012; Ingram, 2018; Willis, 2000).

Whilst masculinities are understood in this chapter as multiple, flowing, and dynamic, there is a need to understand the intersections between education and formations of masculinity in a society. The potential of understanding further how education plays a role in upholding a Hegemonic Masculinity lies in how it can help us, as educators, create ways in which we can disengage men* from patriarchy. To this effect, Frost, Phoenix, and Pattman (2002) have shown in studies in British private schools that the expectations of masculinity that students feel they need to conform to are closely linked to efficiency and achievement orientation. The same study was also conducted in state schools, with different results: masculinity requirements in state schools were associated with having problems with the police, no educational success, deviant careers, and being liked by girls*. Moreover, Helfferich (2009) was able to show in a German state school study that devaluing educational success as 'unmanly' is a relevant strategy for traditional Hegemonic Masculinity in educationally deprived contexts. For some groups, performing masculinity and performing the role of a student seems contradictory. Intersectional analysis by Spindler (2006) also shows that subordinated masculinities themselves often act violently to assure themselves of a powerful position, in the sense of compensating for masculinity. The impossibility of participating at the forefront of Hegemonic Masculinity forces boys* to develop alternative masculine identities that can prove problematic, violent, and toxic.

Understanding masculinities through such a sense of entitlement, aggressiveness, and competition can lead to an endless loop of self-assurance struggles. Men* can feel the need to reassert their manhood time and again, sometimes taking risks that may threaten their livelihood or those of others. This cycle becomes threatening if this fragile self-concept of masculinity is called into question (Bissuti and Wölfl, 2011). The pressure to satisfy certain images of traditional masculinity can subsequently lead to a lack of development of the social skills necessary to deal with oneself and others. For example, some boys* are unable to build sustainable friendships and relationships, to ask for help, to admit to others that they might need help, to assert themselves in life according to their wishes, and much more. In boys*' groups, arrogance and evasive behaviour is instead staged through casualness. Integrating the concept of Caring Masculinities into pedagogical work with young children can offer a space in which boys* can approach their own desires and needs and find ways to live without posing a threat to other people's lives (Bissuti and Wölfl, 2011). This chapter presents Caring Masculinities as an important educational response which challenges dominant forms of masculinity. Caring Masculinities in schooling can help generate men*s' rejection of violence and an understanding of how gender inequalities affect us all.

Theoretical Framework of Caring Masculinities as a Response to Misogyny in Early Childhood Education

Caring is based on the definition of Joan Tronto, who suggested that '... caring be viewed as a species activity that includes everything that we do to maintain, continue, and repair our "world" so that we can live in it as well as possible'

(Tronto, 1993, p.103) and on the concept of care as a human norm which applies to all genders, defined by Nancy Fraser (1996).

In this chapter, the complexities of Tronto's and Fraser's definitions will be taken into account and extended to include the dimension of masculinities. For this purpose, the concept of Caring Masculinities is used, which has been increasingly addressed in research and European policy in recent years (Hanlon 2012, Scambor, Wojnicka, and Bergman, 2013). To avoid essentialist perspectives and meet complex life demands, the concept of Caring Masculinities must be understood in its broadest sense:

> ... Men are not just fathers, and care giving should not be limited to childcare tasks (such as feeding babies, putting them to sleep, helping children with their homework). Care giving involves more: emotional support as well as affection, and it is a deeper kind of attention to the needs of children and others, such as friends, the elderly, neighbours, work colleagues, and family members.
>
> Scambor, Wojnicka, and Bergman 2013, p. 151

Karla Elliott (2016) proposed the rejection of violence and male dominance as well as the integration of values of care as central features of Caring Masculinities. The connection of Caring Masculinities to prevention of gender-based violence and protection of nature should be explicitly mentioned: The foundations of gender-based violence, especially by men*, are countered at an early stage by raising awareness of emotional needs and equal relationships as well as encouraging critical reflection on traditional male expectations. This increases competence in dealing with inner crises that can lead to violence, particularly since men* with sexist ideas about masculinity are more likely to be abusive or violent towards women* (Flood, 2019). An awareness of the social environment and the consequences of one's own actions is created. When boys* critically reflect on traditional expectations of masculinity, there is more room for alternative non-violent ways of conflict resolution. Furthermore, against the backdrop of the current ecological challenges, protection of nature has an important role to play. By increasing the sensitivity and sustainability of men*'s own responsibility, a different approach to nature can be made possible, one that is not only based on exploitation and value creation, but on recognising the importance of nature and the consequences of human overexploitation (Hultman and Pulé, 2018).

When thinking about inequalities of gender, there are various research studies focusing on how these inequalities affect the lives of children in primary school (Renold, 2004; Hine, 2023; Heikkilä, 2019; Hjelmér, 2020), and in the secondary school (Renold, 2018; Hadjar and Aeschlimann, 2015; Bragg et al., 2018). Yet, these inequalities are taking place in early childhood education, and more attention should be paid to understanding how issues of gender emerge. In 2013, a report by the National Education Union (NEU), titled, *Stereotypes Stop You Doing Stuff* highlighted how gender stereotypes continue to go unchallenged even when teacher training in the early years has become more comprehensive. Some of the key findings from the report show how, when it comes to tidying up and apologising for inappropriate behaviour, boys* are challenged less when they refuse, in comparison to girls*. The selected teachers who were willing to challenge gender stereotypes recognised that they tend to focus on challenging girls* much more than challenging boys*, so as not to hurt the boys*' feelings, since girls* are perceived to be more adept at dealing with feelings. The report found evidence of misogyny and that 'many girls* and boys* held quite stereotypical views about each other', with boys* in early primary years using words such as, 'bossy', 'annoying', and 'sexy' to describe girls*. Significantly, the results suggested that 'girls* generally have a higher opinion of boys* than the other way around' (National Education Union, 2013, p. 14).

Additionally, teachers acknowledged that they do not challenge what they viewed as the natural division of play, with digging in sandpits still very popular with boys* and dressing up popular with girls* (National Education Union, 2013). Some of these issues point to the problem with a blind adoption of 'child-centredness' in early childhood education (ECE). The presence of a strong child-centred discourse means that challenges to the traditional gender order are of secondary importance to following the child's 'natural' interests and motivations. Within this ethos there is a tension between challenging the child's construction of the gender binary or following their lead. In addition, many pre-school teachers believe that gender matters are not important to young children, while others argue that young children are too young to be introduced to complex issues such as challenging gender stereotypes (Warin and Adriany, 2017, p. 376).

Importantly, educational research on gender disparities in ECE demonstrates how there is still an androcentric understanding of gender; androcentrism is a worldview in which the man is understood as the centre, standard, and norm and women* and other non-normative genders as a deviation from this norm. This has, for many years, been the dichotomous model that has generated a male-centred positioning towards living beings, where everything has a function and where human beings, particularly males, are top of a hierarchy where we are separated from nature. The male-centred system is the cause of the construction of a society centred on the exasperated pursuit of power, unsustainable growth, competition, the overpowering of the other, and of the woman–nature/man–culture binomial. Within this androcentric and paternalistic rationality, man is understood as the 'light of reason' who exercises control and mastery over 'others', protecting all, as others are considered irrational and vulnerable.

The notion of Caring Masculinities has the potential to disrupt this mentality where masculinity is understood as a binary opposite to femininity and where masculinity is separated from nature. Man's goal has always been to fight and impose himself to have full control over events, for the betterment and progress of mankind. This model has generated a system that imposes a model of masculinity that is toxic to oneself, to others and to the world (Messerschmidt, 2018). The historical moment that initiated this process of androcentralisation of nature was positivism. Positivism is based on a philosophy that emphasised the importance of science and technology and allowed man to have the tools to control nature and the destiny of humanity. The earth has now reached the point of collapse due to the exploitation of resources by mankind for centuries. We are facing what scholars from ecological studies call 'ecocide'. Talking about an environmental crisis, an ecological crisis, does not only imply focusing on purely environmental disasters, linked to the disproportionate use of the resources offered by our planet, and consequently analysing the problem from a biophysical point of view, but it is necessary to use a systematic approach.

The notion of Caring Masculinities can be used as pedagogical practice to create school environments that resemble masculinity formations that care about nature and the environment and so contradict the essentialist pattern of a natural connection between femininity and nature. These aspects are central in Ecofeminism. In its different strands and since its inception, Ecofeminism has argued that a patriarchal and capitalist system perpetuates and legitimises the oppression of women* and the domination of nature (Bernacchi, 2020). As a consequence, they have criticised the neo-liberal economic model and a type of science that conceptualises nature as a machine rather than a living organism and asked for a radical reshaping of socioeconomic models (Merchant, 1979). Along the same lines, ecomasculinities studies, traceable in the theorisations by Hultman and Pulé (2018), focus on the dimension of care as the basis of not only interpersonal relationships but also relations to nature. This thinking ties in with Tronto's (1995) idea of the category of care, according to which:

> caring is often accompanied by a concomitant sense of self-acceptance and responsibility for the wellbeing of others, whether voluntarily/overly imposed or innate [...] care is not limited to human interactions alone, but can be applied to relational exchanges between human beings and our world.
>
> Tronto, 1995, p. 171

Rethinking humanity from a glocal (local and global) perspective implies starting from a new cultural framework that needs to deconstruct the Western capitalist model based on the techno-scientific, male-oriented model. The model of Caring Masculinities places caring at the centre as a system capable of promoting new identity models of masculinity without abandoning this dimension, but through being disloyal to the hegemonic model. In order to do this, we need to start from an analysis of the costs of normative masculinity in education that has an effect on the authentic dimension of men* from childhood.

Through Caring Masculinities, schooling can address a variety of issues and universalise caring beyond its traditional an unequal distribution by gender as it continues to persist. There are very important initial steps that still need to be taken in early childhood education in order to tackle later significant inequalities in education. Tackling gender stereotypes throughout all education, but importantly, in the early years, can help address later issues in education, such as sexual violence and sexual harassment, since 'the more rigidly gendered the beliefs of male adolescents, the more likely they are to practise sexual coercion' and commit crimes deemed to be violence against women* (Lacasse and

Mendelson, 2007, p. 425). Therefore, Caring Masculinities becomes an approach that can help tackle, more holistically, some of the unequal gender relations that are found in education, and which crucially begin in early childhood education.

Mapping Caring Masculinities in Early Childhood Education in Europe – Insights from the ECaRoM Transnational Report

In the ECaRoM project, a review of gender sensitive pedagogy in ECEC services and primary schools has been conducted by examining existing good practices aimed at overcoming gender stereotypes and pedagogical materials with a focus on masculinities, care, and early childhood education (Bernacchi et al., 2022). The selection of countries encompasses diverse European perspectives as it includes partners from Central and Western Europe (Austria, Germany, and Slovenia), Southern Europe (Italy), and from the East of Europe (Bulgaria and Lithuania).

Some countries emphasise that increased gender sensitivity can be observed in ECEC services in recent years. For instance, play areas are diverse and inclusive; children are offered a variety of toys regardless of gender; gender-sensitive colours are used; biological determinism in explanations of gender differences is the exception rather than the rule. Teachers are more equipped with mechanisms for self-reflection, including on hidden curriculum and gender bias. There is also some production of gender-sensitive pedagogical material. However, the review also shows that gender-sensitive pedagogy is not carried out in a systematic way in any country but depends largely on individual teachers' interest in and engagement with gender equality and gender stereotypes. Moreover, the vast majority of the didactical tools are the creations of activists, enthusiasts, and non-governmental organisations rather than systemic actions, while there is an obvious lack of cooperation and networking between NGOs and teachers in ECEC services and primary schools in terms of transferring good practice and practical tools for gender-sensitive pedagogy. Most of the existing gender-sensitive materials target primary schools, while there is a distinct lack of materials addressing children and teachers in ECEC. Most of the materials provide methods, guidelines, and information aimed at teachers, while gender-sensitive didactic tools such as toys, picture books, games etc. aimed directly at children are still scarce.

As a rule, existing pedagogical materials are based on a binary conception of gender and primarily address girls*. Didactical tools aimed at occupational orientation, which prevail among existing materials, generally concentrate on the promotion of STEM subjects for girls*, while materials introducing boys* to EHW professions are not so common. The majority of didactical tools in ECEC services take the form of card sets and memory games which represent different professions and activities for girls* and boys*. One prominent example in primary schools is also the ongoing project Boys' Day (https://www.boysday. at) carried out in Austria and Germany which aims at broadening the spectrum of career choices for boys* who are introduced to care professions in nursing, education, and social work. Addressing masculinities and care is therefore concentrated on the gender sectorial segregation of the labour market. On the other hand, there is very little attention paid to masculinity and care in other life areas such as ecology, social solidarity, intimate relations, and family. In relation to that, picture books and fairy tales emerge as a promising site of a more comprehensive deconstruction of gender stereotypes related to masculinities and care according to the logic of counter-stereotyping. The anti-princess model is often offered to girls*, while boys* are portrayed in situations where they can show their feelings, play with dolls, and not necessarily be heroes. Still, didactical tools for children that address stereotypes about masculinities related to costs of dominant norms on how to be a boy or a man (Messner, 1997), such as body size and shape, restrictions on emotionality and help-seeking, prescriptions of invulnerability, heteronormativity, competitiveness, and violence (Elliott, 2020), are very scarce. Also, the presence of men* educators in ECEC services and primary schools is very limited in all countries, meaning that children learn from an early age that care is fundamentally a female activity. There is therefore an express need to raise their number, although the presence of male educators does not automatically equate to a measure that counters gender stereotypes without the adoption of a gender sensitive pedagogy.

All in all, there is an obvious need for pedagogical material that deconstructs care as an inherent, natural feminine trait and presents it as a universal human activity, as well as material that would highlight the importance of working with emotions, human co-dependency, empathy, and solidarity. The image of care should be enhanced beyond professional and family care. The benefit for individuals, interpersonal relations, and for society as a whole should become evident. The economic and social importance of care work should be made visible.

How to Teach Caring Masculinities – Gender Sensitive Pedagogy

All children and adolescents are under pressure to be accepted as a 'proper'/ 'normal' boy* or 'proper;/'normal' girl* by peers, educators, and parents. Boys* who are not interested in sports or like to wear 'feminine' clothes run the risk of being devalued. Girls* who are loud or not interested in their appearance are often considered unfeminine. Children who are non-binary are usually not noticed or taken seriously. Gender-sensitive pedagogy aims to counteract these socialising constrictions and the accompanying devaluations and discrimination. Gender-sensitive pedagogy therefore means explicitly and implicitly keeping gender in mind in pedagogical work and initiating processes of change – both on the part of the pedagogical staff and on the part of children and parents. In doing so, it is important to be aware that even gender-sensitive pedagogical professionals can reproduce gender norms. Reflection is therefore a continuous process. Central goals of gender-sensitive pedagogy are:

1   the promotion of diverse interests, competencies, and behaviours without gendered constrictions;
2   the alleviation of gender expectations;
3   intervening in and reducing discrimination and violence.

On the one hand, gender-sensitive pedagogy can explicitly deal with topics such as gendered socialisation, expectations of masculinity and femininity, sexism, gender, and sexual diversity by focussing on unequal gendered structures in societies. On the other hand, pedagogical professionals can use gender as an analytical frame, based on which individual diversity and self-determination is addressed, without explicitly using gendered markers. Gender-sensitive pedagogy plays an important role in this process of change. For this, the pedagogical professionals need knowledge (about gender dynamics and socialisation processes), analytical competence with regard to pedagogical action situations and pedagogical needs, adequate methodology, and a variety of tools as well as good working conditions.

Since the focus of the chapter is on childhood education, it is important to specify what caring by children can look like. Examples of caring practices with children include: tidying up toys, preparing and cleaning up after meals, comforting friends, gardening, taking care of animals, offering/giving support to solve conflicts non-violently, considering other opinions and not only one's own, integrating children who are 'outsiders' and supporting other children in everyday practical actions (e.g. tying shoes). So how can these activities be strengthened in pedagogy?

For gender-sensitive pedagogy with a focus on Caring Masculinities, the theory of trilemmatic inclusion by Mai-Anh Boger (2017) is used, based on three dimensions: empowerment, normalisation, and deconstruction. These dimensions systematise the different theoretical paradigms on inclusion, which are always in a contradictory relationship with each other. Adapted for this context, the three named dimensions can very well illustrate the simultaneity needed to empower Caring Masculinities in gender-sensitive childhood and elementary education: the empowerment of caring, the normalisation of multiple masculinities, and the deconstruction of traditional patterns of masculinity. The contrasting nature of the dimensions may also be reflected in pedagogical implementation. Empowerment, normalisation, and deconstruction cannot usually be considered simultaneously within a method, but each can come into focus at different points over the course of a pedagogical unit.

We propose that a gender-sensitive pedagogy should be centred around principles of empowerment for care, such as learning empathy, listening, boundary awareness, and self-care (Boger, 2017). Furthermore, the admission and handling of emotions, coping with crises and failures to live up to the requirements of masculinity, recognition of one's own needs as well as thinking about others, and the consequences of one's own behaviour for others should be taken into account. A framework should be created in which boys* are relieved of the demands of masculinity and in which caring is reinforced and its positive effect clarified. In pedagogy, this can mean addressing emotions, encouraging children to help, involving them in caring activities, establishing mentorships of older children for younger ones, and similar.

Furthermore, the normalisation of diverse masculinities can foster the inclusion of currently othered themes in masculinity, such as, equal relationships, vulnerability, acceptance of (gender) diversity, dealing with the unknown, and creating spaces where boys* can share their experiences and have some relief from the demands of masculinity. In addition, the value and visibility of care should be made clear, along with recognition of the care already provided primarily by women*. Pedagogically, this could be done by providing and using material that shows masculinities in many roles, e.g., in picture books, films, or by acting those roles out.

Last but not least, deconstruction involves interrupting familiar habits and assumptions; it involves questioning dominance, risk-taking, competition, violence, discrimination, devaluation of femininity and care, and the performance and production paradigm.

Pedagogic Example: Caring Dinosaurs

During a capacity building training in the framework of the project 'ECaRoM – Promotion of Caring Masculinities in Early Education and Care' for pedagogical professionals in ECEC, we talked about boys*' attitudes and behaviours*. A female educator reported:

> When I look around, I usually find the boys in the play corner with the dinos. When we hear a loud 'Rrroar!' or 'Wuarg!', we know they are biting the dinos to death again. Everyone wants to play with the biggest dino, the Tyrannosaurus Rex, because he can bite the others the best. So, first there is a fight between the boys* about the Tyrannosaurus Rex, and when that is settled, the other dinos are bitten by the Tyrannosaurus Rex. He always wins because he's the biggest and most dangerous. I often wonder why the boys don't come up with other ideas for playing with the dinos. It can't be that it's always about the biggest and strongest dino.

When we see that the boys*' dinosaurs are always biting each other, it is helpful to offer alternatives. This way, the boys* can discover how the dinos can be used in other ways. We have collected a few ideas for this. These can be used individually or together and should be adapted according to the target group.

- *Expanding skills*: We can look with the boys* at what other strengths the dinos have. What else are the dinos good at and what are they afraid of? What is difficult for them and what is easy – besides biting? To do this, we can create a picture gallery showing the dinos performing different skills.
- *Animal assembly*: In the play corner with the dinos, other animals or play figures can be placed, e.g. horses, fairies, or a llama. If the dinos are just

biting each other, an animal assembly can be called: The animals discuss how they feel about the fact that the dinos always bite each other. Together with the animals, a solution can be sought on how to deal with the violence without creating new violence.

- *Interview*: A reporter (e.g. another animal) could do a report on the dinos biting each other. He asks the dinos involved individually how they feel when they bite each other: How does it feel to be bitten by another dino? Why do you bite the other dino? Furthermore, you can ask how the other, uninvolved animals feel about it. It is good to give the individual dinos names or to ask what the children call the dinos. The more personalised the animals are, the less likely violence is.
- *Taking away*: Agree with the children that dinos that are bitten will die. If the dinos bite each other, one dino is taken away, e.g. for the day. This way, it can be shown that biting has consequences and is not fun in that sense.
- *Cooperation game*: This could be a puzzle or a challenge in which all the dinos have to participate. One possibility would be to set up a scale that weighs as much as all the dinos. The children would have to look at how they create a balance accordingly.
- *Paramedic*: One dino is a paramedic and takes care of the injured dinos. Then the injured animal could be taken to a hospital and cared for: e.g. apply bandages or cure the wounds in bed.

The proposals are not about prohibiting dinos from biting each other. They will probably continue to do so. In general, it is important to make clear that dinos can do more than just bite, and to give them a multi-layered character. Using perspective-taking (What is it like to be bitten by someone else?), emotions can be discussed with the children. It must also be taken into account that hierarchies between the boys* are sometimes negotiated through the dino game. The game may seem like fun, but it is about who comes out on top and is the strongest. If the possibilities of the game are expanded, different types of relationships can be learned and explicit caring skills can be strengthened. The ECaRoM Project developed a manual (https://ecarom.eu/curriculum-and-manual/) where the approach to teaching Caring Masculinities is explained in more detail. An online self-learning platform was also developed as well as lots of pedagogic material like posters, a song, and methods (https://ecarom.eu/).

Conclusion: Care as Essential for All

Care is irreplaceable at both the individual and societal levels. Without care, society would not function as it is. Caring Masculinities takes this into account and focuses on creating a connection between care, boys*, and men*. With this approach the gender care gap, gender-based violence and climate change can be can be addressed simultaneously. Caring Masculinities contradicts the current pattern of growth mentality, androcentralisation, and patriarchy. For this reason, teaching Caring Masculinities is necessary as early as possible.

Pedagogues, especially in ECEC and primary school, have an important role because gender stereotypes are being laid in early years. Some important aspects for gender-sensitive pedagogy in early education are: self-reflection relating to stereotypes and Caring Masculinities, putting forward care as a social value, especially activities that invite boys* to care, and the use of gender-sensitive material and methods, which the ECaRoM project provides. But the recognition of care requires all those involved: children, educational staff, parents, and political decision-makers – and especially boys* and men*.

Note

1 Throughout this article we use the Asterisk* for example when writing about boys*, girls*, men*, women*, or trans*. We do so to point out the constructivist character of gender and gender identities and to show that more than two of these identities exist. Exceptions are fixed terms (e.g. Boys' Day).

References

Bernacchi, E. (2020) 'Ecofeminist reflections on Covid-19'. *Fuori Luogo Rivista di Sociologia del Territorio, Turismo, Tecnologia*, 8,(2), pp. 23–30.

Bernacchi, E., Di Grigoli, A.R., Hrzenjak, M. and Humer, Ž. (2022) *Caring Masculinities in Early Childhood Education and Care Services and Primary Schools in Europe ECaRoM –Early Care and the Role of Men. Transnational Report*. Berlin, Florence and Ljubljana: ECaRoM. Available at: https://ecarom.eu/wp-content/uploads/2022/03/Transnational-report-EcaRom-final.pdf (Accessed 17 March 2020)

Bissuti, R. and Wölfl, G. (2011) *Stark aber wie? Methodensammlung und Arbeitsunterlagen zur Jungenarbeit mit dem Schwerpunkt Gewaltprävention*. 2nd ed. Vienna: Bundesministerium für Unterricht, Kunst und Kultur.

Boger, M.-A. (2017) 'Theorien der Inklusion – eine Übersicht'. Zeitschrift für inklusion – online.net, 01/2017. Available at: https://www.inklusion-online.net/index.php/inklusion-online/article/view/413/317 (Accessed 17 March 2020).

Bragg, S., Renold, E., Ringrose, J. and Jackson, C. (2018) '"More than boy, girl, male, female": exploring young people's views on gender diversity within and beyond school contexts'. *Sex Education*, 18(4), pp. 420–434. doi:10.1080/14681811.2018.1439373.

Budde, J. (2006) Interaktionen im Klassenzimmer – Die Herstellung von Männlichkeit im Schulalltag, in: S. Andresen and B. Rendtorff (Eds) *Jahrbuch für Frauen- und Geschlechterforschung Geschlechtertypisierungen im Kontext von Familie und Schule*, Opladen: Barbara Budrich Verlag, pp. 113–119.

Connell, R. (1999) *Der gemachte Mann. Konstruktion und Krise von Männlichkeiten*. Wiesbanden: Springer VS.

Connell, R. (2005) Globalization, imperialism, and masculinities, in: M.S. Kimmel, J. Hearn, and R. Connell (Eds) *Handbook of Studies on Men & Masculinities*. Thousand Oaks/London/New Delhi: Sage, pp. 71–89.

Elliott, K. (2016) 'Caring Masculinities: Theorizing an emerging concept'. *Men and Masculinities*, 19(3), pp. 240–259.

Elliott, K. (2018) 'Challenging toxic masculinity in schools and society'. *On the Horizon*, 26(1), pp. 17–22. https://doi.org/10.1108/OTH-11-2017-0088.

Elliott, K. (2020) *Young Men Navigating Contemporary Masculinities*. London: Palgrave Macmillan.

Flood, M. (2019) *Engaging Men and Boys in Violence Prevention*. New York: Palgrave Macmillan.

Fraser, N. (1996) Gender equity and the welfare state: a postindustrial thought experiment, in S. Benhabib (Ed.) *Democracy and Difference. Contesting the Boundaries of the Political*. Princeton: Princeton University Press, pp. 218–242.

Frost, S., Phoenix, A. and Pattman, R. (2022) *Young Masculinities*. Basingstoke: Palgrave.

Hadjar, A. and Aeschlimann, B. (2015) 'Gender stereotypes and gendered vocational aspirations among Swiss secondary school students'. *Educational Research*, 57(1), pp. 22–42. doi:10.1080/00131881.2014.983719.

Hanlon, N. (2012) *Masculinities, Care and Equality – Identity and Nurture in Men's Lives*. London: Palgrave Macmillan.

Heikkilä, M. (2019) 'Changing the gender balance in preschools: an analysis of active work carried out by seven Swedish municipalities'. *Education Inquiry*, 10(2), pp. 134–150. doi:10.1080/20004508.2018.1492843.

Helfferich, C. (2009) 'Wer darf mit dem war warum machen? Wie macht und Ohnmacht in jugendlichen Interaktionssystemen hergestellt und erlebt werden und was das mit Bildungschancen zu tun hat'. *Bildung und Wissenschaft*, 63(10), pp. 30–33.

Hine, S. (2023) '"Sometimes there are rules about what girls can do": a rights-based exploration of primary-aged children's constructions of gender in Forest School'. *Education*, 3(13), doi:10.1080/03004279.2023.2168500.

Hjelmér, C. (2020) 'Free play, free choices? – Influence and construction of gender in preschools in different local contexts'. *Education Inquiry*, 11(2), pp. 144–158. doi:10.1080/20004508.2020.1724585.

Holtermann, D. (2019) 'Boys in care work? Vocational orientation towards EHW professions'. *Teorija in praksa*, 4(19), pp. 1069–1086. Available at: https://www.fdv.uni-lj.si/docs/default-source/tip/fantje-v-skrbstvenem-delu-poklicna-orientacija-na-podro%C4%8Dju-izobra%C5%BEevanja-zdravja-in-socialnega-varstva.pdf?sfvrsn=0 (Accessed 12 June 2023).

Holtermann, D. (Ed.) (2022) *Caring Masculinities in Elementary and Primary Education in Germany*. Berlin: Dissens – Institut für Bildung und Forschung e.V. Available at: https://www.dissens.de/fileadmin/ECaRoM/Holtermann__Daniel__2022__Caring_masculinities_in_elementary_and_primary_education_in_Germany.pdf (Accessed 12 June 2023).

Hultman, M. and Pulé, P.M. (2018) *Ecological Masculinities Theoretical Foundations and Practical Guidance*. London and New York: Routledge.

Ingram, N. (2018) *Success, Class, and Masculinities*. Basingstoke: Palgrave Macmillan.

Kimmel, M. (2008) *Guyland: The Perilous World Where Boys Become Men*. New York: Harper.

Lacasse, A. and Mendelson, M. J. (2007) 'Sexual coercion among adolescents: victims and perpetrators'. *Journal on Interpersonal Violence*, 22(4), pp. 424–437.

Merchant, C. (1979) *The Death of Nature. Women, Ecology and the Scientific Revolution*, London: Wildwood House.

Messerschmidt J.W. (2018) *Hegemonic Masculinity. Formulation, Reformulation, and Amplification*. Lanham, MD: Rowman & Littlefield.

Messner, M.A. (1997) *Politics of Masculinities: Men in Movements*. Thousand Oaks: Sage.

National Education Union (2013) *Stereotypes Stop You Doing Stuff: Challenging Gender Stereotypes through Primary Education*. Available at: https://neu.org.uk/sites/default/files/2023-04/Stereotypes%20stop%20you%20doing%20stuff.pdf.

Renold, E. (2004) '"Other" boys: negotiating non-hegemonic masculinities in the primary school'. *Gender and Education*, 16(2), pp. 247–265. doi:10.1080/09540250310001690609.

Renold, E. (2018) '"Feel what I feel": making da(r)ta with teen girls for creative activisms on how sexual violence matters'. *Journal of Gender Studies*, 27(1), pp. 37–55. doi:10.1080/09589236.2017.1296352.

Rieske, T.V., Scambor, E. and Wittenzellner, U. (2018) Aufdeckungsprozesse bei männlichen Betroffenen von sexualisierter Gewalt in Kindheit und Jugend, in: S. Andresen & R. Tippelt (Eds) *Sexuelle Gewalt in Kindheit und Jugend. Theoretische, empirische und konzeptionelle Erkenntnisse und Herausforderungen erziehungswissenschaftlicher Forschung. Sonderheft der Zeitschrift für Pädagogik.* Weinheim: Beltz Juventa, pp. 138–148.

Rieske, T.V. (2012) Feminisierung der Pädagogik? Kritik einer Problemdiagnose. *Betrifft Mädchen*, 25(1), pp. 16–20.

Scambor, E., Jauk, D., Gärtner, M. and Bernacchi, E. (2019) Caring masculinities in action: Teaching beyond and against the gender-segregated labour market, in: S. Magaraggia, G. Mauerer, and M. Schmidbaur (Eds): *Feminist Perspectives on Teaching Masculinities. Learning Beyond Stereotypes.* ATGENDER, London and New York: Routledge, pp. 59–77.

Scambor, E., Wojnicka, K. and Nadja Bergman (2013) *Study on the Role of Men in Gender Equality*, Available at: https://op.europa.eu/en/publication-detail/-/publication/f6f90d59-ac4f-442f-be9b-32c3bd36eaf1/language-en (Accessed 17 March 2020).

Spindler, S. (2006) *Corpus delicti. Männlichkeit, Rassismus und Kriminalisierung im Alltag jugendlicher Migranten*, Münster: Unrast Verlag.

Stuve, O. and Debus, K. (2012) Männlichkeitsanforderungen. Impulse kritischer Männlichkeitstheorie für eine geschlechterreflektierte Pädagogik mit Jungen, in: e.V. Dissens/ K. Debus, B. Könnecke, K. Schwerma, and O. Stuve (Eds) *Geschlechterreflektierte Arbeit mit Jungen an der Schule. Texte zu Pädagogik und Fortbildung rund um Jungen, Geschlecht und Bildung.* Berlin: Dissens, pp. 43–60.

Tronto, J. (1993) *Moral Boundaries: A Political Argument for an Ethic of Care.* New York: Routledge.

Tronto, J. (1995) Women and caring: What can feminists learn about morality from caring?, in: V. Held (Ed.). *Justice and Care: Essential Readings in Feminist Ethics.* Boulder: Westview Press, pp. 101–116.

Warin, J. and Adriany, V. (2017) 'Gender flexible pedagogy in early childhood education'. *Journal of Gender Studies*, 26(4), pp. 375–386. doi:10.1080/09589236.2015.1105738.

Willis, P. (2000) *Learning to Labour: How Working Class Kids Get Working Class Jobs.* London: Routledge.

7 Gender Knowledge and Gender Relations on Higher Education Sport and Physical Education Courses

Philippa Velija and Catherine Phipps

Introduction

In this chapter we consider how the curricula on higher education (HE) sport and physical education (PE) courses – alongside the teaching practices evident – may reinforce and influence gender stereotypes and binary notions of biological sex in PE and school sport. While our interest in this topic comes from our research on gender and sport, it is also related to our combined twenty years of studying and then teaching sport and PE courses at several universities across the UK. During this time, we have reflected on our own research and teaching, engaged in numerous discussions with colleagues around gender knowledge and sport/PE, and considered how our teaching on these topics has been received by colleagues and students. Teaching gender knowledge and challenging students to reconsider ideas around gender is more significant since the rise of high-profile discussions about lad cultures and gender at UK universities (Jackson and Sundaram, 2018). This has prompted us to consider our own experiences and the ways in which the curricula, pedagogies, and teaching spaces may reinforce students' perceptions of gender binaries and essentialist views about gender. With this in mind, we consider universities and university sport/PE courses as being spaces where gender stereotypes can be reinforced and potentially challenged. This is significant as many of the students on these courses will then go on to teach PE and sport in schools (Preece and Bullingham, 2022) and research continues to find that PE and sport reinforce traditional, binary interpretations of gender identity, with beliefs about difference in biological sex drawn upon to justify being a (largely) sex-segregated subject.

In this chapter we discuss the data from an online survey which was distributed to course leaders of any HE sport or PE course across the UK, as well as ten in-depth semi-structured interviews with women students studying on these courses. The survey asked about the gender split of students on the courses the course leaders taught, the course content, where gender knowledge was taught or embedded within a course, and colleagues' experiences of teaching gender knowledge; twenty-eight responses were gathered from course leaders across the UK. The semi-structured interviews were conducted with students studying HE sport and PE courses and asked questions about gender knowledge

DOI: 10.4324/9781003397502-7

in the curricula and their experiences of being women students in often male-dominated classrooms. We utilise figurational sociology as a conceptual framework for understanding 'knowledge' about how sport/PE and gender is selected or ignored in curricula, how gender knowledge is marginalised, and the dominance of specific types of gender knowledge which may reinforce dominant gender relations in sport and PE. Ultimately, this replicates current policies and practices which further establish gender essentialism in sport education.

Figurational Sociology, Power, and Knowledge

In this chapter, we draw on concepts from figurational sociology to understand gender relations as a form of power. We do this because figurational sociology emphasises that human societies can only be understood as long-term social processes of change, and that human life is characterised by interdependent relations which are diverse, shifting, and underpinned by changing balances of power. Elias' book, titled *On the Process of Civilisation* (2012), is an empirical example, examining the processes by which changes have taken place and are central in standards of behavioural expectations (Dunning and Hughes, 2013). Elias (1978) emphasised how human societies are characterised by different degrees of dynamic interplay between internal and external social controls, with the latter evident in relatively complex societies (Velija and Malcolm, 2018). Velija and Malcolm (2018) identify six principles which define a figurational sociological approach; these include specific approaches to macro-micro sociology, objectivity and subjectivity, structure and agency, primacy of process, nature and nurture, and the sociology of knowledge. We will briefly summarise these. Elias' approach to macro-micro sociology was to connect large-scale social processes and emotions. To capture this, Elias used the term sociogenesis, which refers to the process of development and transformation in social relations, and psychogenesis, which refers to transformations in personality or habitus that accompany social change (Goodwin and O'Connor, 2016). Elias stressed how over time people come to perceive and evaluate similar acts in different ways; for example, the exclusion of women and girls from education would be viewed differently today than in previous times. To understand this, we must consider how humans are not fixed entities, but rather behavioural standards of the time impact our emotional responses.

The concept of the figuration is used to respond to sociology's dualism of the terms structure and agency. Figurations refer to groups of interdependent people with asymmetric power relations. Elias' orientation to historical/developmental approaches rejects what he calls sociology's retreat to the present (Velija and Malcolm, 2018). Elias highlights how our view of history is contextually determined and how sociology should focus on long term processes to provide an understanding of how things came to be. Elias' (1939) concept of nature and nurture, through his discussion of 'the hinge', reflects his interest in the physical body and his analysis of its self-regulation over time. His research highlights the ways people are increasingly expected to exercise control over their bodies and how self-restraint is forged in more interdependent environments. He particularly explores how some aspects of the body that seem natural are related to wider social contexts and environments. Finally, Elias' approach to knowledge is that it is a social and historical process that cannot be separated from those creating or sharing it; knowledge cannot be understood as separate from the social conditions in which it is generated and how it comes to be presented as truth (Velija and Malcom, 2018).

Therefore, 'knowledge' exists as part of all interdependent relationships, and it is produced and shared by humans over time. How knowledge is produced and shared in ways that enable established groups to maintain their power is also of concern. Knowledge can have a purpose in which outsiders are encouraged to internalise the view that they should maintain their inferior position (Ernst, 2003). Knowledge is always socially constructed and exists as part of broader power relations. Thinking of knowledge in this way aids a broader social structural analysis of the way power relations influence the relative acceptance of different explanatory accounts (Malcolm, 2021). In *The Established and Outsiders* (1965/1994), Elias and Scotson provide an empirical example of the ways in which power and knowledge are integral in community relations and the ways in which selective knowledge is used to maintain existing patterns of power, which keep some groups in more powerful positions over others. They demonstrate the ways in which established groups may utilise selected knowledge to denigrate outsider groups who have less power to resist a characterisation of themselves based on selective empirical evidence. Within the context of education, Lybeck (2021) utilises Elias' concepts to consider a range of ways that this can aid an understanding of education. Lybeck (2021) identifies how the exclusion or selection of knowledge in the curriculum can be understood as being part of the monopolisation of knowledge by established groups and how there is still a hierarchy of what knowledge is valued, selected, and taught in HE.

Figurational sociology provides a lens for us to understand how the curricula in sport HE courses are designed. It allows us to consider how knowledge is taught, and what is excluded (or marginalised), and consider the way this influences the ongoing social reproduction that situates men and male sport as the norm. In doing so, we argue that knowledge taught on sport and PE courses is not neutral or objective; rather, the decisions about what is taught and the interdependencies between those teaching and those being taught reflects and reinforces wider gender relations in sport and PE. Knowledge is not just imparted; instead, it is taught in classrooms by people, and the connection between curricula, knowledge, and people (and how knowledge is accepted or resisted) can also be understood by considering the way power relations between lecturers and students influence this.

Gender Essentialism, Physical Education, and School Sport

In this section we discuss the gendered structure of PE and school sport, to contextualise how this links to HE curricula and content. PE is still predominantly taught in gender-segregated spaces in secondary schools, with different 'gender appropriate' elements of the curricula (Hills and Croston, 2012). The way the subject is taught promotes binary understandings of gender, mirroring the biologically sexed body. Dominant notions of masculinity and femininity can be seen in PE, with activities considered 'naturally' suited to either the male or female body (Hills and Croston, 2012). This reflects biologically deterministic ideas, where boys and girls are positioned as binary opposites, with different attitudes, behaviours, and abilities, which in turn shapes a gender-differentiated curricula (Gerdin, 2017; Hills and Croston, 2012). For instance, research has suggested some girls may have a restricted PE curriculum compared to boys and may not have access to traditionally masculine sports such as rugby, football, and basketball (Phipps and Blackall, 2021; Velija and Kumar, 2009). Therefore, the notion of gendered physical activity is prevalent in PE (Azzarito and Solmon, 2009).

Importantly, this may also have wider consequences for girls' physical activity levels. For instance, The Youth Sport Trust (YST) Girls Active Report (2017) suggests girls aged 11 to 18 are significantly less physically active than boys, with only eight percent meeting the Chief Medical Officer's recommendation of 60 minutes of physical activity a day, compared to 16 percent of boys. Furthermore, fewer girls placed importance on being physically active as this was considered less relevant to their lives, and a lack of confidence was a key factor influencing activity levels (Youth Sport Trust, 2017). Thus, the current system may not be working to encourage girls to be physically active. Part of this may include rethinking the binary gendered nature of PE with its focus on gender segregation. The knowledge drawn upon to support segregated spaces emphasises difference and is based on biological essentialism which considers the male and female body as needing different physical spaces. To expand, segregated spaces reinforce dominant discourses of gender and gender stereotyping (Gerdin, 2017). They support ideas that boys are always better than girls at sport, that female bodies are subordinate to male bodies, and that boys and girls need separate spaces for physical activity.

Although there may be a perception that PE reflects 'natural' gender differences, PE plays an important role in the social construction of gender in the first instance (Gerdin, 2017), being an environment which enforces, regulates, and trains pupils in gender-appropriate ways (Kettley-Linsell, Sandford, and Coates, 2022). In turn, this privileges some males, as it sustains a normative gendered hierarchy and perpetuates inequities (Hills and Croston, 2012). Binary spaces may also fail to provide students (and teachers) with experiences that help them challenge these gendered discourses (Aartun et al., 2022). In addition to this, gender-segregated PE also operates under the assumption that everyone can be classified as either a boy or a girl (Kettley-Linsell, Sandford, and Coates, 2022). As fluidity of gender cannot usually be seen in PE, school sport, and in wider educational spaces, this creates problems around the inclusion of trans and gender-diverse pupils who need to be accommodated within the binary system (Phipps and Blackall, 2021). For these reasons PE can be understood as a cis-normative and cisgendered space, where trans and gender-diverse students and educators may need to abide by normative gender to fit in (Kettley-Linsell, Sandford, and Coates, 2022).

The reproduction of gender norms has also been found in teacher training; pre-service teachers hold gendered ideas about what male and female bodies can and cannot do, both in terms of their own teaching and their pupils' abilities (McVeigh and Waring, 2021). Those training as PE teachers may therefore hold gender essentialist assumptions (Preece and Bullingham, 2022) and may be complicit in the reproduction of gendered practices, which they have experienced and then reproduce in their own spaces (Gerdin, 2017). PE teachers are often taught on HE sport and PE courses, and therefore what is taught and how it is taught can either reinforce or challenge dominant and essentialist assumptions about gender. While there are no set curricula for HE sport and PE courses, the Quality Assurance Agency (QAA) publish benchmark statements at undergraduate level which outline what students could be expected to know at the end of their studies. In the UK, these often map to Events, Hospitality, Leisure, Sport, and Tourism benchmarks for validation (QAA, 2019). Due to the diversity of knowledge and content across these courses, these benchmarks cover varied topics, which range from knowledge about human responses to sport and exercise; sport performance; health and disease management; and the historical, social, political, economic, and cultural diffusion of sport. However, issues of equity and gender do not directly feature as areas that should or must be discussed as part of the curricula.

While to date, there has been little UK-based research exploring the ways gender knowledge is taught to students, or how that knowledge is received, the work of Serra et al. (2018) interrogates HE sport courses in Spain. They consider how gender knowledge is marginalised, suggesting that curricula continue to reproduce rather than disrupt gender relations. In research looking at HE sport business management courses, Pielichaty (2020) argues that one reason this sector remains male dominated may relate to students not engaging critically in discussions about gender inequity in sport. She argues that, without this, the curricula and classroom do not position students to challenge existing inequities. More recently, Allison and Love (2023) discuss the ways students respond to a gender integrated sport module to challenge gender essentialism. However, through playing a gender integrated sport, they found students continued to understand gender difference as 'natural'. Using the concept of feminist failures, they reflect on the ways in which students' perceptions around gender ideology were not challenged and argue there is a need for students to counteract dominant constructions of how sport should be organised.

The wider context for gender and university-based research has also focused more broadly on lad culture, an area of increasing academic interest and one that impacts on gendered experiences in HE. Lad culture has been defined in a National Union of Students (NUS) report (2012) as 'a group or "pack" mentality residing in activities such as sport and heavy alcohol consumption, and "banter" which was often sexist, misogynistic, and homophobic'. This has become a blanket term to encompass a spectrum of different overt and subtle behaviours, including drunkenness, public rowdiness, sexual harassment, and the objectification and degradation of women. Although intersecting with other inequities (such as homophobia and racism), sexism is argued to underpin lad culture, and the term may encompass behaviours that are commonplace, normalised, and that largely go unchallenged (Jackson and Sundaram, 2018). These examples highlight the ongoing issues around gender and HE, particularly around sport and PE courses.

Without a challenge to dominant ideas about PE and school sport, and alternative ways to deliver and challenge gender binary practices, these practices may continue. In the next section, we discuss data from both the survey and interviews to explore power, curricula, and where gender knowledge is taught on HE sport and PE courses.

PE and HE Sport Courses: Where is the Gender Knowledge?

In a previous paper (Velija and Phipps, 2023), we explored how knowledge around gender in the curricula is compartmentalised and taught in discreet modules. Similarly, in this study, it was revealed the depth of space for exploring gender relations was often limited, with a survey respondent explaining: 'Explicitly, I would say at least once an academic year within the sociology of sport modules. They also perhaps cover gender within the PE and coaching specific modules' (Respondent 4, BA Physical Education and Sport Coaching). Sport and PE courses cover wide-ranging content across several disciplines, and the variety of content means the amount of gender knowledge taught can be difficult to quantify. However, one respondent said 'Infrequently. One week is dedicated to "Gender and Sexuality" in a level 6 ethics module, other mentions are sporadic and not embedded in the module content' (Respondent 18, BSc Sport Coaching). Only one of the courses had a specific module on gender and sport. The others commented that the content was covered across the degree:

RESPONDENT 7, BA SPORTS STUDIES: It's hard to say, but I feel that gender is addressed quite often. Although it doesn't necessarily appear in module descriptors, it still may feature in lectures as a means of addressing module content. It is often the case that when gender is addressed, it is primarily addressed via discussions of women's sport.

However, the above response was unique, and most survey respondents outlined the spaces in the curricula where discussions of gender and women's sport took place as limited to modules based on sociology or sociocultural elements of sport and PE. For instance, respondent 9 (BA Sport and Physical Education) stated: 'Mainly in the socio-cultural strand which has three core modules (one at each level) and two optional modules at level 6. How frequently? It probably gets discussed every 2–3 weeks in some form or another'. The compartmentalisation of gender knowledge was found in the work of Serra et al. (2018) who argued this was problematic as it meant students were not challenged to think about gender in some areas of the syllabus. Another respondent outlined:

RESPONDENT 21, BA SPORT COACHING AND PHYSICAL EDUCATION: There is frequent discussion of women's sport and women athletes throughout the sociological strand of the degree ... with dedicated sessions to gender inequality, discrimination, stereotyping, feminist theory, and other related content. Students are allowed to choose their own topics for assignments in this strand, and a significant proportion (approx. 25–30%) of submissions have explicit reference to women's sport and women athletes within their chosen assignment topics. We also support a number of students (approx. 5–10% of cohort) who complete research projects/dissertations on gender-related topics in relation to women's sport.

Here, the coverage of women sport and gender was quite extensive through the sociological aspects of the degree, but less discussed or considered in other aspects of the curricula. There was a notable difference for those studying sport science who were less likely to have experienced discussions around gender relations in sport, with one student outlining:

FREYA, STUDENT, BSC APPLIED SPORT SCIENCE DEGREE: In applied sport science, we have not discussed anything to do with gender and sport so far in the curriculum. I think this could be incorporated in topics such as anatomy and physiology as men and women are biologically different. But also, in places like psychology where we could discuss approaches to a man training a woman and vice versa rather than not mentioning it at all.

In sport science, the absence of any discussion around gender knowledge means students have no opportunity to question their own or others' views around gender/sex. Instead, the topic is invisible, meaning knowledge about men and male bodies is considered universal. This is problematic because of the need to challenge people's perceptions of gender on courses, to broaden students' knowledge to better understand women in sport, and to see how women are also central to constructing knowledge in this field. Thus, knowledge is limited and centres mainly on male bodies. For example, Respondent 25, who teaches on a BSc Sport Therapy course, noted how students are 'knowledgeable re injury prevalence but not so much with soft skills e.g., comms and also little delivery at present on rehab specific to women's pelvic floor'. The way in which some knowledge and skills are valued over others, and whose bodies are centralised on courses, reflects dominant ideas and practices in sport.

What and whose knowledge is taught should sensitise us to what knowledge is valued. This is significant as Elias emphasises how knowledge is utilised by different groups and explores the way in which power relations influence the acceptance of different accounts (Malcolm, 2021). While active resistance to teaching gender seemed rare, Respondent 6 noted they had experienced this from other HE colleagues teaching physical aspects of sport science:

RESPONDENT 6, BA SPORT DEVELOPMENT AND COACHING: Frequently. Some colleagues from physical science backgrounds often make judgements about what content is covered and whether there is a necessity to cover it at all. There is often some frustration about the use of terms female and women as a result of the social content taught. Physical science colleagues often insist students use the term female in their work and discussions, and when students challenge this or confuse terms, we often experience some frustration from physical sciences staff who place an element of blame on what we are teaching students. Similarly, I have physical science colleagues (physiology mainly) who are very resistant to us teaching anything about trans athletes and intersex athletes, presumably because this does not fit with their binary male/female ideals. I have had many conversations with one staff member who seemingly refuses to accept trans or intersex people exist, but instead there are simply either males or females.

This demonstrates some of the challenges of teaching on sport and PE courses and the variety of knowledge that students experience across multiple disciplines. This makes these courses somewhat different to others, as students cover multiple disciplines with a wide range of perspectives, with different values placed on them. The challenge of teaching gender knowledge amongst disciplines where seemingly 'common-sense' and binary views prevail is clear, and the respondent noted that this was often presented as banter:

RESPONDENT 6, BA SPORT DEVELOPMENT AND COACHING: This is often framed as 'banter' of course and never directly about individuals, but mainly around the merit in teaching and discussing gender in the curriculum. The biggest form of resistance came about 2–3 years ago when BASES accreditation of the BSc Hons Sport and Exercise Science programme was proceeded with the notion that students on this programme could no longer complete a sociological/sociology-based final year project, and as such, any students on this programme that have an interest in women in sport must limit their research to psychological, biomechanical or physiological analyses. However, modules where gender/women in sport is taught remain options for these students. This is sometimes problematic for those students who wish to conduct a social project on women in sport.

We suggest that students may align their initial views about gender (often emphasised in PE and school sport) to disciplinary knowledge that supports separatism and binarism, thus reinforcing their own gender ideologies. Across HE sport and PE curricula, times in which gender knowledge is discussed and challenged may be minimal, thus highlighting the ways in which certain knowledge is selected, resisted, and challenged by other colleagues and students.

Knowledge is therefore taught and shared by people in particular social contexts. Elias' framework is useful to connect the way knowledge is socially received, challenged, or resisted. In their figurations, individuals can choose to accept knowledge that challenges their existing perceptions of sport and PE, or they can reject these in favour of finding other 'knowledge' that may support their existing beliefs. This may be particularly problematic with sport science content whereby biological essentialism is presented as factual, thus positioning 'difference' as a natural phenomenon that cannot be challenged or changed.

The way in which knowledge is framed in sport science research more broadly is challenged by Cowley et al. (2021), who outlines how research on sport and exercise science continues to generalise data from men to women participants. In other words, research is often about male bodies and athletes, further questioning women's place in these spaces. Furthermore, there is still little critical discussion of how men are presented as the universal norm in sport and exercise research, and the ways in which women remain underrepresented. This has wider implications as research centred around men is then taught on sport courses, with little critical discussion of this bias.

These exchanges reflect the ways in which women as a category are marginalised. Annie (Student, BA Sport Coaching and Sport Development Degree) reflected on her course and the dominance of discussions about men and men's sport, stating, 'that's where you start to think like, does anyone actually listen to or watch women's sport?'. The marginalisation of women's sport which is normalised through formal curricula and informal discussions reinforces the notion that men's sport is what is being studied, thus sidelining and 'othering' women athletes and women's sport, as well as limiting knowledge of gender beyond the 'common sense'. As respondent 14 (BSc Sport and Exercise Science) notes, students 'appear far more "liberal" (in the broadest sense of the word) than ever before. However, the subject appears not to be thought about much beyond the obvious'. Some students may recognise that the depth of discussions about gender knowledge are limited. There is a risk that students develop some knowledge; however, as Allison and Love (2023) note, this remains superficial, and may lack a critical analysis of the ways in which gender inequities are embedded in sport and PE.

Students may also discuss or experience gender knowledge alongside learning about other forms of power. For example, in modules on the sociology of sport, students may study gendered power relations alongside disability, race/ethnicity, and social class, amongst other social issues. Colleagues reflected on students' reactions to understanding gender compared to other areas of power and inequity in sport, with the suggestion that these responses were different:

RESPONDENT 5, BA SPORT COACHING AND DEVELOPMENT: Generally, I find students 'get' racism and disability discrimination, but they find it harder to get their heads around gendered discrimination … issues such as sexual abuse/exploitation they understand but sexual or gender harassment less so – it's often trivialised as banter. This has certainly got worse since the programme has come to be dominated by men in recent years.

Knowledge that challenges dominant views around gender may therefore be received differently, with some inequities considered more 'real' than others, highlighting power relations in this context. Students may select (and recognise) some knowledge and aspects of inequity, leading to acceptance of these accounts. However, for the established group who may not recognise particular inequities, certain knowledge may be easier to reject in favour of other accounts. While a small sample, gender knowledge is not a significant part of the curricula for students across the 28 institutions who were included in the study. In the next section of this chapter, we discuss the ways in which gender knowledge is experienced by staff and students.

The Experience of Teaching and Being Taught Gender Knowledge

What is taught is only one part of understanding gender relations on courses, and our research was also interested in colleagues' experiences of teaching gender knowledge. While there was a varied response, a common comment was that the 'value' of learning about gender and sport/PE was questioned by students. For instance, Respondent 1 (BA Sport Management) argued, 'some don't see the value in understanding gender studies'. As students come on courses to study sport or PE, the introduction of topics such as power and gender knowledge can come as a surprise, and students can respond in ways that appear resistant. As Respondent 18 (BA Sport Studies) notes, 'this has taken two forms. One, women's sports are not as relevant. Two, analyses of sport are gender blind'. Experiences of teaching gender knowledge were also mixed and a range of responses from students were demonstrated:

RESPONDENT 3, BSC SPORTS COACHING: You do get quite a few male students who can portray biological reductionist perspectives of gender differences. Sometimes female students can portray similar views. On a few rare occasions you can get a male student expressing a sexist viewpoint. Likewise, the topic of transgender inclusion can sometimes evoke contrasting views, but these are mainly around fairness within sport etc.

While some lecturers noted there was an initial reluctance, this often changed over time. For example, Respondent 20 (BA Sport Management) stated, 'when I first started teaching, there were a couple of "why do we need to do this?" comments, but once you preface the main arguments, they (males) recognise the significance'. However, resistance to the ideas of gender equity in sport are not always straightforward and can be experienced in complex ways. How this is handled may differ depending on the experience and the self-identified gender of the colleague teaching, with Respondent 14 (BSc Sport and Exercise Sciences) suggesting 'I've often contextualised my position as a male lecturer when discussing feminist theory particularly, but despite the very occasional off-colour remark from male students, I've never experienced any resistance to gender issues from any students'. The gender and identity of the person sharing the knowledge may have some significance here and is perhaps not widely considered. Women sharing gender knowledge may be considered biased, something both authors have experienced when delivering sessions. The relationship between the person sharing the knowledge and the content being taught therefore seems significant. Some colleagues experienced resistance to certain ideas and a negative connotation attached to being a feminist. For instance, Respondent 5 (BA Sport Coaching and Development) suggested, 'sometimes I feel male students challenge me directly on the evidence because they believe me to be some sort of radical feminist. I don't think they would be so hostile if it were a male colleague leading the class'. This was something that male colleagues teaching about gender were often aware of, and when asked whether their gender 'mattered' when teaching, one respondent stated:

RESPONDENT 4, BA PHYSICAL EDUCATION AND SPORT COACHING: Sadly yes, I am a male and I cover the history of male and female sport. I also highlight gender inequalities within modern day sport. Generally speaking, this is well received, but I do suspect if a female lecturer were to deliver similar content it might be questioned more or rejected. Unfortunately, this would imply that amongst a student cohort there can be elements where being a male is perceived as being a more authoritative figure on matters of sport. This is clearly not true, but a gendered ideological perception.

The classroom environment highlights that knowledge is not passively accepted, but rather, when gender knowledge is taught, it can be challenged, resisted, or simply ignored. In the cases where lecturers taught gender-based modules as optional, this was well received; this might be because students are choosing these modules and already see the value of learning. It also highlights that the challenge of engaging with gender knowledge can be avoided by those who do not want to accept more inclusive gender practices in sport and PE.

Some students may consider that knowledge about gender is factual, scientific, and/or can be 'evidenced' by their own experiences, suggesting that not all students are ready to discuss or challenge dominant gender relations in sport/PE. For instance:

RESPONDENT 6, BSC SPORT DEVELOPMENT AND COACHING: I do get the sense sometimes that they are worried about saying the wrong thing even though much work goes into creating a safe space for discussion and debate. That said, I've found male students are increasingly challenging the view that women are less privileged, particularly if we are discussing Connell's theoretical ideas on hegemonic masculinity for example, and certainly more so in the past year or so. A number of (male) students still seem to be relatively passive, but there does seem to be an emerging pocket of resistance to the notion that women are under/misrepresented and when this occurs, I sometimes feel there is an element of hostility/defensiveness from them.

This was summarised by Respondent 22 (BSc Sport Coaching) who, when asked about how knowledgeable students are around gender and women's sport, stated, 'knowledgeable at a superficial level, but depth of thought is usually lacking'. It is this depth of thought that may be required to be able to develop more gender inclusive PE and school sport spaces for those that go into teaching. Yet, from our experience, and the data we have collected, there seemed to be little opportunity for transformative ways of thinking about gender, the body, and sport/PE.

For students, the spaces where discussions take place in classrooms are often male dominated. For instance, in 2020/2021, the number of women students studying sport and exercise sciences related degrees was 16,175 compared to 33,440 men (HESA, 2022). This gender split means women students could be made to feel:

FREYA, STUDENT, BSC APPLIED SPORT SCIENCE DEGREE: A bit like an odd one out. But I could sort of, I talked to my dad about it before I actually joined. Because when I came to look around and I had some talks and I was like, not many girls looking to do the course and stuff. And maybe it's because sports are seen as quite a male thing. Maybe. I know my cousin wanted to join a similar course in Manchester and one of the main reasons that she didn't was because there was a lot of boys on that. And it was, they were like really football based type things.

For Jessica, although she felt different to start with, 'now that I've got to know everyone, it's absolutely fine. Like I'm used to, obviously being in sport. I'm used to being the minority' (Jessica, Student, BA Physical Education Degree). While the gender split may differ amongst various sport and PE courses, the students had all experienced examples in which gender and women in sport were problematically framed in classroom discussions. As women students were the minority, their experiences of discussing gender and sport/PE may be minimised or ridiculed. For Emily, this had happened in a classroom session on sport and social issues when one of the students criticised women's sport. She stated, 'I think the biggest quote was like from one of the lads, and he quoted that women's basketball was BTEC basketball' (Emily, Student, BA Sport Coaching and Sport Development Degree). The ability to challenge these comments was not always possible because of the dynamics in the classroom. This meant that women on the course and their views and experiences about gender were not always valued or listened to.

For Indigo, the issue of engaging and working with men was problematic in how it might be seen by others. As she explained in an interview:

INDIGO, STUDENT, BSC APPLIED SPORT SCIENCE DEGREE: it's just I feel like they've got their little group and I don't want to go in and be like the girl that wants … I don't want to be seen as the girl who's going to come and sit with you guys.

The physical dominance of men on the course was then further discussed by Emily later in her interview:

EMILY, STUDENT, BA SPORT COACHING AND SPORT DEVELOPMENT DEGREE: Whenever we like get to like do football or something more masculine, because obviously, when we turn up, most of the girls turn up in their leggings, and like shorts and a T shirt, they turn up in their trackies, and then they take off their hoody, then they will stay in their pack until we call them over to do activities or something like that. They don't like mix with anyone else.

While there is growing literature on the complexity of identities and laddish behaviour (Jackson and Sundaram, 2018; Jeffries, 2020; Phipps, 2017), the definition drawn upon to describe lad culture – outlined earlier in this chapter – was evident in many women students' experiences, especially in relation to the idea of 'packs'. For example, Sati stated:

SATI, STUDENT, BSC APPLIED SPORT SCIENCE DEGREE: it's just mostly guys like. I don't think it really relates to women as much, but it can do. Just like when they're in a group, they're all trying to be like alpha males, just like show off and impress their friends and be intimidating to others.

Thus, laddish behaviours and cultures, in often male-dominated spaces, can also impact classroom dynamics. In other words, the way in which knowledge is shared and how people accept certain accounts are both related to other interdependent social relations.

Conclusion

In this chapter, we have outlined the ways in which curricula are related to power and gender knowledge in HE sport and PE courses. In addition, we have explored what is taught (the curricula) which is decided upon by people in webs of interdependencies, alongside how it is received. As Elias encouraged sociologists to consider how knowledge is produced through human relations and to see knowledge as a social and historical process, it is important to consider the ways in which it can be utilised to maintain power relations between groups. Indeed, HE sport and PE courses cover a diverse range of content, from the physical science subjects to social science topics on sport. However, there are disciplinary hierarchies about what knowledge is needed to become a teacher, and this knowledge can draw on fixed perspectives on the body. On HE sport and PE courses, the place and significance of gender knowledge is at best marginalised and, in other examples, invisible. There is a complex interplay between curricula, lecturers, students, and power when it comes to gender knowledge on these courses. What is taught, how it is taught, and how this knowledge is challenged and resisted within curricula needs a broader analysis and discussion. Without this, the sector wide challenge of addressing gender inequity in sport, and alternative, transformative, and more inclusive ways to deliver PE and school sport seems unlikely.

References

Aartun, I., Walseth, K., Standal, Ø.F., and Kirk, D. (2022) 'Pedagogies of embodiment in physical education – a literature review'. *Sport, Education and Society*, 27(1), pp. 1–13. doi:10.1080/13573322.2020.1821182.

Allison, R., and Love, A. (2023) '"It should have been named women's rights … I was displeased": Teaching about gender ideology in the sport sociology classroom'. *Journal of Hospitality, Leisure, Sport & Tourism Education*, 32, Article 100413. doi:10.1016/j.jhlste.2022.100413.

Azzarito, L. and Solmon, M. (2009) 'An investigation of students' embodied discourses in physical education: A gender project'. *Journal of Teaching in Physical Education*, 28(2), pp. 173–191. doi:10.1123/jtpe.28.2.173.

Cowley E.S., Olenick, A.A., McNulty, K.L., and Ross, E.Z. (2021) '"Invisible sportswomen": The sex data gap in sport and exercise science research'. *Women in Sport and Physical Activity Journal*, 29(2), pp. 146–151. doi:10.1123/wspaj.2021-0028.

Dunning, E. and Hughes, J. (2013) *Norbert Elias and Modern Sociology: Knowledge, Interdependence, Power, Process*. London: Bloomsbury.

Elias, N. and Scotson J.L. (1965/1994) *The Established and the Outsiders*. London/Thousand Oaks/New Delhi:Sage.

Elias, N. (1978) *What Is Sociology?*. New York: Columbia University Press.

Elias, N. (2012) *On the Process of Civilization*. Chicago: Chicago University Press.

Ernst, S. (2003) 'From blame gossip to praise gossip? Gender, leadership and organizational change'. *European Journal of Women's Studies*, 10(3), pp. 277–299. doi:10.1177/1350506803010003003.

Gerdin, G. (2017) '"It's not like you are less of a man just because you don't play rugby"—Boys' problematisation of gender during secondary school physical education lessons in New Zealand.' *Sport, Education and Society*, 22(8), pp. 890–904. doi:10.1080/13573322.2015.1112781.

Goodwin, J. and O'Connor, H. (2016) *Norbert Elias's Lost Research: Revisiting the Youth Worker Project*. London: Routledge.

HESA (2022) *What Do HE Students Study?: Personal Characteristics*. Cheltenham: HESA. Available at: https://www.hesa.ac.uk/data-and-analysis/students/what-study/characteristics (Accessed 10 March 2023).

Hills, L.A. and Croston, A. (2012) '"It should be better all together": Exploring strategies for 'undoing' gender in coeducational physical education'. *Sport, Education and Society*, 17(5), pp. 591–605. doi:10.1080/13573322.2011.553215.

Jackson, C., and Sundaram, V. (2018) '"I have a sense that it's probably quite bad … but because I don't see it, I don't know": Staff perspectives on "lad culture" in higher education'. *Gender and Education*, 33(4), pp. 435–450. doi:10.1080/09540253.2018.1501006.

Jeffries, M. (2020) '"Is it okay to go out on the pull without it being nasty?": Lads' performance of lad culture'. *Gender and Education*, 32(7), pp. 908–925. doi:10.1080/09540253.2019.1594706.

Kettley-Linsell, H., Sandford, R., and Coates, J. (2022) Negotiating gender performances in physical education and school sport: Gender diversity and inclusive practices, in: G. Witcomb and E. Peel (Eds) *Gender Diversity and Sport: Interdisciplinary Perspectives on Increasing Inclusivity*. London: Routledge, pp. 97–116.

Lybeck, E. (2021). *Norbert Elias and the Sociology of Education*. London: Bloomsbury Publishing.

Malcolm, D. (2021) 'Post-truth society? An Eliasian sociological analysis of knowledge in the 21st century'. *Sociology*, 55(6), pp. 1063–1079. doi:10.1177/0038038521994039.

McVeigh, J. and Waring, M. (2021) 'Developing the pedagogical practice of physical education pre-service teachers in gymnastics: Exploring gendered embodiment'. *Physical Education and Sport Pedagogy*. doi:10.1080/17408989.2021.1990246.

NUS (2012) *That's What She Said: Women Students' Experiences of 'Lad Culture' in Higher Education*. London: NUS. Available at: https://www.nusconnect.org.uk/resources/that-s-what-she-said-2013 (Accessed 14 March 2023).

Phipps, A. (2017) '(Re)theorising laddish masculinities in higher education'. *Gender and Education*, 29(7), pp. 815–830. doi:10.1080/09540253.2016.1171298.

Phipps, C. and Blackall, C.J. (2021) '"I wasn't allowed to join the boys": The ideology of cultural cisgenderism in a UK school'. *Pedagogy, Culture & Society*, 31(5), pp. 1097–1114. doi:10.1080/14681366.2021.2000012.

Pielichaty, H. (2020) 'Embedding gender justice in higher education: An example from sports business management'. *IMPact e-journal*, 4(1). Available at: https://hdl.handle.net/10779/lincoln.24387043.v3.

Preece, S., and Bullingham, R. (2022) 'Gender stereotypes: The impact upon perceived roles and practice of in-service teachers in physical education'. *Sport, Education and Society*, 27(3), pp. 259–271. doi:10.1080/13573322.2020.1848813.

QAA (2019) *Subject Benchmark Statement: Events, Hospitality, Leisure, Sport And Tourism*. Gloucester: QAA. Available at: https://www.qaa.ac.uk/the-quality-code/subject-benchmark-statements?indexCatalogue=documents-and-pages-for-sbs&searchQuery=sport&wordsMode=AllWords (Accessed 14 March 2023).

Serra, P., Soler, S., Prat, M., Vizcarra, M.T., Garay, B., and Flintoff, A. (2018) 'The (in)visibility of gender knowledge in the physical activity and sport science degree in Spain'. *Sport, Education and Society*, 23(4), pp. 324–338. doi:10.1080/13573322.2016.1199016.

Velija, P. and Kumar, G. (2009) 'GCSE physical education and the embodiment of gender'. *Sport, Education and Society*, 14(4), pp. 383–399. doi:10.1080/13573320903217083.

Velija, P., and Malcolm, D. (2018) *Figurational Research in Sport, Leisure and Health*. London: Routledge.

Velija, P. and Phipps, C. (2023) '"That's where you start to think like, does anyone actually listen to or watch women's sport?": Gender regimes and students' experiences on higher education sport courses'. *International Review for the Sociology of Sport*, 58(2), pp. 233–252. doi:10.1177/10126902221097824.

Youth Sport Trust (2017) *YST Girls Active Report: Stats Pack for Media*. Loughborough: Youth Sports Trust. Available at: https://www.youthsporttrust.org/news-insight/research/girls-active-2017 (Accessed 14 March 2023).

8 The Neoliberal University and Masculine Values

What About Care?

Isaura Castelao-Huerta

Introduction

When talking about care, reference is often made to reproductive work, as well as feeding, clothing, raising, and looking after, especially for infants, the sick, and the elderly (Comas-d'Argemir, 2019). Care work in provision of services where there is an emotional component involved has also been accounted for (Arango Gaviria, 2011, 2015). Following Molinier and Legarreta, the world 'is built day after day, night after night, through work that knows no limits in time' (2016, p. 5): care work. But care is more than a job, as it involves a whole series of thoughts, actions, and practices that take place when there is an awareness of our vulnerability, the vulnerability of others, and the vulnerability of the world we inhabit in its physical, social, political, economic, symbolic, and psychological dimensions (Izquierdo, 2004). Thus, the ethics of care implies 'granting care a central place in the orientation of our lives' (Izquierdo, 2004, p. 133), in order to achieve the sustainability of our world. According to Gravett, Taylor, and Fairchild, posthuman feminism considers 'care as an in situ practice of mutuality, reciprocity and relationality. As a mode of embodied labour largely seen as women's work, care can be thought of – and enacted – as a move against the conditions of the accelerated academy' (2021, p. 5).

Having said this, the aim of this chapter is to highlight the importance and complexity of care within academia. This will be done by presenting a content analysis of the main discussions and problematisations around care in higher education, keeping in mind that the neoliberal model has permeated all social institutions for more than four decades. This model rewards a stereotypically masculine way of acting that promotes toughness, boasting, individualism, and competition, and downplays the emotional side of life (Acker and Wagner, 2019). Thus, neoliberal academia and the State have manoeuvred to create a marginalised care work sector within the academic staff, devaluing the teaching labour that is necessary to sustain life within higher education (Cardozo, 2017). At the same time, it is necessary to keep in mind that care is mediated by the regulations of gender order: firstly, who has to care, who demands care, who has the right to receive care, whose care is recognised and whose is not; secondly, the practical materialities, the endowment of resources for care, and the costs of lack of care; and thirdly, the emotional and bodily affections of care

DOI: 10.4324/9781003397502-8

which circulate around specific bodies that need care or go beyond them (Breeze and Taylor, 2020a, p. 64).

Fisher and Tronto define care as all activities that we do 'to maintain, continue, and repair our "world" so that we can live in it as well as possible. That world includes our bodies, our selves, and our environment, all of which we seek to interweave in a complex, life-sustaining web' (1990, p. 40). In this way, care is a central component for the physical, psychological, and emotional well-being of the entire population (Esteban, 2017; Faur and Pereyra, 2018). Similarly, Zembylas, Bozalek, and Shefer (2014) state that care is a labour-heavy activity that involves thought, emotion, action, and practical work, thus threading together a complex web, with care practices being changeable through time and space (Askins and Blazek, 2017). Zembylas, Bozalek, and Shefer (2014, p. 204) also highlight the five stages of an ethics of care based on Tronto's contributions: 1. *caring about*: noticing people's needs for care; 2. *caring for*: a person or a group of people must take responsibility for ensuring that care needs are met; 3. *caregiving*: someone takes on the practical work of caring for people; 4. *care-receiving*: responding to the care that is provided by the caregiver; and 5. *caring with*: this is the reiteration of the care process, where habits and patterns of care emerge over time, and where trust and solidarity are developed. On the last point, Askins and Blazek (2017) agree on underlining that care can precipitate a varied reciprocal commitment, providing a basis for mitigating individual challenges and anxieties, thus creating conditions in which the probability of beneficial collective outcomes will improve.

Cardozo (2017) emphasises that university teaching can be considered interactive care work because it facilitates the development of human capacities and because academic staff can develop emotional bonds with their students. Motta and Bennett (2018) highlight three key areas of care within academia: 1. care as recognition – acknowledging the holistic individual; 2. care as a dialogic relationality – where teaching and learning are based on relational pedagogy; and 3. care as embodied affective praxis – where academic staff and students have the same opportunities in the process of teaching and learning as knowers and knowledge generators. Some care practices within academia include listening to students, showing empathy, supporting them, actively encouraging their learning, praising them in appropriate and meaningful ways, having high expectations regarding work and behaviour, and showing active concern about their personal lives (Walker and Gleaves, 2016). As I present below, care in the academic world also includes practices of mentoring and care among colleagues.

Despite their importance, care practices are devalued and naturalised, and they are either unpaid or underpaid (Breeze and Taylor, 2020a), which is a fundamental characteristic of capitalism (Cardozo, 2017). In academia, this undervaluing has been exalted by neoliberal policies, some of which will be explored later. In the next section, I present how academia has undergone a process of neoliberalisation, which resulted in discarding care practices since they are not measurable or quantifiable products. Subsequently, I expose the main care practices within academia, despite their devaluation. I close this chapter with some reflections on the complexities of care in academia.

The Neoliberalised World of Academia and the Precarity of Care

Following Harvey (2007), neoliberalism is a theory of both political and economic practices. Importantly, this chapter also explores how neoliberalism affects the personal domains of our lives too. With reference to care, neoliberalism proposes that human welfare is best achieved by allowing the free development of individual entrepreneurial abilities and liberties within an institutional framework, established and preserved by the State, and characterised by strong private property rights, free markets, and freedom of commerce (Harvey, 2007). Beyond its economic aspect, Brown (2015) underlines that neoliberalism is a rationality that propagates the values and measurements of the market in all aspects of life, including the university. Thus, the university's integration into the neoliberal economy occurs under a process of academic capitalism (Slaughter and Rhoades, 2004), where education is seen as an 'investment' whose objective is to train individuals to succeed in the market (Hernández Gutiérrez, 2016, p. 426). This *casino capitalism*, as shown by Giroux (2016, p. 8), produces a policy where disposability, exclusion, racism, and class gaps have been normalised, which has led to a denigration of 'the other' and an attack on the critical function of higher education (De la Fuente, 2002). Broadly speaking for academia, in addition to prevailing budget cuts (Castelao-Huerta, 2021), the implementation of performance evaluation systems has led to pressures for productivity, efficiency, and the commodification of knowledge: 'as academics we are evaluated on our metrics' (O'Dwyer, Pinto, and McDonough, 2018, p. 243). In that sense, the demands on academic staff to publish have been exacerbated through a work ethic of publish or perish (Feigenbaum, 2007; Rodríguez, Leongómez, and Suárez, 2020). This leads to high demands on research and its subsequent publication (Gómez-Morales, 2017).

Research on the impact of neoliberalism on academia shows how detrimental it has been for faculty members. With the scarcity of resources and performance evaluations (Castelao-Huerta, 2021), faculty conditions are characterised by a heavier workload, short-term contracts, job insecurity, excessive competitiveness, an imbalance of power between managers and faculty, and weakened union power (Ivancheva, Lynch, and Keating, 2019). In many countries, the faculty works more than the time established in their contracts (Gill and Donaghue, 2016; Kenny, 2017; Lipton, 2020). Additionally, Feldman and Sandoval (2018) point out that free time becomes an extension of the working day because it provides an opportunity to catch up with work or, at least, to avoid drowning in the pressures of academic performance. Thus, as personal effort has been capitalised as if it were an economic resource and a factor of production, work and free time are no longer two opposing activities; instead, free time is invested in continuing to work (Gill, 2009; Lemke, 2016). This system produces anxiety and poor health in academics around the world, who are seen as individualised human capital and suffer from stress, feelings of instability, and precarious working conditions (Berg, Huijbens, and Larsen, 2016).

The growing expectations of entrepreneurship, striving in the pursuit of prestige, and the modes of research production (O'Meara, 2007), encourage prioritising individual careers over collective collaboration (Acker and Wagner, 2019). Thus, 'the ideal academic' is conceptualised as a responsibilised and competitive individual with no care obligations (Acker, 1990; Henderson and Moreau, 2020). As Fairweather (1993, 2005) demonstrates, highly paid faculty members spend more time working with graduate students, conducting research, and publishing, while spending less time on teaching activities. This means that spending more time on teaching, particularly classroom instruction, results in lower pay.

The gender order and neoliberal rationality drive most women to perform large amounts of unpaid service: formally, through workload assignments, and informally, through work processes and interpersonal interactions (Gannon et al., 2016; Simien and Wallace, 2022). This service work includes activities related to faculty governance, faculty recruitment, evaluation and promotion, student admissions and scholarships, programme supervision, development and marketing, internal awards, among others (Guarino and Borden, 2017). Women perceive injustice in service loads, and perceived injustice is associated with reduced job satisfaction, increased scholarly isolation, interpersonal workplace conflict, and job stress (Castelao-Huerta, 2022, 2023b; Pedersen and Minnotte, 2018).

At the same time, Chomsky (2013) stresses that a technique of neoliberal indoctrination is to sever the contact of students with the academics. In this regard, Ginn (2014) suggests that there are everyday pressures to treat students as clients, which is why the ability to improve 'employability' is prioritised over the ability to improve collegiality. Thus, pedagogy is used as a tool for demonstrating effectiveness (Naskali and Keskitalo-Foley, 2017), turning academic–student relationships into instrumental interactions where care is considered useless because it is neither quantifiable nor profitable. This results in a 'culture of hierarchy, competition and individualism' that promotes rivalry and generates a hostile atmosphere, which prevails through 'the eradication of cultures of solidarity, care and collectivity' (Motta and Bennett, 2018, p. 634).

The new individualised academic capitalism, as Lynch (2010) underlines, generates an organisational culture marked by a growing egocentrism, highly conditioned loyalties, and a continuously decreasing sense of responsibility towards others, especially towards the students, thus subordinating and trivialising practices that lack market value. This constructs the universities as 'dispassionate and objective emotion-free zones' (Lipton, 2020, p. 205). In this sense, Angervall (2018) and Brown (2015) point out that under the neoliberal paradigm, the hours and care invested in preparing classes and the accompanying work conducted with students seem to lack relevance because what is privileged is hyperproductivity. To this effect, Cardozo (2017, p. 409) underlines that the precarisation of academic work reconstructs teaching as 'poorly paid housework in the marketplace', in which some care for the (university) children and maintain the household (the department or the campus), while others dedicate themselves to more 'productive' work that circulates as highly esteemed in the market.

Thus, the process of the neoliberalisation of academia is strongly linked to the practices developed by academics with their students, as productivist demands that weigh on the faculty have a direct influence on academic demands that are imposed on students due to the imperative of meeting the market's demands for human capital. Lynch (2010) points out that the carelessness in education has its origins in the classical Cartesian view of education, which considers academic work separate from emotional thinking and sentiments, thus focusing on educating an autonomous and rational person, whose relationality is not considered fundamental to their being. Subsequently, she stresses, the separation between facts and values is strengthened, which is endemic to contemporary positivist norms that govern not just the scientific and scientific-social thinking, but also the organisation of higher education. Thus, in neoliberalised academia, the Cartesian view has been sharpened, which leads to marginalising the expression of emotions such as fear and anxiety and to the privileging of dominance, instrumentality, invulnerability, and emotional self-control. Institutionally, care provided to students is not conceived as a key performance indicator as it cannot be measured (Gannon et al., 2016), which is why the materiality of affective work is not recognised and the fact that it is hard and productive work is overlooked (Lolich and Lynch, 2017).

Moreover, Lu (2018) and Jackson (2019) note that in the university context the association of care, emotion, and femininity persists. This results in expectations for the women academics to be kind, understanding, and not too bossy. However, this does not necessarily imply that these women academics are considered 'good teachers'. At the same time, men academics are associated with a detached intellectualism, which reflects the persistence of the gender order within academia. Similarly, it is culturally expected from women that they comply with daily activities of sustaining the university, such as care practices that confront the neoliberal brutality and instrumentalism, which are rarely compensated by progress and promotion policies (Fannin and Perrier, 2017). With these gendered assumptions within the university, neoliberal logics are reinforced as generally it is the men who possess the social and economic permissibility to devote themselves to high workloads imposed by the system, while most women are compelled to take on what the neoliberal system deems worthless: care. Thus, the ideal academic has been constructed as 'care-free' (Henderson and Moreau, 2020, p 72). However, neoliberal academia is sustained by the invisibilised and unrecognised care efforts of, for the most part, women academics. Women academics discover that care is 'interpreted as a lack of productivity that counts against them in promotions processes' (Breeze and Taylor, 2020a, p. 53). As such, 'universities simultaneously repudiate and depend on feminized forms of labor' (Gannon et al., 2016, p. 195), which works against the career aspirations of women academics.

Previous studies show that women academics in higher education are mainly responsible for a wide range of care practices. On the one hand, there is the care provided to partners, children, pets, friends, and relatives (Henderson and Moreau, 2020; Jackson, 2019; Lendák-Kabók, 2022; Magadley, 2021; Moreau and Robertson, 2019; Ortiz Ruiz, 2018; Villar-Aguilés and Obiol-Francés, 2022). On the other hand, there are care practices that occur within academia and allow for sustaining the university life. These include good teaching, kindness, pastoral care, and mentoring activities. In the following, I briefly discuss these care practices.

Gendering Traditional Care Practices and Mentoring in Academia

What can be considered traditional care practices include good teaching, kindness, and pastoral care. Good teaching encompasses course management, teaching with critical feedback and review, flexible pedagogy, thesis supervision, democratic administration, and academic manoeuvrability (Cardozo, 2017; Gaudet et al., 2021; Horncastle, 2011). Good teaching involves special attention to student learning, careful communication, reflection on one's own teaching practices, and timely attention. Good teachers have been characterised as having two important qualities that are far removed from neoliberal productivity metrics focused on academic production. First, they are people who care about their discipline, thereby fostering intellectual transformation and provoking a sense of interest, engagement, challenge, connection, appreciation, and even love. Second, they care about teaching and about students, which strongly influences the students' commitment to the course, their enthusiasm for learning, and their aspirations for the future (Dowie-Chin and Schroeder, 2020). Thus, care is present in the attention, openness, capacity to respond to students' learning needs, and investment in students' well-being. The feeling that the academics care about students, both inside and outside the classroom, facilitates dialogic learning in class (Anderson et al., 2019).

Another traditional care practice is kindness, understood as a feeling of active concern for the life projects of the other, a relational pedagogy (Clegg and Rowland, 2010; Gravett, Taylor, and Fairchild, 2021; Motta and Bennett, 2018; Walker and Gleaves, 2016). In general terms, kindness has been thought to be out of place when talking about higher education since it can suggest a sentimental and unrigorous approach, which focuses on the relational at the expense of ideas. However, kindness can subvert neoliberal assumptions that value utility and cost over other human values. Kindness implies acknowledging differential power, positionality, and student needs, as well as valuing the projects of others instead of just our own (Clegg and Rowland, 2010). This kindness can be shown as solidarity in the face of students' material needs, which leads women academics to search for resources in order to develop research and also to offer some financial support (Castelao-Huerta, 2023a).

When it comes to pastoral care, this involves providing personal attention and emotional support (Dowie-Chin and Schroeder, 2020; Lu, 2018). Some of these practices involve intervening to prevent harm and being open to listening. With these practices, women academics ensure that their students do not drop out of university and can conclude their studies (Castelao-Huerta, 2023a). The COVID-19 pandemic caused distress to be aggravated, which led to an increase in emotional burden due to the need for guidance and support as students required comforting messages (Newcomb, 2021). Nevertheless, Lu (2018) points out an important gender distinction: women academics in her study, who care about emotions and try to build relationships with their students, are not necessarily considered good academics. Generally speaking, good teaching, kindness, and pastoral care are acts of resistance in the face of a performance-oriented academic culture: a way of surviving and finding sense within the existing system (Gaudet et al., 2021).

Moreover, the figure of mentor is fundamental to academic career advancement since mentors are often sources of guidance as well as figures of support and listening (Oberhauser and Caretta, 2019). Mentoring is a care practice with postgraduate students and early-career academics, and it is intensive work that is not necessarily recognised by the institutions, yet many academics consider this activity to be an integral part of their responsibility (Acker and Wagner, 2019). Mentoring occurs when there is a display of attention that evolves over time, especially with a PhD supervisor since supervisors frequently meet with their students on a one-to-one basis, which makes the relationship more personal (Gaudet et al., 2021).

Sometimes mentoring involves collaboration. This encompasses both the way in which early-career academics receive guidance and support from 'veteran' colleagues, and the way in which research grants and teaching staff can rely on the occasional work of doctoral students and postdocs. It should also be noted that within mentoring there are means of 'vital support', such as teaching students to have an international orientation, as well as to be brave and passionate and show solidarity (Lund and Tienari, 2019). Similarly, mentoring involves activities that are necessary to continue in an academic career, such as writing recommendation letters, practices that are neither compensated nor valued because they are not quantified under productivity metrics, in addition to not being limited to the confines of a normal labour shift (Cardozo, 2017, p. 418). Nevertheless, mentoring work is fundamental because it can reclaim and disrupt professional categories and competitive individualism (Breeze and Taylor, 2020b; Moreau, 2017).

Final Reflections: The Complexity of Care

Hierro (1985) points out that the feminist ethics that seeks to lay the foundations for a cultural revolution of everyday life advocates the universalisation of positive 'feminine' values: softness, gentleness, tenderness, sensitivity, patience, receptivity, and a sense of community. At the same time, feminist ethics devalues masculine pseudo-values: competition, performance, will to power, and we might also add, individualism and exacerbated productivity. Thus, a feminist ethics of care that incorporates concern for the well-being of others in academia favours good teaching and produces knowledges that care for the natural world and humanity (Lynch et al., 2020). Following this idea, care practices, mostly provided by women academics, serve to improve the lives of people around them, and to build a much kinder and more united university. Care in teaching is more than just a social relationship with ethical dimensions; it can also be the foundation of an ethically and politically alternative standpoint, with implications for how we see traditional notions of educational development and its policies of higher education (Zembylas, 2017). Care practices are linked to higher attendance, more time dedicated to studies, improved academic performance, and lower dropout rates (Foster, 2008). Moreover, these practices can build 'safe academic spaces' for women, which can be difficult to find considering how universities are masculinised in many ways (Mackinlay and Lipton, 2020). People who care in academia know about the academic, economic, and personal concerns of their students because they know them, listen to them, and get involved in their problems: their relationship goes beyond the classroom, and this allows them to build an academic community (Askins and Blazek, 2017; Zembylas, Bozalek, and Shefer, 2014). Care as a core value counterbalances competitive individuality (Lund and Tienari, 2019). This occurs despite the hostile relations among the academic staff resulting from the implementation of neoliberal policies in higher education (Castelao-Huerta, 2022, 2023b).

While neoliberal policies can lead to individualism, there are still ways in which collective compromise and strategic connectivity improve academia, advocating for careful practices that have a deep impact 'on students' affective and embodied well-being, openness to learning, interest in subject material, capacity to understand and aspirations for the future' (Anderson et al., 2019, p. 16). Situating care at the centre of life is part of a feminist politics of resistance and responsibility within the academia, making it crucial to incorporate affective and ethical practices into knowledge production (Askins and Blazek, 2017). As Horncastle underlines, 'it would be a shame to lose scholars for the reason that they are not cared for' (2011, p. 52). This implies that care activities 'should serve as a reference point instead of the activity carried out in the market' (Carrasco Bengoa, 2013, p. 48).

Nevertheless, it is necessary to emphasise that care is a complex practice, full of tensions and ambivalences (Motta and Bennett, 2018; Zembylas, 2017). The pressure to obtain resources and publish, the increase in administrative tasks, combined with the demands for individual accountability, come into tension with the efforts of many women academics to be kind, affectionate, collaborative, and show solidarity which generates the stress of wanting to do everything right (Acker and Wagner, 2019). Thus, there is an irreconcilable tension between being someone who cares about relationships and having developed a type of competitive individualised agency (Gannon et al., 2016). In certain cases, the efforts of academics to obtain resources allow for the continuation of their students' academic formation, but this also implies entering into the neoliberal game because they dedicate their time to preparing research proposals in order to compete for the scarce funds available. This constitutes an extra workload, which does not yield positive results in most cases, and by undertaking it, they are taking responsibility for the lack of public funding for scientific research (Castelao-Huerta, 2023a). Moreover, it is impossible for academics to fund all of their students, which can result in envy and competition in some cases.

Another important issue is that employment arrangements between academics and students, both formal and informal, can place students in a precarious situation when their rights do not include access to social security and health services. Also, the relationship between early-career and established academics can be oversimplified, either as an exclusively exploitative relationship (researchers and assistants whose careers are just starting are not recognised or compensated for their work, from which more established colleagues benefit) or a relationship of entitlement (established academics are obliged and expected to perform an unrecognised and unrewarded mentoring and support work for their colleagues whose careers are just starting) (Breeze and Taylor, 2020b). In other words, while care practices can be a temporary relief, they do not resolve the problem of university defunding at its roots, and they can help the State to continue to fail to take responsibility for its financial obligations. That is, academics spend 'considerable time and energy' on searching for funding opportunities, which results in 'short-term contracts that ironically left workers so insecure that they would perpetually be searching for another contract' (Acker and Wagner, 2019, p. 14). Care is complex because while 'these forms may be co-opted and put to work in the form of so-called collaboration, networking and plugging the institutional-care gaps in teaching and collegiality', at the same they can 'provide alternatives to neoliberal, gendered and racialized forms of governance' (Gannon et al., 2016, p. 195).

Another complexity of care can be seen in that 'it can lead to acts that by intention are kind but may involve misjudgement and harm to the others' (Clegg and Rowland, 2010, p. 723). In this sense, interventions and questionings about personal situations can be interpreted as harassment if students feel a persistent intrusion into their lives. Thus, these care practices 'can cause tension between sensitive students and even caring teachers when they do not position each other in the same discourse' (Lu, 2018, p. 16). These can also provoke feelings of unfair treatment in other students if they do not receive the same level of attention.

Regarding mentoring, which helps mentees survive and progress through insecurity and uncertainty, it can be partially interpreted as an individualisation of the work of supporting those who are starting their careers and are casual workers, which should be a collective responsibility. Thus, the feminist project of supporting early-career entrants can, ambivalently, do the work of remedying the lack of institutional care and responsibility (Breeze and Taylor, 2020b).

Finally, it should be reiterated that care practices are gendered, as most women are expected to carry them out, thus running the risk of being idealised and poorly recognised (Breeze and Taylor, 2020a). Mentoring as resistance can reinscribe normative assumptions about women as innate nurturers, feeding into the disproportionate responsibility for doing care work, with women 'sacrificing [their own] career gains' to support others and being punished for not providing all the care all the time (Breeze and Taylor, 2020b).

Lynch et al. (2020) highlight the care ceiling, which devalues and silences care-related practices. Furthermore, since care is not a 'submittable' product in the culture of productivity, it cannot be measured or counted. Yet care is productive because it produces a positive response from students (Clegg and Rowland, 2010), and when it occurs between colleagues, it also makes it possible for academics to continue producing within a careless neoliberal system. However, care implies an extra workload, which adds to the teaching, research, and administrative workloads, and thus increases academics' fatigue. As Cardozo underlines, it is essential to 'reclaim the value of caring while recognizing that working "for love" renders us vulnerable to exploitation' (2017, p. 415). In light of this, we can ask ourselves, is it possible to develop an adequate metric for valuing care within academia?

In neoliberalised academia, to prioritise care is to resist (O'Dwyer, Pinto, and McDonough, 2018). Therefore, we must promote a structural change that recognises and values care as an essential practice of higher education: an ethics of care that subverts the hierarchy, defies power, and promotes egalitarianism and collaboration (Acker and Wagner, 2019), thus rejecting the elitism, sexism, and racism that continuously reproduce prevailing academic values (Cardozo, 2017). An ethics of care in academia combines the responsive and empathetic elements of human relationships with the specific responsibility of the institution's mission for student learning and success; it recognises the impact of well-being on student engagement, their willingness to learn, capacity to learn, and success in obtaining the results of learning. This ethics of care, which should be part of the institutional philosophy (Burford, 2013), could foreground reciprocity and interdependence in a communal project of care (Askins and Blazek, 2017).

References

Acker, J. (1990) 'Hierarchies, jobs, bodies: A theory of gendered organizations'. *Gender & Society*, 4(2), pp. 139–158. doi:10.1177/089124390004002002.

Acker, S. and Wagner, A. (2019) 'Feminist scholars working around the neoliberal university'. *Gender and Education*, 31(1), pp. 62–81. doi:10.1080/09540253.2017.1296117.

Anderson, V., Rabello, R., Wass, R., Golding, C., Rangi, A., Eteuati, E., Bristowe, Z., and Waller, A. (2019) 'Good teaching as care in higher education'. *Higher Education*, 79(1), pp. 1–19. doi:10.1007/s10734-019-00392-6.

Angervall, P. (2018) 'The academic career: a study of subjectivity, gender and movement among women university lecturers'. *Gender and Education*, 30(1), pp. 105–118. doi:10.1080/09540253.2016.1184234.

Arango Gaviria, L.G. (2011) El trabajo de cuidado: ¿servidumbre, profesión o ingeniería emocional?, in: L.G. Arango Gaviria and P. Molinier (Eds) *El trabajo y la ética del cuidado*. Bogotá: La Carreta Editores, Universidad Nacional de Colombia, pp. 91–109.

Arango Gaviria, L. G. (2015) 'Cuidado, trabajo emocional y mercado: los servicios estéticos y corporales'. *Revista Latinoamericana de Estudios de Familia*, 7, pp. 99–120.

Askins, K. and Blazek, M. (2017) 'Feeling our way: Academia, emotions and a politics of care'. *Social & Cultural Geography*, 18(8), pp. 1086–1105. doi:10.1080/14649365.2016.1240224.

Berg, L.D., Huijbens, E.H., and Larsen, H.G. (2016) 'Producing anxiety in the neoliberal university'. *The Canadian Geographer*, 60(2), pp. 168–180.

Breeze, M., and Taylor, Y. (2020a) Care(er)ing: Queer feminist career cares, in: *Feminist Repetitions in Higher Education: Interrupting Career Categories*. Cham: Palgrave Macmillan, pp. 49–68. doi:10.1007/978-3-030-53661-9_3.

Breeze, M., and Taylor, Y. (2020b) 'Feminist collaborations in higher education: Stretched across career stages'. *Gender and Education*, 32(3), pp. 412–428. doi:10.1080/09540253.2018.1471197.

Brown, W. (2015) *Undoing the Demos: Neoliberalism's Stealth Revolution*. New York: Zone Books.

Burford, M. (2013) *Meanings of 'Care' in Higher Education: Undergraduates' Experiences*. University of Technology, Doctoral dissertation.

Cardozo, K.M. (2017) 'Academic Labor: Who Cares?', *Critical Sociology*, 43(3), pp. 405–428. doi:10.1177/0896920516641733.

Carrasco Bengoa, C. (2013) 'El cuidado como eje vertebrador de una nueva economía'. *Cuadernos de Relaciones Laborales*, 31(2), pp. 39–56.

Castelao-Huerta, I. (2021) 'Investigaciones sobre los efectos de la neoliberalización de la educación superior pública en América Latina'. *Educação e Pesquisa*, 47, pp. 1–24. doi:10.1590/s1678-4634202147232882.

Castelao-Huerta, I. (2022) 'The discreet habits of subtle violence: An approach to the experiences of women full professors in neoliberal times'. *Gender and Education*, 34 (2), pp. 216–230. doi:10.1080/09540253.2020.1815660.

Castelao-Huerta, I. (2023a) 'Beyond the neoliberalized academy: Caring and careful practices of women full professors'. *Gender and Education*, 35(3), pp. 234–249. doi:10.1080/09540253.2022.2147148.

Castelao-Huerta, I. (2023b) 'Recelos y envidias: violencias sutiles de género en la academia neoliberalizada'. *Debate Feminista*, 65, pp. 273–302. doi:10.22201/cieg.2594066xe.2023.65.2339.

Chomsky, N. (2013) 'El trabajo académico, el asalto neoliberal a las universidades y cómo debería ser la educación superior'. *Bajo El Volcán*, 13(21), pp. 121–134.

Clegg, S. and Rowland, S. (2010) 'Kindness in pedagogical practice and academic life'. *British Journal of Sociology of Education*, 31(6), pp. 719–735. doi:10.1080/01425692.2010.515102.

Comas-d'Argemir, D. (2019) 'Cuidados y derechos. El avance hacia la democratización de los cuidados'. *Cuadernos de Antropología Social*, 49, pp. 13–29. doi:10.34096/cas.i49.6190.

De la Fuente, J.R. (2002) 'Academic freedom and social responsibility'. *Higher Education Policy*, 15, pp. 337–339.

Dowie-Chin, T. and Schroeder, S. (2020) 'Critical, calculated, neoliberal: Differing conceptions of care in higher education'. *Teaching in Higher Education*, pp. 1–15. doi:10.1080/13562517.2020.1749588.

Esteban, M.L. (2017) 'Los cuidados, un concepto central en la teoría feminista: aportaciones, riesgos y diálogos con la antropología'. *QUADERNS-E*, 22(2), pp. 33–48.

Fairweather, J.S. (1993) 'Academic values and faculty rewards'. *The Review of Higher Education*, 17(1), pp. 43–68. doi:10.1353/rhe.1993.0002.

Fairweather, J.S. (2005) 'Beyond the rhetoric: Trends in the relative value of teaching and research in faculty salaries'. *The Journal of Higher Education*, 76(4), pp. 401–422. doi:10.1080/00221546.2005.11772290.

Fannin, M., and Perrier, M. (2019) '"Birth work" accompaniment and PhD supervision: An alternative feminist pedagogy for the neoliberal university'. *Gender and Education*, 31(1), pp. 136–152. doi:10.1080/09540253.2017.1358806.

Faur, E. and Pereyra, F. (2018) Gramáticas del cuidado, in: J.I. Piovani and A. Salvia (Eds) *La argentina en el siglo XXI: Cómo somos, vivimos y convivimos en una sociedad desigual. Encuesta Nacional sobre la Estructura Social*. Buenos Aires: Siglo XXI Editores, pp. 495–532.

Feigenbaum, A. (2007) 'The teachable moment: Feminist pedagogy and the neoliberal classroom'. *Review of Education, Pedagogy, and Cultural Studies*, 29(4), pp. 337–349. doi:10.1080/10714410701291145.

Feldman, Z. and Sandoval, M. (2018) 'Metric power and the academic self: Neoliberalism, knowledge and resistance in the British university'. *TripleC*, 16(1), pp. 214–233.

Fisher, B. and Tronto, J. (1990) Towards a feminist theory of caring, in: E.K. Abel and M.K. Nelson (Eds) *Circles of Care: Work and Identity in Women's Lives*. New York: State University of New York Press, pp. 35–62.

Foster, K.C. (2008) 'The transformative potential of teacher care as described by students in a higher education access initiative'. *Education and Urban Society*, 41(1), pp. 104–126. doi:10.1177/0013124508321591.

Gannon, S., Kligyte, G., McLean, J., Perrier, M., Swan, E., Vanni, I., and van Rijswijk, H. (2016) 'Uneven relationalities, collective biography, and sisterly affect in neoliberal universities'. *Feminist Formations*, 27(3), pp. 189–216. doi:10.1353/ff.2016.0007.

Gaudet, S., Marchand, I., Bujaki, M., and Bourgeault, I.L. (2021) 'Women and gender equity in academia through the conceptual lens of care'. *Journal of Gender Studies*, 31(1) pp. 74–86. doi:10.1080/09589236.2021.1944848.

Gill, R. (2009) Breaking the silence: The hidden injuries of neo-liberal academia, in: R. Ryan-Flood and R. Gill (Eds) *Secrecy and Silence in the Research Process: Feminist Reflections*. London: Routledge, pp. 228–244. doi:10.1515/fs-2016-0105.

Gill, R., and Donaghue, N. (2016) 'Resilience, apps and reluctant individualism: Technologies of self in the neoliberal academy'. *Women's Studies International Forum*, 54, pp. 91–99. doi:10.1016/j.wsif.2015.06.016.

Ginn, F. (2014) '"Being like a researcher": Supervising Masters dissertations in a neoliberalizing university'. *Journal of Geography in Higher Education*, 38(1), pp. 106–118.

Giroux, H.A. (2016) 'Disposable futures: Neoliberalism's assault on higher education'. *Límite*, 11(35), pp. 7–17.

Gómez-Morales, Y.J. (2017) 'El baile de los que sobran: cambio cultural y evaluación académica'. *Revista Colombiana de Antropología*, 53(2), pp. 15–25.

Gravett, K., Taylor, C. A., and Fairchild, N. (2021) 'Pedagogies of mattering: Re-conceptualising relational pedagogies in higher education'. *Teaching in Higher Education*, 29(2) pp.388–403. https://doi.org/10.1080/13562517.2021.1989580.

Guarino, C.M., and Borden, V.M.H. (2017) 'Faculty Service Loads and Gender: Are Women Taking Care of the Academic Family?'. *Research in Higher Education*, 58(6), pp. 672–694. doi:10.1007/s11162-017-9454-2.

Harvey, D. (2007) *Breve historia del neoliberalismo*. Madrid: Akal.

Henderson, E.F. and Moreau, M.-P. (2020) 'Carefree conferences? Academics with caring responsibilities performing mobile academic subjectivities'. *Gender and Education*, 32(1), pp. 70–85. doi:10.1080/09540253.2019.1685654.

Hernández Gutiérrez, R. (2016) 'Trayectoria del neoliberalismo: de la academia al espacio público'. *Revista Mexicana de Ciencias Políticas y Sociales*, 61(227), pp. 423–428.

Hierro, G. (1985) *Ética y feminismo*. México: Coordinación de Humanidades, UNAM.

Horncastle, J. (2011) 'Taking care in academia: The critical thinker, ethics and cuts'. *Graduate Journal of Social Science*, 8(2), pp. 41–57.

Ivancheva, M., Lynch, K., and Keating, K. (2019) 'Precarity, gender and care in the neoliberal academy'. *Gender, Work & Organization*, 26(4), pp. 448–462. doi:10.1111/gwao.12350.

Izquierdo, M.J. (2004) 'El cuidado de los individuos y de los grupos: ¿quién cuida a quién? Organización social y género'. *Debate Feminista*, 30, pp. 129–153. doi:10.22201/cieg.2594066xe.2004.30.1052.

Jackson, L. (2019) 'The smiling philosopher: Emotional labor, gender, and harassment in conference spaces'. *Educational Philosophy and Theory*, 51(7), pp. 693–701. doi:10.1080/00131857.2017.1343112.

Kenny, J. (2017) 'Academic work and performativity'. *Higher Education*, 74(5), pp. 897–913. doi:10.1007/s10734-016-0084-y.

Lemke, T. (2016) *Foucault, Governmentality, and Critique*. Oxon, New York: Routledge.

Lendák-Kabók, K. (2022) 'Women's work–Life balance strategies in academia'. *Journal of Family Studies*, 28(3), pp. 1139–1157. doi:10.1080/13229400.2020.1802324.

Lipton, B. (2020) *Academic Women in Neoliberal Times*. Cham: Springer International Publishing. doi:10.1007/978-3-030-45062-5.

Lolich, L. and Lynch, K. (2017) 'Aligning the market and affective self: Care and student resistance to entrepreneurial subjectivities'. *Gender and Education*, 29(1), pp. 115–131. doi:10.1080/09540253.2016.1197379.

Lu, H. (2018) 'Caring teacher and sensitive student: is it a gender issue in the university context?'. *Gender and Education*, 30(1), pp. 74–91. doi:10.1080/09540253.2016.1171296.

Lund, R. and Tienari, J. (2019) 'Passion, care, and eros in the gendered neoliberal university'. *Organization*, 26(1), pp. 98–121. doi:10.1177/1350508418805283.

Lynch, K. (2010) 'Carelessness: A hidden doxa of higher education'. *Arts and Humanities in Higher Education*, 9(1), pp. 54–67. doi:10.1177/1474022209350104.

Lynch, K., Ivancheva, M., O'Flynn, M., Keating, K., and O'Connor, M. (2020) 'The care ceiling in higher education'. *Irish Educational Studies*, 39(2), pp. 157–174. doi:10.1080/03323315.2020.1734044.

Mackinlay, E. and Lipton, B. (2020) 'The doorway effect: Stories of feminist activism and survival in the neoliberal university'. *Emotion, Space and Society*, 35, Article 100675. doi:10.1016/j.emospa.2020.100675.

Magadley, W. (2021) 'Moonlighting in academia: A study of gender differences in work-family conflict among academics'. *Community, Work & Family*, 24(3), pp. 237–256. doi:10.1080/13668803.2019.1678458.

Molinier, P. and Legarreta, M. (2016) 'Subjetividad y materialidad del cuidado: ética, trabajo y proyecto político'. *Papeles Del CEIC*, 1, pp. 1–14. doi:10.1387/pceic.16084.

Moreau, M.-P. (2017) 'Inhabiting and researching the spaces of higher education'. *International Studies in Widening Participation*, 4(2), pp. 6–10.

Moreau, M.-P., and Robertson, M. (2019) '"You scratch my back and I'll scratch yours"? Support to academics who are carers in higher education'. *Social Sciences*, 8(6), pp. 1–12. doi:10.3390/socsci8060164.

Motta, S.C. and Bennett, A. (2018) 'Pedagogies of care, care-full epistemological practice and 'other' caring subjectivities in enabling education'. *Teaching in Higher Education*, 235), pp. 631–646. doi:10.1080/13562517.2018.1465911.

Naskali, P. and Keskitalo-Foley, S. (2019) 'Mainstream university pedagogy in feminist perspective'. *Gender and Education*, 31(1), pp. 100–116. doi:10.1080/09540253.2017.1315057.

Newcomb, M. (2021) 'The emotional labour of academia in the time of a pandemic: A feminist reflection'. *Qualitative Social Work*, 20(1–2), pp. 639–644. doi:10.1177/1473325020981089.

O'Dwyer, S., Pinto, S., and McDonough, S. (2018) 'Self-care for academics: A poetic invitation to reflect and resist'. *Reflective Practice*, 19(2), pp. 243–249. doi:10.1080/14623943.2018.1437407.

O'Meara, K. (2007) Striving for what? Exploring the pursuit of prestige, in: *Higher Education: Handbook of Theory and Research*. Dordrecht: Springer, pp. 121–179. doi:10.1007/978-1-4020-5666-6_3.

Oberhauser, A.M., and Caretta, M.A. (2019) 'Mentoring early career women geographers in the neoliberal academy: Dialogue, reflexivity, and ethics of care'. *Geografiska Annaler: Series B, Human Geography*, 101(1), pp. 56–67. doi:10.1080/04353684.2018.1556566.

Ortiz Ruiz, F. (2018) 'Los cuidados en el laboratorio y la vida familiar en la academia'. *PAAKAT: Revista de Tecnología y Sociedad*, 8(14), pp. 1–15. doi:10.32870/Pk.a8n14.315.

Pedersen, D.E. and Minnotte, K.L. (2018) 'University service work in STEM departments: gender, perceived injustice, and consequences for faculty'. *Sociological Focus*, 51(3), pp. 217–237. doi:10.1080/00380237.2018.1393607.

Rodríguez, A.M.R., Leongómez, M.V., and Suárez, C.A.A. (2020) 'Mujeres y cuidado: disputas y negociaciones en el espacio académico'. *Cadernos de Pesquisa*, 50(178), pp. 981–999. doi:10.1590/198053147001.

Simien, E.M. and Wallace, S.J. (2022) 'The impacts of exclusion and disproportionate service on women and faculty of color in political science'. *PS: Political Science & Politics*, 56(2), pp. 291–294. doi:10.1017/S104909652200110X.

Slaughter, S. and Rhoades, G. (2004) *Academic Capitalism and The New Economy: Markets, State, and Higher Education*. Baltimore: Johns Hopkins University Press.

Villar-Aguilés, A. and Obiol-Francés, S. (2022) 'Academic career, gender and neoliberal university in Spain: the silent precariousness between publishing and care-giving'. *British Journal of Sociology of Education*, 43(4), pp. 623–638. doi:10.1080/01425692.2022.2042194.

Walker, C., and Gleaves, A. (2016) 'Constructing the caring higher education teacher: A theoretical framework'. *Teaching and Teacher Education*, 54, pp. 65–76. doi:10.1016/j.tate.2015.11.013.

Zembylas, M. (2017) 'Practicing an ethic of discomfort as an ethic of care in higher education teaching'. *Critical Studies in Teaching and Learning (CriSTaL)*, 5(1), pp. 1–17. doi:10.14426/cristal.v5i1.97.

Zembylas, M., Bozalek, V., and Shefer, T. (2014) 'Tronto's notion of privileged irresponsibility and the reconceptualisation of care: Implications for critical pedagogies of emotion in higher education'. *Gender and Education*, 26(3), pp. 200–214. doi:10.1080/09540253.2014.901718.

9   The Body, Male Gaze, and Sexual Harassment in Higher Education

Naomi Davis, Brian McDonough and Jan Parker

Introduction

The body, creative and resourceful, is integral to discovering, examining, and understanding the material, sensorial and social world. Using Merleau-Ponty's *Phenomenology of Perception* (2014) to understand the existential importance of the body, and drawing on Foucault's (2003) notion of 'the gaze' from *The Birth of the Clinic: An Archaeology of Medical Perception*, this chapter examines the ways in which female students manage sexually predatory behaviour in HE spaces. These spaces include classrooms and corridors, campus areas beyond the classroom, and work placements off campus. These three areas connect to social spaces where students, in our research, have described experiences where the body is subject to mistreatments, including [sexual] intimidation; [sexual] harassment and fear, sexual attacks, and other sexual-related interactions. Prohibiting sexually predatory behaviour and stopping gender-based violence in HE not only involves developing better policies and practices (Humphreys and Towl, 2023) but also involves understanding how gendered culture operates across broader society.

The discussion of this chapter is organised into three main parts. The first part provides background to the theoretical concepts used, such as Merleau-Pontian terms like the 'lived-body'; 'la prise' (bodily grip on the social world), and 'gestalt'. It also outlines the notion of the 'male gaze', developed out of Foucault's social theory. The first part also analyses in-class experiences of sexual harassment within HE. The second part of the chapter provides an examination of the ways in which students navigate the patriarchal social spaces in and around university campuses. Drawing on data from female students of different ages and from several UK universities, the chapter reveals how students disclose the body in ways which maximise their safety and avoidance of sexual intimidation, [sexual] harassment, and [sexual] violence. The third part of the chapter provides an analysis of data from students on a social work degree at a British university. These students, working on a placement, have other bodily experiences that they must deal with to remain resilient in their transition from university education to social work employment.

In Foucault's (2003) work, the gaze is a particular form of disclosure, an ensemble or discourse by which the world discloses itself to us. This chapter

DOI: 10.4324/9781003397502-9

shows that much of academia for female university students involves negotiating spaces in which a *male gaze* operates, where students encounter such things as: being looked at [sexually], being approached [for sexual purposes], and being sexually harassed. In Foucault's (2003) work, the ensemble of the gaze encompasses everything and everyone, it is an entirety. As such, the male gaze is not something that merely sits with any specific male but something that is disclosed by women too. With this context in mind, this chapter examines how students negotiate spaces using their bodies. Merleau-Ponty (2014) wrote about the lived-body, referring to the ways in which bodies gesture and connect through inter-corporeality. It is not merely the case that we *have* bodies, but rather that they are *inhabited* and enable us to disclose the world. Merleau-Ponty (2014) distinguishes between the body as object – a physical thing to be weighed and measured, with the lived-body, an existential body. In *The Visible and the Invisible*, Merleau-Ponty (1969) also wrote about the interworld, where our gazes cross and our perceptions overlap. All gazes are existential, but they are not separate from our bodies. For example, from one's 'first step already a style of walking, a gait, is initiated, a rhythm of movement that propagates itself' (Merleau-Ponty, 2014, p.xlviii). The walk of a young female or male student says something about who they are – their intentions and purposes, their sexuality, and expectations, because bodies have style and dispositions, which encompass our moral and ideological assumptions. They are also gendered bodies, which must negotiate with others in the world in particular gendered ways. Merleau-Ponty (2014) explained that our bodies are utilised in such a way as to obtain an optimal gestalt – a way that maximizes our perception, our visibility, so that we attain the ideal focal point for viewing objects and dealing with others in the world. In Merleau-Ponty's (2014) work on perception, the author describes a picture in an art gallery, where viewers stand before the painting to grasp the most enjoyable perspective:

> For each object, just as for each painting in an art gallery, there is an optimal distance from which it asks to be seen – an orientation through which it presents more of itself – beneath or beyond which we merely have a confused perception due to excess or lack. Hence, we tend toward the maximum visibility and we seek, just as when using a microscope, a better focus point, which is obtained through a certain equilibrium between the interior and exterior horizons.
>
> Merleau-Ponty, 2014, p. 137

In the examples we outline in this chapter, it is not paintings that are viewed, but people. In some cases, it is female students who become the object of which male gazers wish to seek maximum visibility. In other cases, it is female students who orient themselves to maintain an optimal distance from male gazers, in these cases positioning themselves to maximize their safety, maintain their self-respect, and prevent violations of their bodies. Another set of cases, less focused upon in this chapter, involve women's gaze at other women and self-

..ation too. We remind the reader that the male gaze is a mode of dis-
..osing the world for all. In this chapter, we draw on Merleau-Ponty's (2014) term *la prise* (p. 497), meaning 'grip' or 'hold', and *en prise*, which literally means 'in gear' (or figuratively 'attuned to'), to denote the understanding involved in bodily movements within HE contexts.

Since bodies do not perceive, and nor are they perceived, in neutral ways, this chapter lays out the way they are disclosed, via the male gaze. In Foucault's (2003) work *The Birth of the Clinic: An Archaeology of Medical Perception*, the author lays out what he calls *le regard medical*, 'a medical gaze', to denote a way of looking at patients within medical practices (or medical worlds). The particular medical gaze, as Foucault (2003) called it, referred to an under-standing of the body as a pure thing, or object, laid out for scientific investiga-tion. Foucault showed that there were particular ways in which bodies could be disclosed. In this chapter, we describe another type of gaze, 'the male gaze'. Although the term 'male gaze' has long been established (See Berger, 2008; Mulvey 1975; Laing and Willson, 2022), few authors to date have used this term to examine the experiences of students in HE. Foucault himself was not the first to use the term gaze. Indeed, Heidegger's (2005) book *The Soujourns: The Journey to Greece*, used the term gaze to illustrate the particular way a tourist sees the everyday world when travelling – an idea taken up in Urry and Larsen's (2011) book *The Tourist Gaze*. Urry and Larsen (2011) also develop the idea of gazers and gazees, to denote the ways in which we look and are looked at.

Classrooms and Corridors: Battles of Sexual Objectification

Gendered battles of social interaction take place in university classrooms and corridors. Universities, just like most other social spaces in education and across society, are patriarchal spaces where men and male values dominate. Male domination is inherent to patriarchal societies where man is considered as default and woman as 'Other' (Beauvoir, 1997, p. 36) and effectively a second-class citizen. Men look, and women are looked at (Berger, 2008). Metaphori-cally speaking, university is a space where gender wars take place, since the 'looking' and being 'looked at' are gendered activities. The sexual objectifica-tion of women can be brutal. Interactions on and around university campuses can range from sexual gazing to intimidation to sexual assault and rape (Towl and Walker, 2019). There is therefore a 'power of corridors' in universities (Hurdley, 2010), where gender battles play out.

Ahmed (2021) pays particular attention to the body in her book *Complaint!*, which examines sexual harassment, bullying, and the abuse of power in HE. Drawing on an account of a student being sexually harassed by an academic, Ahmed (2021, p. 182) reveals the instinctive reactions of the body in certain contexts:

> And he pushed me up against the back of a door and tried to kiss me, and I pushed him away, it was an instinctive pushed him away, and tried to get

out of the room, and it was a horrible moment because I realised I couldn't actually, it was very difficult to operate the latch.

Ahmed (2021, p. 182) adds that 'our bodies can tell us when something is not quite right, when something is wrong'. Yet, in many circumstances, we can conflict with what our bodies are instinctively telling us to do, as Ahmed (2021, p. 183) explains: 'how you are taught to be, polite, considerate, not trouble-some, as a girl, as a student, is how you become more vulnerable, less able to stop someone from pushing the line you need to protect yourself'. In many circumstances, despite the inclination to want to flee from the harasser, 'no' becomes hard to say – the female student does not wish to be antisocial, cause trouble, or be seen as being over the top or paranoid. As a consequence, student victims of abuse find themselves in spaces they do not really wish to be in, like entering a male tutor's office or sharing a taxi with [male] co-students.

The decolletage (the part of a woman's body revealed by a low neckline – as in the cleavage) is one part of the body that is sexually objectified and where there exists a battle, taken up in visual performance, between women's bodies being objectified by being 'ogled at', and thus violated, and avoidance strategies used to prevent violation. Sam, a female student, walks past a group of male students on the way to the toilets pulls over her coat to 'cover up' her cleavage, so the violation does not take place:

SAM: I could see them [male students] staring at my tits. I was walking to class and still had my coat off, having just left the loo, but I quickly put my coat on to cover up. I'm aware I'm being glared at, just because I'm a woman, it makes me sick but what can I do.

Sam sees she is being seen and her body is rendered a sexual object. But men are not the only ones engaged in the male gaze, since fellow female students also look at Sam's low-cut top, some labelling her a 'tart' for being scantily dressed. To understand the 'being looked at', we must appreciate that the sexual objectification of women's bodies stems from how the body is gazed upon. Gazing, in an existential sense, involves a being-with others in which it is disclosed in a particular way. There is a key difference between *vision* – what the human eye is physiologically capable of seeing and *visuality* – how vision is constructed in various ways, in terms of 'how we see, how we are able, allowed, or made to see' (Rose, 2016, p. 2–3). In Merleau-Ponty's (2014) work, the body offers an important way of seeing, as he explains:

the relation between the things and my body is decidedly singular: it is what makes me sometimes remain in appearances, and it is also what sometimes brings me to the things themselves; it is what produces the buzzing of appearances, it is also what silences them and casts me fully into the world.

Merleau-Ponty, 2014, p. 8

s' can make more sense if we consider the ways in
:akes place within university classrooms:

> with this guy and he kept staring at me in every
> irtunity he has, he looks at me. I don't look at him
> igh my peripheral view. For example, if the person
> d the class look at her, he'll take that opportunity
> weird and does make me feel uncomfortable.

The gazer optimises his position and opportunity both in a physical and existential sense, creating sexual intimidation. But in response, the gazee, aware she is being looked at, positions herself in ways that provide what Merleau-Ponty (2014) refers to as an optimal vision, a *la prise*, for avoiding the stare.

Avoiding Sexual Harassment in HE Campus Spaces

The second part of this chapter discusses how women students navigate sexual harassment, particularly the male sexualised gaze, within HE campus spaces outside and beyond the classroom. To make sense of women's lived experience of sexual harassment in HE spaces, we have drawn on the phenomenology of Merleau-Ponty (2014) to examine how women students act in the face of sexual harassment. Merleau-Ponty (2014, p. 497) describes how the body adjusts or attunes itself to become '*en prise*' (literally meaning in-gear or, figuratively, attuned to something) within particular social environments and acting and reacting accordingly with the whole embodied self. This account of the body as central to perception and action leads to an understanding of the nuance and complexity of women's embodied existence within the gendered structures of HE spaces. A nuanced understanding is essential because sexual harassment in HE is not a rare phenomenon. It is a global problem (Bondestrum and Lundqvist, 2020), described by the UK Government as a 'significant issue' (Lewis, 2022). Women aged 16–24 are most at risk of sexual harassment (Office for National Statistics, 2021) and it is common for women HE students to be sexually harassed both within HE spaces (Bondestam and Lundqvist, 2020; Tutchell and Edmonds, 2020; Lipinski et al., 2022) and beyond (Anitha et al., 2021; Roberts, Donovan, and Durey, 2022; Gunby et al., 2022).

Using a methodology known as 'walking interviews' (King and Woodroffe, 2019; Kinney, 2021) conducted in and around English university campuses in 2023, three women undergraduates describe their day-to-day navigations of sexual harassment within HE. Faced with an underlying, and sometimes overt, threat of sexual harassment within the non-teaching spaces, we found these women students sought to avoid or deter sexual harassment with their whole embodied self. Finely attuned to the patriarchal culture of sexual harassment within HE, they protect themselves with a unity of behaviour within their bodily conduct, even with clothes and accessories used in particular ways to help prohibit unwanted sexual attention and to prevent becoming a victim of

sexual and sexist harassment. Hannah spoke about the clothi[ng she wore to]
avoid sexual harassment at university:

> I remember there was a time when I stopped actually wearing dress[es and]
> stuff. Like, maybe I thought if I wear baggy things then I wouldn't loo[k]
> attractive to a man. I was actually wearing really baggy jumpers and lik[e,]
> you know those cargoes, like big blooming ones, and I was wearing my big
> headphones. I just wanted to look invisible and as unapproachable as pos-
> sible, especially in uni sometimes, because these people be crazy, they don't
> understand what 'no' means.

Hannah describes how she uses her clothes to deter sexual harassment by
making herself appear less attractive to male gazers. This is a form of 'safety
work', a strategy that women instinctively or consciously perform as a pre-
cursor to stop violence happening (Kelly, 2012). Having a feminine appearance,
for example by wearing feminine clothes or wearing lipstick or having long
hair, can make women feel unsafe as they navigate public spaces. Adapting
one's appearance to appear less feminine is a form of 'direct safety work', an
embodied practice that many women choose to do to feel safer in public (Vera-
Grey, 2018; Vera-Grey and Kelly, 2020). Hannah utilises this strategy, making
conscious clothing choices to avoid being victimised by, in her own words,
becoming 'invisible'. She stops wearing her typically feminine clothes, her
dresses, and starts to wear baggy jumpers and big blooming cargo trousers,
which hide her body's natural shape, in an effort to make herself [sexually]
unattractive to male students. Furthermore, she wears big headphones, which
signify to others that she does not want to be approached. Wearing clothing
and accessories is a situated bodily practice through which women perform and
which also provides the means for women to negotiate their visibility in public
spaces (Knowles and Melo Lopes, 2023).

Through her strategies of dress, Hannah performs her intentions to go
about the world without being harassed. She minimises her risk of sexual
harassment by managing her sexual appearance within gendered spaces. For
Hannah, these strategies are seen as necessary. Sexual harassment is a normalised practice within HE spaces (Jackson and Sundaram, 2020), and
Hannah views some of the men at university as 'crazy'; they would harass
her if she wore her usual feminine clothes, and if they start harassing her,
they 'won't stop' even if she tells them to, so through her situated bodily
practices Hannah aims to deter sexual harassment before it can even begin.
Hannah's clothes and accessories become a cocoon of safety for her body.
Merleau-Ponty (2014; p. 143) describes how 'the blind man's stick ceases to
be an object for him', it instead becomes an artefact for extending the body,
and in a similar way, Hannah's clothes and headphones become an extension of her body, performing her intentions to inhabit public space without
experiencing sexual harassment.

Catherine also uses her headphones and her bodily demeanour to avoid and deter sexual harassment, as detailed in the following account:

> Sometimes I sense that when I do walk past certain people, there'd be a stare or maybe a potential comment. But when I put my headphones on, I don't need to think about anybody else. I can just focus on that music. They can see that I've got headphones on, they can see that I'm not gonna be able to hear anything if it was said. And yeah, I just sort of look uninterested, really. You can just sort of look straight, headphones on, shoulders up straight, strong, keep walking, type of thing.

Here, Catherine talks about how she instinctively senses in her body which people would be most likely to sexually harass her and what form that harassment might take, such as unwanted stares or comments. When faced with this situation, her intentions are performed through her body to deter potential sexual harassment. As Merleau-Ponty (2014) theorised, auxiliary objects become instrumental extensions of the body which shape one's perceptions and interactions with the world. As an instrumental extension of her embodied self, Catherine's headphones create a barrier, a separation between herself and the world, enabling her to carve out a personal space so she can navigate her surroundings safely. Her headphones shape her perceptions; with the music playing through her headphones, Catherine cannot hear sexualised comments. They take her focus away from the harassment, she does not need to think about anybody else, she can just focus herself on moving past them, on getting past the threat. The headphones also show potential harassers that Catherine cannot hear them, so there is no point in making comments towards her. In this way, her intentions to walk through HE spaces without being harassed are performed. Furthermore, she performs her intentions in how she carries herself. Catherine shows harassers she is uninterested by not interacting with them. She does not look at or speak to male students as she walks past, instead she looks straight ahead and keeps walking, holding her body in a way that signifies she is strong, with her shoulders up straight. Strength is not a characteristic that is typically associated with femininity (Rudman and Glick, 2021), so by adjusting her posture to signify strength, Catherine may be seeking to appear less feminine and so become less attractive to men in order to deter the male sexualised gaze. Traditional gender role expectations presume women to be approachable, kind, and receptive to men, but men often misinterpret friendliness as sexual attraction (Moran et al., 2023), so to avoid harassment women play down their friendliness and femininity:

ROBYN: So I am really lucky I guess, in that I have a resting bitch face. I can easily look very unapproachable, so I really put that on. I walk at people, aggressively, so if there's a bunch of people walking towards me, I won't get out of their way, I'll expect them to get out of mine. So, that attitude of taking no shit, making it seem as if I would cause more problems if they approached me, if they tried to do anything.

Here, Robyn explains how her whole bodily conduct signifies her intention to move through HE spaces without being harassed. Her facial expression, which she describes as a 'resting bitch face', a term used to describe a facial expression that creates an impression of contempt or scorn which can be perceived as unapproachability, is used to show others that she *is* unapproachable. She doesn't just 'not smile' at men as she walks past, or ignore them, but she really 'puts on' her 'resting bitch face', to emphasise her unapproachability to those she comes into contact with. Social gender roles expect women to present as kind and approachable, as amenable and submissive to men's advances (Rudman and Glick, 2021) but Robyn disrupts this social convention with her whole bodily demeanour. Her walk is aggressive, and this is not how women are expected to move through space. Deviating from gender-expected behaviour can elicit more sexual harassment and may sometimes lead to the experience of negative social repercussions known as 'backlash' (Kozlowski and Power, 2022), so Robyn shows others she will 'take no shit'; she wants others to believe that she would cause more problems if they tried to harass her, and in this way, she seeks to avoid sexual harassment by managing others' expectations and behaviours through her whole bodily conduct.

Drawing on Merleau-Ponty's (2014) notions of embodied subjectivity to make sense of the lived experiences of sexual harassment of women students in on-campus non-teaching spaces, our understanding of their worlds was vastly increased, was 'maximised', by using walking interview methodology. By engaging with and communicating with women students in situ, in the very places where sexual harassment had occurred or could occur, their full and whole understanding of sexual harassment became clear and their experiences of sexual harassment in HE spaces began to be mapped out. The bodily strategies described by the women in this research reflect the gendered nature of HE, exposing gendered power dynamics within HE which are perpetuated and reinforced through the male sexualised gaze. The male gaze, which sexually objectifies women, reinforces patriarchy and men's dominance within the 'continuum of violence' that normalises men's power and more extreme forms of violence towards women (Kelly, 1987). As an expression of patriarchal power, sexual harassment limits women's freedoms to exist in public spaces, as women fear both harassment and the more extreme forms of violence it provides the backdrop for (Boyer, 2022). And so, within HE, sexual harassment operates as a mechanism which reserves and shapes HE as a space for men (Jackson and Sundaram, 2020; Phipps, 2020). When HE spaces are experienced by women as spaces in which sexual objectification and harassment is normalised and may routinely occur, it can create an environment that is intimidating and offensive overall, affecting women's physical and mental health, as well as their academic performance and progress as students (Athanasiades et al., 2023, Bondestam and Lunqvist, 2020, Tutchell and Edmonds. 2020). Within this gendered culture, women students are constrained by the patriarchal male sexualised gaze. However, while women students are constrained within the gendered culture of HE, the participants in this research described actions that demonstrate skilful navigations of the male sexualised gaze. They describe practised and adroit adaptations to the gendered culture of higher education in terms of their own experiences of it. In this way, the women students in our research were *en prise* with the culture of sexual harassment within HE; they knew when and where it was most likely to occur, and who was likely to perpetrate it, and they had acquainted themselves with the necessary skills to optimise their grasp of the world of sexual harassment and so avoid or deter it through their situated bodily practices. They minimised their feminine visibility though their clothing choices, they created barriers through headphones, and they carried their bodies to look more strong, unfriendly, or unapproachable to deter and avoid to the male sexualised gaze. In these varied ways, women students skilfully keep themselves safe and manage their own bodies in gendered HE spaces.

Student Work Placements and the Male Gaze

In this part of the chapter, we explore student encounters of the male gaze in social work contexts drawing from the experiences of female students. In many UK universities with social work degrees, the transition from HE into the workplace is supported through a placement, usually within a social work setting. The work placement is an opportunity for students to experience real world learning, providing a readiness for social work practice and enhancing the development of coping strategies in what can be a stressful working environment. This part of the chapter examines the ways in which the male gaze permeates social work placements.

Contrary to the idea that HE placements are inspiring and fulfilling for student participants, many female students on social work placements can find the experience to be emotionally draining, often demeaning, and sometimes acting as a trigger for past traumas. For social work students victimised by the male gaze, many experiences can be devastating as it is unwanted, can be isolating, lowers self-esteem, and has the potential to lead to lost opportunities both educationally and professionally.

It is widely accepted that social work has become a highly stressful working situation (McLaughlin et al., 2023). There is an irony in that social work is referred to as a *helping profession* for those it serves. However, those who train to deliver the service often become casualties of the organisation they work for through professional burnout (Ashley-Binge and Cousins, 2019). Social work practice involves engaging with complex caseloads resulting in traumatic experiences. Scholars such as Ravalier (2019) have long advocated for changes to social work practices since vicarious trauma results in high levels of sickness, absenteeism, and poor workforce retention. The finger of blame predominantly points at the nature of the work, although this narrative tends to overlook how women are positioned as an object of male heterosexual misogyny (Oliver, 2017). To date, there is little discussion in the literature of how the male gaze and the objectification of the female body adds additional challenges for females working in social work contexts. The patriarchal conception of how women working in social work should look and act impacts on how they must navigate their employment. Derogatory sexual comments, harassment, and threats of sexual violence (including rape) are constants for placement students in social work employment, affecting their mental health, resulting in feelings of hopelessness, low self-esteem, and the demise of autonomy and power.

Social work began as a philanthropic activity in the 19th century, becoming a regulated profession in 2001 following the legislation of the Care Standards Act 2000. Since its origins, social work has, numerically at least, been dominated by women. A post-feminist context suggests social work has been subject to dominant male perspectives and the profession is more accurately termed a 'male-dominated, female-majority profession' (Walton, 2022). Ironically, the professional roots of social work are supposedly entrenched in human rights and principles, such as respect for human dignity, transparency, and accountability (Mapp et al., 2019), yet the male gaze permeates the heart of social work practice. Feminist social work is based upon the desire to change societal structures, yet for female social workers, they are themselves targets of macro and microaggressions, experiencing discrimination because of their biological sex (Grant, 2018). Female social workers encounter a different code of morals from male social workers, regularly experiencing sexual assaults and subjected to slurs, violence, and threats from male clients. In studies focusing on the retention of social workers (see the work of McLaughlin et al., 2023), there is criticism of how senior management overlooks the significance and impact of the male gaze on its female workforce. One account from the literature illustrates the context female social workers are confronted with:

> I had a really frightening experience of a young man who tried to attack me in a meeting … So, it was, like, that, sort of, fight or flight thing, and I just literally froze. It was a case where this young man had stabbed his girl-friend to death, had a preoccupation with knives, and an affinity in violence towards women.
>
> McLaughlin et al., 2023, p.1978

This particular social worker reported the incident and then asked to be taken off the case since there was no safety plan put in place for her. Female social work students deal with complex and multi-faceted problems. As students, they do not want to fail their course, so they are more likely to conceal bad experiences from their managers – particularly experiences they have not been able to cope with. Many female social work students try to *contain* their own vulnerabilities, silencing themselves in attempt to take back responsibility. We can see this more visibly through Natalie's recollections of her experience in her first social work placement. Natalie, was a victim of sexual assault in her teens and now has to help a man who is threatening her with sexual violence:

> So, we had a forensic case in which it was a person who had been arrested, they had done their time in prison and been released and then they did it

again, they committed sexual assault. I have a trauma history with this happening to myself, and the circumstances got a little bit close emotionally for me, the person was also phoning up the agency and speaking to me and my colleagues repeatedly and was threatening and using very explicit language.

A social worker has assigned powers and responsibilities to carry out duties according to legislative and policy frameworks. However, rather than feeling empowered to carry out her work under statutory duties, Natalie felt the reverse. She suffered from a loss of autonomy as the male client took control through an onslaught of patriarchal abuse. The process of implementing the social work task became lost as the power shifted away from her. She found herself in a position where she was unable to maintain control of the situation and make decisions. Natalie also felt pressure from the organisation to develop 'a thick skin' to show she was resilient and able to carry out the work of a social worker. This left her with feelings of being inadequate as she was unable to mimic her the behaviours of her colleagues, who appeared to be able to brush off the client's intimidating control and dominating behaviours. The abusive characteristics of the male client triggered adverse memories of a time when she had been a victim of male predatory sexual abuse. The male gaze served to lead her to feel vulnerable and inadequate to the point where she doubted herself. The consequences of this were debilitating, as Natalie continues to tell:

> In the moment with our forensic case, it was very ... I didn't know how much I could share about how I was feeling because I was very new in this, and I felt a bit pathetic that I've just gone to the bathroom and cried for 10 minutes because some guy shouted at me. Like there's a little bit of me that's saying: you're a social worker stop being an idiot. So, it was entirely internal how I was feeling.

For Natalie her experience of the male gaze was one of vitriol and malice. Her experiences with the client triggered adverse childhood experiences and traumatic emotions of shame, self-loathing, and a feeling of being powerless and of being inadequate. Natalie found solace for herself by hiding in secret in the bathroom, removing her body from public view and placing herself behind a locked door, crying to self-comfort and soothe herself. Merleau-Ponty (2014) explains that the body is a physical entity but also an existential one, and so positioning her body out of sight of men is Natalie's attempt to protect herself. Sadly, Natalie's attempt to hide is futile, since discourses like the male gaze are capillary and have no single source, with beginning and end points, but are everywhere (Worthman and Troiano, 2016). The male gaze discloses Natalie's clients as existential threats to her role as a social worker and to her course as a student. Being compelled to conform and endure this position, suffer in silence rather than dealing with it publicly, perpetuates the way women like Natalie are conditioned to endure patriarchal dominance. Like other female social workers, Natalie is expected to be resilient and deal with men robustly, otherwise she would be seen as failing in her work placement and career. Importantly, Natalie is expected to help the male sex abuser, but was unable to give him the care required in her role:

> I was never going to be able to give him the care he needed, I had this massive barrier with him ... because in my head, what was going on for me the whole time was 'you should be in jail'.

Natalie chose social work as a course and career as she felt it would empower her to help people, to support change, find resolutions, keep children safe, and make a difference to people's lives. Social work is viewed as an empowering profession, but the irony is that for Natalie, she is still disclosed as victim, even within her social work career.

Students, like Natalie, embarking on a social work career, often hold a particular idea of social work (as caring and rewarding), but in reality, they encounter it as something very different (Mullaly and Dupré, 2019). A profession driven by the dogma of anti-oppressive practice (Gray and Webb, 2013), social workers are required to provide space for their clients to develop and express their perspective on their needs and priorities. A social worker is seen as the person in authority to help the vulnerable client, but within professional social work practice, students and practitioners are also often the vulnerable ones. They too are often silenced, some of their real views kept discreet, and they become accepting of their vulnerabilities for fear of not being seen as resilient to the emotional complexities they are faced with every day of their working lives.

Another mature female student, called Hayley, is studying to become a professional social worker. During interviews with her, she was asked if the social work degree had supported her to develop resilience to cope with the demands of carrying out the role. Hayley chooses not to speak about her learning on the degree, but rather she reflects on the abuse she had encountered as a young child.

> When I look back on that 8, 9, 10, 11 and 12-year-old self, I see unimaginable and unnecessary pain which surrounded and consumed me. I see those adults who were supposed to care and love me make unsuitable choices, display inappropriate behaviours, and commit felonious acts of abuse time and time again. In their eyes, their actions were acceptable, like a book of unspoken rules; because I was a child and children were always meant to respect their adults and comply with those adult rules.

She recounts how this experience had left her wanting to end her own life. Suicide had felt like a viable option for her younger self. Her recollections of the impact of the abuse presented a picture of a vulnerable existence, one that was devoid of autonomy, without power and control. In her adult life she saw a social work career as something that would equip her to have the power to help others in a similar situation. Hayley saw being a social worker as a way of breaking free from the male gaze, yet sadly, she cannot evade it, since it is as strong as ever on her work placement. Hayley was seeking the power and autonomy she was denied as a child with a right to say 'no'. Whilst a traumatic childhood existence may have been the driving force behind her decision to train as a social worker, in practice female social work students encountering the adverse effects of the male gaze as a child or adult are shown to continuously search for coping mechanisms to manage their work experiences. The male gaze objectifies others sexually and also renders children objects for sexual abuse. The male gaze was present before Haley was even born; it existed throughout her childhood, and it still shapes her experiences now. Preparing to go on her first social work placement, Hayley was asked to write down her thoughts about her emotional resilience and how she would adapt to a social work setting. Hayley once again chose to write about her childhood. Growing up, she experienced adverse childhood experiences (ACES) which included sexual, physical, and emotional abuse. This is how she describes her childhood:

> I fully understand and realise how important becoming a social worker is to me. I was a vulnerable child, with little support/guidance during my formative years. I suffered, unnecessarily because I did not feel I had a voice. I believed that I would never be believed and so the cycle of fear, hopelessness and mistrust overshadowed me like a haunting ghost. A social worker could have empowered me, given me a voice, placed a glimmer of hope into my desolate existence. I thrive to become that social worker one day, to make a difference, no matter how small in a child's life.

For Foucault, 'the gaze' has the task of 'absorbing experience in its entirety' (2003, p. 15), of ceaselessly revealing and disclosing phenomena in such and such a way. Whilst Foucault was describing a medical gaze in his analysis of science and medical practice, we draw on the male gaze within social work practices and educational institutions, to understand how female students are disclosed in male privileged spaces. In social work the relationship of power indifference created by the male gaze, can be seen in the practices that maintain it. There is a cultural norm for social workers and students to 'grow a thick skin' and deny their own vulnerability as the fear of being seen as a failure prohibits seeking help through supervisory processes. The requirement placed on female social workers and students in social work placement settings requires a degree of compliance and acceptance to 'work with' rather than overtly deal with the challenges of patriarchal male dominance and the objectification of women in practice. In other words, the male gaze both subjugates and silences women within social work HE placements.

Conclusion

This chapter explored the ways in which students in HE experience sexual harassment and other gendered forms of behaviour in three spaces: in university classrooms, in on-campus non-teaching spaces, and on student work placements. The first part of this chapter provided a background to the theoretical concepts used, laying out the 'lived-body'; 'la prise' and 'gestalt' from Merleau-Pontian philosophy. But it also outlined the 'male gaze', developed primarily from Foucault. The first part also analysed in-class experiences of sexual harassment within HE, finding that university classrooms are spaces where gendered battles take place. The second part of the chapter examined how students navigated these patriarchal social spaces in and around university campuses. It used a walking methodology to empathise with how female students navigated campus life by disclosing their bodies to maximise their safety and avoid sexual intimidation, [sexual] harassment, and [sexual] violence. The third part of the chapter provided an analysis of data of students on a social work degree at a British university. These students, working on placements, had to use their bodies to deal with a range of experiences in order to become resilient in their transition from university education to social work employment.

The male gaze operates across HE for students on campus, off campus, at student placements and within the world of work. The male gaze permeates society. In many of the social spaces examined in this chapter, women are relentlessly sought after and disclosed as sexual bodies to be violated against. Within the male gaze there is a fear of verbal and physical abuse, and a fear of sexual assault, violence, and rape.

References

Ahmed, S. (2021) *Complaint!* Durham, NC: Duke University Press.

Anitha, S., Jordan, A., Jameson, J., and Davy, Z. (2021). 'A balancing act: Agency and constraints in university students' understanding of and responses to sexual violence in the night-time economy'. *Violence against women*, 27(11), pp. 2043–2065.

Ashley-Binge, S. and Cousins, C. (2020) 'Individual and organisational practices Addressing social workers' experiences of vicarious trauma', *Practice*, 32(3), pp. 191–207. doi:10.1080/09503153.2019.1620201.

Athanasiades, C., Stamovlasis, D., Touloupis, T., and Charalambous, H. (2023) 'University students' experiences of sexual harassment: the role of gender and psychological resilience'. *Frontiers in Psychology*, 14, Article 1202241. Available at: https://doi.org/10.3389/fpsyg.2023.1202241.

Beauvoir, S. de (1997) *The Second Sex*. London: Vintage Books.

Berger, J. (2008) *Ways of Seeing*. London: Penguin.

Bondestam, F. and Lundqvist M. (2020) 'Sexual Harassment in higher education—A systematic review'. *European Journal of Higher Education*, 10(4), pp. 397–419. doi:10.1080/21568235.2020.1729833.

Boyer, K. (2022) 'Sexual harassment and the right to everyday life'. *Progress in Human Geography*, 46(2), pp. 398–415. Available at: https://doi.org/10.1177/03091325211024340.

Foucault, M. (2003) *The Birth of the Clinic: An Archaeology of Medical Perception.* London: Routledge.

Grant, L. (2018) *Feminist Perspectives on Social Work Practice.* Oxford: Oxford University Press.

Gray, M. and Webb, S. (2013) *Social Work: Theories and Methods.* London: Sage.

Gunby, C., Carline, A., Taylor, S., and Gosling, H. (2020). 'Unwanted sexual attention in the night-time economy: Behaviors, safety strategies, and conceptualizing "feisty femininity"'. *Feminist Criminology*, 15(1), pp. 24–46.

Heidegger, M. (2005) *The Sojourns: The Journey to Greece.* New York: State of New York University Press.

Humphreys, C.J. and Towl, G.J. (Eds) (2023) *Stopping Gender-Based Violence in Higher Education: Policy, Practice, and Partnerships.* London: Routledge.

Hurdley, R. (2010) 'The power of corridors: Connecting doors, mobilising materials, plotting openness'. *The Sociological Review*, 58, pp. 45–64.

Jackson, C. and Sundaram, V. (2020). *Lad Culture in Higher Education: Sexism, Sexual Harassment and Violence.* London: Routledge.

Kelly, L. (1987). The Continuum of Sexual Violence, In: J. Hanmer and M. Maynard (Eds) *Women, Violence and Social Control. Explorations in Sociology.* London: Palgrave Macmillan, pp. 46–60. https://doi.org/10.1007/978-1-349-18592-4_4.

Kelly, L. (2012). Standing the test of time? Reflections on the concept of the continuum of sexual violence, in: J. Brown and S. Walklate (Eds), *Handbook on Sexual Violence.* London: Routledge, pp. xvii–xxvi.

King, A.C. and Woodroffe, J. (2019). Walking interviews, in: P. Liamputtong (Ed.) *Handbook of Research Methods in Health Social Sciences.* New York: Springer.

Kinney, P. (2021). Walking interviews: a novel way of ensuring the voices of vulnerable populations are included in research, in: M. Borcsa and C. Willig (Eds) *Qualitative Research Methods for Mental Health.* New York: Springer.

Knowles, C. and Melo Lopes, F. (2023). 'How to dress like a feminist: a relational ethics of non-complicity'. *Inquiry: An Interdisciplinary Journal of Philosophy*, Available at: https://doi.org/10.1080/0020174X.2023.2233014.

Kozlowski, D. and Power, I. (2022). 'Unpacking backlash: Social costs of gender non-conformity for women and men'. *Journal of Research in Gender Studies*, 12(2), pp. 9–32.

Laing, M. and Willson, J. (2022) *Revisiting the Gaze: The Fashioned Body and the Politics of Looking.* New York: Bloomsbury.

Lewis, J. (2022). 'House of Commons briefing: Sexual harassment and violence in further and higher education'. Available at: https://commonslibrary.parliament.uk/research-briefings/cbp-9438/.

Lipinsky, A., Schredl, C., Baumann, H., Humbert, A. and Tanwar, J. (2022) *Gender-Based Violence and its Consequences in European Academia, Summary Results from the UniSAFE Survey.* Report, November 2022. UniSAFE Project no.101006261.

Lloyd, C., King, R. and Chenoweth, L. (2002) 'Social work, stress and burnout: A review'. *Journal of Mental Health*, 11(3), pp. 255–265 Available at: doi:10.1080/09638230020023642.

Mapp, S., McPherson, J., Androff, A. and Gatenio Gabel, S. (2019) 'Social Work Is a Human Rights Profession'. *Social Work*, 64(3), pp. 259–269. Available at: https://doi.org/10.1093/sw/swz023.

McLaughlin, H., Scholar, H., McCaughan, S. and Pollock, S. (2023) 'Should I stay or should I go?: The experiences of forty social workers in England who had previously indicated they would stay in or leave children and family social work'. *The British*

Journal of Social Work, 53(4), pp. 1963–1983. Available at: https://doi.org/10.1093/bjsw/bcac191.

Merleau-Ponty, M (1969) *The Visible and the Invisible*. Evanston: Northwestern University Press.

Merleau-Ponty, M (2014) *Phenomenology of Perception*. London: Routledge.

Moran, J.B., Airington, Z., McGee, E., Murray, D. (2023) '(Mis)Perceiving sexual intent: A mixed-method approach investigating sexual overperception across diverse sexual identities'. *Archives of Sexual Behavior*, 53, pp. 511–524. https://doi.org/10.1007/s10508-023-02748-7.

Mullaly, B. and Dupré, M.(2019) *The New Structural Social Work: Ideology, Theory, and Practice*. 4th Ed. Don Mills, Ontario: Oxford University Press.

Mulvey, L. (1975) 'Visual pleasure and narrative cinema'. *Screen*, 16(3), pp. 6–18.

Office for National Statistics (2021). *Sexual Harassment Report*. Available at: https://assets.publishing.service.gov.uk/government/uploads/system/uploads/attachment_data/file/1002873/2021-07-12_Sexual_Harassment_Report_FINAL.pdf.

Oliver, K. (2017) 'The male gaze is more relevant, and more dangerous, than ever'. *New Review of Film and Television Studies*, 15(4), pp. 451–455. doi:10.1080/17400309.2017.1377937.

Orme, J., (2013) Feminist Social Work, M. Gray and S. Webb (Eds) *Social Work: Theories and Methods*. London: Sage, pp. 90–91.

Phipps, A. (2020). *Me, Not You: The Trouble with Mainstream Feminism*. 1st Ed.. Manchester: Manchester University Press. Available at: http://www.jstor.org/stable/j.ctvzgb6n6.

Ravalier, J.M. (2019). 'Psycho-social working conditions and stress in UK social workers'. *The British Journal of Social Work*, 49(2), pp. 371–390, Available at: https://doi.org/10.1093/bjsw/bcy023.

Roberts, N., Donovan, C. and Durey, M. (2022) 'Gendered landscapes of safety: How women construct and navigate the urban landscape to avoid sexual violence'. *Criminology & Criminal Justice*, 22(2), pp. 287–303. Available at: https://doi.org/10.1177/1748895820963208.

Rose, G. (2016) *Visual Methodologies: An Introduction to Researching with Visual Materials*. London: Sage.

Rudman, L.A., and Glick, P. (2021) *The Social Psychology of Gender: How Power and Intimacy Shape Gender Relations*. 2nd Ed. New York: Guilford Publications.

Towl, G. and Walker, T. (2019) *Tackling Sexual Violence at Universities: An International Perspective*. London: Routledge.

Tutchell, E. and Edmonds, J. (2020). *Unsafe Spaces. Ending Sexual Abuse in Universities*. Bingley: Emerald Publishing.

Urry, J. and Larsen, J. (2011) *The Tourist Gaze 3.0*. Los Angeles, London, New Delhi, Singapore, Washington DC: Sage.

Vera-Gray, F. (2018). *The Right Amount of Panic: How Women Trade Freedom for Safety*. Bristol: Policy Press.

Vera-Gray, F., and Kelly, L. (2020). Contested gendered space: Public sexual harassment and women's safety work, in: V. Ceccato and M. Nalla (Eds). (2020). *Crime and Fear in Public Places: Towards Safe, Inclusive and Sustainable Cities*. 1st Ed. London and New York: Routledge, pp. 217–231. doi:10.4324/9780429352775-15.

Walton, R.G. (2022) *Women in Social Work*. London and New York: Routledge.

White, V. (2009) Quiet challenges? Professional practice in modernized social work, in: Harris, J. and White, V. (Eds) *Modernising Social Work: Critical Considerations*. Bristol: Policy Press, pp. 129–144.

Worthman, C. and Troiano, B. (2016) 'Capillary discourses, fissure points, and tacity confessing the self: Foucault's later work and educational research'. *Journal of Adult and Continuing Education*, 22(1), pp. 46–67.

10 Neoliberal Academic Speeds and the Desire to Slow Down (in) Academia as a Feminist Practice of Resistance

Domitilla (Domi) Olivieri and Iraia Elorduy Alverde

Introduction

In the last 20 years, the university as an institution, in the many parts of the world where capitalism and western neoliberal logics shape politics and social life, has increasingly become the object of study from various critical angles and disciplines (Readings, 1997; Brown, 2011). A significant amount of this scholarship has been dedicated to defining, unpacking, and critiquing the specific functioning of what we call here the 'neoliberal university' (Fleming, 2021; Slaughter and Rhoades, 2000).

> In a market-led system, the student is defined as an economic maximizer, governed by self-interest. There is a glorification of the 'consumer citizen' construed as willing, resourced, and capable of making market-led choices. Education becomes just another consumption good (not a human right) paralleling other goods and the individual is held responsible for her or his own 'choices' within it.
>
> Lynch, Grummell, and Devine, 2012, p. 14

In this chapter we take the university as the object of our study not in its institutional mechanisms as such, but through the lived experiences of those who inhabit it, particularly students and teachers. We aim at making visible the effects and affects of the implicit norms and rationality of neoliberal academia, as a first step towards undoing, or at least questioning, the current institutional academic rationality and its norms. We build on what scholars have amply shown about the contemporary neoliberal university as being increasingly based upon the financialisation of higher education (Lynch, 2006), capitalist models of time management and production (Slaughter and Rhoades, 2004; Berg and Seeber, 2016), and individualism. This translates into a culture and practice of quantified outputs, 'metrics of assessment, quick turn-around of student graduations, grants as forms of excellence, etc.' (Olivieri, 2022, p. 103).

As feminist scholars, our approach is also embedded in an understanding that the mechanisms and logics of this university reproduce exclusions and discriminations along lines of racism, colonialism, sexism, and normative ideas of

DOI: 10.4324/9781003397502-10

ability and gender (Harney and Moten, 2013; Luhmann, 1988). The chapter critically explores how feminist pedagogy helps in 'developing a democratic resistance to injustices [which] is a slow process and systematic critical education is central to it' (Lynch, 2021, p. 270). Our focus is on how academic speed, in terms of fastness and efficient time management, is one of the seemingly necessary logics of the university and on how such speed is imposed upon and internalised by students and teachers alike. The framework we adopt is that of slowness and slowing down (in) the neoliberal university as a feminist practice of resistance, as has been outlined by scholars such as (Gill, 2017; O'Neill, 2014), and as having to do with a logic of care and 'response-able pedagogy', (Bozalek, 2017, p. 44).

> Pedagogy [...] has a specific chronotope that is radically alien to the notion of accountable time upon which the excellence of capitalist-bureaucratic management and bookkeeping depend. Such a pedagogy can provide a notion of educational responsibility, of accountability, that is markedly at odds with the logic of accounting that runs the University of Excellence.
>
> Readings, 1997, p. 151

We address the issue of speeds and slowness also to argue that this neoliberal university assumes one approach that 'fits all', one understanding of the 'ideal' student, teacher or researcher, one standardised model that translates into specific forms of assessments, deadlines, ideas of mobility, 24/7 availability, lack of care responsibilities, etc. Such a 'standard' subject (that works fast and produces numerous and 'effective' outputs) is another version of the patriarchal-modern-colonial rational, autonomous subject that has been criticised by feminist, decolonial, and queer scholars for decades. Therefore, this project on slowness and the neoliberal university cannot but involve how the body and embodied experiences have all to do with how and why this kind of educational institution is not working.

This chapter is the outcome of years of direct observations and 14 interviews conducted in the Netherlands by Iraia Elorduy Alverde. This research is the second step of a broader project started by Domi Olivieri aimed at investigating what it is about the speed and time management logic of the contemporary university that is not working, and what it could mean to slow it down. It should be mentioned that we do not take for granted that slowing down is a feminist or counter-normative strategy *per se*, but we intend to outline how slowing down can translate into a series of strategies to change (our relation to) the university and can allow us to attend to the world, attend to each other, and attend to our bodies differently (Olivieri, 2022).

In the first part of this chapter, we will present how the way we collaborated and executed the research is itself a practice of undoing the demands of academic productivity and speed, and the implicit power relations between students and teachers that the institution imposes. Next, we will analyse some of the outcomes of our research, organised according to themes, all revolving around the issue of speed as a key aspect of the neoliberal rationality of the university. Finally, but crucially, although we have mainly observed and collected the experiences of teachers, researchers, and students, we centralise in this reflection the perspectives of the latter, since the voices of the students remain often unheard in scholarly analyses (e.g. Fleming, 2021). This chapter is the result of a collaboration between a student in the Research Master in Gender Studies programme and an assistant professor in the field of Gender Studies.

Methodology: How We Worked Together

One of us has experienced the speeds of contemporary neoliberal academia for several years and has been grappling with the dilemma of how, and whether, to stay in an institution that (re)produces neoliberal, racist, classist, and gendered oppressions. The other one of us has only recently encountered the neoliberal academic speeds and their multiple financial, physical, and mental health consequences. Neither of us is from the Netherlands. Our personal paths into this project are worth mentioning briefly.

Domi

After working in the university for more than 15 years and having become an assistant professor with a fixed contract and more (managerial) responsibilities, I could no longer ignore the serious personal and political tensions I was experiencing daily in my life and job.

For example, as one of the academic coordinators of the Masters in Gender Studies, I realised there was very little space, if any, for engendering structural changes because all desired adjustments would have to comply with the explicit and implicit institutional requirements for speed, productivity, and financial gains. Thus, I reluctantly ended up trying, and pressing colleagues, students, and myself, to comply with this logic and its demands. These pressures continue to prove to be unsustainable for most of us and certainly do not make for feminist caring and 'care-ful(l) pedagogies' (Thiele, Górska and Türer, 2020, p. 60). On a weekly basis, I have conversations with students who cannot keep up with the required speed of their programme (e.g. because of care responsibilities, visa issues, neurodivergences, and various forms of social discrimination) and suffer because of it.

Iraia

My goal for this research was clear: understanding academic rhythms. Why is the speed of academia so fast? Why are some of us struggling so much with it, while others are thriving? And most importantly, why are teachers — persons in positions of power — not doing anything to change it? These concerns arose after suffering the mental and physical consequences of the current academic speed. At first, I thought that these problems arose due to my lack of organisational skills; however, once I slowed down – which I could do thanks to my privileged position in terms of funding and passport – I realized that these circumstances had nothing to do with me lacking organisational skills, but rather with the institutional neoliberal speeds that are impossible for me to keep up with without compromising my health. To my surprise, I was not the only one struggling; most of my peers were struggling too. Hence, I entered this project with the intention of unfolding the layers of this issue and to try to grasp to what extent the issue was solvable, whose responsibility it was to solve it, and how.

One of the initial goals of this project was to understand whether slowing down was seen as a needed or desirable approach for people (mostly students and lecturers) in the university to deal with or push back against neoliberal logics of speed and productivity. Next, the aim was to map what strategies people employ or could imagine employing to slow down or hamper the university's machinery and make the university more liveable. Instead, we realised that first we needed to know exactly how people experienced the (fast) pace of academic labour and how they made sense of it. Therefore, our intention with this research is to discern how the speed of the university affects the lives of those who inhabit it, before theorising if and where slowness/slowing down can become a political project and not another efficiency-driven strategic rhythm. Another aim of the project was to help us make sense of our own experiences and feel less alone in studying/working in the university.

We decided that doing interviews would have been the most enriching and multi-vocal way to approach this research, given that they are 'particularly useful for getting the story behind a participant's experiences' and the interviewer 'can pursue in-depth information around the topic' that might not have been thought about before (Utibe, 2020, p. 16). Moreover, doing semi-structured interviews, without a predefined length, meant making time to listen to and acknowledge people's experiences that had not been heard or systematically addressed before (DeVault and Gross, 2012, p. 209). Following a feminist qualitative approach, we aimed at giving space to these voices, while being aware that interviews also shape and redesign the research along the way; thus, interviews do not simply constitute data to analyse but are modes of thought and action that inform the research process itself (DeVault and Gross, 2012).

To find and select our interviewees, we followed a snowball sampling approach combined with participatory action research since we were talking to participants from within our own communities. Snowball sampling is usually effective for finding participants who are socially vulnerable and difficult to reach (Liamputtong, 2010). Participatory action research refers to a process of knowledge production with people 'for the express purpose of building power with/by those people' (Gatenby and Humphries, 2000, p. 89). In this case, the convenience of these mixed methods was that the people we reached out to, or who reached out to us, approached us with trust and a commonality of intent from the start. All participants' data is presented in extracts which also show time stamps where applicable, and names of research participants have been anonymised, although almost all of them also agreed to be named if and where that would prove to be useful or necessary.

As the project and the interviews started, more and more people showed interest and wanted to share their experiences. As of the time of writing, we have gathered 14 interviews: six graduate students and two teachers in Gender Studies, one student advisor in the Humanities Faculty, two PhD students and one professor in Mathematics, a PhD student in Anthropology, and a PhD student in Brain Development. The enthusiasm with which our interviews and research were received is confirmation of the need of people in the university – regardless of their field – to be heard and to make sense of what is happening in contemporary Dutch academia.

A Gender Studies Programme in a Neoliberal University: Addressing Expectations, Tensions, Practices of Care and Carelessness

One of the key insights that emerged from our interviews is that students entering a Gender Studies programme arrive with expectations that often remain unacknowledged and unaddressed in the classroom, especially in conversations with the teachers. So much so that they become a source of frustration and tensions among students, in relation to the teachers or in relation to the programme as a whole. Making explicit and giving space to the discussion of such – informed and legitimate but often unfeasible – expectations could be seen as a necessary step in facilitating feminist engagements within neoliberal academia.

Many of the students interviewed (five out of the six Gender Studies students interviewed and many more in our direct observations and informal communications) hold the expectation that a Gender Studies programme is the place within the university where all subjectivities are welcomed, where students and educators can be physically and emotionally safe, where feminist pedagogies – pedagogies of care – are actively implemented, and where activism is part of the everyday practices of learning and relating (Bozalek, Zembylas, and Tronto, 2020). A graduate gender studies programme is also expected to be the place where critical thinking is embraced and flourishes, unencumbered by competitiveness and commodification. In sum, a safer space, where exclusions and oppressions are averted, and where especially marked or marginalised subjects are welcome and cherished. Although these might be the aims and politics of said programme, nonetheless students are soon confronted with unmet expectations, which in turn make them even more frustrated and negatively affected by the logics and speeds of the neoliberal university.

For example, students realize that practices of care are not – cannot be – always their priority or teachers' priority. This might have to do with an awareness of the values and governing rationality of this kind of university, based on market metrics, capital enhancement, and output-oriented effectiveness. This creates a consequent disillusionment with the role and potential of the university in contributing to a more just world and with the working conditions created by these logics, which are incompatible with consistent ethics and pedagogies of care (Lynch, 2021; Bourgault, 2016). From the students' perspectives we have heard statements such as:

> Sometimes it feels like it's merely transactional, right? So, to me, that's also always the bottom line. It's like, I'm a student, I feel like, oh, I need to get something useful out of this. But what is useful about reading *Necropolitics*? It's not in any terms useful. Who the fuck cares if I change the way I think about my love relationships, because I read Berlant, you know? Like, no one cares. Like, it makes no change in how the world keeps reproducing itself.
>
> (M., 23:58–34:10)

Having to deal with a high-pressure approach to work has, at least in humanities and social science faculties, become a consequence of the neoliberalisation of Dutch universities. These dynamics have resulted in teachers having to negotiate with themselves how much care they can put into their teaching, as L., a lecturer at the university explains:

> But it's very difficult to sacrifice teaching. I mean, you have to be a bit more careless, I guess, towards your ... and to have a bit of a thicker skin in how students perceive you or to be less preoccupied with these sorts of things, you know, just be okay, I did my best. This is what I'm paid for. And I know people that, especially Dutch people, who are more attached to this vision of like, I'm doing my best, this is what I'm paid for. I'm not gonna do more.
>
> (L., 15:48).

Many of the teachers and students we have talked to seem to have experienced a moment of being confronted, if not colliding, with the affordances of the university, its systematic reproduction of exclusions and carelessness, and the recognition of how narrow the space for learning/teaching otherwise is, within the institution. We have also observed that a way to reduce falling into carelessness and succumbing to the neoliberal values of competition and efficiency is by facilitating spaces to discuss the tensions and exploitations that both students and teachers experience. Created with the intention of sharing experiences and strategies, these spaces – this research being one such space – at least in part prevent frustrations or resentments, by addressing the role of the institution and our restricted modes of action within it. While these frictions are not exclusively experienced by people in a Gender Studies programme, the hopes and beliefs many entering such a programme hold might play a role in the degree of frustration, hurt, and disappointment many of us feel. That is why, in this chapter, we articulate how the tensions between feminist politics and the institutional mechanisms of the neoliberal university – more specifically its speed – play out in the lives and bodies of people that inhabit that space.

Two larger questions emerge here: what is the place of a Gender Studies programme within a neoliberal university? What is the purpose of the University? The latter question has been amply discussed by scholars such as Readings (1997) and Wright and Shore (2019) in terms of historical changes and coexisting and conflicting values and aims that, more recently, have gone in the direction of neoliberal governmentality (Brown, 2019) and academic capitalism (Slaughter and Rhoades, 2004). The first question, instead, is at the core of the tensions this study has detected, and more space for discussion seems needed among those of us involved in these programmes, transnationally and within our specific campuses. For the sake of this chapter, what is remarkable and a lesson to be learnt is that open conversations between teachers and students about the politics of our academic institutions are a necessary part of 'response-able pedagogies' (Bozalek, 2017, p. 44).

As previously mentioned, we chose to focus our study on one specific aspect of neoliberal universities (in the Netherlands), namely their speeds. While research on slow scholarship has emerged significantly out of fields or theories informed by gender studies frameworks (see, for example, Mountz et al., 2015), the issue of time in academia has been addressed also by other scholars in political theory, law, sociology, etc. Yet, at the start of our research, we thought that it would be mostly students, researchers, and educators in the humanities, and specifically in gender studies, who would feel a strong resonance with our inquiry about slowing down in academia. This assumption was mostly informed by the fact that it is especially humanities faculties, and smaller programmes with a less established disciplinary history, that are known to suffer the most from the budget cuts and 'strategic' restructuring of universities over the last 10 years (Couldry and McRobbie, 2010; Wright and Shore, 2019). This might have been true some years ago. Certainly now, because of the incremental marketisation and quantification of all universities, and the resulting increased workload experienced by almost all academic employees not in the top managerial positions (for the data in Dutch universities, see Universities of the Netherlands, 2020), it appears that there is a widespread urgency in addressing the issue of 'speedy scholarship' (Hartman and Darab, 2012, p. 49).

Yet, we have also observed some specificities in the interviews with those in Gender Studies, in terms of the embodied effects and affects of the fast academic rhythms. These specificities have to do not just with students' and teachers' convictions and expectations, as previously noted, but also with the marginalised social and political positionalities of many of us who choose to specialise in gender studies. We theorise and analyse the structural and systematic conditions of (im)possibility under which certain subjectivities and groups are or have been excluded or oppressed, and the impact these conditions have on our lives and livelihood. Therefore, many of us in gender studies are not only learning theories, debates, and academic writing skills, but we are the very subjects of those theories, experiencing in our lives and bodies the very debates we discuss. We observed that this generates an added layer of involvement among gender studies students with the topics addressed in class, making it harder to 'detach' or 'separate' themselves from the matter studied, and therefore often leading to them becoming less 'efficient' and 'productive' in terms of the fastness required to complete their degrees in time.

The Neoliberal Logic of Speed in Academia Affects us All: Internalising Speed and Slowing Down as a Privilege

Professors and PhD candidates from various faculties and universities volunteered to be part of the project as soon as they found out about it. It all occurred in a very organic way, where people would become immediately very interested and want to be interviewed as soon as they heard that our project was about getting to know the various ways in which students, teachers, professors, and researchers experience and relate to speed, slowness, so called time management, and related personal and political issues. The intriguing aspect of these encounters for us was the spontaneity and very strong interest others showed in the project itself and, above all, the interest they showed once they learnt this research was part of an internship project created by a student and a professor, where the main focus was to listen to their experiences in relation to academic speed. The reason for such interest appeared to be twofold: because these matters are not talked about between teachers and students; and because our interviewees found it remarkable that someone from within the university was honestly interested in hearing those personal experiences of discomfort, suffering, and frustration.

Another aspect that greatly surprised us was how many of the people interviewed acknowledged themselves as 'slow' in relation to academic speed, even people that 'seemed' to be operating comfortably within the neoliberal pace and demands. I think it [slowness] has a positive connotation because I recognize that I am myself slow in most of the things I do' (F, PhD student in Mathematics, 27:42). It appeared that regardless of their professional position in academia or their field – either a student in Gender Studies, an assistant professor or PhD candidate in Mathematics, a PhD student in Brain Development, or a study advisor in the Humanities – they were all searching for ways to deal with the current academic speed while not aligning with it.

> So I think that it takes more hours for me to do things and I guess do the things the way I want to do them because I yeah, I could also go a bit more unprepared in class, or it can be I don't know, more sloppy, or to not always reply to emails, you know, not immediately, then I could do things differently to reduce this. But it's like a choice that I sacrifice, like my free time or achieving higher standards.
>
> (G., Assistant Professor in Mathematics, 11:14)

The interviews conducted with professors and students outside the fields of Humanities and Gender Studies provided a confirmation of the literature on the matter but also showed us the degree to which the neoliberal logics of speed are tangibly experienced and suffered by so many people, regardless of their field, in the Netherlands. And, while it seems that everyone we have interviewed is seeking ways to *slow down in academia*, it is especially those in precarious and marginalised positions that are the most affected. Given that such precarious and marginalised positions are the very reason Gender Studies as a field of study exists, and that many of the teachers and students in the field experience marginalization and forms of social oppressions, it is not surprising that it is from scholars and students in these fields that the pressures of the neoliberal university are felt especially intensely and the yearning to *slow down academia itself* is the strongest.

Many of the students, teachers, and researchers we have interviewed criticise the logic of neoliberal academia in terms of quantifiable measurements of excellence, speed, and competition. Yet, we also found that 12 out of the 14 people interviewed had also internalised these logics to some extent, and always to the detriment of their own sense of adequacy or as a pressure they had to find ways of coping with. The two people who seemed to be less affected by these pressures were not unaware of them, but they found it easier to detach from them, not let them negatively affect their work, or navigate them to their advantage. Out of those 12 interviewees, some students shared how they internalised the speed of progress and mindset of competition and excellence during their studies, to the detriment of their well-being and mental health:

> I just got into this mode of always being behind, and like, you're always running after things. And it was so stressful. I remember during deadlines [...] just being so stressed and depressed. I remember that there were like, at least three, three times 'Oh, it's really, I think like this too much'. Maybe I should just quit because I cannot do this.
>
> (M., 5:51)

> ... what I'm trying, to be gentle on myself, is not to be frustrated. And that's something that I, that it's a very lonely work. Because we are always comparing to each other, it's kind of impossible not to.
>
> (R., 35:06)

While we join those other scholars who advocate for slowing down as a mode of resistance or survival, we also must seriously ask the question: who can afford to slow down? Particularly, when slowing down might entail taking longer to read an article, write a paper, finish a course, answer an email, grade a paper, or write an article. What we have gathered through our study is a wider understanding of how slowing down in higher education institutions becomes a privilege, only available to the very few, as we elaborate further here. One of the major obstacles to 'slowing down' has to do with precarious labour, for example for teachers with short-term temporary contracts or other unstable financial circumstances. The issue of precarity in higher education institutions, in Europe and elsewhere, has been discussed by scholars from various disciplines. Notably, a special issue of *Social Anthropology/Anthropologie Sociale* (2019) shows how '[p]recarity has become an indeterminacy that is now more the norm than the exception' (Loher, Strasser and Stoica, 2019, p. 8) in academia, because of austerity measures, authoritarianism, different regimes of values, and various emergency situations.

According to our experiences, observations, and interviews, from the teachers' perspective – although many of the below-mentioned complications experienced by students are also applicable to teachers' situations – there are specific labour-related constraints that make some of them unable to challenge the logics of quantification and quickness, and the rules and calculations that ensue. In our university, and in many universities in the Netherlands, all teachers are given a set amount of hours to complete certain tasks; and even though it is well known that such calculations are grossly inaccurate as an underestimation, new and temporary hired staff suffer the most by these quantified speeds:

> So when you start teaching, you're basically getting the same time, like people who have been teaching the same courses for many years, whereas you are at the beginning. So then you obviously, you know, put more time into it.
>
> (L., 10.49)

> So it's a sort of well-known fact that you're going to work more than what you get paid for, let's say, it's sort of like seen like a part of the deal.
>
> (L., 12.02).

Felt by Many but Intensified for Those Who 'Fit In' Less: Speed, Neoliberal Standards, and the 'Ideal' Student

Not only have we observed how velocity worsens the financial pressures and inequalities experienced by students and teachers, but in our study, we have identified that one major issue at stake in the academic neoliberal rationality has to do with how the university standardises the idea of 'the student'. This implicit but ubiquitous model of the 'ideal' student is imagined as being Dutch, white, middle-class, able-bodied, neuro-normative, and having access to a comfortable living space and a support network. It is fair to say that a similar standard is also at play in how the neoliberal university relates to teachers and other employees, but we wish to keep the students as our focus. This ideal student also knows how to write papers in an academic jargon, knows some version of standard English, has stability and unambiguous goals in their personal life. Moreover, this student is 'care-free' (Lynch, 2021, p. 148) as they have no responsibility of care towards anyone and are perceived as independent, free, and 'without relational commitments' (ibid, p. 132). Therefore, officially, all students are assessed and approached equally by the university as if they all fit this model of the 'ideal' student, which is obviously not true, and this (re)produces exclusions and inequalities.

One of the many instances where this model of the 'ideal' student is at play is with students who are not familiar with the Dutch academic system. It should be noted that international, especially non-EU, students were highly sought after by universities in the name of 'internationalisation' and to increase the inflow of students and related financial gains dependent upon numbers of students and tuition fees. International students are often seen as not 'fitting in' when they are not immediately aware of the expectations of the Dutch university, concerning how to write papers, approach the readings, handle the deadlines and implicit time-management norms, for example. Talking about the system of grades and assessment, a student explains:

> I feel like we're just assessed differently. I cannot prove this. But I feel like international students or people from non-Dutch backgrounds have the most interesting, thought provoking, roundabout ways of thinking about lived realities. But it seems the most simplistic way of structuring an essay is what will sway an examiner about what is deemed a good essay or not. It's like whether or not you have the structure of beginning, middle, and end done in a very particular academic jargon way like *that* is more important than the kind of ideas that you're trying to put forward or that you're trying to argue for.
>
> (S.C., 21:52)

It is not only non-Dutch students who are disadvantaged by the implicit standards of the 'ideal' student, but one student remarks that:

> If I didn't work round the clock, seven days a week for school, then I couldn't keep up. And it just didn't make sense to me. It was very demotivating for me seeing that. The only people who are quote unquote complaining or protesting about the way things were structured or being assessed were people of colour, and people who aren't from here.
>
> (S.C., 18:23)

For students, financial constraints are often related not only to the availability of financial funds, but also to other social circumstances that have to do with social and economic location and place of origin. For example, international students most of the time do not have a support network when they relocate to the Netherlands, and during their study, they have to negotiate logistic and emotional obstacles that render them more precarious. For example, in terms of housing or the limited available jobs that do not require fluency in Dutch or in learning to navigate the healthcare system, amongst other acculturation processes.

These material conditions affect how and how much time students can dedicate to focusing on studying, as such, it is the students who arrive from non-EU countries who usually face the toughest drawbacks (in general) and obstacles to being able to slow down. Higher tuition fees, scholarships dependent on getting a degree in a limited timeframe, the need to work but the impossibility of doing so on specific visa permits are all factors that make it unreasonable and unimaginable that those students would adopt strategies of slowing down. We have talked to several such non-EU and other international students, and we have heard many stories about their struggles to keep up with the university's speed and quantification of success. In the case of international students who get a student visa and financial support from the Dutch government, such financial help makes it impossible for them to slow down:

> I don't think people fully grasp or understand that if I do not have a certain number of credits every block, my visa status gets into question. I will no longer count as a full-time master's student, if I don't have a certain number of credit hours every month. And when I don't count as a full-time master student, that means I'm violating the terms of my visa. So that means that I have to be enrolled in a certain amount, at least, a certain amount of courses at all times, and thus submit those essays, then be re enrolled, just to fulfil that. I need to also perform productivity for the programme, but also for the government in order to stay in this country.
>
> (S.C., 19:25).

A similar situation occurs with students who need to work while studying to make a living: there is no possibility of slowing down because they need to work a specific number of hours per week to be eligible for and to retain the financial support provided by the government.

> For students who are working, you have to work certain amount of hours a week to get this help. And so, you have to be working *this* amount of hours. Imagine with the pandemic and all the changes in the possibility to work and stuff, so you can get the money, so you can keep studying. So, you can keep living here. So, it's a cycle of hell.
>
> (M., 1:07:04)

In all these cases we encounter the same challenge: if students are provided with financial support from the Dutch government to study and live in the Netherlands, they need to meet a fixed and non-negotiable target of quantifiable performance otherwise they lose such aid. Hence, while slowing down is acknowledged as desirable by many, the reality is that this is not viable for many of the students. The combination of governmental financial support and academic speed, operating by the same logic of capital investment and quantitative outcomes, makes it so that only those with personal or family monetary means, who can afford the tuition fees and the expenses of living in the Netherlands, have the possibility of slowing down.

As if academic speed were not already overwhelming, students of colour and students who 'are not from here' face academic disadvantages, which results in the need to spend even more time on managing and surviving the system. More interviews and more examples would be needed to highlight all the other differences among students and all the other social inequalities that mark a student as 'not fitting in', not being 'from here'. With this chapter and these examples, we aimed at pointing out some of the ways in which the speed of the university – as core to neoliberal rationality – is not only unbearable to many, but it further heightens inequalities, benefitting those who are closest to the 'ideal' subject imagined by the university and making it harder for everyone else to stay and thrive.

Conclusion

This chapter presented some of the voices and reflections we have encountered in our research so far about the normative, neoliberal logic of the university in terms of speeds and time management and the consequences such norms have for students and teachers. During this project, we came to realize there is one overarching problem that coexists with the academic norms of speed and efficiency and that has not yet been explicitly addressed here: the discriminations and exclusions the neoliberal university (re)produces have become normalised, taken for granted, made uninteresting. The pressures and expectations put on students and teachers – that we have outlined in this chapter – have not improved in recent years; the burnouts and dropouts keep repeating every year, and so do our struggles.

Consequently, such challenging working/studying conditions and their consequences have become the foundation of academic life, and that foundation has been normalised, made routine, made invisible, and left unaddressed. This normalisation makes it easier to approach those frictions and struggles with a cynical perspective. From the teachers' perspective, we often hear students' difficulties being normalised; sentences such as 'students are having a hard time, yes, we know, and we know their struggles' are regularly heard in meetings and corridors. Even among colleagues and peers we hear phrases such as: 'being overworked is part of the deal', 'teachers are burned out, we know, we are all burned out'.

Our interviews with students and teachers made clear, we hope, that the damaging effects of university norms and speed need to be acknowledged and challenged. Right now, it is often the teachers who practice pedagogies of care that do the job that the institutions are neglecting. However, this is neither fair nor sustainable. It is unethical to put on those who already have a lot of responsibilities – and often those who carry the burden of economic and social precarity – the added responsibility of caring and trying to solve structural institutional problems. Because care labour is unpaid in our society, teachers do not get extra money, nor extra time, nor structural recognition, for caring. Equally, as a student, you do not receive any form of recognition for the extra labour done to 'overcome' structural problems and perform as the 'ideal' student is expected to. Even if recognition is not the only goal, nor the solution, the consequences of this lack of acknowledgement are felt and must be addressed in terms of restructuring and redistribution.

While plenty of what the interviewees have told us resonates with what other scholars have written about, this project made it clear to us that there is a need for people in the university, in specific geopolitical contexts, and from their situated knowledges, to tell their embodied, affective stories. Identifying the tensions and failures of the neoliberal university through scholars who have analysed the mechanisms and possible solutions to them is crucial, but maybe not enough. It runs the risk of forgetting the specificities of those who, every year anew, are faced with the same challenges and do not yet have the language to talk about them. It also runs the risk of forgetting to take seriously new stories and new lived experiences, in the name of 'we know this already'. It is a feminist practice of care, and the starting point of possible new collective strategies of resistance and refusal, to make space for, and listen to, people's experiences and embodied stories. If we stop doing this, we run the risk of, once again, treating students as numbers: the student as a known entity that struggles homogeneously and predictably and that, like many other similar entities before, will equally survive the university logic and speed ... if they learn to 'fit in'.

As a step in a broader project, instead of immediately trying to find strategies to slow down (in) academia, what we are proposing here is that there is a need for students' stories to be heard, acknowledged, and shared with teachers. And although the stories in this article are not 'the worst-case scenario', and are also not exemplary, they are definitely not exceptional. Finally, 'slowing down' for us, while doing this project, meant not only collaborating – a teacher and a student – but listening, acknowledging, and validating each other's struggles while working together. Most importantly, 'slowing down' meant creating a space for people within the university, specifically students, to address their discomfort, struggles, disappointments, and frustrations, and for us to listen, and take them seriously. In doing so, we also wish to contribute to imagining and plotting new feminist and critical strategies to live (in) the university, if not to refuse and undo what the neoliberal university is and does altogether.

References

Berg, M., and Seeber, B.K. (2016) *Slow Professor: Challenging the Culture of Speed in the Academy*. Toronto: University of Toronto Press.

Bourgault, S. (2016) 'Attentive listening and care in a neoliberal era: Weilian insights for hurried times'. *Etica & Politica / Ethics & Politics*, XVIII(3), pp. 311–337.

Bozalek, V. (2017) 'Slow scholarship in writing retreats: A diffractive methodology for response-able pedagogies'. *South African Journal of Higher Education*, 31(2), pp. 40–57. https://doi.org/10.20853/31-2-1344.

Bozalek, V., Zembylas, M., and Tronto, J. (2020) *Posthuman and Political Care Ethics for Reconfiguring Higher Education*. New York: Routledge.

Brown, W. (2011) 'Neoliberalized knowledge'. *History of the Present*, 1(1), pp. 113–129. https://doi.org/10.5406/historypresent.1.1.0113.

Brown, W. (2019) *In the Ruins of Neoliberalism: The Rise of Antidemocratic Politics in the West*. New York: Columbia University Press.

Couldry, N. and McRobbie, A. (2010) 'The death of the university, English style'. *Culture Machine*. Available at: https://culturemachine.net/interzone/death-of-the-university-couldry-mcrobbie/.

DeVault, M.L. and Gross, G. (2012) Feminist qualitative interviewing: Experience, talk, and knowledge. in: S.N. Hesse-Biber (Ed.) *Handbook of Feminist Research: Theory and Praxis*. 2nd Ed. Thousand Oaks: Sage.

Fleming, P. (2021) *Dark Academia: How Universities Die*. London: Pluto Press.

Gatenby, B. and Humphries, M. (2000) 'Feminist participatory action research: Methodological and ethical issues'. *Women's Studies International Forum*, 23(1), pp. 89–105.

Gill, R. (2017) Beyond individualism: The psychosocial life of the neoliberal university, in: M. Spooner (Ed.) *A Critical Guide to Higher Education & the Politics of Evidence: Resisting Colonialism, Neoliberalism, & Audit Culture*. Regina: University of Regina Press.

Harney, S. and Moten, F. (2013) *The Undercommons: Fugitive Planning & Black Study*. Wivenhoe: Minor Compositions.

Hartman, Y. and Darab, S. (2012) 'A call for slow scholarship: A case study on the intensification of academic life and its implications for pedagogy', *Review of Education, Pedagogy, and Cultural Studies*, 34(1–2), pp. 49–60. https://doi.org/10.1080/10714413.2012.643740.

Lynch, K. (2006) 'Neo-liberalism and marketisation: The implications for higher education'. *European Educational Research Journal*, 5(1), pp. 1–17. https://doi-org.proxy.library.uu.nl/10.2304/eerj.2006.5.1.1.

Lynch, K. (2021) *Care and Capitalism*. Hoboken: John Wiley & Sons.

Lynch, K., Grummell, B., and Devine, D. (2012) *New Managerialism in Education: Commercialization, Carelessness and Gender*. London:Palgrave Macmillan.

Liamputtong, Pranee (2010). *Performing Qualitative Cross-Cultural Research*. New York: Cambridge University Press.

Loher, D., Strasser, S., and Stoica, G. (2019) 'Politics of precarity: neoliberal academia under austerity measures and authoritarian threat', *Social Anthropology/Anthropologie Sociale*, 27(S2), pp. 3–117.

Luhmann, S. (1988) Queering/Querying pedagogy? Or, pedagogy is a pretty queer thing, in: F.P. William (Ed.) *Queer Theory in Education*. Mahwah: L. Erlbaum Associates, pp. 141–155.

Mountz, A., Bonds, A., Mansfield, B., Loyd, J., and Hyndman, J. (2015) 'For slow scholarship: A feminist politics of resistance through collective action in the neoliberal university'. *ACME: An International Journal for Critical Geographies* 14 (4), pp. 1235–1259.

O'Neill, M. (2014) 'The slow university: Work, time and well-being'. *Forum: Qualitative Social Research* 15(3). https://doi.org/10.17169/fqs-15.3.2226.

Olivieri, D. (2022) 'Slowness as a mode of attention and resistance: Playing with time in documentary cinema and disturbing the rhythms of the neoliberal university'. *Contention*, 10(1), pp. 99–114. https://doi.org/10.3167/cont.2022.100108.

Readings, B. (1997) *The University in Ruins*. Cambridge, MA: Harvard University Press.

Slaughter, S. and Rhoades, G. (2000) 'The Neo-Liberal University'. *New Labor Forum*, 6, pp. 73–79.

Slaughter, S. and Rhoades, G. (2004) *Academic Capitalism and the New Economy: Markets, State, and Higher Education*. Baltimore: JHU Press.

Thiele, K., Górska, M., and Türer, P. (2020) Relation(al) matters: Vulnerable pedagogies, care and carriance as (c)air-ful(l)ness in higher education, in: B. Bozalek, M. Zembylas, and J.C. Tronto (Eds) *Posthuman and Political Care Ethics for Reconfiguring Higher Education Pedagogies*. New York: Routledge, pp. 51–65.

Universities of The Netherlands (2020) 'Universities take concerns over work pressure seriously'. Available at: https://www.universiteitenvannederland.nl/en_GB/2020-werk druk-ictu.html.

Utibe, T. (2020) 'Impacts of interview as research instrument of data collection in social sciences'. *Journal of Digital Art & Humanities* 1(1), pp. 15–24. https://doi.org/10.33847/2712-8148.1.1_2.

Wright S. and Shore C. *(2019) Death of the Public University?: Uncertain Futures for Higher Education in the Knowledge Economy*. New York; Oxford: Berghahn Books.

11 Feminist Teaching Practice as Drawing from Oneself

Combining Knowledge, Care and Lived Experiences in the University

Diana Fernández Romero

Introduction

When thinking of teaching, hooks proposes that 'teaching is a performative act' (1994, p. 11); the work of teachers, she points out, should serve as a catalyst to call all involved actors to commit themselves and participate more and more actively in learning. This chapter critically reflects on how teaching at university level needs to open up to feminist pedagogical approaches to disrupt the linear ways in which knowledge is constructed. Returning to hooks (1994), the role of educators is extended into the realm of the social, beyond teaching as instrument or teaching as dissemination of knowledge; hooks argues, 'professors who embrace the challenge of self-actualization will be better able to create pedagogical practices that engage students, providing them with ways of knowing that enhance their capacity to live fully and deeply' (1994, p. 22). Following this call by hooks to challenge the reduction of educators to instruments of knowledge, this chapter explores how feminist pedagogies can contribute to teaching at university level and re-sensitise both students and educators to the ways in which knowledge construction is political and characterised by imbalances of power.

For Manicom (1992), one of the challenges of feminist pedagogy is the transformation of the ways of knowing and acting in/on the world. She especially values attempts to pay attention to experience, to foster collaborative forms of learning, and to reduce relations of authority in the classroom: 'Nonetheless, these practices are full of complexities and contradictions, and must be challenged and deconstructed if the political project of feminism is to be advanced' (Manicom, 1992, p. 366). In her article, the author ponders what a standpoint of feminist pedagogy might be. In this regard, she proposes 'that we ask ourselves the following: "Is what I am doing as teacher enhancing our capacity for transformative practice? In my particular circumstances, what kind of teaching and learning has the most potential to develop a collective capacity to engage in transformative feminist practice?"' (Manicom, 1992, p. 383). Thus, feminist pedagogies refer to both a particular philosophy and a set of classroom teaching practices, informed by feminist theories, based on the principles of feminism, and concerned with what, how, and why we teach and the repercussions of what we teach (Crabtree, Sapp, and Licona, 2009).

DOI: 10.4324/9781003397502-11

However, putting feminist theory into practice in the classroom poses pedagogical challenges and dilemmas (Crabtree and Snapp, 2003; Bustillos Morales and Zarabadi, 2024). Haraway's (1995) position on the need for learning in our bodies argues in favour of situated and embodied knowledge over various forms of irresponsible and unsituated knowledge statements. 'Occupying a place implies responsibility in our practices', affirms Haraway (1995, p. 333). In her 'Politics of Location', Adrienne Rich (1994) insists on a location that is political, not neutral, that cannot be separated from its context of production. In this regard, Haraway (1995) points out that 'regardless of the type of method used, no knowledge is detached from its context or from the subjectivity of the issuer' (p. 346). Questions therefore arise from a decolonial feminist pedagogy concerning what privileges are and how they enable us to 'speak' and 'listen' (Cariño et al., 2017, p. 509). From this perspective, Cerda Monje proposes naming the teacher as an 'agitator of experiences' and as a 'cartographer' whom she locates in the shipwreck 'of intuitive, corporeal, ancestral, experiential knowledge' (2020, p. 45). The author advocates learning methods that attend to the diversity of contexts in which 'experience agitators work, affect and engage' (Cerda Monje, 2020, p. 46).

Stemming from these theoretical reflections, in practice, this chapter proposes to introduce 'feminist pedagogies' in the university by intervening both in course design and in pedagogy itself. With regard to design, one should consider how to critically review competencies; how to develop content and provide models, theories, and examples that address diversity; what bibliography and sources to establish to improve the visibility of female knowledge; what language to use to be inclusive. In terms of teaching practices, we must attend to the relations we promote inside and outside the classroom so as not to reproduce inequalities and to facilitate integration; what the dynamics of participation that favour a critical view are; how we articulate the use of space to be inclusive; whether or not we intervene in the composition of work groups so that the students feel comfortable and free to work and express their ideas; how we design the lecture sessions so that a relationship framework is established where there is empathy and exchange of experiences.

This chapter narrates some of the processes in the creation of basic categories of a rubric designed for two editions of a workshop on the introduction of gendered perspective in university teaching. This rubric was drawn up so that educators could evaluate the Teaching and Curricular Guidelines of their courses from a feminist perspective. Based on the approaches developed above, the professors assessed the following components of their courses: 'Competencies', 'Content Development', 'Forms of Relation', 'Bibliography and Sources', and 'Utilisation of Inclusive Language'. Participants then scored these components following their consideration of gender equality: 'No consideration', 'Some consideration', and 'Comprehensive consideration'. For each of the categories, the participants were asked to contribute reflections and proposals that were shared in the second session of the workshop, which we will present in this chapter.

Methodological Framework

The chapter echoes the collective reflection of 82 university professors who have participated in two editions of the workshop within the permanent training plan for teachers at the Rey Juan Carlos University (Madrid, Spain). The first edition, which brought together 36 attendees, took place in May and June 2021 and was entitled 'Introduction of the Gender Perspective in University Teaching'. The second, in which 46 teachers participated, was called 'Gender Perspective in Teaching: Revision of Teaching Guides' and was carried out in June 2023. The participating professors were from different academic ranks and areas of knowledge, including Psychology, Computer Science, Statistics, Architecture, Economics, Communication, Arts and Humanities, History, Design, Law, Biology, International Relations, Physiotherapy, Occupational Therapy, Language and Literature, Mathematics, Education Sciences, Electronic Technology, and Sign Language, among others. Both editions had similar dynamics: the workshop consisted of two 1.5-hour sessions in two consecutive weeks.

In the first week, participants worked on concepts of feminist theory and pedagogies and the evaluation rubric was presented. This tool proposes, from a feminist critical perspective, reflection on design and pedagogical practices through the revision of the Teaching Guides of the different classes. Thus, teachers were invited to work, over the following week, with the rubric, to examine their syllabi, and to express their concerns and proposals, which served as the basis for a collaborative meeting held in a second session. As noted, in terms of course design, the evaluated components included: competencies, content development, bibliography and sources, and use of inclusive language. Regarding teaching practices, forms of relationship, dynamics of participation, and interactions inside and outside the classroom were reviewed.

In practice, this resulted in two enriching encounters in which professors actively participated in the reorganisation of content, reflection on the concepts, and models and theories we handle, as well as the introduction of new cases, practical examples, and reference sources. For part of the workshop, teachers were invited to demonstrate the silencing of feminist knowledge in different fields (Mora and Pujal, 2009). Similarly, the emotions, affects, experiences, and care practices of everyday teaching in the context of universities were put in dialogue with the differentiation proposed by Izquierdo et al. (2008, p. 17):

> Care is a type of social relationship that is characterized by the action of satisfying the needs of one person by another, being the end of the action and where the face-to-face interaction between caregiver and caregiver is a crucial element in the whole activity. The need is of such a nature that there is no possibility that it can be met by the person being cared for. Providing refers to that type of relationship aimed at achieving objectives, where the purpose is to obtain something, with little attention to the impact that one's own activities have on others. Relationships with people acquire an instrumental character.

It is interesting to note these distinctions between providing and caring, where actions of providing, associated with masculinity, are encouraged above all while caring activities, symbolically linked to femininity, were reported by educators as remaining in the background. In line with these reflections, and in light of feminist pedagogies, a rethinking of the types of actions, practices, and relationships emerged to reflect on what we want to promote and weave into Higher Education.

To approach the testimonies collected in the practices of both workshops as captured in the evaluation rubrics, we utilise Critical Discourse Analysis (CDA) which, as Van Dijk (1999) points out, mainly addresses the way in which the abuse of power, dominance, and inequality 'are practiced, reproduced, and occasionally combated, by texts and speech in the social and political context' (p. 23). We are interested, in this specific case, in approaching the processes of construction of gender discourses and thus taking into account the relationship between dominant and consensual discourses on the one hand and those that resist them on the other (Núñez Puente and Fernández Romero, 2022). We attend to gender discourses that, in their connection with the social, contribute to constituting social structures and in turn are constituted by them (Núñez Puente and Fernández Romero, 2022). By studying the narratives of the participating faculty, we participate in the reflection on the tensions that make up the discourses on gender and how these are contextualised in social practices conditioning their possible transformation (West, Lazar, and Kramarae, 2000).

Feminist Pedagogies, Embodiment and Practice in Relationships

Putting the educational relationship at the centre implies mediating knowledge with the students, entering into their languages, social imaginaries, world views, and, finally, their systems of meaning. From this perspective, the classroom is configured as a space for the constant exchange of knowledge, experiences, and ways of understanding and being in the world. This also implies, however, a continued awareness of the power dynamics that this 'ideal' model of mediation does not escape. As Luke (1992, p. 22) clarifies, the selection, interpretation, and evaluation of all knowledge 'constitute the basic relations of exchange between teacher and student, which are fundamentally immersed, although institutionally limited, in the intersubjective relations of authority, desire, power, and control'. In this regard, Giroux points out that education goes beyond creating an autonomous and critical populace: 'it also appeals to self-reflection and the ability to question power' (2018, p. 9). Therefore, education is crucially about learning how to exercise our own voice as we understand how to speak to power and how power works, particularly in knowledge construction and knowledge instruction. This is how feminist scholarship and feminist pedagogies have been used to provide a tangible framework that educators within the university context can use, not just to be introduced to feminist pedagogies, but more importantly, to reflect on how its inherent challenge to power can reconfigure classroom culture and knowledge creation.

Similar to hooks (1994) and also stemming from a critical pedagogical perspective, Freire (1982) asserts that 'education must begin by overcoming the educator–learner contradiction. It must be based on the reconciliation of its poles, in such a way that both become, simultaneously, educators and learners' (p. 52). In his critique of the 'banking' concept of education, Freire rejects the idea of educating as 'the act of depositing, transferring, transmitting values and knowledge' (1982, p. 52). In this paradigm, 'the educator is the subject of the process; the learners, mere objects' (Freire, 1982, p. 53). If the intention of education is to promote transformation as opposed to adaptation, stimulate criticality, and encourage the creative power of learners, then it would not make sense to conceive the task of the educator as simply giving, delivering, or transmitting her knowledge. If this were the case, according to Freire, this knowledge would cease to come from a 'realized experience to be the knowledge of narrated or transmitted experience' (Freire, 1982, p. 53). Therefore, it is especially important to put oneself into relation, bringing one's own lived experiences and wisdom into contact with those of the students. That is, to 'listen, grant importance, and help bring to light what each student is and wants, with their own experiences and peculiarities' (Hernández Morales, 2001, p. 31). A tall order in a large university.

These proposals involve moving towards a model in which formation provokes doubts, dilemmas, concerns, and insecurities in educational actors; but at the same time, provokes an openness to creation and new manners and possibilities of teaching and learning. In the higher education sector, feminist pedagogies have been discussed as highlighting the 'heteroglossia of pedagogy ... to create a collaborative and liberatory environment' (Bustillos Morales, 2021, p. 216). Feminist pedagogies can be a crucial step in dissolving the traditional power relationships that characterise teaching and learning in university contexts. Similar to Bustillos Morales (2021), this chapter proposes that educators must 'offer students in-class opportunities to negotiate the usual power relationships that characterise traditionalistic pedagogies' (p. 213). Yet, it remains challenging for educators to understand how this could happen in classroom practice, and so this chapter draws from feminist and critical pedagogies to hold a more collaborative and collegiate conversation and introduce pedagogical transformations across faculties.

The project introducing feminist pedagogies centred on Freire's (1982) argument that the basis for pedagogical action is 'dialogue' as an 'existential requirement' (p. 101). This dialogue cannot take place in a context of despair, as Freire points out, because 'if the subjects of dialogue expect nothing from their work, there can no longer be dialogue. Their encounter there is empty and sterile. It is bureaucratic and annoying' (Freire, 1982, p. 106). Holding dialogue through a feminist pedagogy can help educators navigate the complexities of classroom interactions and relationships with students to activate the 'ever-vigilant' in our pedagogical practices (hooks, 1994, p. 86), beyond the institutional apparatus. In this way, feminist pedagogies have been conceptualised and used in the project as a way of recognising the diversity of knowledge, experiences, or ways of feeling that imply the need to de-patriarchalise and de-colonise education (Martínez Martín and Ramírez Artiaga, 2017, p. 85).

Specifically, the 'intersectional feminist pedagogies', according to Troncoso Pérez, Follegati, and Stutzin (2019) refer to pedagogical practices that address social inequalities and power relations from an intersectional approach 'encompassing a wide range of critical black, decolonial, post-structuralist feminist and queer/*cuir* sexual dissidence debates, which allow resisting the depoliticization and (neo)liberalization of feminist demands' (p. 6). Lugones (2005), on the other hand, points to a shift from the logic of oppression to that of resistance in the movement towards a radical multiculturalism of the feminisms of Women of Colour (p. 61).

In line with feminist pedagogies, 'the voices/bodies of those who resist patriarchy and place the relationship between oppressions on the scene' inscribe themselves in this way of understanding feminist pedagogies (Ortega and Villa, 2021, p. 147). Thus, the embodiment of educators becomes an essential part of change, it goes beyond dialogue to incorporate 'the order of the political, the ethical, the cultural, the symbolic and the affective' (Ortega and Villa, 2021, p. 150). This entails, a politicising of education and denouncing, as political subjects, the false neutrality of the neoliberal and academic educational system that brings with it 'a masking of male domination, sexism, patriarchy and ableism where the student—and teacher—are disembodied' (Ortega and Villa, 2021, p. 155). Feminist pedagogical practices imply, on the contrary, bringing lived experience into the classroom that allows teaching from the proximity of problems by allowing them to pass 'through our pains, joys, feelings, through the skin itself' (Ortega and Villa, 2021, p. 154). This would be an exercise in commitment and passion. Following Russell (1997), the true aim of the teaching is 'to *empassion* students with feminist knowledge' (pp. 57–58). In the words of hooks (1994, p. 193):

> those of us who have been intimately engaged as students or teachers with feminist thinking have always recognized the legitimacy of a pedagogy that dares to subvert the mind/body split and allow us to be whole in the classroom, and as a consequence wholehearted.

Feminist praxis thus challenges the sexism adhering to pedagogical practices by promoting the inclusion of the affective in teaching–learning processes (Vázquez Verdera, 2010, p. 180). Giving saliency to feminist pedagogy also involves critical reflections on educators' and students' embodiment, namely that embodiment can reappear as affective in teaching and learning (Hernández, 2006). Valuing the feelings and emotions, relational capacities, knowledge and experiences of educators and students, and the knowledge associated with care implies creating a new school culture that displaces the centrality of knowledge and labour traditionally considered masculine (Solsona, 2008). 'By making our experiences speak – feelings, contradictions, desires – we make the world speak', according to Piussi (2000, p. 110), an important factor in identifying and troubling unequal relations of power in education.

Conesa (2018) asserts that the new managerial model of science and its focus on productivity invokes the figure of a disembodied 'ideal academic' In that context, Conesa (2018) reflects, the 'ethics of care' approach places care at the centre of life, interacting with the notion in a political and philosophical way (See also, Tronto, 1993).

> An ethics of care perspective supports ideas of interdependency and vulnerability. As an analytical approach, it offers the possibility to display and study the genderedness of care across its multiple layers: personal, collective, familial, at the workplace, at decision-making level, within institutions, etc.
>
> (Conesa, 2018)

To be precise, sharing vulnerabilities and concerns in the teaching–learning process in the academy within the framework of an ethics of care is articulated as a strategy to counteract the individualism promoted by neoliberalism in higher education (Rogowska-Strangret, 2019).

In accordance with Pié Balaguer, care 'should take center stage in the act of educational transmission' (2019, p. 105). However, Western culture 'has repressed and excluded care that relates to flows, differences, transitory boundaries, contingency, motherhood, etc' (Pié Balaguer, 2019, p. 105). This repression of care in the figure of the educator in university contexts reduces the educator and classroom dynamics to a rational and transactional exchange, where the educator–student relationship is coopted by institutional processes of monitoring, standardisation and repetition. Counteracting it would imply including 'epistemologies and values associated with the personal and the affective' (Vázquez Verdera, 2010, p. 180) in a teaching as a 'collective and embodied' (López, 2022, p. 304), 'relational practice' (Noddings, 2003, p. 241). As Maceira Ochoa indicates: 'Feminist pedagogy is a pedagogy of subjectivity, autonomy, transgression, being what one wants to be, of inventing oneself' (2008, p. 194). This pedagogy, López adds 'is an opening to new and better ways of imagining collective life' (2022, p. 305). A feminist pedagogy that wrestles with these limits of teaching and learning practice and the usual rationalising embodiments of the educator can generate 'teaching that enables transgressions—a movement against and beyond boundaries. It is that movement which makes education the practice of freedom', as hooks posits (1994, p. 12).

Incorporating the practice of drawing from oneself into teaching, bringing knowledge, learning, experiences, doubts, relationships, emotions, and so on, into the classroom is a relational feminist political practice that is not identified with the bureaucratic codes of rules and power (Piussi, 2000, p. 109). It is, however, a revolutionary praxis that involves speaking in the first person and expressing oneself from one's sexual difference (Montoya Ramos, 2010, pp. 142–143). This positioning is linked to the act of centring educational relationship, being in the classroom with the greatest authority and the least power (Montoya Ramos, 2010, p. 143).

As Luke (1992, p. 22) points out, 'feminist pedagogy' rejects traditional authority and power in the relationship between teacher and student 'and instead demands the establishment of pedagogical encounters characterised by cooperation, sharing, support and giving voice to the silenced'. This, according to Gore (1993, in Luke and Gore, 1993, p. 67), points to how the feminist classroom is marked 'by the rhetoric of freedom, not control'. However, Luke discovers that, in these 'alleged spaces of freedom, the authority of the teacher is frequently disapproved of and, as a rule, the sexual politics of institutionally authorised female authority and power are not debated or questioned'. According to Cigarini, the feminine authority of women in the workplace is rooted in the female difference, 'because, it is said, women have one *additional* competence: the relational one' (Cigarini in Rivera Garretas, 2009, p. 188, emphasis in original). In this regard, García Dauder (2011) brings to the debate how some young female teachers are forced to 'act', especially in their first classes, in order to be respected. That is: to 'disembody' their way of being in the classroom and adopt a masculinised posture of exercising authority. As Crabtree, Sapp, and Licona (2009) explain, in the context of the feminist classroom this issue remains problematic because of the different layers of complexity surrounding the authority of women to teach or the ways in which the student body challenges the authority of female teachers.

In his article 'Authority', Bauer (1990) encourages thinking about authority as an emancipatory strategy. Similarly, Hernández Morales (2001, p. 26) proposes an interesting path on how to spread authority even in the face of the logics of power:: 'the authority to teach is not given to me by being a speaker, not even by knowing much about this or that subject, but by the fact that my students recognise that I have something to contribute to them, something I am willing to exchange. And, in addition, for my ability to recognise what they have and do not have, to give them the floor and be interested in listening'.

It is precisely feminist pedagogy that emphasises the epistemological validity of personal experience, often related to notions of voice and authority: 'Through a critique of the ways traditional scientific and academic inquiry have ignored or negated the lived experiences of women, feminist pedagogy acknowledges personal, communal, and subjective ways of knowing as valid forms of inquiry and knowledge production' (Crabtree, Sapp, and Licona, 2009, p. 7).

Situated Knowledge to Rethink Pedagogical Design and Practices in the University

With the participation of teachers of Higher Education in a theoretical-practical workshop to review university Teaching and Curricular Guidelines, the author aimed to identify and problematise the construction of discourses, normative systems, and forms of subjectivity that contribute to the production and reproduction of inequalities in the educational context of the university. Starting with the premise that 'education for critical consciousness can fundamentally alter our perceptions of reality and our actions' (hooks, 1994, p. 195), the notion of situated knowledge (Haraway, 1995), together with an intersectional gaze, was a generative step. Haraway appeals to learning through our bodies and advocates a doctrine of 'embodied objectivity' (1995, p. 324) that accommodates paradoxical and critical feminist science projects. Her idea connects with an embodied and affective pedagogy that emphasises the pleasure of teaching as an act of resistance (hooks, 2017). This resistance, from an intersectional proposal, implies a political commitment to take into account the situated experiences of the subjects 'produced outside the sex-generic norm and racial, ethnic and class hegemony, among others' (Troncoso Pérez, Follegati, and Stutzin, 2019, p. 11). This fusion of notions helped to reveal and combat the hidden curriculum that is inscribed in the design and implementation of courses in a very bureaucratised university environment.

Precisely in this context, a teacher expressed her reluctance and self-censorship when taking a feminist critical perspective in the face of an environment that was hostile and not always welcoming of these proposals:

> In the classes, I incorporate a critical spirit with an androcentric vision in the world of art and visual culture, but I recognise that I feel a certain fear of expressing the feminist perspective in an explicit way in the teaching guide. The reticence of which I am aware daily around me slows me down, although I know that, in turn, they give it meaning. That is why it is so necessary, not only to learn, but to create spaces of support and make visible and meet other people who are working in the same direction.

Regarding competencies, both general and specific, the rubric encouraged the application of a feminist perspective that would allow us to question to what extent competency design contributes to mitigating or sustaining sexism. Although lecturers have little room for intervention in this area, given that the competencies are predesigned for the different subjects, the exercise led to debate on their apparent neutrality in a patriarchal curricular design typical of the neoliberal university. Among the proposals that were formulated were the need to 'liberate' the imposed competencies and promote the inclusion of cognitive, attitudinal, or instrumental competencies related to the ability to analyse different themes from the feminist and gender perspective. The competency that, in the lecturers' opinion, best fits this purpose is the ability to reason critically and practise self-criticism. In this regard, a lecturer raised the necessity of specifying how to articulate and promote that awareness among students so that it does not remain an empty concept, saying, 'I would try to define more deeply what we mean when we talk about students having a perspective or a critical-analytical capacity'. In this sense, feminist pedagogies contribute to promoting awareness and critical praxis from the recognition of the complexity of relationships and power structures to promote social transformation (Troncoso Pérez, Follegati, and Stutzin, 2019). Particularly stimulating in this context was the initiative of a biology professor who, from an intersectional position, shared that although she could not apply the gender perspective to classroom competencies, in her field she believed it was necessary to promote reflection on the fact that 'all the experiments we see have been carried out with hetero-normative groups of white people. At least having that space for reflection can contribute to mitigating sexism'.

Another of the axes of analysis was linked to self-reflection on the selection of models and theories that explain the phenomena discussed in the classroom. As a group we reflected, both individually and collectively, on whether these materials and the use of examples drive reflections and actions to change the sexist and androcentric conception of being in the world or if they attend to prevention and awareness of sexist discourses across various disciplines. As Haraway (1995) states, modern theories about how meanings and bodies are created allow us not to deny them but to live in meanings and bodies that have opportunity in the future. This idea is reflected in the initiative of a professor of Arts and Humanities to 'not just give examples of women artists' in her classes, but also to incorporate "works in which the discourse breaks with stereotypes". [To] show works made by women, but also those that provide new forms of plastic and conceptual expression, other ways of seeing and understanding the world'. The professors – both male and female – highlighted here the necessity to review course manuals in order to promote the critical review of their contents and thus mediate the pre-existing perceptions of students. The idea of including topics in the curricula that question patriarchal and heteronormative visions was highlighted, with one participant stating:

> I think it is important to avoid 'gender biases' in each subject: not to be carried away by the androcentric inertia of the syllabus (to take for granted a male subject, both as a subject of knowledge and as an object), which does not attend to the particular situation of women but overlooks or undervalues it.

At the same time, it was decided to address intersectionality, to take into account the processes of gender socialisation and to introduce the issue of inequality and power relations into the classroom. In terms of student evaluation, a professor pointed out the importance of 'analysing in a concrete way if the assignments meet the objectives of visibility of reproductive work on an equal footing with productive ones'.

The portion addressing the bibliography and sources was aimed at discerning whether or not the Subject Guidelines provide materials and resources to balance the number of women and men authors in the references and whether female knowledge and experiences are incorporated to recognise their authority. In this regard, Manicom (1992) remarks that the 'attention to women's experiences is a cornerstone of feminist pedagogy' (p. 370). She concludes that 'the feminist claim has been that many women (both teachers and students) have to (re)learn to value concrete, subjective knowledge, and that the academy must be challenged in its consistent devaluing of such knowledge' (Manicom, 1992, p. 370).

After reviewing subject guides, a professor showed her surprise at seeing that the guide for her subject 'overlooks the presence of women as producers of knowledge'. At this point, the faculty agreed that the vast majority of the textbooks they utilise are written by men. From this introspection and subsequent conversation, interesting commitments emerged, such as: incorporating full first names in bibliographies to make female authorship visible; make an effort to find and add relevant references by women or involving women; incorporate female references in statements of exercises and texts provided to students. One teacher expressed her proposal for the following year after reviewing her guide: 'I will include assignments that aren't from a manual but rather incorporate classic and current theoretical proposals'. In terms of involving students and encouraging classrooms to be democratic spaces in which students appropriate projects and conversations in class (Martin, 2017), a teacher pointed to the need to 'push students to look for bibliography related to the subject featuring women authors'.

In the rubric, teachers were also questioned about the use of inclusive language, gendered terms, or the use of neutral or impersonal expressions to avoid the generic masculine grammatical gender (unmarked use of the language in Spanish). They were also asked if, in their teaching practices, they try to grant similar value and respect to all people, attending to diversity and intersectionality and avoiding the use of gendered stereotypes in language in an attempt to decolonise and depatriarchalise the way in which we communicate. Cumes (cited in Cariño et al., 2017) brings up, with regard to black and indigenous women, Spivak's question about whether the subaltern can speak. Her answer is that we speak not only from our voices, but also through our silences and our bodies which, however, are not always attended to or interpreted: 'If knowledge is generated precisely by dialoguing with other truths, how will we do that, if our voice is annulled?' (Cariño et al., 2017, p. 519).

Despite some reluctance, almost all teachers agreed on the need to use inclusive language in guides and teaching materials. The argument also arose that students are sometimes more sensitive to inclusive language than teachers. We discussed which are the most appropriate resources and tools, such as the use of generic terms, using the female grammatical gender first when discussing gendered pairs, or directly applying the feminine grammatical as the generic default. An educator raised the need to choose where and when to include such interventions, and thus 'adapt the type of language to each context. In more resistant classes or groups, I do not always use an inclusive language at first, if that is going to be a barrier. I'll go little by little'.

Professors confessed their difficulties in incorporating inclusive language into classroom dialogue despite efforts to carry it out in written documents. In this context, they evidenced the need to break down the masculine grammatical gender and attend to the diversity of the students through practice, as related by one participant: 'At the beginning of the course I always ask them to tell me how they prefer me to address each one of them'.

The dialogue was especially enriching in terms of self-evaluation and listening to the forms of relation and dynamics of participation and interactions fostered in the classroom. The lecturers reflected on whether or not classroom activities and participation dynamics encourage students to take on any role within a small group regardless of gender, rather than reinforcing gendered stereotypes in terms of decision-making or mediation for consensus. Professors also reflected on power dynamics and authority in the classroom and on thinking of classrooms as spaces for dialogue and freedom.

In this framework, a professor sparked reflection through questions about the type of participation encouraged in the classroom, how students relate in the classroom, and if the degree of involvement is the same according to gender. The idiosyncrasies of some of the highly masculinised degrees led teachers to express their concerns about the attitudes and behaviours of students in these environments:

> The percentage of female students is much lower than that of men and they tend to be less participatory. In general, they have a very cautious attitude in their interventions and are much more insecure than their peers. When it comes to forming groups, it is common for the few women to group together.

Some of the proposed measures were to promote collective (self-)evaluation exercises on the attitudes developed after the completion of projects, taking into account, among other aspects, respect, the composition of the groups to consider diversity and promote horizontality, and the rotation of roles. Some teachers stressed the importance of considering error as a learning tool and claimed doubt to be legitimate in educational spaces of trust.

The lecturers reacted negatively to the fact that classes often focus more on technical aspects than aspects of interpretation and social reach. As an alternative, they proposed implementing methodologies in which 'empathy is the fundamental basis' or that 'give value to care work in the classroom or in teamwork', thus emphasising the relational. From this aspect, we meditated on the necessary analysis of gender differences in groups and launched ideas to think about the suitability of mixed-gender groups and to promote the exchange of roles 'to give all students a voice and confidence in their work even in the face of more dominant profiles in the classroom'. An educator pointed out the importance of mediating in class interventions to review 'the androcentric inertia of giving more credit to the male voice', as well as using reinforcements to compensate for the insecurities of the students, especially those who are more reluctant to participate publicly: 'Respect intervention times and manage rhythms and silences. Girls tend to have a harder time intervening, and if you provide more time they're more likely to do so'. Participants forwarded reflections about the body and emotions in teaching and also about the essential commitment to diversity. They exchanged questions about how to work on emotions that they perceive from students and about what to do about violence in the classroom or how to articulate desire, which can be a taboo subject in education.

In connection with this embodiment, participants addressed the importance of the faculty 'body' and its interaction with the students, attending to axes such as age, gender, race, accent, and so on. In this way, professors pointed to a more collective sense of corporeality in the light of a feminist pedagogy. For hooks (1994), 'most professors must practice being vulnerable in the classroom, being wholly present in mind, body, and spirit' (p. 21). By this she means taking the risk of bringing one's experiences to the debates in the classroom and accepting the challenge of self-actualisation, which, as we have written above, will encourage the involvement of students in their knowledge process (hooks, 1994, p. 22). The author considers it crucial that we learn to enter the classroom 'whole' and not as 'disembodied spirit' (hooks, 1994, p. 193).

In line with intersectional thinking, some participants supported the idea of the university being committed to diversity and generating open, diverse, free teaching reference models. In this regard, they raised doubts about how to handle the diversity of students in the classroom:

> ... there is the paradox in that we want to introduce/make visible issues of racism, ableism, but at the same time we can over-visualise or make vulnerable students that prefer to go unnoticed. 'Good intentions' may not take into account the particular needs of students.

Finally, the teachers asked themselves about how gender mobilises authority or trust in a patriarchal and particularly bureaucratised environment and what kind of practices and links to establish to promote respect and trust. In this sense, the challenge of making visible the 'extra affective work carried out by many women teachers outside the classroom' was put on the table as a commitment to be in relationship and thus give value to what each student brings with them.

Conclusion

The experience of teachers exposed to reviewing their teaching practice following the principles of *drawing from oneself* reveals the importance of incorporating the resources and questions contributed by feminist critical pedagogies to put themselves into play in the classroom, outside the patriarchal and colonial gaze.

Confronting the established order and proposing alternative pedagogies in Higher Education is possible if we understand teaching as a relational practice that allows us to filter that which we exchange in the classroom through our bodily and lived experiences. Activating empathy and emphasising care promotes attending to the diversity of world views that are interwoven in the classroom and respecting the diverse voices of the students and the demands placed on them. Affective work, which is an extra burden for women teachers, nevertheless comes into play with authority and power. A feminist classroom incorporates relational practices to articulate other ways of understanding authority, which resides not so much in the transmission of knowledge, but in the ability to create spaces of tolerance, collaboration, creativity, and freedom.

This ethical-political positioning that is linked to self-actualisation (hooks, 1994) tries to engage students by speaking in the first person, promoting listening and valuing knowledge that goes beyond the actions of providing. This involves an exercise of commitment and passion on the part of those of us who are teachers that must activate an intersectional look at languages, references, models. Moving beyond theory and into practice is part of the performative act that is teaching, in which the dialogue with one's lived experience contributes to transformation, promotes criticality, and fosters creative power in education.

References

Bailyn, L. (2003) 'Academic careers and gender equity: Lessons learned from MIT'. *Gender, Work & Organization*, 10(2), pp. 137–153.

Bauer, D.M. (1990) 'Authority'. *NWSA Journal*, 3(1), pp. 95–97.

Bustillos Morales, J. (2021) 'De-territorialisations for pedagogical co-creation: Challenging traditionalistic pedagogies with students in higher education'. *Journal of University Teaching & Learning Practice*, 18(7), pp. 214–227. doi:10.53761/1.18.7.13.

Bustillos Morales, J. A. and Zarabadi, S. (2024) *Towards Posthumanism in Education: Theoretical Entanglements and Pedagogical Mappings*. London: Routledge.

Cariño, C., Cumes, A., Curiel, O., Garzón, M. T., Mendoza, B., Ochoa, K., and Londoño, A. (2017) Pensar, sentir y hacer pedagogías feministas descoloniales: diálogos y puntadas, in: C. Walsh (Ed.) *Pedagogías decoloniales. Prácticas insurgentes de resistir, (re)existir y (re) vivir*. Tomo II. Serie Pensamiento Decolonial. Quito: Abya Yala, pp. 509–536.

Cerda Monje, C. (2020) 'Re-existencias pedagógicas. Reflexiones sobre la corporalidad en la práctica pedagógica desde una aproximación decolonial'. *Trenzar. Revista de Educación Popular, Pedagogía Crítica e Investigación Militante*, 4(2), pp. 31–51.

Conesa, E. (2018) 'How are academic lives sustained? Gender and the ethics of care in the neoliberal accelerated academy'. *LSE Impact Blog*, 27 March. Available at: https://blogs.lse.ac.uk/impactofsocialsciences/2018/03/27/how-are-academic-lives-sustained-gender-and-the-ethics-of-care-in-the-neoliberal-accelerated-academy/ (Accessed 3 July 2023).

Crabtree, R., Sapp, D., and Licona, A. (2009) Introduction: The passion and the praxis of feminist pedagogy, in: R. Crabtree, D. Sapp and A. Licona (Eds) *Feminist Pedagogy: Looking Back to Move Forward*. Baltimore: Johns Hopkins University Press.

Crabtree, R. and Sapp, D. (2003) 'Theoretical, Political, and Pedagogical Challenges in the Feminist Classroom: Our Struggles to "Walk the Walk"'. *College Teaching*, 51(4), pp. 131–140.

Freire, P. (1982) *Pedagogía del Oprimido*. México: Siglo Veintiuno Editores.

García Dauder, S. (2011) *Proyecto Docente e Investigador. Psicología Social. Especialidad en Género*. Madrid: Universidad Rey Juan Carlos.

Giroux, H. (2018) Prólogo, in: B. Evans, S.M. Wilson, and A. Useros Martín (Eds) *Retratos de la Violencia. Una historia ilustrada del pensamiento radical*. Madrid: Akal, pp. 7–13.

Gore, J. (1993) What we can do for you! What can 'we' do for ' you'? Struggling over Empowerment in critical and feminist pedagogy, in: C. Luke and J. Gore (Eds) *Feminisms and Critical Pedagogy*. New York: Routledge, pp. 54–74.

Haraway, D. (1995) *Ciencia, Cyborgs y Mujeres. La reinvención de la naturaleza*. Valencia: Cátedra.

Hernández, G. (2006) Partir de Sí para Deshacer la Violencia, in: A. Mañeru and A. Maria Piussi (Eds) *Educación, nombre común femenino*. Barcelona: Octaedro Ediciones, pp. 204–209.

Hernández Morales, G. (2001) Un Intercambio de Experiencias Singulares, in: *Relaciona: una propuesta ante la violencia*. Serie de Cuadernos de Educación No Sexista, 11. Madrid: Instituto de la Mujer, pp. 21–34.

hooks, b. (1994) *Teaching to Trangress. Education as the practice of freedom*. New York, London: Routledge.

hooks, b. (2017) *El feminismo es para todo el mundo*. Madrid: Traficantes de sueños.

Izquierdo, M.J. (dir.), Canelles, N., Colldeforns Torres, L., Duarte Campderrós, L., Gutiérrez-Otero Mora, A., Mora Malo, E. and Puig Andreu, X. (2008) *Cuidado y Provisión: el sesgo de género en las prácticas universitarias y su impacto en la función socializadora de la universidad*. Madrid: Ministerio de Igualdad. Instituto de la Mujer.

López, H. (2022) Materiales culturales de memoria. Un acercamiento a la pedagogía feminista en la educación superior, in: M. Fonseca Santos, G. Hernández Rivas, and T. Mitjans Alayón (Eds) *Memoria y feminismos: cuerpos, sentipensares y resistencias*. México: Siglo XXI Editores, pp. 303–330.

Lugones, M. (2005) 'Multiculturalismo radical y feminismos de mujeres de color'. *Revista Internacional de Filosofía Política*, 25, pp. 61–76.

Luke, C. (Comp.) (1992) *Feminismos y pedagogías en la vida cotidiana*. Madrid: Ediciones Morata.

Maceira Ochoa, L. (2008) *El sueño y la práctica de sí. Pedagogía feminista. Una propuesta*. Mexico: CdMx, El Colegio de México.

Manicom, A. (1992) 'Feminist pedagogy: Transformations, standpoints, and politics'. *Canadian Journal of Education/Revue canadienne de l'éducation*, 17(3), pp. 365–389.

Martin, J.L. (2017). And the Danger Went Away. Speculative Pedagogy in the Myth of the Post-Feminist, in: J.L. Martin, A.E. Nickels, and M. Sharp-Grier (Eds) *Feminist Pedagogy, Practice, and Activism Improving Lives for Girls and Women*. New York and London: Routledge.

Martínez Martín, I. and Ramírez Artiaga, G. (2017) 'Non-patriarchal and non-colonial education. Experiences of a feminist teacher training'. *Revista Internacional de Educación para la Justicia Social (RIEJS)*, 6(2), pp. 81–95. doi:10.15366/riejs2017.6.2.005.

Montoya Ramos, M.M. (2010) Traer al aula el saber de la experiencia. Una mediación imprescindible en la nueva civilización, in: M.J. Clavo Sebastián and M.A. Goicoechea Gaona (Eds) *Miradas Multidisciplinares para un Mundo en Igualdad: ponencias de la I Reunión Científica sobre Igualdad y Género*, Girona: Dialnet, pp. 135–146.

Mora, E. and Pujal, M. (2009) Introducción de la perspectiva de género en la docencia universitaria, in: *AA.VV. UNIVEST 09: II Congrés Internacional "Claus per a la implicació de l'estudiant a la universitat"*. Girona: Universitat de Girona, pp. 1–15.

Noddings, N. (2003). 'Is teaching a practice?'. *Journal of Philosophy of Education*, 37(2), pp. 241–251.

Núñez Puente, S. and Fernández Romero, D. (2022). Estudios de género y discurso in: C. López Ferrero, I.E. Carranza, and T.A. Van Dijk (Eds) *Estudios del discurso: The Routledge Handbook of Spanish Language Discourse Studies*. New York and London: Routledge, pp. 302–315.

Ortega, P. and Villa, J.P. (2021) 'La pedagogía crítica: sentires insumisos desde el devenir feminista'. *(Pensamiento), (palabra) y obra*, 26(1), pp. 144–163.

Pié Balaguer, A. (2019) *La insurrección de la vulnerabilidad*. Barcelona: Universidad de Barcelona.

Piussi, A.M. (2000) 'Partir de si: necesidad y deseo'. *DUODA: Estudis de la Diferència Sexual*, 19(1), pp. 107–126.

Rich, A. (1994) Notes Toward a Politics of Location, in: A. Rich (Ed.) *Blood, Bread, and Poetry: Selected Prose 1979–1985.* New York: W. W. Norton & Company.

Rivera Garretas, M.M. (2009) 'Lia Cigarini. Entrevista realizada por María- Milagros Rivera Garretas'. *Duoda: Revista d'estudis feministes*, 36, pp. 181–188.

Rogowska-Strangret, M. (2019) Compartiendo vulnerabilidades Buscando 'fronteras ingobernables' en la academia neoliberal, in: V. Revelles-Benavente. and A.M. González Ramos (Eds) *Género en la educación. Pedagogía y responsabilidad feministas en tiempos de crisis política.* Madrid: Morata, pp. 31–48.

Russell, T. (1997) *Teaching about Teaching : Purpose, Passion and Pedagogy in Teacher Education.* London: Routledge.

Solsona, N. (2008) El aprendizaje del cuidado en la escuela, in: M. GarcíaA. Calvo, and T. Susinos (Eds) *Las Mujeres Cambian la Educación. Investigar la escuela, relatar la experiencia.* Madrid: Narcea, pp. 199–228.

Troncoso Pérez, L., Follegati, L., and Stutzin, V. (2019) 'Más allá de una educación no sexista: aportes de pedagogías feministas interseccionales'. *Pensamiento Educativo. Revista de Investigación Educacional Latinoamericana*, 56(1), pp. 1–15.

Tronto, J. (1993) *Moral Boundaries: A Political Argument for an Ethic of Care.* New York: Routledge.

Van Dijk, T.A. (1999) 'Análisis crítico del discurso'. *Anthropos*, 186, pp. 23–36.

Vázquez Verdera, V. (2010) 'La perspectiva de la ética del cuidado: una forma diferente de hacer educación', *Facultad de Educación. UNED Educación XX1*, pp. 177–197.

West, C., Lazar, M.M., and Kramarae, C. (2000). El género en el discurso, in: T.A. van Dijk (Ed.) *El discurso como interacción social. Estudios del discurso II. Una introducción multidisciplinaria.* Barcelona: Gedisa, pp. 179–212.

12 Teaching Sexuality Education in China During Times of Uncertainty

Zixi Zuo

Introduction: Understanding Sexuality Education in China

There has been global awareness about the importance of lifetime sexuality education which supports and protects sexual development, as well as teaching young people the skills required to enjoy and explore their sexuality and have safe, healthy relationships (UNESCO, 2018; Ringrose, 2016; Allen and Carmody, 2012; Tolman, 2012; Fine and McClelland, 2006). One of the key debates is the discourse of pleasure and young people's desires while shifting the focus from the dangers and negativity of sexuality (Allen and Carmody, 2012; Tolman, 2012; Lamb, Lustig, and Graling, 2013). Elsewhere, there has been increasing academic acknowledgement of sexual competences that centralises consensuality and sexual autonomy, such as sexual communication skills and perceptions of healthy relationships (Palmer et al., 2017; Fine and McClelland, 2006). Fine and McClelland (2006), for example, encourage young people to develop 'skills to express political and sexual agency ... in order to undertake critical analysis, trusting conversation, help-seeking and finally to negotiate risk and pursue pleasure' (p. 327). Yet a body of feminist research continues to question the contemporary sexual liberalism and pluralism in many Western contexts. Without addressing patriarchal society, the challenges of sexuality, such as increasing awareness towards women's sexual agency and mutuality, are not only uneven but also reproduce traditional gendered roles and expectations (Powell, 2010; Tolman, 2012). Under the conditions of pervasive sexualisation and self-sexualisation, representations of desiring women are entangled with the latest production to induce male desire.

Compared with their Western peers, Chinese young people are facing a different stigma in a context where strict moralised public discourse on youth sexuality coexists with the sexual liberalism and pluralism prevalent in many Western contexts. In the US context, researchers' support of comprehensive sexuality education positions young people as agentic sexual subjects with specific rights and responsibilities, promotes sexual diversity, interrogates heteronormativity, and focuses on unplanned pregnancy and exploring young people's understandings of pleasure and desire (Allen and Carmody, 2012; Tolman, 2012; Lamb, Lustig, and Graling, 2013). Whereas in the Chinese educational

DOI: 10.4324/9781003397502-12

environment, the discourses on sexual diversity and gender equality reflect social historical and contextual variability and have been consistently negotiated, (re)interpreted, and reproduced by practitioners (Jeffreys, 2006; Sigley and Jeffreys, 1999; Zheng, 2005). Some recent sexuality researchers and educators are providing informative and structured sexuality education for young people, drawing upon existing resources from the Western contexts, including positive framework sexuality education for adolescents (Jolly, 2016), comprehensive sexuality education in Chinese higher education (Huang et al., 2009), and empowerment sexuality education (Fang, 2012). The fight for institutional legitimacy and recognition for teaching comprehensive sexuality education and destigmatisation in Chinese educational systems continues (Zhao et al., 2020; Wei, 2020; Li, King, and Winter, 2009). The practice of teaching sexuality education in China is closely associated with sexuality politics, state power, and omnipresent heteronormative culture.

In alignment with the sex politics and sociocultural shifts in China, the sex/sexuality education promoted under the Chinese modernisation agenda has placed a strong emphasis on reproductive and physiological knowledge. Despite a discursive explosion around sexual-related discourses at the end of the Mao period, discussions of sex and sex education continue to be limited and remain sensitive topics in reform China (Hershatter, 1996). Sex education at school was almost non-existent during the Mao period, and information related to reproduction was only given to women and men in the form of marriage manuals and reproduction brochures (Ruan, 1985). The sex education in the early 1980s normally had a general focus on physiological processes, such as puberty, alongside a warning tone about engaging in premarital sex (Li and Wang, 1992). Sex education was used to target young people in their understanding of how their reproductive rights and practices were a matter of state policy and only validated if they married under the first marriage law. This was intensified with the one-child policies implemented by the Chinese government in 1978, which produced associated prohibitions for 'early date, early sexual behaviour, and uncontrolled childbirth' (Shen, 2015, p. 96). *Zaolian* (early love) has been institutionalised as a peculiar social problem in response to reproductive policies in the 2000s,[1] using human scientific discourses, particularly in the form of eugenic science and sexology (Shen, 2015). Therefore, the main agenda of sex education in schools is to help young people establish a correct outlook on love, marriage, family, and reproduction – which further supports and sustains the heterosexual, married ideals and social stability (Aresu, 2009).

Moreover, this alignment of school policy, ideology, and educational practices promotes abstinence for heterosexual marriage and discourages critical education about power, desires, and potential dangers. With a particular emphasis on 'moral discipline', the adolescent sex education in China has kept its warning attitude towards premarital sex, and girls'/women's sexuality unsurprisingly continues to be seen as problematic and harmful (Peng, Yi, and Yu, 2022; Jiang, 2003; Chen, 2017. Moreover, the prohibitive attitude towards 'early love' or teen romance, has intertwined with a strong emphasis on meritocracy, which leads to many schools' sexuality education portraying early adolescent relationships as harmful to students' education, taking their attention away from studying (Jolly, 2016). Therefore, any distraction (such as teenage romance or sexual behaviours) would potentially jeopardise their success and divert them from middle-class trajectories and their educational future (Zarafoneties, 2017; Liu, 2014).

Under the educational institution's discourse of early love and moralistic attitudes towards sexuality, the bodies of young women not only bear the consequence of limited sexuality education and public safety net of resources, but are also placed under threat of economic, social and sexual vulnerability. From a Foucauldian perspective, young women's sexuality is governed through a morality which is justified by the meritocratic promise of education and becomes a designated dense transfer point for relations of power, where women's sexual identity interacts with the state – through law, policy, and public institutions (Foucault, 1990). This sense of morality and the coupling of education with a suitably disciplined attitude to early teenage love works as a disciplining effect on young people's identities, which can also victimise them and leave them feeling guilty if things go wrong. To this effect, in their strong opposition to the 'moralizing ideology' (p. 301) in public policy regarding sexuality education, Fine and McClelland (2006) criticise the way moralising discourses function to privatise bad choices, thus absolving public institutions of taking responsibility for the negative outcomes of poor sexual health.

In the Chinese context, the continuing controversy around sexuality education, based on a strong emphasis on positivist approaches and moralistic discourses, has further hindered the development of inclusive gender and sexuality education. Under the current political climate, the marginalisation of feminist and sexuality research in Chinese higher education institutions has imposed restrictions on providing reflexive, comprehensive sexuality education, but also ambiguity regarding women's rights advocacy, gender equality and diversity. This is widely evident in sexuality education instructors' lack of practical experience in teaching education that is sensitive to queer issues (Huang et al., 2009). As Huang et al. (2009) examined the practices of sexuality education in Chinese universities, they observed an overall persistent, ambiguous attitude from university authorities – they embrace an open attitude towards teaching sexuality-related knowledge while they continue to emphasise scientific-focused knowledge rather than the cultural and social aspects of sexualities. The latter, which includes feminist and queer research, is considered sensitive and controversial (Huang et al., 2009). In the current political climate, universities constructed courses with limited expertise on LGBTQ issues, which, in turn, they downplay to avoid any potential 'radical' elements – justified by how they have to carefully consider the potential negative responses on the course curriculum (Wei, 2020; Huang, 2018; Cui, 2023). It is unsurprising that this strategically self-censored conversation on sexuality-related topics is limited to superficial and scientific discussions, while the unbalanced structure of power remains untouched, not to mention other sexual constructs such as sexual competence (Palmer et al., 2017), dating and relationship violence, or sexual communication skills. Without comprehensive rights-based sexuality education or a sufficient safety-net of resources, young people are educated to derive their identity from heterosexual and potentially patriarchal relationships, performing their familial roles, and bearing children (Kam, 2013; Fincher, 2016; Luo, 2017) leading them to a more constrained and heteronormative script about love and intimate relationships.

Love and Relationship Courses in Chinese Universities

Given the growing demands from university students to access relationship advice (China Youth Daily, 2020; Du, 2020), the love and relationships courses and similar products have been adopted into the higher education systems and have proliferated during the last decade. The earliest reported 'Studying Love Advice' course was introduced at Renmin University of China in Beijing, by Deng Hu, a student well-being and consultant lecturer, in 2002 (Qin, 2011). Later in 2011, the Beijing Education Committee began the first official trials on promoting a healthy relationships course as a part of the compulsory course, called University Students Well-Being Education (Deng, 2011). The curriculum for the course first started among the Beijing higher education institutions to teach university students how to start a relationship. The syllabus of the course starts with dealing with the most common relationship issues among college students, integrated with related love and relationship theory, aiming to 'teach the college students to love themselves, express, accept, reject, maintain love and face break-up' (Deng, 2011, para. 4). The course also includes teaching about homosexuality, which was regarded as a taboo topic in the Chinese context. Among all the modules of Massive Open Online Courses (MOOCs) from Chinese higher education institutions, Studying Love Advice, one of the most popular courses, has 27 thousand auditing students online: 'Studying Love Advice is a manual to help you find Mr Right', the description states on the Studying Love Advice on the MOOCs website (Zhang, 2018, para. 2).[2]

Most of the lecturers from the taped classes on MOOCs come from a psychological background; they have not been professionally trained in the fields of sexuality and gender. Perhaps due to this, one of the frequent references from these courses is the famous Kinsey report on human sexuality (Kinsey, Pomeroy and Martin, 2003; Kinsey et al., 1998). Kinsey reports were first translated by Chinese scholars in the 1990s, while similar Kinsey-type surveys began to flourish and be accorded confidence in modern scientific thought (Liu, 1986). The sexology study blends with the discourses of subjectification and transforms individuals into responsible and self-choosing subjects with provided scientific knowledge (Wong, 2016. This scientific knowledge essentialises gender differences between men and women by employing a 'popular paradigm' to rationalise problems in (heterosexual) relationships and correlate sexual morals with biological predisposition. For example, in an open-access virtual online platform, a 'love expert' says in her recorded course, 'Men are innately afraid of physical infidelity, as it may discontinue their patrilineal bloodline' (Zhang, 2018, 00:03:01). Similar accounts can be traced back to the evolution of 'self-help' books[3] and 'relationship science' about modern marriage that emerged in the late 20th century (Gill, 2009; Ward, 2020)and can still be seen in the recent relationship advice in Chinese media (see also Sun and Lei, 2017).

Methodology

This research focuses on an emerging elective course in Chinese universities which will be referred to in this chapter through the pseudonym 'Studying Love Advice', where the lecturers (typically student well-being counsellors) offer dating advice to the students. The goal of this study was to explore the controversial positions of the university as the primary site of an educational institution in young people's constructions of gender and sexuality. To achieve this goal, I conducted online interviews with counsellors who worked in the student well-being centres at two different universities located in central China, Wuhan – University N and University H. This research is based on interviews with the leading lecturers of a course called Love and Relationship Psychology and subsequent observations that were agreed to in the spring term of 2020.

The data discussed in this paper is drawn from the interviews with the course lecturers, the observation of the courses, and fieldnotes. The semi-structured interview was designed to encourage the participants to discuss some key themes, including: 1) their perceptions of young people's healthy relationships; 2) their experience working as love and relationship lecturers as well as counsellors in the student well-being centres; and 3) their designing of the course's curriculum and approaches to the sensitive topics, such as gender equality, LGBT issues, and sexual behaviours of college students. Every interview lasted for one to one and a half hours, was conducted in Chinese, and later transcribed verbatim by the researcher. The class observations took place online, and for ethical considerations, the observation of the class was only recorded by taking notes during and after the classes. The participants' data used in this research have been carefully processed and pseudonymised to protect the privacy of research participants.

After the initial data collection and processing, this research employs a feminist critical discourse analysis to explore the controversies associated with young adults' sexuality education in the context of higher education. Similar to CDA (critical discourse analysis), feminist critical discourse analysis, or FCDA, views discourses as an element of social practice, dialectically associated with society and discursively influenced by it. FCDA also highlights patriarchy as an omnipresent schema surrounding these discourses (Lazar, 2007). FCDA (Lazar, 2007) offers a flexible and discursive method to understand the production of knowledge, ideology, and power relations, which I find particularly useful for this research. Three major discourses emerged after analysis: 1) (re)essentialising gender differences; 2) ambiguities of the gender equality; and 3) responsibilisation of women's sexuality. The article provides a culturally grounded and ingenious approach to studying sexuality education in a non-western context, while identifying the compromise and potential progress in current sexuality education in Chinese higher education.

Meanwhile, the meaning of uncertainty in the title lies within the diminished face-to-face interactions, unconventional teaching environment, and unprecedented situations of the public health emergency at the time – early January 2020, when Wuhan became the epicentre of the massive outbreak of COVID-19. Hoping to stop the outbreak, Chinese authorities put the entire nation into lockdown. Wuhan had been put under an extremely strict curfew – every public facility and institution, including universities, closed until further notice. Later in that spring term both the universities where I planned my data collection field trips announced that they would start the semester online, including elective courses like Studying Love Advice. The university students and lecturers were facing not only increasing isolation but also pressure to maintain and resume their studying/teaching.

Now is a timely point to reflect on the limitations and possibilities of the existing and often overlooked relationship courses in Chinese universities. The emergence of relationship-focused courses mirrors the cultural authorities that normalise (hetero)sexual conducts but also has to navigate the inter-relations among the state regulatory power, university policy, and educational practices. Examining these sexuality-related courses, I pay particular attention to the discourses associated with young people's sexuality, responsible choices, dating, and relationship advice. With the aim of exploring the practices of teaching sexuality education, this research offers reflections on alternative approaches to young people's sexuality education in China and, at the same time, probes into the positions of the university on addressing sexuality education on campus.

(Re)essentialising Gender Differences

It is worth noting that in contemporary Chinese, *xing* is the word most commonly used to refer to both 'sexuality' and 'sex' (see also the debate on the conceptualisation of sexuality in China, Ruan, 2013; Pan and Huang, 2011; Sigley and Jeffreys, 1999). In everyday usage of Chinese, the distinction between biological sex and gender is minimal, and both terms, gender and sex, can be referred to with the word, *xing bie* '性别'. The linguistic confusion of the concepts of gender and sex, however, only partly explains the (re)essentialising of gender difference observed in the three courses by presenting sexuality as biological sexual development which in turn explains the distinctions between women and men.

As it happened, in the online taped courses mentioned earlier, the lecturers in the observed courses explained the difference between men and women using the Kinsey-type survey combined with evolutionary psychology. For example, both Guang Han and Li Ping use the psychological basis of men's active sexual drive to explain intimacy issues, such as jealousy, adultery, and cheating. Li Ping's first lecture exemplifies this further:

From an evolutionary perspective, women normally choose those (young men) who have enough financial resources – economic status and professional achievement; while young men chose those (young women) who can produce their offspring – physical figure, appearance, and age.

Li Ping, Lecturer, Powerpoint slides from the first class – 'What is Love'

The usage of evolutionary psychology in explaining sex/gender differences can be traced back to the earliest references to Darwinism in the early 1870s during the Chinese semi-colonial and semi-feudal periods. These Darwinian principles, namely, the 'struggle for existence' and 'natural selection' reached their climax in the mid 1890s, and were appropriated by the Chinese enlightenment intellectuals in the name of facilitating China's social evolution towards modern nations (Rocha and College, 2012). In addition, eugenicist protagonists legitimated some feminist arguments, such as freedom of marriage and love, with progressive sociological beliefs (sexual selection) during the earliest Chinese feminist enlightenment (Hershatter, 2007; Shen, 2015). Later in the Republican period, new biologising discourses, in relation to reproduction, sexual health, and family continued to add to the eugenics beliefs concerning the future of the race and the nation (Barlow, 2004; Dikötter, 1998). The pioneer thinkers (mostly male feminist theorists) value women's substantial responsibility for not only the perpetuation of the family but also for the very survival of China.

However, the widespread use of social Darwinism and adoption of scientific sexuality discourses without any criticality nowadays can further solidify the age-old centrality of the male in conventional heteronormative thinking. Particularly in the example above, divisive discourses such as men being valued for their economic status and women being valued for their youth and appearance is a major traditional dating ideology that is frequently reiterated in the course discussions. On the superficial level, this statement is self-evident in its interpretation of the 'evolutionary perspective', namely, the evolutionary psychology, which is quoted by Li Ping in the later section of her class, explaining that women lean towards men with resources and qualities of potential being a 'good father', while women's health and youth are their more favourable points. However, the problem with the discipline of evolutionary psychology in explaining modern young people's dating patterns is that it does not take into consideration the complexity of individual development and self-identification, nor does it mention the influence of present-day societies and socioeconomic backgrounds. Therefore, the biological underpinnings of the evolutionary psychology that these lecturers mentioned leave little space for reflexive individual experience within the traditional ideologies, not to mention interracial relationships, consensual non-monogamy or polyamory, or other intimate relationships of marginalised groups.

On another level, these traditional Darwinist discourses that present women's beauty and men's wealth as the prototype for an ideal match communicate the rehearsal of the continuing patriarchal standards in China. The statement objectifies feminine qualities through fertility potential and appearance, and so it essentialises traditional feminine qualities (a dutiful wife and loving mother or *xiangqi liangmu*) (Evans, 1997). These perceptions embed the stereotype that beautiful young women are bonded with rich, resourceful, and powerful men (normally older than they are), who also perceive women (and their youth) as one of the resources that justify male power and wealth. This reinforces the beauty myth that women's value relies on their looks which can be perceived as a form of currency and power in patriarchal gender relations (Ma, 2022) while, in contrast, men are valued for their entrepreneurial qualities and ability to provide and protect financially (Wong, 2020; Liu, 2019). These social evolutionary principles again disguise patriarchal ideologies as along with gender binarism and agism under seemingly scientific discourses.

Ambiguities of Gender Equality and Diversity

The lecturers' visions of a more progressive relationship included the notions of gender diversity and equality, yet maintained various levels of ambiguity and flexible rhetorical discourses. Whilst the courses seek to show some openness to balanced equality (not equity) by including some liberal ideologies in order not to be labelled anti-feminist, they continue to have very divisive and ambiguously sexist recommended readings, such as John Gray's (1992) *Men are from Mars and Women are from Venus*. As one of the classic relationship book writers, Gray (1992) writes about the importance of communication in a (heterosexual) relationship to bring it back into balance; many of his claims are outdated and limited to a specific timeframe and context.

Therefore, the value of equality plays a rhetorical central role in the promotion of a healthy relationship prescribed in the Studying Love Advice course. These relationship advisers are identifying with a circumscribed definition of feminism, they are nonetheless accepting of some of the central tenets of the feminist and queer movement, one of which is, namely, that women and men are born equal and deserving of the same opportunities in life. Another is the right to sexuality, which implies the freedom to express one's sexual orientation and sexual desire without fear of persecution, victimisation, or discrimination. These lecturers responded to the call for gender equality in their classrooms by increasing symbolic representations. For example, in the session for sexual intimacy, Li Ping carefully replaced the term 'premarital sex' with 'safe sexual behaviour' to delink the causal relations between sex and marriage and destigmatise sexual behaviours out of wedlock. At one of the sessions on the course, titled the Truth about Sex and Happiness, she also actively replaces 'girlfriend/boyfriend' with more neutral words such as 'partner' or 'other half' (*linyiban*) when she refers to either side of a relationship (fieldnote, 13 April 2020). Elsewhere in the course, the lecturers made an effort to break down the conventional belief that monogamous heterosexual marriage is the legitimation for sexual behaviours. In Guang Han's courses, he often used example pictures of both heterosexual and LGBT couples in the course slides, and always corrected students' language use and reminded them to make more gender and sexuality inclusive word choices.

Arguably, the endorsement of feminism (or liberal feminist ideas) is far more than the simple level of replacing the words or pictures that depict the hetero-sexual normative relationship with more diverse or neutral wordings. Here the discourse of gender equality is manipulated with flexibility within the intimate spheres (as the course focuses on students' romantic relationships) as well as the public sphere (the ways that the gender equality concept was taught by the lecturers in the classroom). During the interview, Guang Han said:

> ... but I would not necessarily call myself a feminist. I agree with some of the feminist opinions, but I don't believe in the existence of so-called feminism and patriarchy. Because once it comes to feminism, we would have to admit there is patriarchy, which means that we think it is an issue and we need to solve it. To be more precise on the definition (of myself), I would rather say I am supportive of gender equality for sure. I would like to call myself an LGBTQ-friendly counsellor. No matter whether they are women, men, non-binary or queer, I think they are all equal.
>
> Online interview, 20 October 2019

Interestingly, despite listing examples of non-conforming relationships or emphasising LGBT-inclusive language use, Guang Han exhibited opposing views, drawing from the Western–Chinese conflict. In the lecture titled Love and Marriage, he listed non-conforming relationships, such as cohabitation and non-monogamous relationships, then commented, 'Don't get me wrong, these are just emerging social phenomena from other rotten capitalist societies' (fieldnote, 19 May 2020). Concerning students who would take these listed examples from their lecturer as encouragement of these behaviours and relationship patterns, he drew a clear line between what are 'acceptable' and 'abnormal' behaviours in the Chinese social context for young university students. The term 'rotten capitalist' was frequently used in the mid-1980s when referring to 'abnormal' sexualities that are associated with 'bourgeois behaviours' (Evans, 1997, p. 212). Previous ethnographic study of the construction of ideal citizenship, desire, and identity in everyday life have revealed hybrid social-neoliberal forms of ideologies that govern through the desires of individuals (Jeffreys, 2006; Rofel, 2007). The constructions of some sexual activities and relationships as 'other' means they are treated as a source of deviant, danger, formed by rotten Western forces, which are productive of deep moral panics prevalent in different historical periods (Honig, 2003). Wong (2016) concludes that such divisive discourse exhibits an anxiety about social problems and sexual issues during the Chinese open market reformation period. The highly emphasised terms, such as 'Western', 'foreign', or 'capitalism' often circulated in the courses become a helpful tool for categorising 'good' or 'evil', 'right' or 'wrong', which intensify a hierarchal ordering of the expression of sexual desire. The above example conflicts with the gender equality (not equity) discourses that the lecturer employs, since it endorses the hetero-normative culture by downplaying the existence of a gender hierarchy ('they are all equal' – Guang Han) and essentialising heterosexuality through labelling certain sexual expressions and desires as good, traditional Chinese and others as evil, non-conventional Western.

On the institutional level, the example reveals that the current silence and unsupportive institutional environment is another major concern for sexuality education in Chinese universities. On the one hand, as Huang (2018) observed, sexuality-related courses are in a grey area in Chinese universities, where they are 'tolerated' by the authorities 'with an attitude of "opening an eye and closing an eye"' (p. 293). This allows (limited) openness to talk about queer issues in a highly heteronormative space. On the other hand, this muted and unsupportive environment also leads to the major obstacles for the courses – as the materials and course content are entirely based on the lecturers' own epistemology on sexuality and related topics, while a range of self-surveillance techniques are operated in the digital classroom space. Particularly, despite their years of expertise in counselling, the lecturers may not be trained or even willing to address gendered power dynamics in a classroom.

Furthermore, the ongoing struggles of the current Chinese feminist movement have been entwined with negative connotations and misogynistic discourses. Both in the online and face-to-face environment, the lecturers have faced vulnerability that reflects the impact of the feminist backlash on Chinese social media, especially when addressing women's rights and queer issues. For example, after listing the examples of non-conforming relationships mentioned above, Guang Han said half-jokingly and half-sarcastically, 'Please don't take screenshots of this course, I don't want to be famous'. Underpinning this banter lies the multiple intermediate grey areas in the overarching pro-gender-equality stance as well as strategic self-censorship, where the stigmatisation is attached to the speakers who have any visible connection to LGBT studies or sex topics (Irvine, 2014). Fundamentally, the restrictions and 'speaker's burden' (Irvine, 2005, p. 236) is shaped by social and cultural schemes regarding sexuality, the cognitive and affective bias of the instructor, and amplified by the digitally mediated classroom.

Numerous scholars have observed that the persistent system of patriarchy plays a crucial role in facilitating the widespread dissemination of overt sexism in cyberspace (Banet-Weiser and Miltner, 2016; Xie et al., 2022; Marwick and Caplan, 2018). Guang Han's concerns resonate with existing educational research on heteronormative campus culture in Chinese context (Cui, 2023). Cui (2023), in his research on the experience of Chinese queer academics, finds that heteronormative forces operate in interpersonal interactions and institutional practices and might result in self-censorship to conform the expectations of the university's leadership and students. Whereas in this case, given the unique political climate on feminist and queer politics, Guang Han's concerns can be contextualised in a heteronormative campus climate. He has to navigate the students' potential homophobic reaction (take screenshots and post them online) while, at the same time, experiencing increased vulnerability because of his openness towards queer issues in the digital environment where he can potentially be attacked because of his speech. In the worst scenario, claiming to be a feminist or supporting LGBT rights in public is seen as a challenge to social and political stability which would attract groups of antagonists.

Responsibilisation of Women's Sexuality

The notion of responsibility is another emergent discourse when addressing young people's sexual behaviours. The discourse of responsibility is not value-free but reflects complex ideologies combining conservative gender norms with contemporary neoliberal values and patriarchal social values – 'a dual emphasis on both restraints and self-autonomy … in the construction of ideal sexual subjects' (Wong, 2016, p. 5). The discourse of responsibility conveys messages that urge women to uphold the sanctity of monogamous marriage and protect standards of sexual behaviour by regulating their conduct. Meanwhile, this discourse intertwines with the transformation of enterprising, self-choosing, responsible subjects. In the following example, Li Ping expressed that acknowledging the consequences of having sex is the responsibility of women, as expressed on one of her slides (fieldnote, May 2020) stating the three principles relating to sex:

1   With protections,
2   Mutually respected,
3   Be responsible for yourself.

This is continued in the next slide, where Ms L advises the girls to:

1   Fully understand your attitudes toward sex and the potential consequences.
2   Avoid any possibility [for example, staying out late and then having to get a hotel room with your boyfriend, she added] if you are not ready.
3   If you are ready, it means that sexual experience will not damage your well-being, your future relationships and marriage, or society.

Apart from the importance of protected sexual practices as part of the responsibility of women, Li Ping further stresses the importance of awareness of the potential consequences, with the condensed message to 'be responsible' and 'be ready'. The statements once again burden young women with the responsibility to fully understand their sexual attitudes, which could only occur when young women know what embodied desire feels like (Tolman, 2012). Female sexual agency has metamorphosed from autonomous self-determination, with one's life knowable, to notions of deeply implicated projects of self-regulation, with the neoliberal ideas of 'being free' and 'making a responsible choice.' Emphasising women's responsibility in terms of sexual behaviour and the power of femininity, where girls and young women are encouraged to take the position of confident, independent women who can dismiss all criticisms and judgments (Dobson, 2014), overlooks the very double standards that women are subjected to in society.

Moreover, the problem with focusing on individual responsibility and tactics is that it often ignores the structural societal aspects of gender inequality. The endorsement of the over-individualistic approach promotes the exercise of one's goals and desires and assumes that any woman can simply opt out of the systems of victim-blaming and the normalised sexist discourses in which they have grown up and been educated. The unequal relations and the missing discourse of female desire again has denied women an opportunity to be autonomous sexually desiring subjects (Fine, 1988; Tolman, 2005; Allen and Carmody, 2012). Moreover, the gendered apportioning of responsibility expressed in the course reproduces an idealised image of women who need to strike the right balance between acting innocent and unaware of sexual desire while also acting as the gatekeepers of their sexuality ('avoid any possibility of staying in a hotel room with your boyfriend'). Avoiding sex before marriage arguably comes from a sense of self-protection but the responsibility has been left mainly to women, since men's desire was seen as uncontrollable (Evans, 1997; Holland et al., 1998). The avoidance of discourses of desire and gender inequality in the course continue to position the young women within the unbalanced structures of power in a sexual relationship, since they have not been encouraged to recognise their desires, fears, and pleasure nor the complicated context of sexualisation. Instead, they are instructed in managing themselves while considering the dominant prevalence of the sexual desire of men.

Additionally, discourses of responsibilisation of women's sexuality in Chinese contexts continue to objectify women under the persistent patriarchal value system. As some black feminist theorists have reminded us, the specific embodied intersections where young women live are varied by race, ethnicity, class, disability, sexuality, and socioeconomic background (Crenshaw et al., 1995). In the unique social cultural and political context, Chinese youth's sexual subjectivity, especially young women's, is facing multi-layered constraints because of objectification and stigmatisation under the contemporary patriarchal heteronormative regime, where the prioritisation of heterosexual marriage remains unquestioned. The responsibilisation of women's sexuality in China bears the imprint of Chinese reproductive politics and regulatory power of the state (Xie, 2021). For example, in her research on young women's attitudes towards premarital pregnancy, Xie (2021) argues that stigma associated with women's premarital choices remains powerful and undergoes transformation into a pragmatic and self-responsible discourse. By shifting responsibilities to capable neoliberal subjects, individuals can govern themselves in ways deemed appropriate by the regime. College students, in their early adulthood, face twofold dilemmas: on the one hand, they are expected to shoulder responsibility for autonomous decision-making and be capable of asserting their true desires; on the other hand, they are facing continuing pressure to conform to standards of appropriate moral and sexual ideology (Pei, Ho, and Lun, 2007; Evans, 1997).

Without addressing the complexities of sexual culture and practices, the advice inadvertently avoids the discourses of gendered power dynamics, which further reiterates the unbalanced gender relationship, especially when knowledge of safe sex practices is not sufficiently provided, and nor are scenarios of consent discussed. The 'responsible to yourself' advice given to the students inadvertently trails off into futilities. Hence, Chinese women are facing multi-layered damage because of objectification and stigmatisation under China's contemporary patriarchal marriage regime and state regulatory power over women's reproductive bodies.

Conclusion

Through examining the narratives and banter, and the dating advice from the Studying Love Advice course in two different universities in Wuhan, China, I argue that the course's focus on promoting desirable healthy relationships still underpins a prioritisation and privileging of heteronormative relationships. Despite employing an egalitarian rhetoric in favour of LGBT-inclusive and gender equality discourses, the current course fails to provide critical perspectives on societal and cultural aspects of gender construction, and the core ideology of the relationship courses remains conservative. This study has shown that the course's content prioritises heterosexual romantic scripts and solidifies the existing gender hierarchy. Nonetheless, the courses serve as a reflective platform, unveiling the dominant gender discourses of youth culture. The author argues that the teaching of love and relationships in universities is influenced by the intersection of educational practices, institutional heteronormativity, and the political climate in China, which contribute to the uncertainty of the sexuality education classroom.

These findings are consistent with existing educational research on sexuality education in Chinese higher education institutions (Wei, 2020; Huang et al., 2009; Cui, 2023), which shows that, despite the development of a certain openness in the universities, means of self-surveillance and censorship prevail. This chapter highlights the emerging controversies from the narratives of the lecturers and the course content and suggests that the courses are influenced by complex past and present sociocultural contexts in China. By unpacking the complex discourses and controversies reflected in the course, this study reveals a hybrid regime of socialist-neoliberal political rationality, which is both authoritarian and encourages self-governing autonomy to construct an ideal sexual subject (Sigley, 2007). At the same time, these lecturers have to negotiate with gendered discourses and sociopolitical constraints, under the structural heteronormativity, while facing unexpected challenges during the uncertain time of COVID-19. However, the analysis only partially represents the experience of implementing these relationships courses. What has not been addressed is the students' perspectives and how they react to these ambiguous and sometimes controversial gendered discourses and exercise agency facing the conflicting ideologies in their relationships.

Lastly, this research sheds light on the necessary tasks for developing affirmative gender-inclusive love and relationship courses that shift the focus from the dangers and negative sides of young people's sexuality. Encouraging young people to develop healthy sexuality and relationships necessitates addressing a clear, conscious articulation of desires, criticality, and sexual competence (Palmer et al., 2017). Thus, it is vitally important to develop an alternative and culturally grounded approach of sexuality education and establish appropriate teaching training support in Chinese universities.

Notes

1 In contrast with the prohibition of 'early love and early marriage', the family planning campaigns encouraged late marriage in the 1990s with eugenic slogans such as 'late marriage, late childbirth, fewer and better' (*'wanhun wanyu,shaosheng yousheng'*). This relates to the governmental pursuit for a high-quality population and China's modernisation project in the early 2000s (Greenhalgh, 2003)
2 The virtual learning platform, MOOC (Massive Open Online Courses) offers free online courses that are provided by higher-tier Chinese universities and are available for anyone to enrol. At the time of writing this chapter, this course has been registered for over ten thousand times and is also one of the highest rated courses in this platform.
3 John Gray's (1992) *Men are from Mars and Women are from Venus,* has been a popular reference in all love and relationship courses observed by the author.

References

Allen, L. and Carmody, M. (2012) '"Pleasure has no passport": Re-visiting the potential of pleasure in sexuality education'. *Sex Education*, 12(4), pp. 455–468. doi:10.1080/14681811.2012.677208.

Aresu, A. (2009) 'Sex education in modern and contemporary China: Interrupted debates across the last century'. *International Journal of Educational Development*, 29(5), pp. 532–541. doi:10.1016/j.ijedudev.2009.04.010.

Banet-Weiser, S. and Miltner, K.M. (2016) '#MasculinitySoFragile: culture, structure, and networked misogyny'. *Feminist Media Studies*, 16(1), pp. 171–174. doi:10.1080/14680777.2016.1120490.

Barlow, T. (2004) *The Question of Women in Chinese Feminism.* Durham, NC: Duke University Press.

Chen, Z. (2017) 'Perceptions and attitudes of Chinese journalists about gender equality: A national survey'. *Global Media and China*, 2(3–4), pp. 211–231.

China Youth Daily (2020) 'Near Ninety Percent of Students Support Romance Courses in Chinese Universities' ['近九成大学生支持学校开设恋爱课'], *China Youth Daily*, 12 October. Available at: http://zqb.cyol.com/html/2020-10/12/nw.D110000zgqnb_20201012_1-08.htm (Accessed 12 February 2023).

Crenshaw, K., Gotanda, N., Peller, G., and Thomas, K. (1995) *Critical Race Theory: The Key Writings That Formed the Movement.* New York: New Press.

Cui, L. (2023) 'Heteronormative classrooms under surveillance: Gay academics' concerns about addressing queer issues in China'. *Journal of LGBT Youth*, 20(1), pp. 129–142. doi:10.1080/19361653.2021.1997692.

Deng, X. (2011) 'Colleges and Universities in Beijing to Offer Mental Health Classes for College Students to Teach Love' ['Beijing Gaoxiao jiang kaishe daxuesheng xinli jiankangke jiaotanlianai']. *Chinese Academy of Sciences*. Available at: http://www.isl.cas.cn/kxcb/kpwz/201104/t20110418_3117648.html (Accessed 3 March. 2023).

Dikötter, F. (1998) 'Reading the Body: Genetic Knowledge and Social Marginalization in the People's Republic of China'. *China Information*, 13(2–3), pp. 1–13. doi:10.1177/0920203X9801300201.

Dobson, A.S. (2014) 'Performative shamelessness on young women's social network sites: Shielding the self and resisting gender melancholia'. *Feminism & Psychology*, 24 (1), pp. 97–114. doi:10.1177/0959353513510651.

Du, X. (2020) 'Chinese Students Favor College Course on Romance and Relationships'. *Sixth Tone*, 12 October. Available at: https://www.sixthtone.com/news/1006280/chine se-students-favor-college-course-on-romance%2C-relationships.

Evans, H. (1997) *Women and Sexuality in China: Dominant Discourses of Female Sexuality and Gender since 1949*. Cambridge, Polity Press.

Fang, G. (2012) 'Sexuality Education in the Chinese University on the Basis of Human Right and Gender Equality' ['jiyu xingrenquan yu xingbie pingdeng de gaoxiao xing-jiaoyu']. *Chinese Youth Research*. 3(1), pp. 92–96.

Fincher, L.H. (2016) *Leftover Women: The Resurgence of Gender Inequality in China*. London: Zed Books.

Fine, M. (1988) 'Sexuality, schooling, and adolescent females: The missing discourse of desire'. *Harvard Educational Review*. 58(1), pp. 29–54. doi:10.17763/haer.58.1. u0468k1v2n2n8242.

Fine, M. and McClelland, S. (2006) 'Sexuality education and desire: Still missing after all these years'. *Harvard Educational Review*. 76(3), pp. 297–338. doi:10.17763/haer.76.3. w5042g23122n6703.

Foucault, M. (1990) *The History of Sexuality: An Introduction*. Volume I. Trans. R. Hurley. New York: Vintage.

Gill, R. (2009) 'Mediated intimacy and postfeminism: A discourse analytic examination of sex and relationships advice in a women's magazine'. *Discourse & Communication*, 3(4), pp. 345–369. doi:10.1177/1750481309343870.

Gray, J. (1992) *Men Are from Mars and Women Are from Venus*. New York: Thorsons.

Greenhalgh, S. (2003) 'Science, modernity, and the making of China's one-child policy'. *Population and Development Review*, 29(2), pp. 163–196. Available at: http://www.jstor.org/stable/3115224.

Hershatter, G. (1996) Sexing modern China, in: G. Hershatter, J. Lipman, and R. Stross (Eds) *Remapping China Fissures in Historical Terrain*. Redwood City: Stanford University Press, pp. 77–93.

Hershatter, G. (2007) *Women in China's Long Twentieth Century*. Berkeley: University of California Press.

Holland, J., Ramazanoglu, C., Sharpe, S., and Thomson, R. (1998) *The Male in the Head: Young People, Heterosexuality and Power*. London: Tufnell.

Honig, E. (2003) 'Socialist Sex: The Cultural Revolution Revisited'. *Modern China*, 29 (2), pp. 143–175. doi:10.1177/0097700402250735.

Huang, Y. (2018) 'Sexuality Research and Sex Politics in 21st Century of Mainland China'. Available at: https://sxpolitics.org/trendsandtensions/uploads/capitulos/6-china.pdf.

Huang, Y., Suiming, S., Peng, P., and Gao, Y. (2009) 'Teaching Sexualities at Chinese Universities: Context, Experience, and Challenges'. *International Journal of Sexual Health*, 21(4), pp. 282–295. doi:10.1080/19317610903307696.

Irvine, J.M. (2005) *Disorders of Desire: Sexuality and Gender In Modern American Sexology*. Philadelphia: Temple University Press.

Irvine, J.M. (2014) 'Is sexuality research "dirty work"? Institutionalized stigma in the production of sexual knowledge'. *Sexualities*, 17(5–6), pp. 632–656. doi:10.1177/1363460713516338.

Jeffreys, E. (2006) *Sex and Sexuality in China*. 1st edition. London and New York: Routledge. doi:10.4324/9780203967065.

Jiang, X. (2003) 'Psychological Analysis of the Phenomenon of "Teenage Puppy Love"' ['qinshaonian zaolian xinli xianxiang qiantan'], *Journal of Guangxi University for Nationalities (Philosophy and Social Science Edition)*, z1, pp. 253–254. Available at: https://doi.org/10.3969/j.issn.1673-8179.2003.z1.083.

Jolly, S. (2016) 'Positive approaches to sexuality and new normative frames: strands of research and action in China and the USA'. *Sex Education*, 16(3), pp. 294–307. doi:10.1080/14681811.2015.1091767.

Kam, L.Y.L. (2013) *Shanghai Lalas*. Hong Kong: Hong Kong University Press. Available at: http://www.jstor.org/stable/j.ctt2854g8.

Kinsey, A.C., Pomeroy, W.B., Martin, C.E., and Gebhard, P.H. (1998) *Sexual Behavior in the Human Female*. Bloomington: Indiana University Press.

Kinsey, A.C., Pomeroy, W.R., and Martin, C.E. (2003) 'Sexual behavior in the human male'. *American Journal of Public Health*, 93(6), pp. 894–898.

Lamb, S., Lustig, K., and Graling, K. (2013) 'The use and misuse of pleasure in sex education curricula'. *Sex Education*, 13(3), pp. 305–318. doi:10.1080/14681811.2012.738604.

Lazar, M.M. (2007) 'Feminist critical discourse analysis: Articulating a feminist discourse praxis'. *Critical Discourse Studies*, 4(2), pp. 141–164. doi:10.1080/17405900701464816.

Li, L., King, M.E., and Winter, S. (2009) 'Sexuality education in China: The conflict between reality and ideology'. *Asia Pacific Journal of Education*, 29(4), pp. 469–480. doi:10.1080/02188790903309066.

Li, Y. and Wang, X. (1992) *Their World* ['Tamende shijie']. Shanxi Renmin Press.

Liu, D. (1986) 'Sexual science and the four modernisations' ['Xing kexue yu si hua jianshe']. *The Probe*, 5, pp.76–79.

Liu, F. (2014) 'From degendering to (re)gendering the self: Chinese youth negotiating modern womanhood'. *Gender and Education*, 26(1), pp.18–34. Available at: https://doi.org/10.1080/09540253.2013.860432.

Liu, F. (2019) 'Chinese Young Men's Construction of Exemplary Masculinity: The Hegemony of Chenggong'. *Men and Masculinities*, 22(2), pp. 294–316. doi:10.1177/1097184X17696911.

Luo, W. (2017) 'Television's "leftover" bachelors and hegemonic masculinity in post-socialist China'. *Women's Studies in Communication*, 40(2), pp. 190–211. doi:10.1080/07491409.2017.1295295.

Ma, H. (2022) 'Inner and outer beauty: exploring female beauty in contemporary China'. *Journal of Gender Studies*, 1–13. doi:10.1080/09589236.2022.2070463.

Marwick, A.E. and Caplan, R. (2018) 'Drinking male tears: language, the manosphere, and networked harassment'. *Feminist Media Studies*, 18(4), pp. 543–559. doi:10.1080/14680777.2018.1450568.

Palmer, M.J., Clarke, L., Ploubidis, G.B., Mercer, C.H., Gibson, L.J., Johnson, A.M., Copas, A.J., and Wellings, K. (2017) 'Is "sexual competence" at first heterosexual intercourse associated with subsequent sexual health status?'. *The Journal of Sex Research*, 54(1), pp. 91–104. doi:10.1080/00224499.2015.1134424.

Pan, S. and Huang, Y. (2011) *Sexuality* ['Xingshehuixue']. Beijing: China Renmin University Press.

Pei, Y., Ho, S.P., and Lun, N.M. (2007) 'Studies on Women's Sexuality in China since 1980: A Critical Review'. *Journal of Sex Research*. 44(2), pp. 202–212. doi:10.1080/00224490701263868.

Peng, H., Ye, T., and Yu, H. (2022) 'Physiological, psychological and rights analysis of the phenomenon of early love among minor students' ['weichengnianxuesheng zaolianxianxiang shengli xingli yu quanli fenxi'], *Teacher Education Forum*, 05, pp. 19–26. Available at: https://doi.org/10.3969/j.issn.2095-5995%20.2022.05.003.

Powell, A. (2010) Consent: Negotiating consensual sex, in: *Sex, Power and Consent: Youth Culture and the Unwritten Rules*. Cambridge, Cambridge University Press, pp. 86–105. doi:10.1017/CBO9780511777080.005.

Qin, Z. (2011) 'A double life of a psychotherapist' ['yige xinli zixunshi de A mian he B mian']. *China Youth*. Available at: http://zqb.cyol.com/html/2011-11/16/nw.D110000zgqnb_20111116 1-10.htm (Accessed 23 March 2023).

Ringrose, J. (2016) Postfeminist media panics over girls' 'Sexualisation': Implications for UK sex and relationship guidance and curriculum, in: V. Sundaram and H. Sauntson (Eds) *Global Perspectives and Key Debates in Sex and Relationships Education: Addressing Issues of Gender, Sexuality, Plurality and Power*. London: Palgrave Pivot, pp. 30–47.

Rocha, L.A. and College, E. (2012) 'Quentin Pan 潘光旦 in The China Critic'. *China Heritage Quarterly*, 30(31). Available at: http://www.chinaheritagequarterly.org/features.php?searchterm=030_rocha.inc&issue=030 (Accessed 21 February 2023).

Rofel, L. (2007) *Desiring China: Experiments in Neoliberalism, Sexuality, and Public Culture*. Durham, NC: Duke University Press.

Ruan, F.F. (1985) *Sex Knowledge Handbook* ['xingzhishi shouce']. Beijing: Kexue Jishu Wenxian Chubanshe.

Ruan, F.F. (2013) *Sex in China: Studies in Sexology in Chinese Culture*. New York: Springer. Available at: http://public.ebookcentral.proquest.com/choice/publicfullrecord.aspx?p=5575836.

Shen, Y. (2015) 'Too young to date! The origins of *zaolian* (early love) as a social problem in 20th-century China'. *History of Science*, 53(1), pp. 86–101. doi:10.1177/0073275314567437..

Sigley, G. (2007) Sex, politics and the policing of virtue in the People's Republic of China, in: E. Jeffreys (Ed.) *Sex and Sexuality in China*. London and New York: Routledge. pp. 51–69.

Sigley, G. and Jeffreys, E. (1999) 'On "sex" and "sexuality" in China: A conversation with Pan Suiming'. *Bulletin of Concerned Asian Scholars*, 31(1), pp. 50–58. doi:10.1080/14672715.1999.10415730.

Sun, W. and Lei, W. (2017) 'In search of intimacy in China: The emergence of advice media for the privatized self'. *Communication, Culture & Critique*, 10(1), pp. 20–38. doi:10.1111/cccr.12150.

Tolman, D.L. (2005) *Dilemmas of Desire: Teenage Girls Talk about Sexuality*. Cambridge, MA: Harvard University Press.

Tolman, D.L. (2012) 'Female adolescents, sexual empowerment and desire: A missing discourse of gender inequity'. *Sex Roles*, 66(11–12), pp. 746–757. doi:10.1007/s11199-012-0122-x.

UNESCO (2018) *International Technical Guidance on Sexuality Education: An Evidence-Informed Approach*. Paris: UNESCO

Ward, E.J. (2020) *The Tragedy of Heterosexuality*. New York: New York University Press.

Wei, W. (2020) 'The normalization project: The progress and limitations of promoting LGBTQ research and teaching in mainland China'. *Journal of Homosexuality.* 67(3), pp. 335–345. doi:10.1080/00918369.2018.1530883.

Wong, D. (2016) 'Sexology and the making of sexual subjects in contemporary China'. *Journal of Sociology*, 52(1), pp. 68–82. doi:10.1177/1440783315587799.

Wong, M. (2020) *Everyday Masculinities in 21st-Century China: The Making of Able-Responsible Men.* Hong Kong: Hong Kong University Press.

Xie, K. (2021) Premarital Abortion, What Is the Harm? The Responsibilisation of Women's Pregnancy Among China's 'Privileged' Daughters, in: K. Xie (Ed.) *Embodying Middle Class Gender Aspirations: Perspectives from China's Privileged Young Women.* Singapore: Springer, pp. 79–110.

Xie, X., Cambazoglu, I., Berger-Correa, B., and Ringrose, J. (2022) Anti-feminist misogynist shitposting: The challenges of feminist academics navigating toxic Twitter, in: P.J. Burke, J. Coffey, R. Gill, and A. Kanai (Eds). *Gender in an Era of Post-truth Populism: Pedagogies, Challenges and Strategies.* 1st Ed.. London: Bloomsbury. pp. 131–156. doi:10.5040/9781350194625.

Zarafoneties, N. (2017) *Sexuality in a Changing China: Young Women, Sex and Intimate Relations in the Reform Period.* Routledge research on gender in Asia series. London; New York:Routledge.

Zhang (2018) *Love Psychology* ['aiqing xinlixue']. Icourse163 [Online Video]. Available at: https://www.icourse163.org/course/WHUT-1002552002?from=searchPage&outVendor= zw_mooc_pcssjg (Accessed: 21 Feb 2023).

Zhao, P., Yang, L., Sa, Z., and Wang, X. (2020) 'Propriety, empowerment and compromise: challenges in addressing gender among sex educators in China'. *Sex Education*, 20(5), pp.552–567. doi:10.1080/14681811.2019.1705779.

Zheng, W. (2005) '"State Feminism"? Gender and Socialist State Formation in Maoist China'. *Feminist Studies*, 31(3), pp. 519–551. doi:10.2307/20459044.

13 Rethinking Young Women's Sex Education

Sexual Vulnerability and Affective Relations

Rachel Levi Herz and Miri Rozmarin

Introduction: Vulnerability, Affect, and Sex Education

Sex education today reflects a neoliberal dichotomous discourse that sharply distinguishes between young women's active, wilful sexual acts and their sexual vulnerability and risks (Gonick et al., 2009). The neoliberal discourse on sexual empowerment encourages young women to express their sexuality freely. However, it promotes free choice and personal responsibility in a manner that undermines the systematic social inequalities that shape individuals' surroundings and limit their ability to manage their vulnerability (Gilson, 2016). This neoliberal approach that dominates sex education focuses on affirmative sexual consent, which often preserves gender role division, according to which young men are educated to receive consent and young women are educated to provide consent (Kipnis, 2017). In this neoliberal atmosphere, young women often distance themselves from narratives of victimhood – even when they experience violence –to prevent being stigmatised as vulnerable and, therefore, as lacking the ability to act (Bay-Cheng, 2019).

This study challenges the dichotomous discourse on sex education by offering an alternative approach to illuminate the complex relationship between vulnerability and sexual expression. It uses the Israeli case study of 'attacking', which is slang to describe a heterosexual practice performed in nightclubs by adolescents and young people. By approaching young women's vulnerability as an affective pattern, this chapter demonstrates how heightened vulnerability serves as a resource for relationality and collectivity that supports young women's sexual expression. This analysis draws on vulnerability-based principles to rethink gender-based sex education.

Affect theory emphasises the centrality of connections between bodies as constitutive of people's sense of selfhood and their individual expressions. Therefore, it serves as an alternative to perspectives that focus on stable boundaries, subjects, and identities (Grosz, 2005). Affective responses are embodied in immediate experiences that may be primary emotions, such as rage, passion, repulsion, pleasure, or bodily sensations (e.g. freezing, crying, or shivering). Interactions between bodies occur in an in-between space that is material, imaginary, normative, or social. These aspects influence how bodies

DOI: 10.4324/9781003397502-13

affect each other. Thus, what may be perceived as an immediate experience is influenced by social location. Moreover, although affect may be associated with momentary influence, it can exert a significant impact and shape patterns of feelings, thoughts, dispositions, or capacities, influencing how an individual is affected by certain conditions (Brennan, 2004; Watkins, 2010). Therefore, bodies situated differently socially may be influenced differently by their interactions with certain bodies or their surroundings. However, rather than assuming that categories such as gender, race, and class are solely stable power structures, this approach illuminates how these constructs also operate as microdynamics between bodies, resulting in new possibilities for action (Pedwell and Whitehead, 2012). Hemmings (2012) conceptualised one of these transformative possibilities in what she called affective dissonance, which refers to the experience of the gap between the sense of self and social framework that attributes meaning to one's actions.

This chapter uses affect theory to elucidate how young women's sexual expression emerges in 'attacking' spaces. It locates young women's affective responses and relationships –particularly, their experiences of affective dissonance, a dissonance between the sense of self and the actual possibilities of its expression and validation (Hemmings, 2012, p. 154) –to reveal how they engage in these vulnerable situations in transformative manners. The focus on affective responses challenges the neoliberal focus on individuality, self-sufficiency, and choice, and allows a more complex understanding of sexual expression than the dichotomies that shape the main social discourses regarding young women's sexuality and sex education (Paasonen, 2018).

Further, this chapter discusses the common use of the term 'vulnerability' in educational discourse, which refers to the levels of exposure to risk and harm of children and young adults from different sociocultural marginal groups (Eurofound, 2012). From this perspective, the goal of educational practices and pedagogy is to reduce vulnerability as much as possible and promote resilience, understood primarily as independence. Nevertheless, the theorisation of vulnerability has been developed over the past 20 years as a path to rethinking the basic features of human subjectivity and the meaning of the concepts of equality, well-being, and resilience. Vulnerability theory stresses that human subjects are relational, social, and embodied. People depend on other people and social institutions for continual support and care to sustain themselves (Butler, 2004; Fineman, 2008). Although vulnerability is a shared human condition in a neoliberal culture that associates resilience with being an active, independent, and self-mastering individual, it is also closely associated with failure. Being labelled as vulnerable implies the role of a passive victim (Fineman, 2013). Accordingly, vulnerability may become a source of shame and trigger violence to restore a sense of independence and resilience (Bracke, 2016; Butler, 2004).

In the context of young women's sexuality, prominent educational and social discourse contrasts sexual empowerment and sexual expression with sexual vulnerability and risk (Bay-Cheng, 2015; Lamb, 2010). These discourses assume that young women express their sexuality only when they do not face risks.

Moreover, these approaches are associated with vulnerabilities to concrete threats and, therefore, tend to overlook the subtle forms of vulnerability. The normative expectation that young women are responsible for their safety and act freely downplays their ongoing exposure to slut-shaming and other forms of normative gendered judgement. Social judgement regarding sexuality applies to social expectations for balanced, empowered, active, and under-control sexual behaviour (Bay-Cheng, 2015; Gill and Scharff, 2011), and underlines that any space and practice of sexual expression are characterised by intensified vulnerabilities. Gender-based vulnerabilities are among the most persistent forms of social vulnerability that shape the lives of women and minorities (Gilson, 2022). Focusing on vulnerability allows researchers to expand the knowledge of how the conditions of inequality, discrimination, and precarity influence the sense of selfhood and being. Moreover, this focus provides insights into the emotional resources for transformative processes (Gilson, 2014, Rozmarin, 2021).

This study focuses on vulnerability as an affective response of bodies to their surroundings, demonstrating how vulnerability operates as a resource for young women to manage risk while developing their abilities to express themselves sexually. By critically applying the vulnerability theory framework to education, this chapter aims to demonstrate how vulnerability serves not only as a resource of shame but also as an affective resource for acting in certain ways. Therefore, while injurious forms of neglect and exposure to violence must be reduced, the perspective of vulnerability-based education emphasises two major points. First, the ideal of resilience as independence and individual achievement may be harmful because it overlooks and, occasionally, stigmatises the several ways in which people are dependent on others to sustain their well-being (Gilson, 2022). Second, an individualised approach towards vulnerability also excludes the possible resources for managing the harmful social conditions of marginalised groups.

There is emerging interest in theories of vulnerability within pedagogical and educational theories, predominantly for preventing gender-based and sexual violence. These theories aim to offer tools that facilitate boys' and young men's acknowledgement of the unethical nature of gender-based violence. These approaches argue that acknowledging one's own and others' vulnerabilities is the key to establishing ethical sexual relations. Sustaining ethical sexual relations requires the awareness of (a) how one's actions increase the vulnerability of others and (b) shared corporal vulnerability (Cover, 2014). Further, vulnerability operates in education as a crucial resource for recognising social inequalities and developing individual and collective responsibility (Corbella and Uİcar, 2022). Additionally, on the basis of the realisation of vulnerability as a shared human condition, some educational initiatives relate to vulnerability as a resource for developing a disposition for openness to differences (Mcleod, 2012).

Sex education for young people commonly embraces a neoliberal normative framework that promotes sexual autonomy and affirmative sexual consent through a procedural individualised logic that often neglects the relational and communicative manifestations of young women's sexual experiences (Gilbert, 2018). This framework is dominant in Israel. Since 1987, the Israeli Ministry of Education has included sex education under the responsibility of the Psychological Counselling Service (in Hebrew – SHEFI) of the Ministry of Education (Sinai and Shehade, 2018). According to the SHEFI website[1], the most important challenges to be addressed are intimate relationships, choice and consent, gender and sexual identities, sexual assault, and pornography. SHEFI's primary objective is improving the sexual health of adolescents and young people and encouraging them to practise safe sexual behaviour. This objective is achieved through the central programme of 'Life Skills' developed by the Department of School Counseling at the Ministry of Education. This programme is available with specific adjustments for different state education systems in Israel – specifically, secular Jewish, Orthodox Jewish, and Arab. The programme focuses on risk prevention in the lower grades (3rd–7th); such as, relationships and sex education, and the prevention of teenage pregnancy and sexually transmitted diseases; and in the upper grades the focus shifts to the prevention of sexual violence (Ben-Ami and Erhard, 2017). Furthermore, several non-governmental organisations offer sex education programmes to schools as part of the Ministry of Education GEFEN system for supplementary education programmes. These programmes focus on LGBTQ+ sexual identities, sexual consent, and gender equality but are at the discretion of school principals. Thus, owing to significant differences in the socioeconomic, national, political, and religious characteristics of Israeli schools, Israeli schools have different sex education curricula.

Sexual consent and risk prevention are undeniably important and serve as healthy conditions for young women's sexual expression (Coy et al., 2016). However, focusing solely on these aspects and on the individual as solely responsible for achieving these conditions may also cloud how practices of consent echo gender norms (Halley, 2016). Therefore, this analysis of the case study of 'attacking' reveals how vulnerability – a shared relational connection and response to exposure to harm – shapes young women's actions and serves as a resource for sustaining self-expression.

The Case Study of 'Attacking' and Methodology

'Attacking' is a common Israeli heterosexual practice performed primarily by secular, middle-class, young Jewish people in nightclubs for adolescents and young people. This act is performed in accordance with clearly defined rules for initiating casual sexual interactions. During parties, young men approach young women and touch their bodies – often from behind – to initiate kissing, close dancing, or making out. Young women respond either by continuing the sexual interactions or by rejecting these attempts. 'Attacking' differs from 'hitting on' someone in general because it occurs only in specific spaces, such as nightclubs, usually between strangers, and by making immediate physical contact. It occurs in large regional parties wherein anonymity is maintained, the space is dark and shrouded with smoke, and massive alcohol consumption is observed. It has some characteristics in common with hook-up culture, particularly not being prior acquaintances and gender role division, and some situational and concrete elements, such as high accessibility to possible sexual partners and intense alcohol consumption (Allison and Risman, 2014).

'Attacking' has a clear gender role division – young men are expected to initiate sexual interactions, and young women are expected to respond to these attempts. These gender roles match the normative Israeli cultural expectations of young men being the initiators of casual sexual interactions and the parallel expectations of young women to respond to their attempts and behave as gatekeepers (Shulman et al., 2009). Moreover, these attacks echo Israeli cultural connections among the military, sexual assault, sexuality, and gender (Levin, 2011). Despite these violent connotations, young people perceive 'attacking' as normative and acceptable. Furthermore, as their narratives reflect, young women find in 'attacking' possibilities of sexual expression and pleasure.

As a case study, 'attacking' offers valuable insights into how young women express themselves sexually in environments governed by objectifying practices. Looking through the lens of vulnerability and affective responses allows for going beyond the association of young adults' sexuality with risk management, personal responsibility, and sexual consent. This study aims to illustrate how young women navigate spaces of intense vulnerability and shape their sexual selfhood and preferences by revealing the affective relations that support their sexual expression and vulnerabilities. Drawing on these findings, we outline the principles of vulnerability-based education.

Data were derived from 39 in-depth semi-structured interviews with young women. The selected quotes were translated from Hebrew to English while preserving the meaning of the cultural subtexts. All interviewees were given pseudonyms for the data analysis. The research topic presented to the interviewees was flirting at nightclubs and parties. All interviews started with the question, 'What can you tell me about your experience at nightclubs?' This question invited interviewees to narrate their stories, reflecting their experiences during adolescence and early adulthood. Other questions referred to body responses; sexual expression, relations and interactions; and the perception of 'attacking'. The interviews were conducted using the framework of 'critical respect' that holds both hermeneutics of trust towards the interviewees' narratives that describe their active coping in the world and a critical standpoint in relation to power structures and gendered inequalities (Gill, 2007).

Findings

An analysis of 'attacking' emphasises several social spaces in the lives of young women wherein various violent manifestations are perceived as normative. Moreover, it emphasises the complexities of social expectations that construct sexual and social vulnerabilities. The following section discusses three main themes regarding young women's sexual expression in 'attacking' spaces: (a) manifestations of sexual subjective expression in spaces of intensified vulnerability; (b) a dissonance between affective responses and the perception of the normativity of the practice; and (c) alliances based on joint vulnerability. We show how these themes reveal young women's awareness of their vulnerability and suggest alternative educational tools to empower them to manage their intensified vulnerability while expressing their sexuality in varied social spaces.

Sexual Subjective Expression in Spaces of Intensified Vulnerability

The interviewees described 'attacking' as situations wherein a young man 'finds someone he likes' (Lia) and attempts to sexually interact with her by 'trying to hug her from behind' (Tia). Ronny says that she projects 'something sexual' while 'attacking'. She emphasises how, unlike in other social spaces, she feels 'comfortable enough to actually be sexual'. Ronny continues to describe how she experiences different sexual interactions that 'don't make you feel bad or remorseful because you don't attach much importance to them'. The promiscuous boundaries of 'attacking' spaces allow her sexual expression, which is perceived as inappropriate in other social spaces. Although this sexual practice affirms traditional gender roles and has an objectifying aspect, the interviewees described how they found it possible to gain sexual experience and social recognition.

NICOLE: To do more than kissing and with more than five men. We also had our lists of who we wanted to kiss, whom we kissed [...] like kissing someone a year below in school, kissing someone a year above, and flirting with the bouncer. It was a time when we were more sexually aroused.

Nicole's quote echoes a neoliberal discourse that encourages young women to express their sexuality freely. Moreover, it demonstrates the permissive social boundaries in 'attacking' spaces that allow young women to fulfil their sexual curiosity despite their vulnerability and objectification in these spaces.

In 'attacking' spaces, young women establish social and sexual values as attractive targets for sexual interactions. Sahar describes how 'your ego rises when you get a lot of "attacking" attempts', and she recalls the competition between young women when someone feels that no one attempts to 'attack' her. This competition also encourages young women to experience more casual sexual interactions while participating in 'attacks'.

Nevertheless, despite neoliberal expectations of empowered sexual expression, young women have limitations in their sexual behaviour (Bay-Cheng, 2015). These limitations result in young women's intensified vulnerability, expressed through the following three main manifestations in 'attacking' spaces: (1) gender role division that restricts them to responsive positions, (2) strict social judgement of their sexual behaviour, and (3) constant unsolicited touching as a result of 'attacking' attempts (Levi Herz and Rozmarin, 2023).

Spaces of 'attacking' express the normative gender role division, according to which young women are expected to be passive, and men are expected to be active and pursuing. This gender role division requires young women to respond to 'attacking' attempts according to their choice and social expectations. This duality reflects the complexities of the neoliberal concept of choice, which does not consider young women's sexual and social vulnerability. Young women accept that, irrespective of their sexual endeavours, they will be 'attacked'. The inevitability of their vulnerability appears to be a given.

MOR: Boys are horny, so they are allowed. Everyone knows that they are horny and expects them to be horny, so they are allowed whatever they want. However, girls should wait gently for someone to approach them. It's like a princess who needs to be rescued. Girls are gentle and don't initiate sexual interactions. That's the boy's job.

According to Mor, young women are expected to maintain a delicate balance between their wish to fulfil sexual urges and their social expectation to behave in a feminine manner. If young women participate in 'attacking' not according to these expectations, they face strict social judgement and even defamation.

Moran demonstrates strict social judgement when she says that 'other girls are looking at you and expect you to be hard to get, otherwise you're a slut – that's your definition'. Moran's quote reflects the perceived social image of descendant feminine sexual behaviour that young women internalise to prevent being stigmatised negatively. Young women internalise gender role division and social judgement of their sexual behaviour, but young men 'behave like they are not aware of their surroundings because they aren't afraid something bad will happen to them' (Sharon). This quote suggests that young women are constantly aware of possible harm and risks while participating in 'attacking' and, thus, experience intensified vulnerability.

Constant 'attacking' attempts lead to a feeling of loss of autonomy that increases uncertainty and vulnerability and requires constant awareness of the surroundings in the leisure space. Gilly also describes how she and her friends feel like 'easy prey' and refers to the young men constantly touching them. An unsolicited touch may result in feelings of fear and inferiority.

DEBBY: It's like I'm never in a safe position [...] every second someone can force me. This is a type of loss of control and fear. It is just that men are approaching you, and they're stronger. I am especially small {laughter}. It's a fear. So, I take it into account that if I go there, this is my starting point.

Debby emphasises that young women realise that if they want to be part of the social game of 'attacking', they need to accept their responsive and vulnerable position. This positionality results in young women's constant conscious need to manage uncertainty, risk, and loss of control.

That young women are aware of their intense vulnerability when expressing sexuality is critical when rethinking vulnerability-based sex education. The official educational curriculum affects the social meaning of gender roles and relations but often ignores relational manifestations and focuses on individua-lised discussions of young women's vulnerability (Vanner, 2022). Specifically, the focus of sex education on choice and affirmative sexual consent intensifies the social expectations of personal responsibility, encouraging young women to distance themselves from narratives of victimhood (Bay-Cheng, 2015). There-fore, young women's awareness of their constant vulnerability serves as a tool to empower them to manage this social and sexual vulnerability.

Young Women's Experience of Affective Dissonance

Young women's awareness of affective responses may serve as an important resource in sex education. Although neoliberal discourse encourages young women to view themselves as active sexual individuals, embodied affective responses may add important information regarding the risks of certain situa-tions. As presented in the previous section, young women's sexual expression in 'attacking' spaces is entangled with the wish to fulfil the norm successfully and gain social value, fulfil sexual curiosity, and manage their vulnerability. More-over, the findings reveal that young women experience an affective dissonance conflict gap between their sense of self as part of the social framework, which attributes meaning to their actions, and the embodied sense of self that emerges through affective responses.

Further, the findings indicate that the experience of affective dissonance arises from two main gaps – specifically, (a) the gap between affective responses and the perception of the normativity of 'attacking', and (b) the gap between conflictual affective responses that arise simultaneously. Therefore, dissonant feelings are normalised as part of a social game, even when the body signals different risks.

OFIR: There's a positive aspect to it because it's an expression of interest. It doesn't matter if it's pleasant or not. Usually, it gives you a good feeling for two seconds that someone is interested in you. And then, it's like: 'OK. It's not pleasant'. But in general, it gives you a good feeling.

Ofir describes an ambivalence towards 'attacking' that reflects young women's internal conflict when they are compelled to express their sexuality while experiencing intensified vulnerability. Her quote illuminates the dis-sonance between the positive sense of gaining affirmation of her social value through participation in 'attacking' and the affective responses that arise at the instant of physical contact. This dissonance reveals how the possibility to act sexually emerges in an attempt to balance the desire for social recognition with the desire to feel secure.

Additionally, the interviewees describe different moments of recoil, stagnation, and disgust at the moment of the initial contact of 'attacking'. Nira shares how when someone she does not know touches her, she experiences 'this stagnation – your body freezes but you continue'. This stagnation is a reaction to the uncer-tainty that accompanies unsolicited contact with no earlier acquaintance or communication. Although Nira accepts social rules as normative, her body signals reluctance. Nevertheless, despite her affective responses, she keeps performing and participating in 'attacking'.

As mentioned earlier, different affective responses often occur simultaneously. Shira describes how 'when someone spanks my ass, there's a momentary shrinkage – it's a reflex, but then the feeling of euphoria takes over'. She explained that the euphoric feeling is the result of both satisfied sexual desire and a feeling of empowered self-worth. Considering that participating in 'attacking' serves as the 'desirability index', young women establish their social value as sexually attractive targets and are satisfied when they fulfil the norm successfully.

Moreover, the dissonance between the two sets of experiences – the affirmation of social value as a sexual being and affective responses to unsolicited touch – is not a passive state but a dynamic process. The interviewees share how they acknowledge this dissonance and process the different affective responses that arise while participating in 'attacking'. In addition to reluctance, they also experience pleasure and satisfaction.

MICHAL: You come to dance beautifully, and to look good, and you're sexy, there's nothing to do about that. You're not trying too hard; you're just hot and sexy. And you dance and then things like that ['attacking'] just happen to you, and they just come and cling to you.

Despite the passive language that Michal uses ('things just happen to you'), she repeatedly describes affective responses of sexual arousal and pleasure. The mix of these experiences in relation to the objectifying practice leaves young women in a responsive position, but this position, nevertheless, allows for self-expression. The interviewees' descriptions highlight how young women are aware of the dissonance between affective responses of recoil and their wish to participate in 'attacking'. Being aware of these responses without dismissing them as irrelevant is an important step in growing the critical awareness towards the normative practices that shape sexual possibilities for young women. By serving as an affective sign of harmful yet normative situations, affective dissonance can gradually become a motivation to act in ways that enhance self-attentive sexual behaviour.

Thus, sexual education should consider that from the perspective of young women, no real separation exists between the embodied affective sense of self and normative social validation in spaces of normalised sexual vulnerability. To empower young women to manage their vulnerabilities, educators should acknowledge affective dissonance as a point of departure for the growing awareness of this reality. This awareness of their reactions can inspire a personal search for self-attaining sexual expressions.

Interviewees shared how they processed these affective responses as resources to shape their sexual expression. Yamit describes how 'there is a moment of "Oh my God!", but then I look at who is standing behind me, and I have more tools to analyse the situation'. Her quote reveals how affective dissonance marks young women's vulnerability to – and potential for – harm. However, it also demonstrates subjective sexual preferences and becomes an aspect of processing situations in a manner that informs young women when and how to act. When Nicole states that 'slowly you get proportions [...] you understand what is pleasant and what is not', she emphasises the process of maturing and shaping one's sexual expression.

Thus, affective dissonance serves as an educational tool that informs young women regarding the process of finding ways to express themselves sexually. Learning how to be aware of these affective messages and drawing insights into one's actions can be productive steps for young women to learn how to express themselves sexually in spaces of intensified vulnerability.

Alliances Based on Joint Vulnerability

The awareness of young women to their vulnerability is also a resource for relational actions that expand their spaces of sexual expression as they engage in 'attacking'. The findings reveal relationality and collectivity in alliances between young women based on mutual trust and unwritten 'agreement' regarding joint decisions and actions. Young women jointly decide whether to look for sexual interactions or respond to specific 'attacking' attempts and communicate during parties to fulfil these decisions. These alliances support two main objectives – namely, (a) subjective sexual expression and (b) protection from unwanted interactions. The manifestation of these alliances can also challenge the individualised perception towards young women's vulnerability and reflect on strategies for managing vulnerability and uncertainty.

The interviewees describe how they dance in a circle, which supports responses to 'attacking' attempts. This spatial manifestation increases the ease with which friends communicate. Nina shares how when she dances with her friends' circle, they have 'girl power, so no man can break us apart'. She adds that 'if we want to interact with someone, we give each other the freedom to do so'. Nina reveals how the circle empowers young women to feel confident in expressing themselves sexually and realise the neoliberal demands for sexual empowerment. Therefore, the circle reflects the educational possibilities of relationally empowering young women to manage their shared vulnerability.

To fulfil the 'agreement' amongst the circle, young women use intimate language that includes mimics, gestures, and signs expressing their wishes and emphasises their embodied affective responses:

KIM: She opens her eyes, a second to look aside or 'yes' with her head, raising her eyebrows, a wink, a smile, something that makes you understand, and then you keep away, but stay nearby. The second she signals you "too much" or gives you the face ... so usually, we come like a mass of ... Boom! On the man, take her and run away, like fighters.

Kim's description of the nuances of this intimate language reveals how it allows young women to express their desires, passions, and fears such that their friends would know how to respond to the situation. Intimate language and mutual agreement demonstrate vulnerability-based alliances that keep young women alert and attentive to their friends' affective responses and offer them a means to support their subjective expressions.

The collectivity among young women also allows attentiveness to the embodied affective responses:

MORAN: I come to these parties with the purpose of 'attacking', so my ass is touched voluntarily. I have this [female] partner, and we stand out. And we dance provocatively and sexily with each other. And the boys are looking, and then each of us interacts with someone else, and while we kiss, we smile at each other.

Moran's description reveals intimate attentiveness when she and her friend dance together, maintain eye contact, and smile at each other while sexually interacting with young men. Their affective relationships made them feel sufficiently confident to express their sexual desires. Moran describes how she remains attentive to her friend's affective responses to evaluate whether she wants to continue sexual interactions. This attentiveness may result in joint actions to protect friends who interact sexually.

MIA: Especially Debby was constantly coming to pull my shorts down. I was wearing shocking 'f*** me' shorts, and every time they rode up, she came to pull them down. And I was kissing and kissing [...] and I even brought my leg up {demonstrating} and Debby came and took my leg down, saying, 'What the hell do you think you're doing?'

Debbie negotiates with Mia to maintain a balance among her sexual wishes, social expectations, and potential harm. Their alliance allows Mia to be in a safe position to express herself. This collectivity supports the possibility of navigating between different affective responses and social judgements such that young women can assign their own meaning to the practice, expanding their sexual expression. This relational navigation within conflictual expectations and different affective responses reveals how vulnerable positionality serves not only as a source of shame but also as a resource for acting in certain ways.

These relational networks and their attentiveness offer another practical tool for sex educators. Learning the power of relational networks can help girls and young women negotiate their vulnerabilities while being able to sense and express their sexuality. Educators' awareness of the duality of young women's vulnerability can serve as a basis for planning and implementing more comprehensive sex education principles that jointly consider their vulnerability and ability to express their sexuality.

Conclusion

The findings reveal how young women's sexual expressions emerge within conflicting wishes, demands, and expectations, including sexual curiosity, desire for social recognition, and the need to manage intensified vulnerability. While participating in 'attacking', young women experience dissonance between different embodied responses – specifically, sexual desire and possible harm and risk. Moreover, the practice creates dissonance between the perception of normativity and affective responses that mark reluctance. Thus, the awareness of intensified vulnerability and affective dissonance serves as a resource for learning one's subjective sexual desires.

Intensified vulnerability constructs collectivity that supports the understanding of social situations, reduces uncertainty, acquires new knowledge of one's wishes and abilities, and increases the ability to act. Vulnerability-based alliances reveal how young women's sexual expressions emerge relationally rather than individually. These alliances allow young women to show reflexivity towards themselves and others, express joint strategies and actions, and offer responses that are more sensitive to themselves and to the situation. Therefore, this case study highlights the importance of relationships and interactions as supportive resources for young women's sexual expression in spaces of intense vulnerability (Cover, 2014).

These findings suggest that the neoliberal approach towards sexual empowerment and education of young women, which contrasts vulnerability and sexual expression, does not understand how young women are attuned to their affective responses as a resource for sexual expression. Thus, an alternative notion is offered that does not regard young women's vulnerability as a negation of their ability to express themselves sexually. These insights may be valuable for vulnerability-based education, which aims to empower young women beyond the necessary emphasis on consent and safety.

Based on our findings, we outline educational principles that may facilitate vulnerability-based sexual education initiatives aiming to develop the affective and relational aspects of vulnerability as a productive resource for sexual expression. This educational approach strives to enable educators to use tools that support young women's learning to act in spaces of intense vulnerability while exploring their subjective sexual expressions.

This alternative approach yields the following principles:

- Sex education should raise awareness of the intensified vulnerability that young women experience in numerous social spaces, specifically regarding the following three factors: gender role division, restrictive social judgement regarding their sexual behaviour, and objectifying social practices. This principle expands the focus of affirmative consent to educate young women regarding the causes of their sexual and social vulnerabilities. Raising this awareness may result in the following two main outcomes: (a) ascribing new meaning to gender roles and relations and (b) teaching young women how to harness this awareness to manage their vulnerability and express their sexuality.

- Sex education should provide tools for attentiveness to bodily responses as a hermeneutical resource. Learning to identify and name different responses can help young women develop their awareness of how social expectations shape their feelings and actions in different social spaces. Moreover, these guided explorations of affective responses should help young women process the affective dissonance that arises when managing intensified vulnerability. Affective attentiveness can become a resource for critical awareness towards objectifying practices and social expectations. Thus, identifying moments of affective dissonance can be crucial for building new self-narratives.
- Based on the first two principles, the third offers a reference to vulnerability as a positionality that allows creativity and joint strategies based on collectivity and relationality. Strengthening vulnerability-based alliances through sex education enables the recognition of relationships that allow embodied attentiveness and expands the possibilities of sexual expression. This principle offers a critical reference for young women's vulnerability without diminishing their subjective expression but establishes another understanding of the relations that support it (Gilbert, 2018). Therefore, it challenges social expectations that encourage young women to distance themselves from narratives of victimhood. This principle offers young women the possibility of acknowledging their vulnerability without feeling incapacitated or negatively tagged.

This study is based on the experiences and knowledge of young secular Jewish–Israeli women regarding specific social practices. To expand the understanding of these principles, continued research may facilitate further analysis of young women's subjective expressions in relation to other social spaces and the cultural practices of different ethnic, socioeconomic, religious, and cultural groups.

This research was supported by the Israel Science Foundation grant No. 2540/20.

Note

1   https://cms.education.gov.il/EducationCMS/Units/Shefi/Hitpatchut/Hitarvut_Bm iniout_Vepgia/TochniyotHitarvuthatabhata.htm

References

Allison, R. and Risman, B.J. (2014) '"It goes hand in hand with the parties": Race, class, and residence in college student negotiations of hooking up'. *Sociological Perspectives*, 57(1), pp. 102–123.

Bay-Cheng, L.Y. (2015) 'The agency line: A neoliberal metric for appraising young women's sexuality'. *Sex Roles*, 73, pp. 279–291.

Bay-Cheng, L.Y. (2019) 'Agency is everywhere, but agency is not enough: A conceptual analysis of young women's sexual agency'. *The Journal of Sex Research*, 56(4–5), pp. 462–474.

Ben-Ami, E. and Erhard, R. (2017) 'LGB youth in the education system: Protective factors and coping mechanisms with homophobia'. *Society and Welfare*, 37(2), pp. 317–342.

Bracke, S. (2016) Bouncing back: Vulnerability and resistance in time of resilience, in: J. Butler, Z. Gambetti, and L. Sabsay (Eds) *Vulnerability in Resistance*. Durham, NC: Duke University Press, pp. 52–75.

Brennan, T. (2004) *The Transmission of Affect*. Ithaca: Cornell University Press.

Butler, J. (2004) *Precarious Life: The Powers of Mourning and Violence* London: Verso.

Corbella, L., and Úcar, X. (2022) 'Exploring ethics in social education and social pedagogy from Honneth and Butler's recognition theories'. *International Journal of Social Pedagogy*, 11(1), pp. 1–15.

Cover, R. (2014) 'Sexual ethic, masculinity and mutual vulnerability: Judith Butler's contribution to an ethics of non-violence'. *Australian Feminist Studies*, 29(82), pp. 435–451.

Coy, M., Kelly, L., Vera-Gray, F., Garner, M., and Kanyeredzi, A. (2016) From 'no means no' to 'an enthusiastic yes': Changing the discourse on sexual consent through sex and relationships education, in: V. Sundaram and H. Sauntson (Eds) *Global Perspectives and Key Debates in Sex and Relationships Education: Addressing Issues of Gender, Sexuality, Plurality and Power*. Basingstoke: Palgrave Macmillan, pp. 84–99.

Eurofound (2012) *NEETs – Young people not in employment, education or training: Characteristics, costs and policy responses in Europe*. Luxembourg: Publications Office of the European Union.

Fineman, M.A. (2008) 'The vulnerable subject: Anchoring equality in the human condition'. *Yale Journal of Law & Feminism*, 20(1), pp. 1–23.

Fineman, M.A. (Ed.). (2013) *Vulnerability: Reflections on a New Ethical Foundation for Law and Politics*. Farnham: Ashgate Publishing.

Gilbert, J. (2018) 'Contesting consent in sex education.' *Sex Education*, 18(3), pp. 268–279.

Gill, R. (2007) 'Critical respect: The difficulties and dilemmas of agency and "choice" for feminism: a reply to Duits and van Zoonen'. *European Journal of Women's Studies*, 14, pp. 65–76.

Gill, R. and Scharff, C. (2011) *New Femininities: Postfeminism, Neoliberalism, and Subjectivity*. Basingstoke: Palgrave Macmillan.

Gilson, E.C. (2014) *The Ethics of Vulnerability: A Feminist Analysis of Social Life and Practice*. New York: Routledge.

Gilson, E.C. (2016) 'Vulnerability and victimization: Rethinking key concepts in feminist discourses on sexual violence'. *Signs: Journal of Women in Culture and Society*, 42(1), pp. 71–98.

Gilson, E.C. (2022) Sexual injustice and willful ignorance, in: M. Gross and L. McGoey (Eds) *Routledge International Handbook of Ignorance Studies*. London and New York: Routledge, pp. 257–268.

Gonick, M., Renold, E., Ringrose, J., and Weems, L. (2009) 'Rethinking agency and resistance: What comes after girl power?'. *Girlhood Studies*, 2(2), pp. 1–9.

Grosz, E. (2005) *Time Travels: Feminism, Nature, Power*. Durham, NC: Duke University Press.

Halley, J. (2016) 'The move to affirmative consent'. *Signs: Journal of Women in Culture and Society*, 42(1), pp. 257–279.

Hemmings, C. (2012) 'Affective solidarity: Feminist reflexivity and political transformation'. *Feminist Theory*, 13(2), pp. 147–161.

Kipnis, L. (2017) *Unwanted Advances: Sexual Paranoia Comes to Campus*. New York: Harper.

Lamb, S. (2010) 'Feminist ideals for a healthy female adolescent sexuality: A critique'. *Sex Roles*, 62, pp. 294–306.

Levi Herz, R. and Rozmarin, M. (2023) 'Affective Dynamics and Young Women's Sexual Subjectivity: The Case Study of the Israeli Practice of "Attacking"'. *Young*, 31(5), pp. 499–516. doi:10.1177/11033088231165582.

Levin, D.S. (2011) 'You're always first a girl: Emerging adult women, gender, and sexuality in the Israeli army'. *Journal of Adolescent Research*, 26(1), pp. 3–29.

Mcleod, J. (2012) 'Vulnerability and the neoliberal youth citizen: A view from Australia'. *Comparative Education*, 48(1), pp. 11–26.

Paasonen, S. (2018) 'Affect, data, manipulation and price in social media'. *Distinktion: Journal of Social Theory*, 19(2), pp. 214–229.

Pedwell, C. and Whitehead, A. (2012) 'Affecting feminism: Questions of feeling in feminist theory'. *Feminist Theory*, 13(2), pp. 115–129.

Rozmarin, M. (2021) 'Navigating the intimate unknown: Vulnerability as an affective relation'. *NORA: Nordic Journal of Feminist and Gender Research*, 29(3), pp. 190–202.

Shulman, S., Walsh, S.D., Weisman, O., and Schelyer, M. (2009) 'Romantic contexts, Sexual behavior, and depressive symptoms among adolescent males and females'. *Sex Roles*, 61(11), pp. 850–863.

Sinai, M. and Shehade, F.M. (2018) 'Let's (not) talk about sex: Challenges in integrating sex education in traditional Arabic society in Israel'. *International Journal for the Advancement of Counselling*, 41(1), pp. 361–375.

Vanner, C. (2022) 'Education about gender-based violence: Opportunities and obstacles in the Ontario secondary school curriculum'. *Gender and Education*, 34(2), pp.134–150.

Watkins, M. (2010) Desiring Recognition, Accumulating Affect, in: M. Gregg and G.J. Seigworth (Eds) *The Affect Theory Reader*. Durham, NC: Duke University Press, pp. 269–286.

14 The Need for Inclusive Relationships and Sex Education (RSE) to Respond to 'Risky' Youth Online Practices

Groomed with Cisheteronormativity

Scott David Kerpen

Introduction: Uncertain Futures in the Face of Intensifying Hostility against Gender and Sexual Difference

LGBTQIA+ people have long struggled to be seen and heard against marginalisation. Such struggles manifest with particular intensity for LGBTQIA+ youths dependent on adults within adult-centred worlds (Singh, 2012), which operate to constrain the organisation and flow of young people's bodies, identities, and desires. Constructions of childhood innocence circulate to deny and marginalise the experiences of LGBTQIA+ youths (Walton, 2021). However, tired old efforts to 'protect' and separate childhoods from queerness are futile, actively harming young people by failing to acknowledge their realities. The question is not whether or not young people explore gender and sexuality; it is rather *how* they come to explore such things, which demands recognition to reduce harm and encourage safer practices. This chapter builds on longstanding calls for reliable, relatable, and relevant youth-centred education and resources (Buckingham and Bragg, 2004; Renold and McGeeney, 2017) to critically engage with questions around online risk in the face of current opposition to acknowledging young people's emerging gender and sexual agencies. Drawing on two case studies from a participatory PhD research project on queering cisheteromasculinity in the digital age, the chapter considers how efforts to erase LGBTQIA+ youths, far from protecting young people, produces desires to be seen and heard that led two participants in the United Kingdom – a gay male and a trans female youth – to be caught up in sexually exploitative encounters and relationships. The chapter conceptualises sexual exploitation not simply as a matter of force of coercion, undermining youths' *felt* agency, but rather as something relationally constituted, with youths drawn to encounters with predators because of circumstances, through what Pearce (2013, p. 52) describes as 'a social model of abused consent'. Flipping populist narratives of LGBTQIA+ activists grooming kids, the chapter highlights how cisheteronormativity renders such youths vulnerable to exploitation, playing an active role in the process of grooming them.

LGBTQIA+ youths have long taken to the internet to explore identities and desires displaced and marginalised offline, with or without the recognition and

DOI: 10.4324/9781003397502-14

support of those around them (McKenna and Bargh, 1998; Hillier and Harrison, 2007). As Gross (2003) identifies, support networks online can literally be a lifeline for distressed queer youths with nowhere else to turn. Against uncertain futures, with growing social and political hostility towards LGBTQIA+ visibility in and around children (Cumper et al., 2023), such opportunities for identity exploration and validation online are as pertinent as ever. When critically engaging with questions around online risk, opportunities to be seen and heard online cannot be ignored. There are opportunities in taking risks, and risks in not taking opportunities, urging consideration of what Livingstone (2008, p. 393) describes as 'risky opportunities'. Failing to acknowledge emerging gender and sexual agencies when considering online risk and harm is part of the problem, not the solution, as it removes the ability to analyse the allure of risky practices. Thinking beyond reductive accounts of risk versus opportunity, structure versus agency, the chapter draws on Wetherell's (2012) notion of affective practice to consider how risks and opportunities are relationally constituted and embodied, often emerging simultaneously so. This is further embellished by thinking with Neimanis' (2017) metaphor of 'bodies of water', conceptualising bodies and desires as emergent and fluid against cisheteronormative efforts to restrain and contain them. In this way, gender and sexual agencies, while not detached from broader questions of power, are understood to be in perpetual flow, even if that means flowing into troubling waters. In recognising this, the chapter problematises childhood innocence and protection narratives. However, it does not completely evade questions surrounding protection, which by itself is problematic in a context where gendered, racialised, and classed hierarchies deem some youths more worthy of protection and safeguarding than others (Walton, 2021).

Before considering how risks and opportunities are relationally produced online, it seems essential to consider the current social, cultural, and political context in which LGBTQIA+ bodies are often situated. Young people have long been forced to navigate heteronormativity – a sexed order that normalises and naturalises reproductive heterosexual relationships as default (Warner, 1991). Such heteronormativity, in centring reproductive sexuality, is both cisnormative and patriarchal, situated within a binary 'heterosexual matrix', reducing men and women to oppositional reproductive roles (Butler, 1990). As Warner highlights, constructions of a queer other against such normative forces are pervasive, emerging in efforts to understand and organise not only gender and sexuality but also childhoods, which are positioned outside of an 'adult world' of queer expression, even though children are routinely exposed to heterosexual relationships and measured against gender norms assigned to their *cisheterosexualised* bodies at birth. As Renold (2007) identifies in their ethnography of a primary school in England, children learn to value heterosexual expression young, facing pressures, in some instances, to anxiously perform heterosexuality for status among peers. However, such expression is not questioned because it aligns with normative developmental narratives. Young people must navigate what Walton (2021, p. 335) describes as 'restrictive linearity', i.e., normative linear developmental narratives, which selectively other queerness as 'future oriented … [and] out of reach of the child'. Such narratives see notions of queerness in childhood 'granted only in retrospect', demanding 'queers remain "closeted" until the temporalities of innocence and childhood are outgrown' (Walton, 2021, p. 336).

Recent reforms working towards more inclusive compulsory sex and relationship education across the United Kingdom have been met with much opposition (Cumper et al., 2023). Trans people are navigating ontological erasure, facing intensifying TERF wars (Pearce Erikainen and Vincent, 2020), which position them, particularly trans women and girls, as a threat to their cisgender counterparts. Gender affirming care for trans children has come under institutional attack (Pearce, Erikainen, and Vincent, 2020), despite an evidenced need for gender affirming care to tackle gender minority stress among trans youths (Horton 2022). Moreover, there are efforts to restrict children's access to gender non-conforming images more broadly. Drag queens, even those reminiscent of pantomime dames, have been othered as sexual predators (Chabot and Helkenberg, 2022). Such panic fails to consider how drag, like any art form, can be expressed in age-appropriate ways. Moreover, it conveniently ignores how the adult drag performances it selectively extrapolates from are often a mere reflection of pop culture, with drag queens imitating female pop stars who routinely perform in front of children without being labelled sexual predators and paedophiles. Such constructions of a dangerous, predatory queer 'other' are nothing new. However, they are re-intensifying at an alarming rate, with many calling to censor queerness from childhoods (Cumper et al., 2023), and this has been actualised in Tennessee's recent bill criminalising any performance deemed to impersonate men or women (Tennessee General Assembly, 2023). Meanwhile, the likes of Andrew Tate, who has become a figurehead for the alt-right, have risen to fame within what Ging (2017, p. 1) describes as the online 'manosphere', reacting against progress that decentres white affluent cisgender heterosexual men. A poll from the organisation Hope not Hate (2023) worryingly documents Tate's rising popularity among male youths in the United Kingdom. In the aftermath of Brexit and Trump, where borders and divisions, both actual and metaphorical, are intensifying against historically marginalised groups, there is an urgent need to validate and affirm difference.

Towards Reliable, Relevant and Relatable Education: Responding to Online 'Risk'

This chapter builds on longstanding calls for more reliable, relatable, and relevant sex and relationship education (Buckingham and Bragg, 2004). It validates gender and sexual difference to afford safer explorations of desire (Renold and McGeeney, 2017), working with rather than against digital media and technology and young people's digital practices (Scarcelli, 2018). LGBTQIA+ youths in the United Kingdom have long felt underrepresented in sex and relationship education (Bradlow et al., 2017). Despite recent reforms making 'age-appropriate' LGBT-inclusive education compulsory (DfE, 2019; CfW, 2022), actualising inclusive education remains an issue. Work with educational professionals in England reveals barriers faced in delivery due to time constraints, inadequate training, and fears of backlash from parents (Cumper et al., 2023). Additionally, the current guidance for England leaves what is deemed 'age-appropriate' open to much interpretation within an adultist framework. With adults often woefully out of touch with young people's sexual practices (BBFC, 2019), such room for interpretation risks much content being delivered long after young people have become sexually active.

Efforts to 'protect' children not only harm and marginalise those that do not conform to cisheteronormativity, contributing to hostile environments linked to stress and other negative mental health outcomes (Bradlow et al., 2017; Horton, 2022); they also make children more vulnerable. Constructions of childhood innocence are self-fulfilling, failing to provide young people with knowledge and resources necessary for safer practices. Censoring access to information, knowledge, and resources around gender and sexuality simply does not work. Firstly, content filters rely on stark generalisations, routinely under-blocking access to adult spaces and over-blocking age-appropriate information and resources affirming queer youths (Lawrence and Fry, 2016). Additionally, children can access content through friends with unfiltered access (Martellozzo et al., 2016). Moreover, tech-savvy youths are able to bypass filters (CleanBrowsing, 2022). While research conducted by Livingstone et al. (2017) suggests that young people's technical knowledge and abilities to bypass filters may be overblown, their data focuses on young people in general, failing to consider how marginalised youths may be more invested in developing such knowledge and skills. As such, parents, educators, and policymakers must arguably work with rather than against young people in determining what is age-appropriate, providing knowledge and resources responsive to needs and desires, which, in many instances, will be actualised with or without adult support.

Beyond Online Risk versus Opportunity

There has been much concern around the implications of digital media and technology for marginalised youths, made present in work around the likes of cyberbullying (Bradlow et al., 2017); misinformation, hate, and extremism online (Ging, 2017); and, as is the case for this chapter, sexual exploitation (Bryce, 2011), especially of queer youths. Ybarra and Mitchell (2016), in a quantitative study of US adolescents aged between 13 and 18, document that lesbian, gay, and bisexual (LGB) identifying youths are significantly more likely than their heterosexual counterparts to be sexually active online with people five or more years older, particularly YMSM (young men who have sex with men). Mitchell, Ybarra, and Korchmaros (2014) question the idea of the internet being a safer place for LGBT teens, highlighting the disproportionate levels of sexual harassment such youths face. Such figures and experiences are indeed concerning. However, focusing on risk limits analyses of what LGBTQIA+ gain through online encounters, including non-age-appropriate encounters. Risks must arguably be considered *with* opportunities to understand the relational context from which risky practices emerge.

As highlighted, the internet can be a lifeline for LGBTQIA+ youths. It has enabled youths to come out and disclose their marginalised status at a safer distance from potential hostility offline (Gross, 2003; McKenna and Bargh, 1998). It has afforded opportunities for making and sustaining queer connections and communities against queer diaspora (Gross, 2003). Such connections often materialise offline, whether that be through enabling queer countercultures and activism (McLean 2013) or facilitating hook-ups and dates (Gudelunas, 2012). Such connections, when affirming difference and enabling non-normative forms of expression, can work to de-marginalise bodies (McKenna and Bargh, 1998), promoting belonging and resilience in the face of adversity faced from both within and outside the LGBTQIA+ community on/offline (Singh, 2012). Additionally, the internet enhances possibilities of participating in the production, consumption, and distribution of knowledge (Jackson, Bailey, and Welles, 2018) that challenges *harmful and risky* binary narratives. While queer youths face many challenges online and are routinely exposed to hate speech and bullying (Bradlow et al., 2017), affirmative connections established online afford opportunities for navigating hostility both on and offline.

Such opportunities do not float free from risk. As such, this research contributes to a body of work urging researchers, policymakers, and practitioners to consider 'risky opportunities' (Livingstone, 2008, p. 393) to better understand exactly what motivates young people to engage in risky practices and enter exploitative relationships without explicit force or coercion. More specifically, it builds on a smaller body of work around opportunities afforded through sexually exploitative encounters and relationships, particularly as it stands for LGBTQIA+ youths. As Kort (2018) identifies, adult online spaces, and the relationships forged therein, can afford gender and sexual minority youths belonging against the likes of bullying and erasure offline. Likewise, Kvedar (2020), while placing an emphasis on risk, acknowledges the need to consider how adult spaces like Grindr afford LGBTQIA+ minors with outlets for exploring gender and sexuality that are denied to them elsewhere. As Pearce (2013) identifies in their work on child sexual exploitation more broadly, much exploitation occurs without explicit acts of force or coercion; recognising what is afforded through such encounters is necessary for addressing wider dynamics that render some more vulnerable to exploitation than others. Acknowledging such agential possibilities configured through connecting online, even in problematic encounters, is crucial for understanding why so many LGBTQIA+ youths end up in such spaces. Moreover, it is essential for developing inclusive pedagogy that provides information and resources to reduce harm and provide safer opportunities for youths to explore gender and sexuality.

Methodology

This chapter draws on data generated *with* two participants through bio-graphical relational map interviews conducted as part of an ethically approved doctoral study on queer youths' mediated gender and sexual lived experiences and practices across South-West England and South Wales. Participants, a convenient sample of queer youths aged between 18 and 25, recruited through dating/hook-up apps and local LGBTQIA+ events and venues, were asked to create a timeline, mapping out the people, places, spaces and things that had mattered, positively or negatively, to their experiences and practices of queering normative expectations around gender and sexuality. The maps were then used as elicitation tools for conducting the interviews. The method was inspired by Bagnoli's (2009) relational map interviews, where participants were asked to create a map of important people and role models in their lives. However, as Bagnoli's maps only focus on human relationships in the present, the method was modified to a) consider material and spatial relations reconfigured through the use of digital technology and b) account for relational constraints and shifts, providing important context for grappling with the situated, embodied nature of the differentiated mutually constitutive risks and opportunities discussed. The maps afforded a creative mode of expression, enabling the participants to reflect on the relationally constituted nature of their experiences, drawing connections between key sites, events and relationships that may have otherwise been difficult to verbalise on the spot. As Bagnoli (2009, p. 560) argues, such mapping 'engages participants on another level from verbally answering questions ... [enabling them to think] differently about issues ... [to] elicit information which would possibly have remained unknown otherwise'. The method was also participatory in nature, in that it centred around what mattered to the participants. As such, it pushed back against limitations of 'structured approaches to design and data collection ... [which] inevitably rely on researchers' assumptions and value-judgments' (Kerpen and Marston, 2019, p. 5). Prior to participation, the participants were provided with a detailed description of the nature of the study and what their participation involved, including their right to withdraw and refuse to answer questions at any time, before providing informed written consent. All data presented has been pseudonymised.

The research design was implemented as such due to a number of ethical and pragmatic concerns. The decision to restrict participation to youths over 18 worked towards mitigating potential issues around younger participants being unable to open up about online activity deemed legally and/or developmentally inappropriate. However, more importantly, the decision reduced potential safeguarding and well-being concerns surrounding discussing such activity, which may have required adult intervention undermining younger youths' ability to provide informed consent. In short, working with older youths afforded greater opportunities for responsibly exploring sensitive and intimate topics. The participatory design, again motivated by pragmatic and ethical considerations, was attuned to not only what mattered to the participants but how what mattered came to matter. Locating bodies and making sense of online practices in the digital age is no easy task, presenting many ontological, epistemological, methodological, and ethical challenges. As Miller (2011) notes, bodies and desires are increasingly hypermediated, configured through seemingly infinite possibilities of connecting with people, places, spaces, and things beyond situated and contextual constraints of geographical time and place. Bodies and desires are simply far less spatially–materially organised than they once were (Murphy, 2011), making it difficult to draw definitive conclusions about any given individual, group, or practice. As such, the participatory design served to capture the highly variable and differentiated nature of bodies and desires in the digital age. It provided opportunities for generating data from diverse sites of meaning-making (Hine 2015). However, again more importantly, it worked towards giving marginalised youths a voice, pushing back against more structural research designs guided by expert knowledge and authority that has long resulted in data being collected and analysed through normative frameworks (Kerpen and Marston, 2019). Finally, the broad, open-ended nature of the approach afforded opportunities for participants to share sensitive, intimate, and challenging information without being expected to do so, thus reducing the risk of invading privacy and triggering participants through questioning.

The approach pushed back against work drawing definitive conclusions around digital spaces and practices in favour of understanding *how* spaces and practices come to be relationally constituted in contradictory ways through connections within, between and across multiple sites, both on and offline.

Turning to affect, i.e., an immanent capacity for people, spaces, places and things to simultaneously both affect and be affected by one another, (Massumi, 2002), existing not separately but rather actualised through coming together (Deleuze and Guattari, 1983), it approached digital media and practices as sites of potential. However, attuned to questions of embodiment, always relationally reconfigured but nevertheless sill constrained to varying degrees (Neimanis, 2017), the approach moves away from affect as a verb, i.e., to affect and be affected, towards affective as an adjective, imbued in narratives and meaning-making practices. Drawing on Wetherell's (2012) notion of affective practices, it accounts for how such practices, while relationally constituted, often 'stabilise, solidify, and become habit' (p. 14) through an 'ordering of bodily possibilities, narratives, sense-making, and local social relations' (p. 20). As such, it provides scope for thinking about how marginalised bodies and desire, however unstable and fluid, come to be located, relationally, in ways rendering them vulnerable.

Risky Opportunities against Cisheteronormativity: Understanding Youths' Online Experiences to Rethink RSE

In line with existing literature on LGBTQIA+ youths, digital communication afforded a lifeline for the participants in this project, enabling life to flow and flourish in excess of normative positions and constraints. All but one of the participants came out online before doing so offline, with the anonymity of digital space enabling disclosure of marginalised characteristics without dis-turbing affective ties with friends and family. Of course, such embodied prac-tices still mattered offline, even before the participants came out to friends and family. Many such practices are affirming, enabling marginalised groups to develop resilience and pride against stigma and shame (Singh, 2012). However, the finer details of such affirming practices are beyond the scope of this chapter, which instead turns to risky and exploitative practices produced *with* such opportunities. The relative anonymity that enabled the participants of this study to come out also rendered them vulnerable. Two participants entered exploitative encounters and relationships. However, these encounters, while indeed exploitative, characterised by uneven power relations, emerged as affirming against cisheteronormativity. Acknowledging such affirmation is vital for understanding the allure of these encounters and relationships, which, as discussed, is especially strong among LGBTQIA+ youths. Failing to look beyond victim/abuser narratives is to fail to consider how exploitation is rela-tionally constituted, with abusers taking advantage of vulnerabilities that are systematically produced. While it may be comforting to locate power and accountability solely in the hands of abusers to be punished and removed from society, the cases of exploitation to be explored urge researchers, practitioners, and policymakers to grapple with the discomforting reality that cisheter-onormativity renders LGBTQIA+ vulnerable to sexual exploitation by failing to account for young people's felt gender and sexual agencies.

Adele, a UK-based Jewish trans woman, reflected on her early experiences of digital communication, which had enabled a digital gender transition to take place.

> When I was 15/16, I started getting involved on the internet. I'm lucky because I've always looked a little bit androgynous, so if I wear a little bit of make up and do this [poses], I looked very feminine. So, I had a fake Facebook account pretending to be a girl on Facebook.

The coming together of her androgynous appearance, makeup, an internet connection, social media, the anonymity and control of information such media affords, strangers, and a camera actualised possibilities of being seen as a girl. Adele was not out at the time, not even to herself. However, being seen as a woman still mattered to her. As Adele explains, 'it was gender affirming. It was nice because I was getting attention. I didn't realise it at the time but being recognised as a girl made me feel really good', affirming her desire to explore gender beyond normative constraints. The shifting spatial–material–temporal modalities of becoming with digital technology enabled Adele to be seen the way she wanted to be seen, displacing opportunities for others to deny and invalidate her existence by masking attributes that may have otherwise seen her classified as male. The intensity of such affirmation was arguably enhanced by the mode of communication. Adele was not just telling people she was a girl via anonymous chat, she was giving up a degree of control that such chat affords in visually displaying herself in the flesh through photographs and live streams on webcam, facilitating a stronger sense of presence (Jones, 2005). Giving up such control arguably enabled a transition to take place that was read, embodied, and felt as more real.

Such affirming opportunities of being seen online were set against Adele's hostile home environment, where she was denied the ability to exist in her own body. Adele felt othered and shamed by her father and by boys in school for her feminine mannerisms and voice, to the point where she was forced to act and speak in a more masculine way. As Adele explains:

> My dad was very unhappy with how feminine I was. I've always flung my hands around and away, I would go back to speaking normally … I've always been a bit effeminate, and I used to get, I've always had a very sort of lispy voice, and he used to try and make me not do that, which wasn't very nice … I have a lot of resentment towards him because of it … He tried to get me to talk like him … but it didn't feel natural. It basically reached a stage where I would speak a certain way around him … I've always been a bit effeminate, and I used to get bullied quite a lot at school because of it …

The cisheteronormative naturalisation of gender expression and gender identity, reduced to genitalia, restricted Adele's naturally emerging expression. Ironically, it demanded that she consciously perform gender in ways that did not come naturally. Unlike the queer activists *accused* of sexualising children for affirming difference and deconstructing gender norms, whether that be drag queens reading to children (Chabot and Helkenberg, 2022) or advocates for LGBTQIA+ inclusive education more broadly, Adele's father and the bullies were actually seeking to sexualise her body into a culturally fetishised gender binary. Nevertheless, such efforts to contain her body, like any effort to contain and restrict desire, failed, with connections online enabling her body to flow and emerge in excess of cisheteronormativity. Furthermore, the pull of such opportunities for affirmation were only intensified by restraints elsewhere. Nevertheless, such need and desire for affirmation rendered Adele vulnerable, as she was willing to take affirmation from wherever she could.

Adele offered recollections of when she used to use live-streaming with strangers through Chatroulette.com and Omegle.com, which randomly matched users on webcam. At just fifteen years old, Adele's desire to be seen and heard against cisheteronormativity was actualised through encounters with predatory men. As Adele narrates:

ADELE: I used to wear makeup and pretend to be a girl on chat roulette … I would have guys sort of like hitting on me, and I found that really nice … I didn't do anything sexual.

INTERVIEWER: Did they know you were underage?

ADELE: Usually no. Sometimes I'd go 'ha I'm 15', but I usually just let it happen.

INTERVIEWER: What did they do when you told them?

ADELE: Usually just continue as if they hadn't heard or make some sort of shocked gesture then continue anyway … It wasn't even sexual for me. I was just entirely alone, and I felt like they accepted me and that is ultimately what I was after.

Concerningly, these encounters had enabled Adele to be seen, affirming something that had been violently opposed by her father and the bullies in schools. They had made Adele feel desired, wanted, and accepted in a context where she was otherwise othered as undesirable.

Adele's online practices were deeply affective, affording narratives of pride against shame, re-writing the script her father tried to force her to follow and enabling desire to flow in excess of efforts to contain it. RSE needs to take note of such experiences; it needs to recognise gender variability and challenge such violent cisheteronormative efforts to marginalise it. The cisheteronormative educational context in which Adele found herself, whether that be formal education at school or informal education at home, was risky, limiting opportunities for safely exploring gender in age-appropriate ways. In this context, 'risky' online practices were felt by Adele as a safer means of exploring gender. RSE had the potential to affirm difference, producing an inclusive environment, cutting through cisheteronormative rhetoric and constraints materialising in children's homes. However, instead, for Adele, school emerged as a site of exclusion, reproducing normative constraints leaving her with limited places to turn.

In another case, Sajid, a British cis gay Muslim sought connection on a website called Chat Avenue when he was thirteen years old.

SAJID: Chat Avenue … was one of the first online platforms I used to speak to gay people … I wasn't out at the time and so it was kind of one of the easiest ways to chat to people … I did reach a period where I was like, 'Oh, I wish there was an easier way to like actually meet people who are gay' … There were no real gay people in my school, and I went to school with my brother and sister so that was a bit awkward.

The anonymity of the internet afforded Sajid the opportunity to actualise a desire for connection with likeminded others, emerging against constraints of geographical space where a reported absence of out gay people coupled with a desire to remain closeted, particularly around religious family members, limited opportunities for exploring sexuality. Some of the connections he forged online were with others of a similar age; however, others were with men much older.

SAJID: When I look back, it was probably really inappropriate because I was 13 and most of them were obviously much older… Everyone was looking for sex … There was a guy, in his thirties, who I spoke to quite a lot. He used to pay for my phone credit if I went on cam for him … I think about it now and I'm like, 'that was so inappropriate', but I used to do that a lot …

While Sajid's early encounters are concerning to say the least, it must be acknowledged that, by his own admission, they emerged against limited opportunities for exploring sexuality in age-appropriate ways, fuelled by a desire to see and be seen. The intensity of such desires to see and be seen were made particularly present in Sajid's conflicted position. While, upon reflection, Sajid knew the older men were predatory, he expressed a deep emotional attachment to and investment in the encounters. He reported feeling 'nostalgic just looking back at it'. To ignore the desire caught up in these encounters would be to reinforce the very constructions of childhood innocence that produce such vulnerabilities. Sajid was exploited, but so was his desire for connection – a desire for connection intensified by cisheteronormative constraints that limit age-appropriate exploration. It seems vital to acknowledge such desires to address the allure of such encounters for many LGBTQIA+ youths, encounters which young people enter into with feelings of agency, irrespective of their ability to consent.

The exploited bodies and desires of such LGBTQIA+ youths are not and cannot be contained. In fact, it is these very efforts to contain them that rendered the participants vulnerable. History has shown us that attempts to erase gender and sexual variance are futile. Desire has always flowed beyond normative constraints; the question is *how* it flows and whether it flows with information, knowledge, resources, and skills to affirm gender diversity and promote safer practices. Efforts to cisheterosexualise bodies, denying any possible presence of queerness, saw Adele and Sajid flow into troubling waters to actualise possibilities of affirmation denied elsewhere. The encounters provided them with a sense of place against placelessness. While it may be discomforting to acknowledge such affordances, what is more concerning is the fact that such affordances exist. A denial of such youths' emerging gender and sexual agencies only operates to further cisheterosexualise young people, producing the very normative constraints that queer youths seek to escape despite risks and costs. Going online is not without risk, but neither is existing in adultist offline worlds that routinely sexualise young people's bodies in accordance with fetishised cisheteronormative ideals. Given the current political climate, seeking to further deny and erase queerness from childhood, questions around risky practices produced with cisheteronormativity are heightened. Protecting children demands recognising them, working with them rather than against them or on them. Pretending children are devoid of gender and sexual agency does not stop desire, but it does push explorations of desire out of view, rendering kids vulnerable.

Such cases contribute to scholarship pushing for recognition of 'risky opportunities' (Livingstone, 2008), building on work emphasising a need to consider the affordances of risky practices and exploitative relationships for queer youth to address the wider cisheteronormative contexts that render them vulnerable (Kort, 2018; Kvedar, 2020). It is vital to adopt a critical approach to narratives surrounding protecting and censoring childhood that, ironically, result in a failure to protect children from online predators. Efforts to restrict LGBTQIA+

inclusive education only threaten to further limit age-appropriate opportunities for validation and affirmation, intensifying the allure of adult content and spaces. As such, this research builds on ongoing calls for reliable, relatable, and relevant 'experience near ... [and] co-produced' youth-centred education and resources (Renold and McGeeney, 2017, p.35), working with rather than against young people's digital practices (Scarcelli, 2018) to reduce harm and enhance knowledge for navigating risk. However, more importantly, it facilitates the co-production of open inclusive educational settings, affirming marginalised bodies, identities, and desires to afford age-appropriate outlets for being seen and heard. Renold, Edwards, and Huuki (2020) have made great strides in this area, making young voices matter to the recent legislation and policies in Wales. Through the AGENDA initiative, deploying a range of creative and participatory activities, they have worked with young people, teachers, third-sector organisations, and policymakers to develop youth-centred research, learning, and activism. The initiative has given voice to 'micro-political moments' of resistance (Renold, Edwards, and Huuki, 2020, p. 441), affording opportunities for young people to anonymously express desires and struggles to policymakers, maximising opportunities for outing issues without outing young people themselves. Such development of RSE is of course an ongoing process, demanding continual observations of what matters to young people. However, such centring of young people's voices in policymaking is, at present, unevenly distributed, both internationally and within the United Kingdom. As discussed, new legislation in England continues to leave what is deemed age-appropriate open to interpretation within an adultist cisheteronormative framework. Coupled with the ongoing challenges surrounding implementing inclusive education in an increasingly hostile landscape (Cumper et al., 2023), making such young people's voices matter is as important as ever.

Conclusion

To conclude, the deeply affective practices considered in this chapter build on and defend longstanding calls for reliable, relevant, and relatable youth centred education, working with rather than against young people's identities and desires in response to concerns around online risk. Constructions of childhood innocence and efforts to censor and restrict young people's access to knowledge and resources emerged as part of the problem, not the solution. Failure to recognise young people's emerging identities and desires not only marginalises those that are *cisheterosexualised* other, it also actively renders them vulnerable, contributing to social, cultural, and institutional barriers that limit access to resources for navigating risk and connecting in age-appropriate ways. The case studies discussed reveal exploitation relationally produced and enabled with cisheteronormativity. Sexual predators exploited the participants. However, they equally exploited desires to be seen and heard against restraints and risks elsewhere. The *cisheterosexualisation* of the participants' bodies, preoccupied with their reproductive organs, played an active role in a relational context that groomed them. Efforts to contain such bodies emerged as futile, demonstrating how young people's desires can flow and be actualised with or without the support of parents, educators, and/or peers.

A failure to validate and provide space for age-appropriate explorations of identity and desire offline did not contain queerness. Bodies still flowed, finding ways to connect and explore desire in whatever ways they could. Digital communication reconfigured material–spatial–cultural relations, opening possibilities for bodies, identities, and desires to emerge in excess of cisheteronormative constraints of geographical time and place. Such opportunities emerged as particularly strong for Adele when enabling a digital gender transition to take place. However, such opportunities were not without risk, actualised through exploitative encounters. The intensity of such desires for affirmation emerged as particularly strong for Sajid, who continued to derive pleasure from them as an adult. Such pleasure and felt agency are discomforting. However, what is equally discomforting is the relational context through which that pleasure emerged, denying age-appropriate outlets for recognition. In the context of the current hostility and panic around LGBTQIA+ inclusive education and gender affirming care for children, coupled with intensifying geographical and metaphorical borders against marginalised groups created by alt-right populism, such concerns around failing to recognise young people remain pertinent. As those refusing to cisheterosexualise children's bodies are labelled groomers, those preoccupied with defining and organising children's bodies are gaining power, ironically trying to groom children into thinking and behaving according to their desires, all while ironically rendering them vulnerable to actual sexual exploitation.

References

Bagnoli, A. (2009) 'Beyond the standard interview: The use of graphic elicitation and arts-based methods'. *Qualitative Research*, 9(5), pp. 547–570. doi:10.1177/1468794109343625.

BBFC (2019) 'Children see pornography as young as seven, new report finds'. Available at: https://www.bbfc.co.uk/about-us/news/children-see-pornography-as-young-as-seven-new-report-finds (Accessed: 15 November 2023).

Bradlow, J., Bartram, F., Guasp, A., and Jadva, V. (2017) *School Report: The Experiences of Lesbian, Gay, Bi and Trans Young People in Britain's Schools in 2017.* London: Stonewall.

Bryce, J. (2011) Online sexual exploitation of children and young people, in: Y. Jewkes and M. Jar (Eds) *Handbook of Internet Crime.* London: Routledge, pp. 351–374.

Buckingham, D. and Bragg, S. (2004) *Young People, Sex and the Media: The Facts of Life?* Basingstoke: Palgrave Macmillan.

Butler, J. (1990) *Gender Trouble.* London: Routledge.

CfW (2022) *The Curriculum for Wales – Relationships and Sexuality Education Code.* Cardiff: Welsh Government, Available at: https://www.gov.wales/sites/default/files/publications/2022-01/curriculum-for-wales-relationships-sexuality-education-code.pdf (Accessed: 20 February 2023).

Chabot, R. and Helkenberg, D. (2022) The discourse of drag queen story time challengers and supporters, in: *Proceedings of the Annual Conference of CAIS / Actes du congrès annuel de l'ACSI*. doi:10.29173/cais1253.

CleanBrowsing (2022) 'How kids are bypassing porn content filters'. Available at: https://cleanbrowsing.org/help/docs/how-kids-are-bypassing-porn-content-filters/ (Accessed: 4 February 2023).

Cumper, P., Adams, S., Onyejekwe, K., and O'Reilly, M. (2023) 'Teachers' perspectives on relationships and sex education lessons in England'. *Sex Education*, pp.1–17. doi:10.1080/14681811.2023.2171382.

Deleuze, G. and Guattari, F. (1983) *Anti-Oedipus: Capitalism and Schizophrenia*. Minneapolis: University of Minnesota Press.

DfE (2019) *Relationships Education, Relationships and Sex Education (RSE) and Health Education*. London: Department for Education. Available at: https://assets.publishing.service.gov.uk/government/uploads/system/uploads/attachment_data/file/1090195/Relationships_Education_RSE_and_Health_Education.pdf (Accessed: 20 February 2023).

Ging, D. (2017) 'Alphas, Betas, and Incels'. *Men and Masculinities*, 22(4), pp. 1–20. doi:10.1177/1097184X17706401.

Gross, L. (2003) The gay global village in cyberspace, in: N. Couldry and J. Curran (Eds) *Contesting Media Power: Alternative Media in a Networked World*. Lanham: Rowman & Littlefield, pp. 259–272.

Gudelunas, D. (2012) 'There's an app for that: The uses and gratifications of online social networks for gay men'. *Sexuality and Culture* 16(4), pp. 347–365. doi:10.1007/s12119-012-9127-4.

Hope not Hate (2023) 'Hope not hate's latest polling on Andrew Tate'. Available at: https://hopenothate.org.uk/andrew-tate/ (Accessed: 13 April 2023).

Hillier, L. and Harrison, L. (2007) 'Building realities less limited than their own: Young people practising same-sex attraction on the internet'. *Sexualities*, 10(1), pp. 82–100. doi:10.1177/1363460707072956.

Hine, C. (2015) *Ethnography for the Internet: Embedded, Embodied and Everyday*. London: Bloomsbury.

Horton, C. (2022) 'Gender minority stress in education: Protecting trans children's mental health in UK schools'. *International Journal of Transgender Health*, pp. 1–17. doi:10.1080/26895269.2022.2081645.

Jackson, S.J., Bailey, M., and Welles, B.F. (2018) '#GirlsLikeUs: Trans advocacy and community building online'. *New Media & Society*, 20(5), pp. 1868–1888. doi:10.1177/1461444817709276.

Jones, R. (2005) '"You show me yours, I'll show you mine": The negotiation of shifts from textual to visual modes in computer-mediated interaction among gay men'. *Visual Communication*, 4(1), pp. 69–92. doi:10.1177/1470357205048938.

Kerpen, S. (2019) 'Digital empowerment: Whose empowerment? On the limits of gender and sexuality in the digital age'. *Information, Communication & Society*, 22(13), pp. 2024–2029. doi:10.1080/1369118x.2019.1604786.

Kerpen, S. and Marston, K. (2019) Heteronormativity, in: P. Atkinson, S. Delamont, A. Cernat, J.W. Sakshaug, and R.A. Williams (Eds) *SAGE Research Methods Foundations*. London: Sage. doi:10.4135/9781526421036767642.

Kort, J. (2018) *LGBTQ Clients in Therapy: Clinical Issues and Treatment Strategies*. New York: W.W. Norton & Company.

Kvedar, J. (2020) 'Back to the grind: Rethinking Grindr's accountability for user content'. Available at: https://gould.usc.edu/why/students/orgs/ilj/assets/docs/29-3-Kvedar.pdf (Accessed: 10 January 2023).

Lawrence, E. and Fry, R.J. (2016) 'Content blocking and the patron as situated knower: What would it take for an internet filter to work?' *The Library Quarterly*, 86(4), pp. 403–418. doi:10.1086/688030.

Livingstone, S. (2008) 'Taking risky opportunities in youthful content creation: teenagers' use of social networking sites for intimacy, privacy and self- expression'. *New Media & Society* 10(3), pp. 393–411. doi:10.1177/1461444808089415.

Livingstone, S., Davidson, J., Bryce, J., Batool, S., Haughton, C., and Nandi, A. (2017) *Children's Online Activities, Risks and Safety: A Literature Review by the UKCCIS Evidence Group*. London: LSE.

Martellozzo, E., Monaghan, A., Adler, J.R., Davidson, J., Leyva, R., and Horvath, M.A. H. (2016). *A Quantitative and Qualitative Examination of the Impact of Online Pornography on the Values, Attitudes, Beliefs and Behaviours of Children and Young People*. London: Middlesex University.

Massumi, B. (2002) *Parables for the Virtual: Movements, Affect, Sensation*. London: Duke University Press.

McKenna, K.Y. and Bargh, J.A. (1998) 'Coming out in the age of the internet: Identity "demarginalization" through virtual group participation'. *Journal of Personality and Social Psychology*, 75(3), pp. 681–694. doi:10.1037/0022-3514.75.3.681.

McLean, N. (2013) 'Digital as an enabler: A case study of the Joburg Pride 2012'. *Feminist Africa*, 18, pp. 25–42.

Miller, V. (2011) *Understanding Digital Culture*. London: Sage.

Mitchell, K., Ybarra, M.L., and Korchmaros, J.D. (2014) 'Sexual harassment among adolescents of different sexual orientations and gender identities'. *Child Abuse & Neglect*, 38(2), pp. 280–295. doi:10.1016/j.chiabu.2013.09.008.

Murphy, P.D. (2011) Locating media ethnography, in: V. Nightingale (Ed.) *The Handbook of Media Audiences*. Oxford: Blackwell, pp. 380–401.

Neimanis, A. (2017) *Bodies of Water*. London: Bloomsbury.

Pearce, J. (2013) A social model of 'abused consent', in: M. Melrose and J. Pearce (Eds) *Critical Perspectives on Child Sexual Exploitation and Related Trafficking*. Basingstoke: Palgrave Macmillan, pp. 52–68.

Pearce, R., Erikainen, S., and Vincent, B. (2020) 'TERF wars: An introduction'. *The Sociological Review*, 68(4), pp. 677–698. doi:10.1177/0038026120934713.

Renold, E. (2007) 'Primary school "studs"'. *Men and Masculinities*, 9(3), pp. 275–297. doi:10.1177/1097184x05277711.

Renold, E., Edwards, V., and Huuki, T. (2020) 'Becoming eventful: making the 'more-than' of a youth activist conference matter'. *Research in Drama Education: The Journal of Applied Theatre and Performance*, 25(3), pp. 441–464.

Renold, E. and McGeeney, E. (2017) *Informing the future of the Sex and Relationships Education Curriculum in Wales*. Available at: https://www.cardiff.ac.uk/__data/a ssets/pdf_file/0016/1030606/informing-the-   future-of-the-sex-and-relationships-educa tion-curriculum-in-wales-web.pdf (Accessed: 10 April 2020).

Scarcelli, C.M. (2018) Young people and sexual media, in: P.G. Nixon, and I.K. Düsterhöft (Eds) *Sex in the Digital Age*. London: Routledge, pp. 35–44.

Singh, A. (2012) 'Transgender Youth of Color and Resilience: Negotiating Oppression and Finding Support'. *Sex Roles*, 68, pp. 690–702. doi:10.1007/s11199-012-0149-z.

Tennessee General Assembly (2023) 'Senate Bill 0003'. Available at: https://wapp.capitol.tn.gov/apps/BillInfo/default.aspx?BillNumber=SB0003 (Accessed: 20 April 2023).

Walton, E. (2021) 'The queer child cracks: Queer feminist encounters with materiality and innocence in childhood studies'. *Childhood*, 28(3), pp. 333–345. doi:10.1177/09075682211026948.

Warner, M. (1991) 'Introduction: Fear of a queer planet'. *Social Text*, 29, pp. 3–17.

Wetherell, M. (2012) *Affect and emotion*. London: Sage Publications.

Ybarra, M.L. and Mitchell, K.J. (2016) 'A national study of lesbian, gay, bisexual (LGB), and non-LGB youth sexual behavior online and in-person'. *Archives of Sexual Behavior*, 45(6), pp. 1373–1373. doi:10.1007/s10508-016-0767-6.

15 Gendering and Transforming Engineering Education

A Philosophical Perspective on the Gendered Limits of Choice

Sebastian Bernhard and Carmen Leicht-Scholten

Introduction

Gender equality is a fundamental aspect of the Sustainable Development Goals formulated by the United Nations (United Nations, 2022), and given the fact that STEM-related professions are a crucial part of the sustainable transformation, ⊠[f]ailing to bring in the minds and perspectives of half the population to STEM […] stifles innovation and makes it less likely that we can solve today's challenges⊠ (Kesar, 2018, p. 2). However, despite visible progress (Anger et al., 2021; European Commission, 2021) made by initiatives to fix gendered numbers, culture, and knowledge of STEM education and professions (Leicht-Scholten, 2007; Steuer-Dankert et al., 2019), these numbers remain unequal (Stem Women, 2021); something especially true for women who are faced by intersectional forms of injustice, such as *Women of Colour* (True-Funk et al., 2021). What further contributes to this inequality is that approximately 40 per cent of the women who break through some of the initial inequalities and choose to step into engineering education, eventually leave the field (Fouad et al., 2017).

These circumstances lead researchers to question why, despite '[s]tudy after study find[ing] that women have [equal abilities] in STEM subjects […]' (Corbett, 2015, p. 34) and despite the efforts of gender-inclusive initiatives, women are still less likely to choose a STEM programme (Stoet and Geary, 2018), or, additionally, why they leave in such high numbers (Fouad et al., 2017). Yet, as Miner et al. (2018) highlight, focusing on this phenomenon through what they call *individual lenses* or *individual choices* is truncated in that it ignores the larger social context of these issues. In contrast to this truncated individual lens, we are going to address the stated phenomena through the application of a *social-structural lens*, as recommended by Miner et al. (2018). While doing so, we are going to show that there are socioculturally produced gendered limits of choice within such processes of decision-making. As the chapter discusses, this is due to sociocultural construction processes that stereotypically associate engineering with masculinity (Carberry and Baker, 2018; Verdín et al., 2018) and, thereby, contribute to the formation of a professional culture and identity that can be defined as *hegemonic masculine* (Silbey, 2016) and *oppressive*.

DOI: 10.4324/9781003397502-15

Methodology

Coming from an analytical perspective of philosophically informed *Science and Technology Studies*, this chapter will develop its discussion through the following steps.

First, we will conduct a literature-based analysis, synthesising findings from research focussing on the gendered nature of engineering culture. Second, we will present a feminist philosophical perspective focussing on the gendered limits of choice in oppressive contexts. Together, these results will function as a foundation for acknowledging the respective limits of choice in the context of engineering. This will pave the way for a conclusion introducing possible ways to gender and transform engineering education by sensitising for these issues and developing measures to counteract harmful forces of gender oppression within engineering culture and identity.

On the Gendered Nature of Engineering Education and Culture

To sketch a picture of the gendered nature of engineering culture, we must draw on the stated perceptual relation between engineering culture and broader society, since 'society's perception of a given context reflects their understanding as a summation of experiences and interactions with the given context' (Carberry and Baker, 2018, p. 218). Therefore, it comes as no surprise that engineering culture is perceived to be hegemonic masculine (Carberry and Baker, 2018) since '[engineering remains] the most male-dominated field in STEM' (Silbey, 2016). This perception is further reinforced by the fact that current studies, e.g. (Cech, 2022), show that white, able-bodied heterosexual men continue to be favoured within engineering culture in a way that cannot be explained other than through privilege. This includes systematic advantages such as better social inclusion, higher salaries, better or higher positions, and more respect within the profession and its culture (Cech, 2022). What we can infer given these circumstances, is that '[t]he established masculine culture of engineering [helps] to propagate these notions resulting in a perceptual cycle that recruits and retains only those who fit the established cultural mold' (Carberry and Baker, 2018, p. 219). Based on this and further intersecting stereotypes depicting women as social caregivers and men as rational actors (Bem, 1981; Manne, 2017), engineering is constructed in a manner that relies on and, further, reproduces a gendered dichotomy between being *people-focussed*, stereotypically associated with *femaleness*; versus *technology-focussed*, stereotypically associated with *maleness* (Faulkner, 2000). Although both aspects are fundamental, the latter is considered to be what engineering is fundamentally about (Faulkner, 2000).

As Faulkner (2014) further highlights, this threatens the identification of women as real engineers. Connected to that, for instance, young people stereotypically think of the natural engineer as being male (Master, Meltzoff, and Cheryan, 2021) and communicate knowledge about stereotypes depicting women as weak and non-natural engineers (Campbell-Montalvo et al., 2022). What further contributes to this is the societally shared meritocratic assumption that brilliance is a prerequisite for engineering (Deiglmayr, Stern, and Schubert, 2019) and that only outstanding individuals succeed in becoming real engineers (Carberry and Baker, 2018). Yet, in contrast to Seron et al. (2018), who note that this appears to be exclusively a meritocratic rather than a hegemonic masculine ideology, Deiglmayr, Stern, and Schubert (2019) emphasise that this has a gendered component. Namely, as their results show, women tend to emphasise such beliefs about the necessity of brilliance more than men and, based on societal stereotypes associating meritocratic brilliance with men rather than women (Criado-Perez, 2020), show higher levels of uncertainties over belonging in engineering culture (Deiglmayr, Stern, and Schubert, 2019). This is in line with Fiske et al. (2002) highlighting that competence is negatively associated with the stereotypical picture of women as warm and socially orientated caregivers.

Further, since meritocracy itself has a clear gender bias with mostly men being thought of as *the meritocratic individual* (Criado-Perez, 2020), it can be concluded that this meritocratic ideology interferes with ideological aspects of hegemonic masculinity (Criado-Perez, 2020). However, this is still compatible with Seron et al.'s (2018) findings which point to how women who enter engineering and adopt a meritocratic ideology are 'unlikely to be active agents of change promoting greater gender integration' (pp. 134–135). Because, while Seron et al. (2018) think that this is merely due to meritocratic beliefs, this adoption can be interpreted as a special form of mediating the gendered forces of engineering culture via 'extra layers of practitioner identity work [as well as] gender identity work' (Faulkner, 2014, pp. 193–194). Additionally, this can even be interpreted based on the oppressive ideology of *good* vs. *bad women* (Beauvoir, 2011; Manne, 2017). This is because, as Seron et al.'s (2018) findings indicate, women try to establish their identity as *good engineers* and *good women* by opposing *bad women's* feminist 'voice of complaint' (Seron et al., 2018, p. 133) because this voice is said to be 'not only out of step with the presumed political neutrality of engineering but may be interpreted by some as threatening the objectivity of engineering itself' (Seron et al., 2018, p. 137).

Based on these insights, it further comes as no surprise that not only is the construction of engineering culture itself gendered, but so are the given interactions within this culture (Male et al., 2018). As Male et al. (2018) report, gendered interactions within engineering culture contain interactions that demean women, draw attention to their gender, are based on their gender, impose gendered expectations, or marginalise femininity and stereotypical feminine interests. Furthermore, because of such gendered interactions, female engineers report witnessing and experiencing (micro-)aggressions against other women and themselves (Campbell-Montalvo et al., 2022). For example, they inform researchers about being psychologically harmed by being ridiculed, isolated, or even physically assaulted and harassed by peers, professors, instructors, guest speakers, or even customers (Campbell-Montalvo et al., 2022; Fouad et al., 2017). So, in addition to rendering them invisible as engineers (Faulkner, 2014), the gendered nature of engineering threatens women's psychological and physiological well-being, if they are visible as women within the hegemonic masculine culture of engineering (Murphy, Steele, and Gross, 2007).

Yet, men tend to minimise the presence and prevalence of such phenomena (Campbell-Montalvo et al., 2022) or even neglect the stated issues while claiming that engineering is allegedly already diverse (Kent, John, and Robnett, 2020) or apolitical (Cech, 2013). Therefore, ideologies of depoliticisation (associated with anti-feminism) and meritocracy (associated with beliefs about brilliance) intersect and hinder the consideration of social justice (Cech 2013). As stated, female engineers try to deal with this by performing additional identity work (Faulkner, 2000, 2014). However, due to the demonstrated male bias, women report struggling to establish a strong and consistent engineering identity, while men report having such an identity even before starting to study engineering (Carberry and Baker, 2018; Cech, 2015), which highlights a gendered temporality of engineering identity. As a result, female engineers tend to be less confident (Cech et al., 2011) despite having abilities that are at least equal to those of their male counterparts (Corbett, 2015). Additionally, this leads to female engineers questioning their standing in engineering themselves (Faulkner, 2014; Vila-Concejo et al., 2018), resulting in many women leaving the field (Fouad et al., 2017; Silbey, 2016). To cope with such effects, women tend to seek affirmation (Silbey, 2016) or, additionally, appear to establish a routine story in which they try to legitimise their identity as an engineer (Appelhans, 2020). Yet this risks highlighting their gender identity and the related stereotype of women not being naturally capable of doing engineering (Faulkner, 2014).

Since all of this evolves out of the larger sociocultural perception of the engineering culture, it can be concluded that this perception leads to 'influences on women's and men's behavior that originate from larger societal structures that lead to gender inequality in [engineering culture]' (Miner et al., 2018, p. 275). However, to explore further whether the socioculturally produced gendered nature of engineering culture leads to gendered limitations of choice, we must sharpen the focus of our lens. Because as soon as 'the concept of choice is activated, people perceive individuals as responsible for their actions and life outcomes, regardless of social circumstances' (Miner et al., 2018, p. 279). Yet this not only reduces the complexities but is especially critical in the context of the shown meritocratic individualist culture of engineering by, for example, framing the issue of unequal numbers in engineering/STEM as a result of allegedly autonomous choices made due to women allegedly being less interested (Kent, John, and Robnett, 2020; Miner et al., 2018). Consequently, in the following step, we will present a perspective of feminist philosophy challenging this, in Theodor W. Adorno's terms, *naïve ideal of purely self-directed autonomous individuals* (O'Connor, 2013).

A Philosophical Perspective on the Gendered Limits of Choice

The most crucial precondition for an individual x to make a preferred choice to (not) do or (not) become z is having the autonomous ability to do so, or, to put it differently, being free from restriction y (or a set of y's) when choosing (not) to do or (not) become z (List, 2022; MacCallum, 1967). As this shows, the concept of choice further activates a discourse around freedom, autonomy, and preferences (List, 2022; MacCallum, 1967). Thus, the condition of being free to choose z is related to what is called *positive* or *internal freedom*, meaning that an individual x is autonomously self-directed (Cudd, 2006; MacCallum, 1967). However, this is connected to the latter condition of being free from restrictions, constraints, or interferences on choosing or becoming z, usually named *negative* or *external freedom* (Cudd, 2006; MacCallum, 1967). Despite some liberal theorists thinking about this in an either-or fashion (Baehr, 2021), the logical structure of choice indicates a triadic picture of x *being free from* y *to (not) do or (not) become* z (MacCallum, 1967). In connection with the basic liberal principle of a basic right to choose following one's preferences (List, 2022), this is also in line with the subjective comparative evaluation of an individual x who *prefers* to (not) do or (not) become z_1 instead of z_2 (Hansson and Grüne-Yanoff, 2022). Given this, it can be concluded that, in the classical picture, a choice C is free if and only if there is an individual x who is able to choose to (not) do or (not) become z_1 based on a subjective comparative preference among $z_1...z_n$ without external interference y influencing the individual choice to (not) do or (not) become z_1.

This is echoed by feminist philosophers (Stoljar, 2022). However, they have criticised this exact idea of fully self-governed and self-directed individuals, despite it being privileged (Anderson, 2003 – referring to Mendus, 2000; Stoljar, 2022) and legislated for, e.g., in *The Declaration of Human Rights* (United Nations General Assembly, 1948). This is because the 'account of autonomy as self-authorship can only be partially true [since] the self is vulnerable also to the demands of time and variables of gender in shaping the stories of our lives' (Anderson, 2003, p. 153). What is meant by that is that the individual, as Adorno (2003) and Foucault (1980) highlight, is situated in a social totality which negates the possibility of fully self-governed individuals because of the necessity of taking over a social role. Since such roles are mediated through historically evolved ideas and norms, the necessity to take over such a role leads to a constraining identity (O'Connor, 2013). Further, in taking over a social role (which mostly occurs through socialisation), we are continuously marked by this historically evolved social totality, drawing our remaining autonomy into complicity with it (O'Connor, 2013). This is especially noticeable in the context of gender, as it is used as a so-called primary frame to organise society and relations therein (Ridgeway, 2011). This is done through the discursive historical and temporal construction of stereotypical knowledge about a given gender role (Butler, 1999; Ridgeway, 2011). Therefore, the role and the knowledge about it tend to collapse into a normative picture of what it is like to be a member of a given gender, leading to the gender role being enacted in a process of *doing gender* (Butler, 1999).

As this implies, the construction of reliable knowledge that allows for the consistent coordination of social encounters introduces an external regulatory force, pressuring the gendered individual to internalise the discursively generated picture (Butler, 2004; Ridgeway, 2011). However, this comes not only with behavioural constraints but also with a discursively generated material reality of what a gendered body should look like (Butler, 2011). Therefore, as Foucault (1980) stresses, power is a repressive but at the same time creative force, helping to produce social knowledge, norms, and materiality alike (Chambers, 2008). Yet, at the same time, it powerfully suppresses reality to create this discursively built consensus in the form of self-validating practice, norms, and beliefs that form what Foucault calls a power/knowledge regime (Chambers, 2008; Foucault, 1980). Therefore, normative practices and beliefs are either enforced explicitly or internalised, due to force or unconsciously (Chambers, 2008).

Yet, whether internalised or enforced, this shows that those things are *cultural* and do not adhere to the meaning an individual wants them to have (Chambers, 2008). This further leads to the circumstance that a certain behaviour or state of our body tends only to feel right to us if it aligns with a given norm or practice (Chambers, 2008). This latter aspect further intensifies if we consider that in the context of gender, there are strong regulatory processes enforcing given gender norms (Manne, 2017; Ridgeway, 2011). However, these processes often only become explicit if there is a *need* to push an individual back into place (Manne, 2017; Ridgeway, 2011). As this illustrates, if an individual does not want to be policed, the individual must silently adhere to and internalise the given norms (Chambers, 2008; Cudd, 2006). So, in the case of gender, we can see an interplay between explicit and implicit, repressive but at the same time creative powerful forces acting upon the individual and its alleged self-directedness.

If we now trace this back to the topic of choice, we must further acknowledge that all choices take place within this forceful sociocultural totality, too (Chambers, 2008). What this indicates is that despite being able to autonomously choose, acts of choice will not diminish the existence of deep-seated inequalities, such as gender inequalities (Chambers, 2008). Understanding this allows for introducing further insights into gendered oppression (Cudd, 2006; Ingrey, 2016). However, since for example, *The Universal Declaration of Human Rights* (United Nations General Assembly, 1948) ensures political equality for women, gender oppression shall, in this case, not be understood as taking place in the political sphere (Welch, 2012). Rather, it shall be understood as a form of *social oppression* taking place in a sphere where individuals (inter-)act as individual members of (chosen as well as unchosen) social groups (Cudd, 2006; Welch, 2012). In this sense, it 'is a function of unequal power' (Welch, 2012, p. 26) that occurs at the level of social practice by 'the privileging of men over women' (Ingrey, 2016, p. 1067). Thereby, such systemic relations of unequal power can, in a Foucauldian sense, be thought of as the outcome of a historic discourse in which mainly men have been involved in the creation of truth and reality, helping them to institutionalise their privilege (Beauvoir, 2011) while enforcing this constraining reality upon othered social groups (Welch, 2012).

Therefore, while oppression is primarily a group-based form of social injustice, its adverse freedom-limiting impact hits individuals (Cudd, 2006; Ingrey, 2016). As indicated by this, there is an objective and subjective side to oppression. Whereas subjective oppression refers to an individual feeling oppressed, objective oppression refers to objectively exciting circumstances that account for oppression (Cudd, 2006). Therefore, feeling oppressed does note necessarily mean an individual being able to connect the given feelings to oppression. At the same time, an individual can be oppressed without feeling oppressed. Accordingly, these two aspects must be kept analytically separate to avoid confusion (Cudd, 2006). Therefore, it is necessary to further separate material and psychological oppression. Material oppression occurs if an individual is physically harmed by violence or economic domination. Psychological oppression occurs if an individual is oppressed by harmful or threatening mental or emotional states (e.g., including fear, trauma, stress, or diminished self-image) that result from an unjust or oppressive reality (Cudd, 2006; Welch, 2012). However, the forces involved in oppression can either be direct or indirect. Direct forces of oppression affect the individual externally and include intentional acts of physical or psychological violence or the destruction of material resources (Cudd, 2006). In the context of gender oppression, this mostly refers to gender violence (Cudd, 2006) or sexual terrorism against women in the form of 'threats of violence, flashing, street hassling, obscene phone calls, stalking, coercive sex, pornography, prostitution, sexual slavery, femicide, sexual abuse, incest, and sexual harassment' (Welch, 2012, p. 35). Further direct forces are economic restrictions on opportunities such as e.g., (group-based) employment discrimination. Taken together, these direct forms of gender oppression account for an institutionalised systemic practice of oppressive violence, which causes 'terror and trauma not only in the immediate victims and their families but also in the other members of the social group, who quite rationally take themselves to be equally at risk' (Cudd, 2006, p. 117).

Through this and further sexist ideologies, framing this unjust construction of reality as natural (Manne, 2017), the oppressive system ensures its existence by enforcing the construction or pushing for its veiled internalisation (Cudd, 2006; Welch, 2012); it can be presumed that this is how e.g., *unconscious biases* enter our minds. Therefore, the aspect of internalisation especially refers to indirect forces of oppression, which function through the shaping of social beliefs and desires following the oppressive reality that internally affects individual choices at the level of affective and cognitive psychological processes in reaction to external forces (Cudd, 2006). Therefore, respective choices tend to align with the directly enforced or unconsciously internalised oppressive reality, resulting in an internally motivated external reproduction or enactment of it (Cudd, 2006). So, once internalised, oppressed individuals uphold their oppression by subjecting themselves to it, by making choices that further reinforce or intensify it; either because they are threatened by negative direct effects or because they simply (unconsciously) accept the state of things as their natural reality (Cudd, 2006; Welch, 2012). Therefore, it might either be rational for individuals to make choices that align with their oppressive reality (Cudd, 2006) or for this oppressive reality to skew their preferences (Welch, 2012); however, it might also be reasonable to assume that both options coexist.

If we now trace this back to the classical picture of choice stated above, we can conclude that there are gendered limits of choice within a societal reality marked by oppression. Whether this accounts for the gendered engineering culture too shall be analysed in the upcoming section.

Discussion – Engineering and the Gendered Limits of Choice

To begin with, we must highlight that, as Mellén and Angervall (2021) show, the current market, despite emphasising a logic of free choice (following the ideal of *free choice*), reproduces a gendered logic (following the idea of *gendered choice sets*). This is probably because societal constructions of work and the practice thereof are interwoven with an ideological construction of gender (Davies et al., 2018; Miner et al., 2018). This results in accordingly *gendered subjects*, who function autonomously, yet still reproduce the gendered nature of society, reflected in inequalities such as the ones that characterise engineering (Mellén and Angervall, 2021). Therefore, instead of a *logic of free choice*, we can see a *gendered logic of choice*, which has a crucial influence on individuals choosing educational programmes and professions (Quadlin, 2020). Taken together with the gendered nature of engineering culture discussed previously, this has a significant influence on the decision to choose engineering as a major. Even if women develop and show the same preferences for this major, they frequently choose not to enter engineering education (Cardador, Damian, and Wiegand, 2021; Quadlin, 2020). The stated reasons for this circumstance trace back to women choosing under the influence of the broader stereotypical picture of them allegedly being less capable of performing engineering-related tasks and, further, being socially oriented caregivers (Verdín et al., 2018).

Due to such stereotypes and their interwovenness in the creation of gendered subjects and professions, women frequently rather opt for, or are pressured to opt for, subjects and professions that fit better with their gendered identities (Kent, John, and Robnett, 2020; Stoet and Geary, 2018). As Davies et al. (2018) highlight, this often results in them earning less money than men since the unjust, oppressive, gendered construction of work comes along with less pay in the context of feminine-coded work; this, of course, accounts for economic/material oppression. Given this, we can understand such decisions as a clear case of *indirect oppression by choice* (Cudd, 2006). This is because in making these decisions, women contribute to their oppression by making choices that follow the influence of external forces and result in them reinforcing and manifesting their external material oppression.

Further, this decision often goes hand in hand with another phenomenon, namely, how oppressed individuals come to possess lower levels of self-esteem, as stated above. What is meant by that, is that even though women have at least equal abilities in engineering-related subjects such as maths or physics, they rate their competence lower than men do, show higher levels of uncertainty, and receive less recognition (Godwin et al., 2016). This, most probably, traces back to the baseless perception of a stereotypical incompatibility between femaleness and competence or brilliance. As Godwin et al. (2016) and Verdín et al. (2018) highlight, this low self-esteem, resulting from gendered and sexist sociocultural constructions, leads to women choosing engineering education less often than men. Yet, the respective stereotype does also influence the women who, nevertheless, decide to choose engineering, since a reason they give for doing so is because they, in contrast to (most) men, want to use their future degree towards social ends, like helping others (Cardador, Damian, and Wiegand, 2021; Verdín et al., 2018). Of course, this is in line with the stereotypical picture of women as socially orientated caregivers. However, connected with remarks on the devaluation of *the social* within engineering culture, it further comes as no surprise that a lot of women who enter engineering with this end in mind report high levels of frustration in their careers (Silbey, 2016). This results from them not being able to do engineering for social ends to the degree they wished and contributes to women leaving the field (Fouad et al., 2017).

As illustrated above, this shaky standing, taken together with the hegemonic masculine construction of engineering culture and identity, further results in a hostile culture for women, in which they get physically as well as psychologically assaulted. Considering such assaults in addition to what was defined as direct forces of physical or psychological oppression, it is clear that these assaults count as oppressive external forces of gender violence or sexual terrorism. These disadvantages contribute greatly to women's decisions to leave the field, and the culture of engineering exacerbates already unjust sociocultural conditions for female engineers (Fouad et al., 2017; Silbey, 2016). As indicated by this, the threatening, gendered environment of engineering culture creates a barrier to the option of choosing engineering as a major, whether it is to avoid forces of oppressive gender violence or fears of becoming isolated. Accordingly, women self-exclude even when they have the interest and the talent for a career in engineering. Therefore, it can be concluded that the hostile gendered nature of engineering culture and its gendered practices greatly affect practising female engineers directly and potential ones indirectly.

Further, there are institutionalised forms of gendered practice unjustifiably harming or discriminating against female engineers as a social group merely due to them being women while benefiting a privileged group of male engineers (especially white, able-bodied, and heterosexual men) (Cech, 2022). Accordingly, we can conclude that engineering culture does not only seem to be governed by a hegemonic masculinity paradigm but also by myriad forms of gender oppression. As discussed, this results in a female individual's choice to become an engineer being externally and internally influenced by direct and indirect forces of physical and psychological forms of gender oppression that affect subjective comparative preferences. Therefore, we can infer that there are gendered limits of choice in the context of engineering. Consequently, this has a crucial influence on how the account of personal responsibility and the practice of choice is used to explain away inequalities in engineering and other STEM subjects. It becomes clear that, in contrast to those who would claim that personal responsibility underpins the inequalities in engineering/STEM, there are both micro and macro sociocultural processes which must be addressed, since the most damaging inequalities are not the result of autonomous choices resulting from personal responsibility.

Acknowledging this might be threatening, especially to those engineers who claim that their profession is objective and apolitical (Miner et al., 2018). Accordingly, the engineer's meritocratic, objective, masculine, and apolitical identity can be understood as an oppressive tool veiling and reinforcing oppression by forcing its internalisation. If we want to disrupt the gendered culture of engineering, we must tackle the very core of the gender-oppressive nature of engineering to foster real autonomous choices and an inclusive non-harmful culture. In the upcoming conclusion, we will provide potential pathways to resolve these issues, which allow for the preservation of autonomy as an ideal of a just culture and education to counteract gender oppression.

Conclusion

As discussed, there are several gendered limitations of choice within engineering culture. These result from culture, together with identity-influencing ideologies of gender, meritocracy, objectivity, and being apolitical, generating a realm of gender oppression disrupting the very conditions of free autonomous choices. However, acknowledging this allows for paving educational initiatives to counteract this oppressive culture by, as done here in the first step, fostering an analytical consciousness that allows individuals to become critical readers of their own lives in relation to external forces such as norms and other social actors (Anderson, 2003; O'Connor, 2013). In the second step, individuals must be enabled to become constructive authors being able to write their own lives in a way that allows them to oppose and counteract restricting external forces (Adorno, 1996; Anderson, 2003). A way of doing so might be to motivate a level of critical self-esteem that would allow individuals to resist playing along with the restrictive system by opposing e.g., its behavioural role-based norms (Adorno, 1996). Yet, if forced to play along, this shall be done while being aware of the wrongness of doing so, allowing it to change its character towards a negative form of autonomy by critiquing, resisting, and shaping these external forces to individual conditions (Adorno, 1996). This, of course, goes hand in hand with oppressed and privileged individuals unlearning deep-seated social norms and identity-shaping aspects by learning about the unjust hierarchical arrangement of society, cultures, and group-based roles (Cudd, 2006). Further, the direct institutionalised forces shown can be tackled by political or economic initiatives that introduce laws and investments to forcefully counteract oppressive institutionalisations. While the latter can be done almost immediately, the former will take long-lasting efforts of educating and mobilising oppressed and privileged individuals alike to counteract such deep-seated forms of oppression (Cudd, 2006).

Therefore, it can be concluded that to challenge the existing inequalities in engineering education, we must further educate engineers about the oppressive gendered nature of engineering culture and identity while, at the same time, supporting the development of a critical consciousness opposing oppression by non-internalisation and cultural transformation. We argue this could potentially be done by 1) informing engineers about the oppressive nature of and inequalities in engineering culture (as done in this chapter) and 2) empowering students towards solidarity to foster a form of collective political power in the sense of Arendt (2015), allowing them to shatter the meritocratic individualist nature of engineering culture and identity that currently preserves oppression. Further, this could additionally be supported by educating them towards forceful forms of non-violence in the sense of Butler (2021) or by developing a context-sensitive forceful ethical framework imposing clear behavioural guidance to counteract oppression. Systematically developing such an approach would not only gender engineering but also open engineering to all people who do not fit current gender stereotypes, and, therefore, would make engineering more inclusive.

Acknowledgement

Funded by the Deutsche Forschungsgemeinschaft (DFG, German Research Foundation) under Germany's Excellence Strategy – EXC-2023 Internet of Production – 390621612

References

Adorno, T.W. (1996) Probleme der Moralphilosophie, in: T. Schröder (Ed.) *Nachgelassene Schriften. Abteilung IV: Vorlesungen, Band 10.* (Bd. 10). Frankfurt am Main: Suhrkamp.

Adorno, T.W. (2003) *Negative Dialektik.* (Suhrkamp Taschenbuch Wissenschaft, 1706). Frankfurt am Main: Suhrkamp.

Anderson, P.S. (2003) 'Autonomy, vulnerability and gender', *Feminist Theory*, 4(2), pp. 149–164. doi:10.1177/14647001030042004.

Anger, C., Kohlisch, E., Plünnecke, A., and Institut der Deutschen Wirtschaft (2021) *MINT-Herbstreport 2021: Mehr Frauen für MINT gewinnen - Herausforderungen von Dekarbonisierung, Digitalisierung und Demografie meistern, Gutachten für BDA, MINT Zukunft schaffen und Gesamtmetall.* Available at: https:// www.iwkoeln.de / studien/ christina- anger- enno- kohlisch- axel- pluennecke- mehr- frauen- fuer- mint-gewinnen- herausforderungen- von- dekarbonisierung- digitalisierung- und- demografie-meistern.html.

Appelhans, S. (2020) 'Unpacking the elevator pitch: Women's narratives in engineering', *2020 ASEE Virtual Annual Conference Content Access Proceedings, 2020 ASEE Virtual Annual Conference Content Access*, Virtual Online: ASEE Conferences. doi:10.18260/1-2–35434.

Arendt, H. (2015) *Macht und Gewalt.* 25th edn. München: Piper.

Baehr, A.R. (2021) 'Liberal feminism', Stanford Encyclopedia of Philosophy, Spring 2021 Edition. Available at: https://plato.stanford.edu/entries/feminism-liberal/.

Beauvoir, S. de (2011) *The Second Sex.* London: Vintage.

Bem, S.L. (1981) 'Gender schema theory: A cognitive account of sex typing', *Psychological Review*, 88(4), pp. 354–364. doi:10.1037/0033-295X.88.4.354.

Butler, J. (1999) *Gender Trouble: Feminism and the Subversion of Identity*. New York/London: Routledge.

Butler, J. (2004) *Undoing Gender*. New York/London: Routledge.

Butler, J. (2011) *Bodies That Matter: On the Discursive Limits of 'Sex'*. (Routledge classics). Abingdon: Routledge.

Butler, J. (2021) *The Force of Nonviolence: An Ethico-Political Bind*. London: Verso.

Campbell-Montalvo, R., Kersaint, G., Smith, C.A.S., Puccia, E., Skvoretz, J., Wao, H., Martin, J.P., MacDonald, G., and Lee, R. (2022) 'How stereotypes and relationships influence women and underrepresented minority students' fit in engineering', *Journal of Research in Science Teaching*, 59(4), pp. 656–692. doi:10.1002/tea.21740.

Carberry, A.R. and Baker, D.R. (2018) *The Impact of Culture on Engineering and Engineering Education*, in: Y.J. Dori, Z.R. Mevarech, and D.R. Baker (Eds) *Cognition, Metacognition, and Culture in STEM Education*. (Innovations in Science Education and Technology). Cham: Springer, pp. 217–239.

Cardador, M.T., Damian, R.I., and Wiegand, J.P. (2021) 'Does more mean less? Interest surplus and the gender gap in STEM careers', *Journal of Career Assessment*, 29(1), pp. 76–97. doi:10.1177/1069072720930658.

Cech, E.A. (2013) The (mis)framing of social justice: Why ideologies of depoliticization and meritocracy hinder engineers' ability to think about social injustices, in: *Engineering Education for Social Justice*. Dordrecht: Springer, pp. 67–84. Available at: https://link.springer.com/chapter/10.1007/978-94-007-6350-0_4.

Cech, E.A. (2015) 'Engineers and engineeresses? Self-conceptions and the development of gendered professional identities', *Sociological Perspectives*, 58(1), pp. 56–77. doi:10.1177/0731121414556543.

Cech, E.A. (2022) 'The intersectional privilege of white able-bodied heterosexual men in STEM', *Science Advances*, 8(24), eabo1558. doi:10.1126/sciadv.abo1558.

Cech, E.A., Rubineau, B., Silbey, S., and Seron, C. (2011) 'Professional Role Confidence and Gendered Persistence in Engineering', *American Sociological Review*, 76(5), pp. 641–666. doi:10.1177/0003122411420815.

Chambers, C. (2008) *Sex, Culture, and Justice: The Limits of Choice*. University Park, PA: Pennsylvania State University Press.

Corbett, C. (2015) *Solving the Equation: The Variables for Women's Success in Engineering and Computing*. Washington DC: AAUW.

Criado-Perez, C. (2020) *Invisible Women: Exposing Data Bias in a World Designed for Men*. London: Vintage.

Cudd, A.E. (2006) *Analyzing Oppression*. New York: Oxford University Press.

Davies, S.G., McGregor, J., Pringle, J., and Giddings, L. (2018) 'Rationalizing pay inequity: Women engineers, pervasive patriarchy and the neoliberal chimera', *Journal of Gender Studies*, 27(6), pp. 623–636. doi:10.1080/09589236.2017.1284048.

Deiglmayr, A., Stern, E., and Schubert, R. (2019) 'Beliefs in "brilliance" and belonging uncertainty in male and female STEM students', *Frontiers in Psychology*, pp. 1–7. Available at: https://doi.org/10.3389/fpsyg.2019.01114.

European Commission (2021) *She Figures 2021: Gender in Research and Innovation Statistics and Indicators*, Luxembourg: Directorate-General for Research and Innovation – Publications Office of the European Union. Available at: https://data.europa.eu/doi/10.2777/06090.

Faulkner, W. (2000) 'Dualisms, Hierarchies and Gender in Engineering', *Social Studies of Science*, 30(5), pp. 759–792.

Faulkner, W. (2014) Can Women Engineers be 'Real Engineers' and 'Real Women'?. In: E. Waltraud and I. Horwath (Eds.) *Gender in Science and Technology*, Bielefeld: Transcript Verlag, pp. 187–204.

Fiske, S.T., Cuddy, A.J.C., Glick, P. and Xu, J. (2002) 'A model of (often mixed) stereotype content: Competence and warmth respectively follow from perceived status and competition', *Journal of Personality and Social Psychology*, 82(6), pp. 878–902. doi:10.1037/0022-3514.82.6.878.

Fouad, N.A., Chang, W.-H., Wan, M. and Singh, R. (2017) 'Women's Reasons for Leaving the Engineering Field', *Frontiers in Psychology*, 8. doi:10.3389/fpsyg.2017.00875.

Foucault, M. (1980) Power/knowledge, in: C. Gordon (Ed.) *Power/knowledge: Selected Interviews and Other Writings, 1972–1977*. New York: Vintage Books.

Godwin, A., Potvin, G., Hazari, Z., and Lock, R. (2016) 'Identity, critical agency, and engineering: An affective model for predicting engineering as a career choice', *Journal of Engineering Education*, 105(2), pp. 312–340. doi:10.1002/jee.20118.

Hansson, S.O. and Grüne-Yanoff, T. (2022) 'Preferences', Stanford Encyclopedia of Philosophy, Spring Edition 2022. Available at: https://plato.stanford.edu/entries/preferences/.

Ingrey, J.C. (2016) Gender oppression, in N.A. Napels et al (Eds) *The Wiley Blackwell Encyclopedia of Gender and Sexuality Studies*, London: Wiley, pp. 10067–11069.

Kent, S.R., John, J.E., and Robnett, R.D. (2020) '"Maybe these fields just don't interest them." Gender and ethnic differences in attributions about STEM inequities', *International Journal of Gender, Science and Technology*, 12(1), pp. 97–121.

Kesar, S. (2018) 'Closing the STEM Gap: Why STEM classes and careers still lack girls and what we can do about it'. Available at: https://query.prod.cms.rt.microsoft.com/cms/api/am/binary/RE1UMWz.

Leicht-Scholten, C. (2007) *"Gender and Science": Perspektiven in den Natur- und Ingenieurwissenschaften*. (Gender studies). Bielefeld: Transcript Verlag.

List, C. (2022) 'Social Choice Theory', Stanford Encyclopedia of Philosophy, Winter 2022 Edition. Available at: https://plato.stanford.edu/archives/win2022/entries/social- choice/.

MacCallum, G.C. (1967) 'Negative and Positive Freedom', *The Philosophical Review*, 76(3), pp. 312–314. doi:10.2307/2183622.

Male, S.A., Gardner, A., Figueroa, E.,and Bennett, D. (2018) 'Investigation of students' experiences of gendered cultures in engineering workplaces', *European Journal of Engineering Education*, 43(3), pp. 360–377. doi:10.1080/03043797.2017.1397604.

Manne, K. (2017) *Down Girl: The Logic of Misogyny*. New York: Oxford University Press.

Master, A., Meltzoff, A.N., and Cheryan, S. (2021) 'Gender stereotypes about interests start early and cause gender disparities in computer science and engineering', *Proceedings of the National Academy of Sciences of the United States of America*, 118(48). doi:10.1073/pnas.2100030118.

Mellén, J. and Angervall, P. (2021) 'Gender and choice: differentiating options in Swedish upper secondary STEM programmes', *Journal of Education Policy*, 36(3), pp. 417–435. doi:10.1080/02680939.2019.1709130.

Mendus, S. (2000) Out of the Doll's House: Reflections on Autonomy and Political Philosophy, in: S. Mendus (Ed.) *Feminism and Emotion*. London: Palgrave Macmillan, pp. 127–139.

Miner, K.N., Walker, J.M., Bergman, M.E., Jean, V.A., Carter-Sowell, A., January, S. C., and Kaunas, C. (2018) 'From "her" problem to "our" problem: Using an individual lens versus a social-structural lens to understand gender inequity in STEM', *Industrial and Organizational Psychology*, 11(2), pp. 267–290. doi:10.1017/iop.2018.7.

Murphy, M.C., Steele, C.M., and Gross, J.J. (2007) 'Signaling threat: How situational cues affect women in math, science, and engineering settings', *Psychological Science*, 18(10), pp. 879–885. doi:10.1111/j.1467-9280.2007.01995.x.

O'Connor, B. (2013) *Adorno*. (Routledge philosophers). Abingdon, Oxon: Routledge.

Quadlin, N. (2020) 'From major preferences to major choices: Gender and logics of major choice', *Sociology of Education*, 93(2), pp. 91–109. doi:10.1177/0038040719887971.

Ridgeway, C.L. (Ed.) (2011) *Framed by Gender: How Gender Inequality Persists in the Modern World*. New York: Oxford University Press.

Seron, C., Silbey, S., Cech, E., and Rubineau, B. (2018) '"I am Not a Feminist, but…": Hegemony of a Meritocratic Ideology and the Limits of Critique Among Women in Engineering'. *Work and Occupations*, 45(2), pp. 131–167. doi:10.1177/0730888418759774.

Silbey, S.S. (2016) 'Why do so many women who study engineering leave the field?'. 23 August. Available at: https://hbr.org/2016/08/why-do-so-many-women-who-study-engineering-leave-the-field.

Stem Women (2021) 'Women in STEM | Percentages of women in STEM statistics – Stem Women'. 8 June. Available at: https://www.stemwomen.com/women-in-stem-percentages-of-women-in-stem-statistics.

Steuer-Dankert, L., Dungs, C., Muller, C.B., Leicht-Scholten, C., Gilmartin, S.K., and Sheppard, S. (2019) 'Expanding engineering limits: A concept for socially responsible education of engineers', *The International Journal of Engineering Education*, 35 (RWTH-2019–02452), pp. 658–673. doi:0269.

Stoet, G. and Geary, D.C. (2018) 'The gender-equality paradox in science, technology, engineering, and mathematics education', *Psychological Science*, 29(4), pp. 581–593. doi:10.1177/0956797617741719.

Stoljar, N. (2022) 'Feminist Perspectives on Autonomy', Stanford Encyclopedia of Philosophy, Winter 2022 Edition. Available at: https://plato.stanford.edu/entries/feminism-autonomy/.

True-Funk, A., Poleacovschi, C., Jones-Johnson, G., Feinstein, S., Smith, K., and Luster-Teasley, S. (2021) 'Intersectional engineers: Diversity of gender and race microaggressions and their effects in engineering education', *Journal of Management in Engineering*, 37(3), p. 4021002. doi:10.1061/(ASCE)ME.1943-5479.0000889.

United Nations (2022) 'THE 17 GOALS | Sustainable Development'. 16 December. Available at: https://sdgs.un.org/goals.

United Nations General Assembly (1948) *The Universal Declaration of Human Rights (UDHR)*. New York: United Nations.

Verdín, D., Godwin, A., Kirn, A., Benson, L., and Potvin, G. (2018) 'Engineering women's attitudes and goals in choosing disciplines with above and below average female representation', *Social Sciences*, 7, 3(44), pp. 1–25. Available at: https://doi.org/10.3390/socsci7030044.

Vila-Concejo, A., Gallop, S.L., Hamylton, S.M., Esteves, L.S., Bryan, K.R., Delgado-Fernandez, I., Guisado-Pintado, E., Joshi, S., Da Silva, G.M., Ruiz de Alegria-Arzaburu, A., Power, H.E., Senechal, N., and Splinter, K. (2018) 'Steps to improve gender diversity in coastal geoscience and engineering', *Palgrave Communications*, 4(1). doi:10.1057/s41599-018-0154-0.

Welch, S. (2012) *A Theory of Freedom: Feminism and the Social Contract*. (Breaking Feminist Waves Series). New York: Palgrave Macmillan.

Index

Framework for Guidance and Action for Comprehensive Sexuality Education 68
Fraser, Nancy 3, 77
free choice 222–4
Freire, Paulo 34, 50–51, 53, 154
Friedan, Betty 12
Frost, S. 76
fundamental attribution error 13

Gamergate 16
García Dauder, S. 157
gay rights movement 30–31
'gaze' 4, 117–33; and student work placements 125–9
Gender 3.0 63–6, 70
gender binarism 173
gender blindness 97
gender discourse terminology 10–11
gender diversity 61–2
'Gender and Diversity in Schools' 63–6
gender essentialism 90–93
gender hybridity 10
gender knowledge 88–102; being taught gender knowledge 97–100; figurational sociology 89–90; gender essentialism 90–93; location of 93–7; reinforcing stereotypes 88–9
gender norms 187
gender ontologies 9–29; *see also* various gender ontologies
gender oppression 216
gender performativity 17
gender relations on sport/PE courses 88–102
gender role conformity 20–21, 188–9, 195–6
gender studies programmes 138–41
gender violence 221
gender-segregated school subjects 88–9, 91–2
gender-sensitive pedagogy 80–83
gender/sex intelligibility 62
gendered behaviour 130
gendered choice sets 222–4
gendered culture 124
gendered limits of choice 215–28; *see also* gendering engineering education
gendered nature of engineering 216–18
gendered social interaction battles 119–21
gendered structure of PE/sports 90–93
gendering engineering education 215–28; autonomous ability to choose 219–22; engineering and gendered limits 222–4; gendered limits of choice 216; gendered nature of engineering 216–18; limits and culture 224–5
gendering traditional care practices 108–9

Genres of Man 9
GEP *see* Girls Empowerment Project
German Youth Research Institute 64–5
Germany 61–73
Geschlechtlichkeit 67
Gestalt 117–20
Gibb, Nick 33–4
Gill, R. 135
Gill-Peterson, J. 20
Ging, D. 201
Ginn, F. 106
girl power 14–16, 193
Girls Active Report 91
Girls Empowerment Project 52
Giroux, H.A. 105, 153
Giugni, M. 22
Godwin, A. 223
'good queers' 19–20
good teaching 108–9
Gore, J. 157
Gove, Michael 33
Gravett, K. 103
Gray, John 173
Grindr 203
groomed with cisheteronormativity 199–214
grooming 199–200
Gross, L. 200
Guattari, F. 21
Gunaratnam, Y. 47
Guy Code 75

Halberstam, J. 3, 18, 35
Halperin, David 30
Hamilton, T. 18, 20
Haraway, D.J. 22, 151, 158–9
Harvey, D. 105
haunting of gender 22
HE *see* higher education
HE sport and PE courses 88–102
hegemonic masculinity 75–6, 215–24
Heidegger, M. 119
Helfferich, C. 76
helping professions 125
Hernández Morales, G. 157
Hesse, Eva 37
heteronormativity critical agency 32, 61–73, 200; ambivalences/limitations of 63–6; enabling diversity 66–9; exploration of 62–3; paradoxes of in/visibility 70–71; third positive gender marker 61–2; towards diversity inclusion 69–70
heterosexual matrix 6, 11, 17, 20, 200
hierarchisations 71
Hierro, G. 109

Milton Keynes UK
Ingram Content Group UK Ltd.
UKHW020846270824
447372UK00003B/37